PATRIOTIC PACIFISM

PATRIOTIC PACIFISM

Waging War on War in Europe 1815–1914

SANDI E. COOPER

New York · Oxford
OXFORD UNIVERSITY PRESS
1991

Oxford University Press

Oxford New York Toronto
Delhi Bombay Calcutta Madras Karachi
Petaling Jaya Singapore Hong Kong Tokyo
Nairobi Dar es Salaam Cape Town
Melbourne Auckland

and associated companies in
Berlin Ibadan

Copyright © 1991 by Oxford University Press, Inc.

Published by Oxford University Press, Inc.,
200 Madison Avenue, New York, New York 10016

Oxford is a registered trademark of Oxford University Press

Library of Congress Cataloging-in-Publication Data
Cooper, Sandi E.
Patriotic pacifism: Waging war on war in Europe, 1815–1914 / Sandi E. Cooper.
p. cm. Includes bibliographical references and index.
ISBN 0-19-505715-5
1. Peace movements—Europe—History.
2. Pacifism—History.
· I. Title.
JX1952.C615 1991
327.1′72′094—dc20 90–14202

9 8 7 6 5 4 3 2 1

Printed in the United States of America
on acid-free paper

Preface

Somewhere in the late 1950s in a graduate seminar entitled "Europe at the Cross-roads" conducted by A. William Salomone, I began to wonder why the leadership of Europe in 1914 chose a path tantamount to suicide. It seemed peculiar that rational men managing successful societies in control of much of the globe risked everything in a battlefield gamble. This curiosity became a research interest on the broader question of war and peace in history. The bipolar world of the 1950s, the nuclear arms race and the Vietnam War transformed this research interest from abstract intellectual history into a living subject.

My personal encounter with broad war/peace conundrums was given a context and a community of scholars when the Conference (now Council) on Peace Research in History (CPRH) was formed in 1964. Several hundred historians, shocked by the assassination of President John F. Kennedy, created this novel scholarly group that brought together specialists in antiquity, Asia, Europe, and the United States to explore a host of new questions that challenged traditional diplomatic history: Why did some wars not happen? How did wars end? Why did some people struggle to prevent wars from happening or work to stop those in progress? How could the social bases of war-making be understood? The historians attracted to the CPRH probed the record to reveal and analyze historical causation in ways that diplomatic history, the usual repository of wisdom about the coming of war, often considered tendentious or irrelevant. Members of the CPRH recognized the advantages of collaborative projects. It was a welcome relief from the often-mindless competition of graduate schools and university departmental life—a professionalism that did not depend on "destroy thy neighbor." A decade later it was a spirit appropriated by feminist scholars—for a time.

Having dutifully memorized the same five long-range and immediate causes of World War I (from sixth grade through graduate school), I was amazed to discover that a group of people lived in pre-1914 Europe who had worked strenuously, though unsuccessfully, to prevent that war. Despite all the rhetoric about the balance of power deterring any one state from aggression, there had been citizens and a few political leaders who did not believe that that balance would work. They wanted a better, more secure institutionalization of an organized peace. Their labors and the work of their predecessors back to the end of the Napoleonic Wars are represented in the following pages. They were the patriotic pacifists of continental Europe.

I have had much help. Besides all those who wrote on this subject earlier, there are special colleagues and friends who provided crucial intellectual and emotional support that ensured closure on this project. I want to thank, especially, Irwin Abrams, Berenice Carroll, Charles Chatfield, Blanche W. Cook, Stephen J. Stearns, and Solomon Wank on this side of the Atlantic; on the other side, in particular, Peter van den Dungen, Nadine Lubelski-Bernard, and Werner Simon offered indispensable and generous information, support, and leads. Werner Simon was unfailingly gracious and helpful as I raced through the archives in Geneva. At The College of Staten Island–C.U.N.Y., Jerry Mardison in the library continued to smile, despite my requests for obscure journals and out-of-print books. In addition to friends and colleagues, I have had important material help— from the National Endowment for the Humanities, the Professional Staff Congress–City University of New York research grants, and the United States Institute of Peace.

I took too long to finish this book. My dear friend and original cheerleader, A. William Salomone, died in 1989 before this book appeared. He really wanted to see it, and I am profoundly saddened that he did not.

Nancy Lane at Oxford University Press is the best editor anyone can have.

John, Lisa, Ann, Melani, and Mena Cammett make up the best family anyone can have. Their self-sufficiency and independence were a great gift. John is a historian, too, and there is no way to measure how I have benefited from his storehouse of learning as well as his unique capability to be both critic and *compagno*.

New York   S.E.C.
October 1990

Contents

PATRIOTIC PACIFISM

Introduction

In 1989–1990, as the *fin de siècle* of the twentieth century begins, Europeans again seriously debate the possibility of transforming their continent from a geographic expression to a formal political-cultural community. If they succeed, they will realize a recurrent dream of their nineteenth-century ancestors. A German executive, relishing the fruits that the [re]awakening giant will pluck, observed that what was *about* to happen was what *should* have happened in 1914:

> The European challenge is to restore the Europe of 1914, when Europe was the biggest economic power in the world and had the best-educated population, one that is twice the population of the United States and four times the population of Japan.[1]

Apart from its Euro-chauvinism, the remark is interesting for its view of the twentieth century. The two world wars are cast as monumental mistakes, tragic deviations from the rational direction of earlier evolution. As the twentieth century closes, Europeans have begun to reweave some of the broken threads of a nineteenth-century consciousness that realized the distinct advantages of transnational collaboration and collective security over suicidal warfare and aggressive nationalisms. Such arguments had informed the persistent campaigns waged by peace activists from 1815 to 1914. On 2 August 1914, as German troops poised to violate Belgian neutrality, a longtime Belgian peace activist gloomily predicted, "The Americans, the Chinese and the Japanese are preparing to profit from the ruination of Europe."[2]

World War I destroyed a host of expectations. Before 1914, a united Europe with a tribunal at The Hague and with cultural and political capitals at Brussels and Strasbourg was a favored futuristic vision of citizen activists seeking a peaceful

3

solution to the intractable problem of Alsace and Lorraine, France and Germany. The dream of a world made small by aviation and speedy communications figured in a pacifist utopia published in 1893, *Un Peu Plus Tard* by Edmond Potonié-Pierre, as well as in debates of international peace congresses. A single monetary system; the elimination of customs; a unified European educational system; history syllabi that celebrated human achievements (not military victories); and an ethos that cherished national and ethnic diversity (as Giuseppe Mazzini championed) stimulated the work of men and women who were frequently dismissed as utopians in the atmosphere of overheated nationalisms. The promise of reduced armories, of militias replacing professional and conscripted forces, of the conversion of armament plants into factories for civilian goods attracted adherents on the Continent from the time of the Napoleonic Wars down to the very last moment of peace on 31 July 1914. A profound change in the making of foreign policy, one that required open parliamentary votes on treaties and an end to secret alliances, became a demand at nearly every convention of peace activists in France and England—certainly this was true after the Dreyfus affair and the Boer War. (It was first articulated at The International Congress of Societies of Friends of Peace in Paris in 1878.) The benefits of a reduced military budget were anticipated by peace crusaders decade after decade, from Jean-Jacques, comte de Sellon, in Geneva during the 1830s down to Norman Angell in 1912–1913. By 1914, two distinct currents of peace activism flourished in Europe. Socialist internationalism has been studied so frequently that it is often considered to be the only one. The second approach, a secularly based internationalism, derived from religious and humanistic ideals and reinforced by social science analyses, was developed by a diverse community of middle-class, sometimes conservative, sometimes radical, voices.

Prior to the nineteenth century, the organization of a permanent peace among European states sporadically attracted the interest of an occasional ruler, minister, or philosopher interested in formalizing collective security among Christian rulers. From Dante Alighieri and Desiderius Erasmus through Jean-Jacques Rousseau, and Immanuel Kant, proposals for amphictyon councils among civilized (i.e., Christian) nations sprung either from moral and humanistic motives or from practical need—exhaustion after years of war. Where Erasmus's arguments in *The Complaint of Peace* echoed humanistic values, the project of Maximilien de Béthune, duc de Sully, the minister of Henri IV of France, reflected the pain of thirty years of torturous religious warfare. Similarly, the project of the Abbé de Saint-Pierre (Charles-Irénée Castel) in 1714 responded to the half-century of warfare that Louis XIV had unleashed in Europe.[3] Peace projects have mainly interested scholars and theorists; they never replaced the preference of dynastic rulers for what they understood as Niccolò Machiavelli's recipes for success. With the exception of the curious utopia of Louis-Sébastien Mercier, *Memoirs of the Year 2500* (1770), proposals for preserving peace ignored the internal structures of nations. Mercier's futuristic vision of France imagined a peaceful revolution shaped by enlightened, secular philosophy that persuaded men to create a just society and an international order.[4] In general, the right of the ruler to govern, to declare war, and to make peace was unchallenged in most pre-1789 prescriptions.

Peace as an issue to the anonymous subjects of the dynastic states of the Old Regime engaged the hearts and minds of very specific religious sects, groups formed in the upheavals of the Protestant Reformation. From George Fox in England, who shaped the first Quaker commitment "not to study war no more," across the European continent to communities of Mennonites and Brethren, a powerful Christian pacifist message developed that brought into being the weapon of nonviolent resistance. Committed, stubborn, willing to suffer martyrdom, communities of Christian pacifists rarely proselytized among nonbelieving neighbors. Persecuted, they frequently worked out arrangements with governing authorities to perform alternative service during war (e.g., medical aid) or to buy exemption through heavy fines and taxes. That they did not become a model for wide-spread opposition to war is a truism.[5] In the centuries of their creation, pacifist religious sects struggled to preserve the rights of their own members and not to challenge the structure of state and society. Christian pacifism and antimilitarism of the post-Reformation era, based on a re-interpretation of Gospel and tradition, largely defined "pacifism in the strict sense of an unconditional renunciation of war by the individual."[6]

During the French Revolution a connection was forged between prescriptions for both international peace and domestic justice. In their very different ways, Anacharsis Cloots (Jean-Baptiste du Val-de-Grâce, baron de Cloots, 1755–1794) and Immanuel Kant (1724–1804)[7]—both envisioning peace amid the ideological upheavals of the Revolutionary Wars—concluded that the establishment of republics governed by enlightened citizens was the essential precondition. The state was conceived as a moral community; governments were legitimate if they abided by a social contract. This was a sea change in political thinking that reflected the new era, not simply the victory of moral philosophy as Mercier had hoped. Thus, the political environment for the development of peace as a citizen's issue was formed in the late eighteenth century as revolutions swept the Atlantic shores.

During the nineteenth century, along with countless other issues—from public health to national liberation—peace became a citizen's mission—a subject of private conferences, of specialized periodicals, of national and international societies, of university and school curricula, and of challenges to parliamentary candidates. Small numbers of citizens, usually middle class and educated, gathered the courage to challenge the making of foreign policy by the elite corps surrounding executive authority. They offered a different vision of a Europe of the peoples that had no need of war. Overall, activists were unconscious of themselves as a class-based phenomenon until the formation of socialist parties and internationals in the 1860s. Many Continental partisans of organized peace defined their work as completing the unfinished business of the French Revolution.

With the Napoleonic Wars, a subtle shift in war/peace thinking occurred as political economists elaborated the relationship among warfare, militarism, and poverty. Analyses that focused on the political possibilities of a permanently organized peace continued to appear, but the context altered. During the nineteenth century, a new definition of citizenship slowly replaced the older status of subject. Loyalty to a nation of one's peers knit a new civic consciousness among Europeans. Advocates of organized international peace no longer addressed appeals to twenty-five rulers and prime ministers. Peace was claimed as a citizen's right as well as a necessity of modern life. It was promoted as the *desiderata* of *all* social classes that well-run governments must struggle to establish.

From a subject fitfully addressed by intellectuals and gifted public leaders, peace became the property of organized citizen movements. Intellectually, peace thinking moved from the province of philosophers to that of political economists and sociologists. From the social sciences, activists borrowed statistical and qualitative arguments to construct an arsenal in defense of peace.

Peace movements began in Great Britain, the United States, and the city of Geneva following the Treaty of Vienna (1815) and the end of twenty-five years of war and revolution. In nations that were relatively prosperous, where a tradition of citizen activism had been established, where a certain limited tolerance for political dissent existed, where multiple Protestant sects coexisted (however unhappily), and where a titled aristocracy commingled with moderate middle-class critics, peace societies were born. Peace societies also grew where a substantial portion of the economy shifted to commercial, financial, and industrial activity (including the commercialization of agriculture). The conditions required for private peace organizations were described by Ernesto T. Moneta in 1910:

> The pacifist idea is the product of free nations. Only where government is the creation of peoples who have conquered their own freedom, even by force, do citizens have the possibility of instilling in others the love of the Good and the hatred of arrogance . . . [and to] communicate through speech and press to the public.[8]

Thus, in Spain, Portugal, the Balkans, and tsarist Russia before 1905, peace societies were paper organizations of tiny groups of urban professionals. In contrast, by 1900, they commanded respectable followings in Great Britain, France, Scandinavia, the Netherlands, Belgium, Switzerland, and Italy. They were present in the Germanies and the Hapsburg Empire. Members tended to be progressive, liberal, sometimes radical (i.e., democratic in nineteenth-century usage), and occasionally socialist. (Socialist internationalism sprang from different roots than did peace activism.)

If truth is the first casualty of war, peace movements are a close second. Peace activists who labor during peacetime to educate fellow citizens against the necessity of war are vulnerable on every level when war breaks out: they can be imprisoned as potential traitors; they can withdraw to deal with the profound psychological crisis of living with a world that has thoroughly rejected their ideals; they can be ejected from teaching and parliamentary posts. Many retreat into embarrassed silence at the first artillery boom. During the nineteenth century, certainly until 1871, the fate of peace organizations among private citizens was in the hands of those who declared and waged wars. Membership in peace societies and at peace congresses usually evaporated when the boys marched or sailed away to fight. Peace movements that attempted to stop wars in progress were either crushed by governments or vilified by contemptuous, "patriotic" citizens.

The first section of this study of nineteenth-century movements on the European continent—a chronological overview—falls into three parts that reflect cycles of growth, collapse, and revival. In the first period, 1815 to 1850, peace activity took root in Europe. Introduced initially in a British, then an Anglo-American campaign anchored in religious precepts, peace activism attracted a small, educated, and articulate Continental clientele only when secular, pragmatic rational language replaced Gospel truth. The first entirely indigenous Continental peace organization was begun in Geneva in 1830, but the personality of its founder, Jean-Jacques, comte de Sellon, was so overwhelming that the group barely survived his death (1839). In Belgium and France during the 1830s and 1840s, peace arguments were developed by political economists, Fourierists, and Saint-Simonians. Progressive intellectuals and politicians formed serious societies to study and propagate arguments. The first stage of peace organization in Europe really came to a close with the counterrevolutions of 1850, the Crimean War, and the American Civil War—though a few faithful individuals plodded on. The mid-century counterrevolutions and wars wrecked efforts at creating an international network of peace activists that united peoples on the Atlantic shores.

Peace activism in the years from 1850 to 1870 developed a new sophistication after recovering from the wounds of the midcentury. In those years, when nation making and democratic stirrings forced changes in the lingering old regimes, a new generation of European activists interested in organizing peace grew up. By the end of this twenty-year period, two very distinct Continental groupings formed. The first, moderate to conservative, took its inspiration from liberal economics, admired Richard Cobden, and was broadly interested in the evolution of global markets and free trade. In the midcentury, Frédéric Passy, a student of the economist Frédéric Bastiat, rose to prominence as the chief European spokesperson of this position. The second grouping—more flamboyant, democratic, proud of its Jacobin roots, and anticlericalism—attracted Giuseppe Garibaldi, a radicalized Victor Hugo, John Stuart Mill (briefly), and a host of European democrats in exile. Formed in tandem with the First International, The International Workingman's Assocation, this second group tried, initially, to coordinate with working-class leaders in formulating demands. In the late 1860s, tensions stirred by the wars of German unification galvanized the creation of international peace societies led by both types of peace thinkers. A lively international debate among conservative, radical, and socialist voices crossed European borders to the consternation of conservatives and the papacy. With the Franco-Prussian War, the Treaty of Frankfurt ending that war, and the Paris Commune, the democratic peace movement was sundered. The alliance of German, Swiss, Italian, French, Dutch, Belgian, and British peace democrats disintegrated as did the First International, leaving an open field for the new aggressive nationalisms, social Darwinian theory, protectionism, and overseas imperialism. Continental states enlarged standing armies and created the concomitant arms race of the forty-four years of "peace" from 1871 to 1914.

In this last segment of the nineteenth century, European peace movements rose from the ashes of the Franco-Prussian War in a steady trajectory of development that lasted until 1914–1915. Peace organizations were formed in nearly every nation during these decades, spreading into the newly formed states of Italy and Germany as well as the Scandinavian nations. Where older groups existed, especially in France, Belgium, and Great Britain, newer ones joined them to represent new constituencies—workers and women, in particular. As the century wore on, groups of teachers, students, and university professors formed peace societies; full-time professional peace organizers and lecturers worked to spread the message. By the end of the 1880s, parliamentarians interested in organizing international peace began to hold their own meetings. On the centennial of the French Revolution, peace activists from the Continent and Great Britain finally formalized the century-long dream seeded in the initial Anglo-American peace crusade. A permanently organized movement was launched.

The years from 1889 to 1914, a quarter-century filled with crisis and threats to the breakdown of peace, were also a twenty-five-year period of unremitting growth of both national and international peace movements. A true international peace movement was formed, organized in two "peace internationals," in the years 1889 to 1891. One, consisting of members of parliaments, exists to this day as the Interparliamentary Union. The second, composed of private citizens, convened the "annual" Universal Peace Congress from 1889 to 1939 (except for the war years) and opened the Bureau international de la paix in 1891. On the eve of World War I, the president of the *bureau,* the Belgian senator, Henri La Fontaine, estimated that over a million people (mainly European and American) belonged to the movement. The movement became an organized transnational lobby with headquarters in Switzerland and Belgium.

In the quarter-century, 1889 to 1914, the two peace internationals—their lively national and regional sections, their affiliate organizations and the occasional supportive general or politician—debated and refined the positions that came to be known as liberal internationalism and Continental pacifism. The second half of this study explores the main principles and strategies developed by the citizen and parliamentary movements in those twenty-five years. The various proposals for the peaceful resolution of international conflict, broadly synthesized as arbitration, provided the diverse peace membership with its common denominator. Attitudes toward arms reduction and the difficulties of its attainment constituted a second major axis of peace thinking before World War I. Pacifist analyses of war and its role in history underlay the beliefs of modern patriotic pacifism. The internal evolution of the movements is charted as they gradually dropped their cautious and conservative tactics for assertive and critical campaigns to confront contemporary reality. On the eve of the Great War, efforts to join forces with the Second (Socialist) International increased, a recognition that the peace internationals would not succeed if they only focused on diplomats, ministers, rulers, presidents, and a few influential entrepreneurs and academics. Simultaneously, the enthusiasm of women activists in the international and national movements was a new ingredient that lifted spirits at the end of the century.

Not all the problems constricting the success of the movement rose from external circumstances. Within the community of international peace activists, profound political and national differences surfaced that reflected the cultural and political values of the activists. How the movement coped and failed to cope with these differences is very much a part of the story.

This book ends with a short epitaph that describes what happened to the close-knit community of international activists in 1914 and 1915 and, briefly, in the years that followed. It sets the stage for the new types of peace movements that were born in World War I and that functioned in the interwar years. Perhaps this overview of the nineteenth century will provide perspective to those who are planning for the twenty-first century.

A considerable number of unfamous people populate the following pages. Too many of these characters will remain unsatisfactory stick figures or disembodied spirits—sometimes for lack of information and sometimes because of the pressures of compressing a century's worth of unfamiliar material between two covers. Most of the peace activists scattered across the Continent are "disappeared" people. Occasionally, a voice comes through: a man who struggled for years against the arms race and worked to rename a street in Perpignan "rue de la Paix — quai Nobel" to counter the many streets named for battles.[9] There was the poor provincial teacher, a Monsieur Fayette, who scrimped to provide his students with copies of the *Almanach des jeunes amis de la paix* in 1892 to balance the crass nationalism of their history primers.[10] A saddened Belgian student member of the Circle des étudiants pacifistes reported, in 1915, that his fellow students at the Institut Solvay had no "fears . . . about giving their blood for the defense of their land of birth and most sacred rights." Those that were not captured or killed when the Germans entered Belgium were fighting with other armies in order to bring about world peace in the end.[11] They put their prewar dreams of a peaceful Europe out of mind until the conditions for a durable peace were possible after the Germans were driven out. They were fighting to make the world safe for peace.

Invariably, the history of peace movements or the arguments of peace activists inspire "realist" reactions, ranging from mildly critical to enraged. Who can take seriously such a flawed, failed movement that crumbled when World War I broke out? Is there something questionable about a scholar who spends a decade trying to restore these people and their organizations to the historical record—perhaps she is a fellow traveler? Neither the activists in the movement nor this particular author confused possibilities with realities. The peace community was acutely aware of its restricted impact: the power of those in boardrooms, classrooms, editorial rooms, and cabinets to trivialize their arguments; the compelling attraction of vulgarized social Darwinism to intellectuals and much of the public; its inability to cut one military budget request in any European parliament; its total incapacity to alter hostile, derogatory images of pacifism in the press and among many intellectuals. Although Continental peace activists believed that the international economy, culture, and value system of Europeans was a promising base for legal and political collaboration, they did not believe that a new European polity would automatically evolve by predetermined historical necessity. Human agency was crucial; the future did not evolve, it was shaped. The forces making for disaster might well succeed. After 1889, peace activists reflected increasing sensitivity to the dangers of a full-scale Continental war that might pit two alliances against each other: the Triple Alliance of Austria-Hungary, Germany, and Italy and the Dual Alliance of France and tsarist Russia (joined in an entente in 1904 and in 1907 expanded with the addition of Great Britain). If anything, they were prophetic about the probable outcome of a future war among the "civilized" nations. Pacifists understood that they represented one side of a struggle for the soul of Europe and that they could easily lose. Their awareness of possible failure fueled painful debates over how to make propaganda and education more effective.[12]

Continental peace activists developed several specific versions of pacifism, none of which usually pleased British and American absolute religious pacifists nor, for that matter, Leo Tolstoy, who had developed his anarchist and absolutist Christian pacifist position by the late nineteenth century. The European pacifist generally qualified his or her antiwar and propeace position with various exceptions for self- and national defense. Most Continental peace activists refused to abandon the right to fight for national independence or to end oppression. Tolstoy tolerated no exceptions. Quite simply, he insisted, "the way to do away with war is for those who do not want war . . . to refrain from fighting."[13] The formation of an international peace movement required that the distinct and sometimes conflicting forms of pacifist analysis learn to live within the parameters of the same organization. Only between 1889 and 1914 have pacifists from so many nations ever succeeded in that kind of association. It was not an easy experience, and the divisions cemented into place by nationalism and the nation-state finally destroyed the experiment.

Nonetheless, the struggle waged by peace campaigners reveals that not everyone was engaged in creating the long- or short-term causes of the Great War. Among concerned Europeans, especially after the *fin de siècle,* an awareness took root that a transnational European civilization was in the making. It needed protection from traditionalist, myopic, and militarist forces. The new civilization required an organized system for the preservation of peace. That was the essential thrust of Continental pacifism or liberal internationalism.

Two world wars, the rise of fascism, and the Cold War buried the optimistic nineteenth-century international peace movement in obscurity. Its history, diverse to begin with, is a challenge to reconstruct. Surviving sources are scattered across two continents. In some instances, records were destroyed: inadvertantly, as in the Parisian fire at the Hôtel de Ville during the Commune (1871), or deliberately, either by Fascists or to protect people from Fascist and Nazi violence from the 1920s through 1945.[14] Nonetheless, the peace movements of the century that began with the Napoleonic Wars and ended with World War I left sufficient tracks behind, so that future generations can appreciate the alternative paths that they cut.

I

THE ORGANIZATION
OF NATIONAL AND
INTERNATIONAL PEACE
MOVEMENTS IN EUROPE
1815–1914

1

The Debut of European Peace Movements, 1815–1850: From Elite Prescriptions to Middle-Class Participation

Nothing inspires interest in a durable international peace quite as effectively as decades of murderous, debilitating warfare. In April 1792, France, in its third year of revolution, went to war against the Hapsburgs and eventually all the crowned heads of Europe. In the next twenty-three years, ending with the Battle of Waterloo, there were few years of peace as the peoples of Europe and, eventually, the new United States battled for a host of new causes, such as liberty, national freedom, the rights of neutrals, and the abolition of feudalism, or in defense of older causes, such as privilege, imperial control and the salvation of the old regimes. The wars commingled ideological and material motives. At the end, besides the traditional diplomatic meeting to shape the formal peace, there was an unexpected outcome: a critical citizen consciousness that challenged the necessity as well as morality of this presumably legal form of mass murder.

In 1814–1815, exhaustion finally overwhelmed whatever initial enthusiasms had prompted the original mobilizations of men and nations. From Moscow to Madrid, corpses, cemeteries, and battlefields abounded, endowing future generations with memorabilia sufficient for a century of holidays and patriotic celebrations. Rural villages housed larger numbers of marriageable young women than available men, creating a legacy of spinsterhood as well as a dramatic increase in the numbers of hungry orphans and widows. Twenty-two years of warfare overturned centuries of privilege and tradition that, in 1815, hastened to reassert its legitimacy and authority at a congress of the victors and the restored rulers in Vienna.

A few farsighted thinkers and realistic politicians recognized that the wars of the French Revolutionary and Napoleonic years had changed the relationship between war and politics forever. Dynasts had once waged war almost at whim;

that game was now too dangerous to play. War threatened thrones and toppled the social order. It disrupted commerce and destroyed harvests, undermining economies in nations where populations had learned to express their discontent. In 1815, the possibility of eliminating or, at least, controlling the outbreak of war among civilized peoples preoccupied three unrelated groups of Europeans: the international political and diplomatic elites, individual writers and intellectuals alert to socioeconomic changes, and, finally, citizen activists.

The Congress of Vienna, which sat in 1815 to liquidate the consequences of a generation of war and revolution, produced an ambiguous legacy. Its leading participants, representing the great powers of the day—Russia, Prussia, the Austrian monarchy, Great Britain and, finally, France under the restored Bourbon monarch—were obviously engaged in an attempt to restore the temporal and spiritual reality of the Old Regime as closely as possible. But these powers also talked of creating a permanent congress system, encased in a Holy Alliance, that would convene periodically in peacetime, to resolve international tensions. Friedrich von Gentz, a participant in the Vienna meeting as chief adviser to Count Klemens, Fürst von Metternich, the Austrian host and plenipotentiary, went so far as to claim:

> The political system existing in Europe since 1814 and 1815 is a phenomenon without precedent in the world's history. In place of the principle of equilibrium . . . , the counterweights formed by separate alliances . . . there has succeeded a principle of general union, uniting all the states collectively with a federating bond.[1]

The motives for this "federating bond" were not altruistic—they were antirevolutionary. The determination of the monarchs to retain their thrones was formalized in the 1820 Protocol of Troppau; this obliged the congress system to intervene against revolution and uprisings. After 1821, when troops representing the Congress of Europe repressed Neapolitan and Spanish revolutionaries, this intention could not be mistaken. In theory, the congress system was formed to keep peace; in reality, it established an interstate system to intervene against revolution.[2]

The impact of over two decades of warfare on contemporary life intrigued intellectuals and reformers. Writing in the early nineteenth century, the founders of modern schools of political economy—liberal and socialist—examined the effects of warfare on economic growth. The liberal theorist, Jean-Baptiste Say, influenced at least two successive generations with his views on the depressive impact of war on development.[3] As Napoleonic glory deteriorated into increasing privation, both Charles Fourier and Henri de Saint-Simon fashioned their well-known criticisms. Saint-Simon prepared a memorandum for the diplomats at Vienna on ways to preserve the peace.[4] The difference between these analyses of the effects of war and the earlier peace projects—such as the classic proposals of King George of Bohemia, Éméric Crucé, the duc de Sully, William Penn, and the Abbé de Saint-Pierre—was their emphasis on the domestic impact of war. Peace projects designed by thinkers before the nineteenth century had offered technical propositions for preserving dynastic sovereignty within a European governance structure.[5] The new socioeconomic theorists had a different agenda. Saint-Simon and Augustin Thierry, who offered the Congress of Vienna a project for organizing a governance in Europe, believed that a new stage in human history was about to begin, one based on entirely novel economic and technological realities. Concerned with encouraging the natural evolution of modern history fueled by the powerful driving forces of commerce and industry, nineteenth-century thinkers subjected war and peace to statistical analyses. They quantified destruction; they counted the lost labor hours; they estimated the quantity of capital lost to investment; they observed sociological correlations between arms races and social unrest or militarism and the crime rate. As the century progressed, the study of war was enriched by insights from sociology, both positivist and organicist.

The third response catalyzed by the generation of warfare was unique. Private citizens, many of whom had begun to transform Enlightenment ideas into civic organizations, were horrified by tales of battlefield carnage, and they turned to creating societies of "friends of peace." The reformist impulse, which inspired private intiatives for domestic causes, took up arms against man's oldest profession. From the Quaker meetings and the pulpits of progressive clergy, an insistent chorus of antiwar protest began to swell on both sides of the Atlantic.[6] The initiative was largely Anglo-American. In 1815–1816, organizations that evolved into the London (later British) Peace Society and the American Peace Society began their long careers in antiwar propaganda. Unlike religious practitioners of absolute pacifism, the new "friends of peace" launched campaigns to persuade a larger public. They wanted to do more than bear personal Christian witness against evil. In England, opposition to William Pitt the Younger's war against the French Revolution provided experience in lobbying the government against official foreign policy, a relatively new form of citizen action.[7]

Unlike other reform societies, the "friends of peace" confronted the daunting necessity of implanting their message across national boundaries into countries with no traditions of constitutional government, citizen participation, or dissenting religious presence. The Anglo-American crusaders began their struggle as the Congress of Vienna concluded and Tsar Alexander I of Russia announced the formation of the Holy Alliance, based on Christian principles.

The founding fathers of the American and British peace movements were surprised and delighted to discover that initiatives against war began almost simultaneously in London, New York City, Massachusetts, and Warren County, Ohio. The London Society for the Promotion of Permanent and Universal Peace was launched by William Allen, Joseph T. Price, William Crawford, and John and Thomas Clarkson—men with distinguished experience in philanthropic and humanitarian causes, notably against the slave trade.[8] Across the Atlantic, the American organizers included David L. Dodge and the Reverend Noah Worcester.[9] The fact that peace societies were formed on both sides of the broad Atlantic nearly simultaneously and without mutual knowledge seemed to be the work of the hand of God.

The struggle undertaken by the small Anglo-American peace crusade to convert both their own compatriots as well as Continental Europeans was waged bravely, devotedly, and against odds that proved insurmountable. English agents traveled to the Netherlands, Belgium, western Germany, and particularly to France throughout the 1820s, 1830s and 1840s—lecturing, holding private meet-

ings with eminent scholars and (usually) Protestant divines, underwriting translations of tracts on the un-Christian nature of warfare, and inviting promising
Continental figures to London. English efforts were reinforced in the 1840s with
the arrival of Elihu Burritt from the United States—the "learned blacksmith" particularly appealed to French and Belgian liberals. Precisely how significant or
influential were these Anglo-Saxon initiatives? There is no certain answer. At the
end of the century when a permanent, internationally organized peace movement
functioned, its leaders often paid polite lip service to their Anglo-American pioneers but also distanced themselves from the absolutist religious prescriptions of
the founders.

In 1821, the London Peace Society hailed the birth of the Société de la morale
chrétienne in Paris, launched by reform-minded aristocrats and bourgeoisie—
many Protestant. The Duc de la Rochefoucauld-Liancourt, who had traveled in
Britain and North America, as well as Alexandre de Laborde, another widely traveled gentlemen, headed a society committed to reform causes, including peace.
French politics in the 1820s, particularly the struggle to oust the ultraconservative
Bourbon regime, soon absorbed the Protestant and liberal Catholic membership
and the original objectives, including peace, of the *société* were shelved. The group
became a center of political opposition. Following the July Revolution of 1830,
when Louis-Philippe was installed as a Constitutional monarch, a number of the
members of the organization, including François Guizot, the new prime minister,
assumed leadership positions, and the *société* itself lost much of its purpose. Not
until 1841 was peace to reappear in its considerations.

The first continental society devoted to peace appeared in Geneva in 1830, the
work of a reform-minded, Protestant noble with long experience in public service:
Jean-Jacques, comte de Sellon (1782–1839).[10] Sellon's leadership of the Société de
la paix de Génève lasted till his death when, despite efforts by his daughter, Valentine de Sellon, the group became inactive.

Born into an illustrious family of Huguenot origins who had come to Geneva
to escape French persecution, Sellon grew up as an admirer of the Enlightenment
and of progressive change but as an enemy of popular participation associated
with the French Revolution. The writings of Cesare Beccaria, especially *Crimes
and Punishments,* and the model of Tuscany under the enlightened Hapsburgs in
the late eighteenth century persuaded Sellon that the death penalty was a grave
error, and immoral and counterproductive form of punishment. After Napoléon's
empire collapsed, Sellon's political career on the Genevan governing council
ended because of his identification with the French leader. By the 1820s, however,
Sellon, pursuing his favorite cause, the abolition of the death penalty, reentered
political life with a flourish. His campaign was directed at the Genevan government as well as toward a larger European public through a stream of broadsides,
essays, pamphlets, private letters and lectures. This was a men of energetic commitment, unafraid to pursue an unpopular cause.

In 1829–1830, he took up the peace cause as the logical extension of his campaign against the death penalty. Sellon insisted that both causes were politically
safe issues; he was not a disguised Jacobin. "Friends of peace," he argued "have
only one line of conduct to follow: to make an appeal to religious principles and

demonstrate, with patient perseverence, the evils of war."[11] Sincere in his belief that the peace cause transcended class and political identification, Sellon sent his appeal forward to all national groups, to all educational levels, to both sexes, to any occupation.

He was not alone in claiming that peace was a humanitarian, apolitical issue. British pacifists and French reformers had also made the same assertion. In 1819, the organizers of the London Peace Society announced:

> With party politics, the friends of peace have nothing to do. The cause is a *religious,* not a *political* one, and the moment we lose sight of the one, and in any way verge toward the other, the best pillar of support is lost.[12]

Similarly, the founders of the Parisian Société de la morale chrétienne maintained that their purpose was to forward "the progress of civilization" and "to diminish the causes of intestine discords and foreign wars by opposing party hatred and the prejudices of an extravagent and blind patriotism."[13] The profession that the cause was apolitical was meant to calm conservatives.

The British, French, and Genevan patrons of the peace cause did not intend that peace societies include citizens from every social level. Membership was mainly liberal middle and upper class. The London organizers were blunt. In 1819, they published an anonymous letter in the *Herald of Peace* that recommended recruiting the lower classes into peace agitation. The letter charged that the peace society

> ignored that particular grade of society by whom its views might be expected to be most materially advanced; I meant the *lower* classes. For who are the persons that constitute the physical materiél [*sic*] in any army? unquestionably, the poor, the dissolute and the comparatively ignorant.[14]

If the lower classes could be "prevailed on . . . to refuse the selling of themselves, . . . in vain, would kings declare war when deprived of the physical means" of fighting.[15] The author urged the peace society to undertake a campaign of mass organizing to teach resistance and refusal.

To this proposal, the leaders of the London Peace Society issued a flat rejection. Ending war was the work of the ruling classes who control politics and view the army as "a regular and honourable profession . . . for their own aggrandizement."[16] This attitude remained relatively unchanged for several decades, leading during the 1840s to a serious split in Great Britain between middle-class, religiously based peace activism, and that segment of the Chartist movement, led by Thomas Cooper, that embraced antiwar positions.

A similar belief that reform must come from the enlightened privileged classes characterized the work of the Parisian group under Rochefoucauld-Liancourt as well as Sellon's Genevan *société*. Sellon particularly admired the changes that occurred when educated gentlement pooled their talents to create useful things, such as dredging canals, widening the locks on Lake Geneva, cutting paved roads into the Alps, improving the productivity of farms. As an example of that kind of commitment, Sellon gave generously of his personal fortune and time, publishing a variety of journals, annuals, and pamphlets, as well as organizing meetings. He engaged in a voluminous correspondence, including an interesting series of letters to his sister's son, the young Camillo di Cavour,[17] and to the exiled Louis-Napoléon.[18] He was not bashful about describing the work of the *société* and inviting support, even from people he hardly knew.[19] But he did not convene public meetings as did the Saint-Simonians, for instance, a practice he disliked. None of the proceedings of the Genevan *société* record any discussion or voting on resolutions. Sellon wrote and publicized the *société's* positions.

Although Sellon was well aware that peace societies existed in England and the United States, he seems not to have borrowed from their growing arsenal of publications. Informed by his own views of history and contemporary issues, he combined a moral and practical approach to his attack on war. Using a utilitarian approach, he argued that just as the death penalty never deterred crime, war never brought peace. The new political economy of Europe, demonstrated that "a beneficial revolution of . . . industrialism and economics" was replacing the "warlike and monarchical spirit" of the past.[20] The reduction of military expenses would provide means for social and cultural services that the "new age" desperately needed. Considering the often-degraded condition of the poor, Sellon fervently urged popular education, which reduced military expenses (the peace dividend) would make possible. He looked with an envious eye on Sweden, the United States, and Scotland, where public lectures, circulating libraries, and Sunday school classes reached out to the uneducated. (He was especially impressed with South Carolina, where, he believed, a Monsieur Grimké used the Sunday school classes for peace education.)[21] Besides education, savings on military expenses would allow vast improvements throughout Europe: desperately needed highways, canals to connect the Mediterranean and Red seas, museums of natural history, botanical gardens, public works, funds "to help the poor without creating more poverty," repairs on crumbling churches, creation of chairs of political economy at universities, and perhaps even the extension of the "sweetness of civilization" to the barbaric peoples of the globe.[22] Were the three million men currently under arms to be released into the labor market, Sellon argued that they could be employed at once on useful projects, "building bridges, roads, canals, penitentiaries for the rehabilitation of criminals and [possibly] the colonization of Africa."[23] His hope was for the peaceful penetration of Africa, and he denounced the method used by the French government in Algiers in 1830: military invasion.

Sellon plumbed European history for proof that military force rarely achieved its objectives. "Did a standing army save Louis XVI or Charles X?" he noted sarcastically.[24] What conqueror could manage to hold onto territories by force once their populations demanded freedom? Sellon asked. "European peoples are so attached to their national independence, to their *nationality,* that holding onto conquests is no longer feasible," he wrote, clearly recalling the recent Napoleonic experiences in Switzerland, Spain, Austria, Prussia, southern Italy, and the Netherlands.[25] Military force had not preserved the union of Belgium with the Netherlands in 1830, nor was it much use in keeping Greece attached to the Ottoman Empire.[26] He expected that the French invasion of Algeria would eventually lead to profound enmity rather than prosperity and trade. In Sellon's view, European desires to bring both Christianity and commerce to Africa were not likely to succeed if the means were warfare—the murder of potential customers hardly made their survivors likely to be interested consumers.

Sellon was one of the first peace thinkers who wanted the congress system proposed in 1815 at Vienna to become a pacific reality, "If the Holy Alliance had this aim, it would indeed be holy; it would have far better insured the inheritance of thrones and the duration of empires."[27] In the 1830s, Sellon gave considerable thought to developing a governance system for Europe that was consonant with national realities, the rule of a talented elite, and overall European traditions. He established competitive prize-essay contests to encourage thinking on the subject; in 1836, Professor Sartorius of Zurich won a four-hundred-franc medal for his contribution.[28]

Sartorius's proposal reflected Sellon's ideals, "I dare to propose," wrote Sellon, "the creation of a permanent Congress, not to dethrone sovereigns, but to deliver peoples from the burden of war."[29] The congress had to agree on an agenda with three main topics: (1) a declaration of human rights that rejected capital punishment; (2) a promise to transform standing armies into militias or national guards; and (3) the establishment of a permanent tribunal for the arbitration of disputes among nations.[30] The jurisdiction of this congress and its offspring, the tribunal, would cover the international relations among states, not domestic differences between citizens and government. In Europe, the congress would have to represent "national clusters" and not individual nations, given the problem of small states and big powers. Thus, France would represent a cluster that included Spain, Portugal, Italy, Belgium, and the Swiss Romande; the German Confederation would represent the Netherlands, German Switzerland, Sweden, and Denmark; the Russians would represent the Slavic and Greek peoples. Possibly, Great Britain would be represented by the German voice, but Sellon was not clear on this point. In the 1830s, the Germans had created the *Zollverein* and had a reputation as a pacific people. The French had been the adventurous militarists, threatening the peace from the days of Louis XIV through Napoléon.

For Sellon, the heart of an organized peace was a permanent international tribunal staffed with trained jurists. Sellon was not certain that the absence of a defined body of international law was sufficient reason to delay calling the congress and establishing the tribunal. He lobbied widely to have his project receive a hearing—with Louis-Philippe after 1830; the Duke of Buckingham, Louis-Napoléon (in exile); the scholarly academies in France; and the Parisian Société de la morale chrétienne. Given his belief in the right and responsibility of elite actors to fashion the future, his method of communication was perfectly logical.

Sellon did little to insure the permanence of the Genevan *société*. After his death, a member of the *société* noted:

> The Count de Sellon, by his own indefatigable zeal, had too much accustomed [us] to remain inactive; and since the loss of [our] leader, who acted for [us] all, [we] have been unable to continue the publication of [the] *Archives*.[31]

Valentine de Sellon appeared at a congress of peace activists in 1878 to remind a new generation of her father's work.[32] It is not possible to trace a direct connection between Sellon's peace *société* and the many organizations founded in Switzerland later in the century. But Sellon's writings were an uncanny collection of ideas that prefigured most of the thinking of Continental peace activists for decades to come.

In Paris, during the 1830s, the president of the Société de la morale chrétienne, the Marquis Frédéric Gaëtan, son of the duc de la Rochefoucauld-Liancourt, continued his father's tie to the London Peace Society.[33] In the Chamber of Peers, the marquis energetically protested massacres of Arabs at El Ouffla and demanded cuts in the French military budget.[34] But the *société* did not take up an anticolonial campaign. Finally, in 1841, after the London Peace Society promised to fund a prize essay on "The Best Means to Advance and Obtain the Benefit of Universal and Permanent Peace," the *société* agreed to organize a competition. A war scare in 1840 followed by an outpouring of popular emotion when Napoléon's remains were returned to the Invalides in 1840, an occasion when sentiment for past military glories reached manic proportions in Paris.[35]

The winner of the competition was the publicist and political economist, Constantin Pecqueur, an author in debt both to Fourier and Saint-Simon.[36] Unlike Sartorius, Pecqueur was disinterested in institutionalized approaches to organizing peace. Pecqueur attacked the subject by surveying the major proposals of all the previous thinkers—from Eméric Crucé to Jeremy Bentham—and then ignoring them. Only Saint-Simon spoke a language relevant to contemporary times. Pecqueur examined the decades since 1815 and was able to report on the positive outcome of twenty-five years of peace. The development of technology, industries, agricultural productivity, and the dramatic appearance of the steam engine in transportation were sufficient proof of the flowering of human possibilities when the land was not wrecked by warfare. Still, even in peacetime, too much wealth was devoted to maintaining standing armies. He proposed that these disciplined groups of trained men not be disbanded. Instead, they could be mobilized to defeat difficult natural challenges (e.g., building railways over the Alps). Soldiers with nothing to do became bored and decadent. Stories from Algeria indicated serious morale problems in the military. Pecqueur as well as his contemporary, Ferdinand Durand, both urged the use of armies for public works developments.[37]

From Fourier, Pecqueur integrated a belief in the possibility of human associations. The ability of peoples to extend and expand communities meant nationalism was a passing stage on the road to a larger universal organization. The creation of the German economic community in the 1830s, the *Zollverein,* was striking proof of the possibilities of human association. Although nations were useful structures to defend peoples against aggression, they would become passé if the normal course of evolution continued. (To Pecqueur there was no question that defensive war remained legitimate, a typical view among Continental peace thinkers.) The requirements of a new global economic order would force the creation of a pacific Europe.

With this analysis, Pecqueur proposed a different approach than the British peace community.[38] The absolute value of a peaceful world was not a moral imperative, it was a pragmatic requirement of modern social and economic forces. The achievements of the years since 1815 were proof. A future of international organization would evolve from the natural tendency of human groups to enlarge their associations and commingle their cultures. Pecqueur paid no attention to the practical issue of how to get the diplomats to sit down at a table and design some logical system. He identified a sweep of history and was disinterested in housekeeping details.

During the 1840s, in particular, the Saint-Simonian legacy that surfaced among French writers, journalists, and political economists brought peace issues to consciousness and probably had more impact than direct appeals to humanitarian or Christian objectives. Analyses similar to Pecqueur's appeared in the writings of Gustave d'Eichthal, Frédéric Bastiat, Michel Chevalier, Charles Lemonnier, Gustave de Molinari, and Joseph Garnier. In France, newspapers such as *Le Globe, La Presse, La Réforme,* and the prestigious *Journal des économistes* were much more influential than a proliferation of peace committees would have been.[39] D'Eichthal, for instance, echoed Pecqueur's prediction that traditional warfare seemed to be disappearing from advanced cultures, replaced by "expeditions" and "police actions" abroad. War, he observed, "now tends to take on an amphictyonic [*sic*] character."[40] Distant military expeditions that killed "uncivilized" people rarely provoked liberal criticism.

In 1844, in Paris, the Saint-Simonienne, Eugénie Niboyet[41] followed up Pecqueur's prize essay by establishing the first newspaper on the Continent devoted to peace issues, thereby fulfilling another of the ambitions of British peace activists. Niboyet was influenced by the fact that a "world" congress of peace activists had met in London in 1843 and issued public calls for support. Niboyet, a member of both the Paris-based Société de la morale chrétienne and a Saint-Simonian "church," appeared destined briefly in the early 1830s for a high position in the latter organization.[42] A feminist and trained journalist, she launched *La Paix des deux mondes,* which appeared from February through October 1844, followed by *L'Avenir,* equally short-lived. Though the former paper lasted less than one year, the issues aired in it were significant and touched on the growing differences between peace activists and their ideologies.

She, too, was impressed by the results of thirty years of peace in Europe. Although prosperity was not evenly distributed, nonetheless, it was visible everywhere. "Progress," observed Niboyet, "the light of peoples, has no need of cannons or rifles to advance; the conquests of industry are achieved without striking a blow."[43] This vision enraged partisans of France's glorious military past and unleashed bitter militarist attacks. She was charged with treasonable instincts for describing the British Peace Society in glowing terms; her arguments in favor of reduced arms expenditures added fuel to that fire. Niboyet responded by insisting that France's real glory would come from superior economic performance, one that would overshadow other European nations and produce preeminence through peaceful prosperity.[44]

Her admiration for British peace activists changed dramatically when Niboyet realized that "those certain Christians" who denounced all war as illegitimate were the same people who refused to admit the inequality of the distribution of wealth. Misery among the poorest classes had to be alleviated by vast projects of public works, she argued, and rich, selfish people—no matter how pacific—were not useful additions to the cause. Peace without recognition of social justice at its heart, to Niboyet, was fraud.[45] This position placed her closer to the English Chartists than to the classicial arguments of the British Peace Society. The appeal sent by William Lovett to French workers in 1844, for instance, called out, "Brothers . . . while the Ocean separates us, we are nonetheless united by the justice of our principles and the similarity of our interests." He continued by reminding French workers of their mutually spilled blood at the opening of the century, a sufficient sacrifice "between two peoples who, by the superiority of their intelligence, ought to be leading the world to freedom."[46] Lovett's appeal urged French workers to support peaceful solutions, including arbitration, to international conflicts. That sort of language closely reflected the ideals that Niboyet represented. Both she and the radical Chartists pointed to a new direction in peace thinking, one that did not sink roots in peace societies until 1867. In any case, financial insolvency ended her attempt to popularize the peace cause through journalism.

It was not the religious message from Britain that impacted on Continental consciousness during the 1840s as much as the successful crusade led by the energetic Richard Cobden (1804–1865)[47] and the Anti-Corn-Law League. The success of this organization was closely studied in western Europe. Indeed, an entire tradition of French pacifism was molded by Cobdenite views, gradually replacing the Saint-Simonian analysis in significance. This tradition, begun by Frédéric Bastiat, was articulated by Frédéric Passy (1822–1912) who eventually was co-winner with Henri Dunant (1828–1910) of the first Nobel Peace Prize (1901).[48] British peace thinking made converts among the Belgian economists and political thinkers, for example, Émile de Laveleye and Auguste Visschers.[49]

The indefatigable British crusaders, failing to spawn peace societies across the Channel, turned to yet another propaganda method in the 1840s: the international congress. The successful, well-attended World Anti-Slavery Convention held in London in 1840 had publicized the horrors of slavery, and peace activists decided to adapt the congress model. In 1843 in London, the First General Peace Convention was called—a meeting that could be called *international* because 26 delegates came from the United States and 6 from Europe, out of a total of 334 delegates, mainly Britons. Religious and theological assumptions dominated the meeting, which was "to deliberate upon the best means under the Divine blessing to show the world the evil and inexpediency of the spirit and practive of war, and to promote permanent and universal peace."[50] Within this framework, however, the papers and speeches addressed contemporary and historical reality. Much like the antislavery meeting, this congress permitted women to be seen, but not heard.

The British speakers took the occasion to voice ringing denunciations of overseas violence against non-European peoples. At one session, Charles Hindley, M.P., attacked French destruction of the rule of Queen Pomare IV in Tahiti, British action "for the purpose of pressing a deleterious drug upon the people" of China and war in Afghanistan "to press the people to pay allegiance to a foreign power."[51] The theme was continued by other speakers who wondered how heathen peoples would ever be converted by Christian swords. How could a handful of British soldiers ever expect to control Afghan borders with hundreds of people "hidden in the caves and fastnesses of that country," asked another participant.[52]

The congress heard a paper that reviewed the history of war, which noted that the last time France enjoyed a long period of peace was in the previous millennium under the early Capets. Since then, the more monies were spent on armaments, the more wars were fought. The French delegate, the Marquis de la Rochfoucauld-Liancourt, demonstrated a direct correlation between increases in crime and criminality and war scares, with particular reference to 1840.

The congress favored arbitration clauses and a high court of nations to keep the peace in Europe but hesitated to endorse the favorite American project, a congress of nations—an idea urged by William Ladd in a widely circulated essay on the subject.[53] Denunciations of armaments and the increase in budgets for weapons passed easily. The peace congress found time for tactical details: how women might be more effective as local petition organizers; how ministers might be more influential in their communities. An open meeting of two thousand at Exeter Hall (London) closed the congress. The organizers of the peace congress thought of it as a great success but had no plans to repeat the exercise.

Only after the American "learned blacksmith," Elihu Burritt, arrived in Britain in 1846 was another peace congress initiated. Burritt wanted Paris, but the 1848 revolution forced a move to Brussels, where Auguste Visschers agreed to help organize a meeting. Visschers, prominent as an exponent of public education and the abolition of the death penalty, was an admirer of Richard Cobden and free trade thinking.[54]

The Second International Peace Congress, which sat in September 1848, followed an agenda shaped by liberal political economics, especially free trade formulations. One young British recruit to the movement, the devout Henry Richard (1812–1888) who was to succeed Cobden as head of the British Peace Society, was troubled by the absence of any reference to Christian injunctions.[55] The 1848 meeting revealed that if religious peace activists wanted to participate in a European-wide movement, they would have to exchange the sermon for the speech.

The program of the international peace movement at Brussels emphasized arbitration as the best strategy for the resolution of conflicts among nations. Arbitration did not damage national sovereignty nor did it require that the historic diversity of domestic institutions in European nations be challenged. Burritt, however, wanted delegates to center the campaign for peace on the idea of a congress of nations. American delegates offered their own constitution as a model, proposing that Europeans create a court that would allow a potential case such as *Ohio* v. *Pennsylvania* to be settled without civil war. Europeans, including Cobden, realized that on a continent where absolute monarchs bordered constitutional states, an American-style Supreme Court was not a realistic proposal. To create a federal system among European states would require years of warfare. Burritt was the first of many U.S. peace crusaders to be disappointed by the European reception of American recommendations.

Further difficulties arose over the issue of "disarmament"—a word freighted with different meanings. One delegate, Spanish publicist Ramón de la Sagra, vehemently denounced any support for arms reduction on a continent where there was no other means of preserving the social order. He warned peace delegates that they were wandering dangerously close to the revolutionary proposals of radical democrats. Uncomfortable, the delegates settled on innocuous language to urge arms reduction in principle on the governments of "Christendom." Before departing, the delegates voted to sponsor a prize-essay competition on the best ways to establish and preserve international peace. The prize was eventually awarded to a young Belgian lawyer, Louis Bara, whose achievement was honored in 1849 at the Third International Peace Congress, which did get permission to meet in the French capital.[56]

The Paris Peace Congress which opened in August 1849, surpassed the expectations of its organizers. Of all the midcentury international congresses, it came to be memorialized as the apex of the movement, a rich source of peace-movement lore and legend in future decades. The hopes of the Anglo-American peace societies for Continental participation were fulfilled in 1849.

Permission to hold the congress in Paris was wrung from a nervous police chief only after pressure from eminent personages: Alexis de Tocqueville; Victor Hugo; Francisque Bouvet; the archibishop of Paris; Isadore, grand rabbi of France; Horace Say, a councilor of state; Joseph Garnier, the editor of the *Journal des économistes;* leaders of the Société de la morale chrétienne; Michel Chevalier; a reluctant Alphonse de Lamartine as well as a number of eminent entrepreneurs. Sponsors swore that the meeting would not deal with current issues and politics.[57] (This promise was impossible to keep.) Originally the archbishop was to preside, but illness intervened and Victor Hugo stepped in.

The participation of so many notables—including several eminent Belgian scholars; a contingent of British M.P.s, led by Richard Cobden; French economist Frédéric Bastiat; French journalist Émile de Girardin; and an American delegation that even boasted two former slaves—encouraged more respectful press treatment than was usual, though the presence of somberly dressed English Quakers and Quakeresses strained the ability of French journalists to control their sarcasm. This was the first time that people from the Germanies, Italies, and the Netherlands also came, though as individuals not as organized groups. One estimate calculated about six hundred delegates and between one thousand and two thousand spectators in the salon at the Chausée d'Antin.[58] The motives for the participants differed. Bastiat, for instance, confided privately that the political climate in France demanded that steps be taken to insure international peace. The looming fiscal crisis that threatened national stability, in his view ought to be met by increased taxation, but such a solution would "increase the sufferings of the people, already so overwhelmed and so irritated against the rich by the dangerous insinuations of socialism." Bastiat feared a coming social upheaval. The only logical way out was "by a reduction of our War expenditures."[59]

Hugo's opening speech has become the best-known document of the nineteenth-century peace movement. He predicted the evolution of a United States of Europe based on the historic past of most of France and other parts of Europe. Whereas once war raged from "commune to commune, city to city, province to province" and once "Lorraine, Picardy, Normandy, Brittany, the Auvergne, Provence, Dauphiny and Burgundy were separate entities," they had since become one nation—France.

A day will come when you, France; you, Russia; you, Italy; you, England; you, Germany—all of you, nations of the continent, will, without losing your distinctive qualities and your glorious individuality, be blended into a superior unity and constitute a European fraternity, just as Normandy, Brittany, Burgundy, Lorraine, Alsace, have been blended into France.[60]

Hugo came close to violating the rules of the meeting by addressing contemporary tensions. Had the United States of Europe already existed, he argued, the end of European revolutions, the wastage of human life, the misery of the French lower classes, and the agonies of the Italians and Hungarians in 1849 would all have been avoided. The 128 million francs spent since 1815, during so-called peacetime, to pay for military equipment was that much wealth not invested in markets and ideas, in the elimination of misery, and in the construction of needed transportation and communication improvements.[61] His speech reflected an eclectic set of intellectual traditions: Fourierist and Pecqueurian notions of the infinite possibilities of human associations, liberal economic analysis of the misuse of capital for the military in place of peaceful investment, a fundamental belief in an idea of progress leading humankind toward betterment. He shared some of the Saint-Simonian views of bringing development and civilization to backward areas and, much like Sellon, he believed in the possibility of a multinational federated structure for Europe. Hugo utterly ignored the fact that the French model of unification required centuries of warfare in which one royal family eliminated rival feudal armies to create the nation.

Hugo's public association with the movement brought prestige to the peace cause and established it as one of his most important interests for the rest of his life. Later, during his exile on the isle of Guernsey (where he moved to protest the creation of the Second Empire under Louis-Napoléon), Hugo planted an oak tree that he named The United States of Europe.

During the three days of the congress, orators declaimed; resolutions were barely debated. The Anglo-American delegates sat politely through the drama that unfolded. Thus 1849, year of counterrevolution—when tsarist troops were destroying Lajos Kossuth's Hungarian republic, when Austro-Croatian troops were tearing apart the Venetian and Lombard countryside to restore Hapsburg authority, when the Roman republic of Mazzini and Garibaldi was under assault from French troops on behalf of the papal restoration—was a difficult year to keep current politics out of a peace congress. One aim of the congress organizers was to demonstrate that Catholic and Protestant liberals and conservatives, monarchists, and republicans could articulate common positions on peace because peace was a neutral issue transcending party politics. This belief was tested and frayed in 1849. The French liberal politician Francisque Bouvet denounced reactionary papal politics and defended the new Roman republic; Jean Gaspard, the Abbé Deguerrey, as representative of the Parisian archbishop, flared back that revolutions, brought in by "foreigners" and outside agitators (Mazzini and Garibaldi) "give to a nation whose political education is yet unfinished, a species of nourishment which it is not fitted to receive."[62] The Russian repression of Budapest produced a plea at the congress for a resolution of denunciation, a proposal buried in committee—but both Bouvet and Cobden clearly stated their feelings. The former, an enthusiastic organizer of the congress, confessed that the news from Budapest nearly convinced him to stay home, so anguished was he to hear of men

> forced to give up the noble and heroic struggle they were maintaining for the legitimate independence of their country, while at the same time Venice is writhing in the agonies of a certain death, and the Roman Republic . . . is perishing together with the last hope of Italy.[63]

Bouvet was convinced that however evil war was, the threat of barbarism from the north (Russia) and of the resurrected medieval papacy in the south endangered Western civilization even more.

Cobden, too, was profoundly disturbed. Horrified at the repression of the government of his friend Kossuth, he read from the proclamation of the Austrian general Julius Haynau, who promised to execute "on the spot . . . without distinction of condition or sex" any resister. Any resisting commune "*shall be leveled to the ground* to serve as a frightful example of the punishment for resisters." Cobden compared Haynau to Attila and characterized the Austrian army as a modern version of fifth-century Goths.[64] Thus, two of the organizers of the peace congress were unable to contain their rage. D'Eichthal, who attempted to argue the pacific origins of the Holy Alliance, was shouted down.[65] Peace was not an issue that could be separated from European politics.

Proposals for arms limitation did not arouse unanimous enthusiasm either. To persuade liberals that the reduction of arms would not aid repressive states, the journalist Émile de Girardin, editor of *La Presse,* proposed an amendment that condemned wars "for ambition or conquest," thus leaving open the right to use weapons in self-defense. The English delegation, led by Joseph Sturge,[66] wanted the congress to assert an absolute position, and it took all the charm and influence of Hugo to navigate a compromise. Hugo urged the congress to send a message to governments that requested a reduction of arms: this issue remained an area where Continental and British pacifists would disagree for decades to come.

De Girardin presented a remarkable analysis of the costs of military preparations. His statistical tables illustrated the fact that European states, including Turkey, spent over one-third of their budgets on military and naval items during peacetime and that, for an example, the French forces in 1848 (a year of peace) were larger than they had been at any time during Napoléon's wartime conscriptions. He denounced the persistently growing "blood tax" of Louis-Philippe's era, which cost well over six billion francs. In contrast to the size of British land forces (he ignored the navy), France was risking bankruptcy.[67] De Girardin argued the misuse of capital in a nation that should be building rails, public works, and factories and fulfilling the promise made during the revolution for mass education was unconscionable.

Frédéric Bastiat demonstrated the weight that militarism placed on the unemployed and the working poor, not only through conscription but also because of tax burdens they carried. He flatly declared that military outlays were the main source of the social conflict between the middle- and lower-classes; his most devoted pupil, Frédéric Passy, worked on versions of that theme for the rest of the century.[68] Cobden also addressed the economics of militarism and war, noting that without war loans, General Haynau and others would be unable to equip their forces, "My object is to promote peace by withholding the sinews of war," he explained. Banks and crediting institutions must refuse loans when war scares broke out.[69] (This proposal appeared sporadically in the next half-century, but no one ever succeeded in persuading financial authorities to act on it.)

Generally, polite silence greeted the American speakers who tried to encourage Europeans to work for Burritt's congress of nations. Liberal French and Belgian citizens could not envision sitting at the same table with representatives of the east European monarchies; after several days of sitting at the Paris congress, the American delegates finally grasped that their constitution could not be fitted into the European states system.

The talented Hugo found a positive note on which to close the congress. He observed that the meeting was ending on the same date, 24 August, that had been the first day of the Saint Bartholomew's Day massacre in 1572, a bloodbath when Catholic killed Protestant in France. Let us hope, urged Hugo, that "this day will be a memorable day, may it mark the end of the effusion of human blood, massacre and wars [and] inaugurate the commencement of the reign of peace and concord on earth."[70] When the congress closed, delegates went to celebrate at a large party hosted by Alexis de Tocqueville, and then a number of Continental delegates traveled back to England to participate in well-attended meetings in London, Birmingham, and Manchester, where the work of the Paris congress was publicized and praised.[71]

The midcentury organizers tried to follow up their success by holding the 1850 meeting in Frankfurt, where a similar agenda was presented. Bastiat was too ill to come, but many of the newly recruited French participants did attend—notably de Girardin and Garnier; Cobden, Visschers, and Burritt came from Britain, Belgium, and the United States, respectively. Threat of the impending war with Denmark over Schleswig-Holstein lay heavily on the meeting; indeed, a German speaker pleaded with the meeting to vote a resolution on the situation in Holstein, where war was about to break out between Dane and German. The organizers of the meeting, however, silenced him for addressing "present political events."[72]

Despite the dismal political picture in 1850, organizers were initially optimistic, pleased that five hundred English delegates came to Frankfurt and that, again, every religious party was represented.[73] The Lutheran consistory had given the Paulskirche (Saint Paul's Church) to the congress. This was the first international congress with significant German participation and the first time that the proceedings were complicated by the necessity of making frequent translations among English, French, and German speeches. Much of the agenda repeated that of 1848 and 1849. De Girardin pointed out that government policies will foment revolutions as long as armed peace exists. Cobden bluntly proposed that if diplomats could not prevent outbreaks of war, then they should recognize their failure and allow neutral umpires (arbitrators) to take over the task.[74] In place of merely advocating his congress of nations, Burritt, this time, urged that a convocation of nations occur in order to establish the principles of a code of international law.[75]

To avoid splintering controversies, the meeting steered clear of thorny issues. In 1850, speakers were prohibited from discussing the fate of Schleswig-Holstein, for instance. But congress organizers wove controversial issues into innocuous-sounding, generalized resolutions of principle. De Girardin; Theodor C. Creizen-ach, a German delegate; Edward Miall; and Cobden and Burritt led an attack on interventionist states by insisting that nonintervention in the affairs of other nations become the public law of Europe—the "principle of non-intervention" had to be held sacrosanct and inviolate.[76] To the revolutionary exile Théodore Karcher, this was absurd. Only by the liberation of oppressed peoples would peace ever have a chance in Europe, he observed, echoing the opinion of most midcentury democrats:

> To abolish war, first oppression must be abolished .... Sincere, loyal partisans of [genuine] peace must—above all—struggle energetically to push nations into *the final battle,* that of the oppressed against oppressors. When all nationalities will be masters of their destinies, they will learn how to respect and guarantee their mutual rights.[77]

A similar attack on peace philanthropists came from E. Antoine, who was appalled at Cobden's parliamentary initiatives in London to curb arms expenditures. As Cobden had once quoted Haynau, so Antoine used the warnings of General Joseph Radetzky, whose manifestos posted in Italian towns offered torture and death to resisters, "At the moment when despots are assembling their forces throughout Europe to prepare the final struggle, can you seriously propose that throwing away armaments will introduce peace and liberty to the world?"[78] European democrats, radicals and nationalists, such as Mazzini and Garibaldi and their admirers considered the peace cause of the midcentury as potentially as dangerous as the oppressors' forces. An Italian patriot, Mauro Macchi, summarized the problem a few years later:

> No one wants war for its own sake but it is not our fault if the world is overwhelmingly afflicted by injustice that cannot be destroyed except by arms. ... Those who do not approve of the current European order must well invoke them as the only means to assure the conquest of national independence and universal freedom.[79]

In the early 1850s, the Anglo-American aspirations, most recently mobilized by Burritt and Cobden in international peace congresses, began to lose their momentum. The unity of the international peace movement was a fragile reed. Profound gulfs divided Anglo-American peace crusaders and Continental free trade liberals from Continental democrats who considered European peace as the last stage of national liberation, inseparable from human rights and justice.

British activists, many drawn from antislavery societies, were drawn to another cause. As the British Empire began to climb across the Hindu Kush, march toward the China seas, and push onto the African veldt, peace activists leveled attacks on the mistreatment of overseas natives. In 1851, for instance, a branch of the British Peace Society vociferously publicized the vicious abuse of the Kaffirs in South Africa, the repulsive policy of forcing opium on the Chinese, and the violence brought by British arms against the Afghans.[80] This same movement refused to take a position on behalf of the Roman republic, which was destroyed by French troops who restored Pope Pius IX in 1849. Henry Richard disliked the use of violence by patriots on behalf of Italian unification in 1849–1850; a decade later, he opposed the American Civil War and offered no solution to freeing the slaves. Mazzini, who fled to London exile after the Roman republic fell—where he was lionized by the liberal community—specifically warned against peace congresses until all Europeans were freed. He believed in a future unity of Europe, but it was to be a Europe of the peoples.[81]

This, too, was the vision advocated by the Fourierist theorist, Victor Considérant, who called on progressive Europeans from the middle and working classes to form an alliance in order to crush the militarist feudal remnant in power, that is, to complete the French Revolution. A peaceful Europe, he held, could not exist without this last crusade.[82] (Considérant, however, did not call for a physical campaign, but rather for an alliance of ideas, language, and political organization.) For their part, Anglo-American organizers and their Continental liberal adherents refused to support the national liberation movements of the midcentury.

After 1820, the importation into Europe of a peace movement shaped by Anglo-American organizers sometimes helped stimulate local initiatives.[83] But the years following the counterrevolutionary wave of 1849 were not propitious. The division in the movement between Anglo-American and Continental viewpoints was unbridgeable. Louis Bara, who won the 1848 prize-essay contest established at the Brussels meeting, typified Continental thinking when he insisted that the use of arms in self-defense was entirely justified.[84] Peace activists from the "satisfied" parliamentary states (Britain, the United States, Belgium, and France) insisted that a new future would evolve without violence to satisfy the national longings of the peoples.[85]

By midcentury, debates about an organized peace became part of the agendas of middle-class reformers. Control of the subject by a small elite, initially defended by the London, Parisian, and Genevan societies, was replaced by appeals to a broader constituency. Private citizens concerned with an array of projects for the improvement of society learned to discuss and consider alternatives to the arms race and international war. The subject moved from the pens of intellectuals, the pulpits of dissenting clergy, and the secret communiqués of diplomats to a wider community.

2

Peace Movements
and the Challenge of Nationalism
1850–1889

1850–1871: The Struggle to Create a Continental Peace Movement

To the exhilarated organizers of the 1849 Paris International Peace Congress, a future for annual conventions of "friends of peace" seemed assured. Expecting to repeat their success, they had convened in the Paulskirche in Frankfurt in 1850. By 1851, however, when organizers called for a congress in Manchester, political reality intruded. Continental participation dwindled. The "international" meeting had become mainly British.

For the next two decades, peace movements on both sides of the Atlantic underwent persistent battering. During the 1850s, 1860s, and 1870s—with the remarkable exception in 1867–1871—a few, hardy, isolated campaigners struggled against ridicule and indifference. The volcanic political terrain following the revolutions and counterrevolutions of 1849–1851 drove peace from the agendas of many potential supporters.

When Louis-Napoléon, president of the Second Republic, precipitated the coup d'état in December 1851 and declared the Second Empire, the most influential Continental contingent, French liberals, abandoned the peace cause for more immediate issues. Some, such as Victor Hugo, fled into exile; others, particularly Émile de Girardin, chose to believe the imperial device, *L'Empire, c'est la paix.* (Despite his motto, in 1854, the pacific emperor along with the British government joined in the Crimean War; in 1859, he helped the Sardinian royal house to drive Austria out of northern Italy. However, in 1862, Louis-Napoléon refused to send any help to the Polish revolutionaries who were crushed by the tsar's troops.)

The Crimean War (1853–1856), launched in a frenzy of jingoism, wrecked peace societies and destroyed the parliamentary careers of the internationally renowned Richard Cobden and John Bright. American peace activists, of course, were rent by the debate over abolition in the 1850s and then by the Civil War during the 1860s. Italians, engaged in the final acts of the Risorgimento, were hardly interested in discussing permanent peace while Austrian troops occupied their land. From 1866 through 1871, the wars of German unification (and French humiliation) concluded decades of simmering and overt national and international violence. The Franco-Prussian War undermined French peace activism for a generation and eliminated peace activism in Germany. But it encouraged it elsewhere, notably in smaller states: Switzerland, the Netherlands, and Belgium. In short, the political turmoil of nation making deflected peace agitation. The days when British or American peace agents organized Continental congresses of peace activists were over, though occasionally the British Peace Society funded a sporadic initiative. Though peace groups tried in 1878 and sporadically in the 1880s to revive the international meetings, not until 1889 were there sufficiently stable conditions.

No matter how hostile the political climate, peace as a cause always attracted stubborn, loyal individual advocates. No matter how discouraging public indifference and official repression might be, a few activists continued to struggle to fashion a new consensus. In Europe, Edmond Potonié (1829–1902), the son of a Parisian entrepreneur who was a friend of Victor Hugo, assumed that role. The Potonié home had been the organizing center for the 1849 international congress in Paris. In 1850, Edmond attended the Frankfurt congress, where he met Richard Cobden who reinforced Hugo's admonitions to the young man. Both urged Edmond to carry on a "noble struggle against the monstrous, brutal and human ignorance which causes men to arm against each other."[1]

During the 1850s, Potonié, impressed by Cobden's Anti-Corn-Law League, struggled to duplicate its success internationally. Thus Potonié set out to find backers throughout Europe.[2] Traveling on business, originally for his father's enterprise, the young Potonié developed a network of acquaintances, became fluent in German, and learned some Italian. Gradually, he modified the liberal economics absorbed from his father's circle and adopted a cooperative, mutualistic socialist approach. This shift, during the 1860s, did not mean an irrevocable split with liberal supporters and Potonié continued to solicit John Stuart Mill, the German Hermann Schulze-Delitzsch (founder of banking societies among workers), Frédéric Passy, and the Prussian progressive politician and doctor Rudolf Virchow.[3] Belgian worker-intellectuals who were involved in establishing the International Workingman's Association (the First International) in 1864–1865 printed and distributed appeals and articles.[4] Potonié obtained some financing from Henry Richard.[5] This eclectic mix demonstrated a fluidity of political alignments during the 1860s and the possibility that young socialist and labor groups could support a program initially developed by middle-class political circles in the area of peace and internationalism.

Potonié called his international effort the Ligue du bien public. Its program attacked monopolies and ruinous taxation; it appealed for individual freedom (i.e., civil liberties); and it concluded with a call for an organized peace. Founded between 1863 and 1865, the *ligue* hoped to complete the work of the interrupted peace congresses that had petered out during the 1850s.[6] The anomaly that Continental armies continued to increase, despite the Peace of Paris (1856), provoked Potonié's outrage. Nearly a million men remained in arms in tsarist Russia and nearly a half-million each in Austria and Prussia. This absurd waste ought to have compelled rational leaders to develop a new international system, Potonié argued. (Not all his working-class supporters agreed, worried that disarmament might leave them prey to the tsar.)[7]

Unlike all previous peace societies, the *ligue* urged a social program of self-help collectives, credit societies, international expositions of workers' products, a free press, freedom of religion, separation of church and state, abolition of the death penalty, state-sponsored compulsory elementary education, and, eventually, equality of the sexes.[8] This sweeping call for social change cooled the support from Passy, Cobden, Visschers, and de Molinari but not that of the Belgian Catholic pacifist J.-B. Coomans,[9] editor of *La Paix*. An ardent nationalist, the Italian C. F. Gabba, complained that the *ligue* cared little to "free oppressed nationalities [as] a primary condition before international peace [could] be established."[10] Potonié's program for a peaceful Europe, much as Niboyet's earlier approach in *La Paix des deux mondes,* traveled a path to international peace based on social justice. But, in common with liberal and conservative peace activists, he was insufficiently sensitive to the pull of nationalism.

Until his death in 1902, Potonié never waivered from his commitment to social justice, democracy, and peace. Indefatigable as a crusader in print and in person, he was stymied by censorship and police repression when he tried to reach a French audience. The extent of Potonié's network across Europe cannot be determined, for in 1868 the French police seized his papers, and they have disappeared.

The wars for Italian unification (1859–1860), the anger among progressives over tsarist repression of Poland (1863–1864), and the Seven Weeks' War between Prussia and Austria (1866) did not produce a sympathetic response among moderate and liberal peace activists. Instead, they called for a European federation. French intellectuals who took this position came from both socialist and liberal quarters, which included Pierre-Joseph Proudhon, Émile de Girardin, Frédéric Passy, and Michel Chevalier. In 1859, Passy argued that nothing of permanent political value came from military solutions—an oblique way of denouncing the wars of Italian unification conducted with aid from the French emperor.[11] To address political problems, Passy insisted, Europe needed a "permanent congress to oversee the general interests of humanity," which included an international police to "assure against oppression" and disorder. In those years, Passy defined disorder as socialism.[12] Proudhon's *War and Peace* (1861) considered national self-determination an obstruction to real historical change.[13] Émile de Girardin could not believe that it mattered much whether Milan was ruled by Turin or Vienna—as long as it was ruled well. He fully backed Louis-Napoléon's decision not to help the Poles. Chevalier called for a European federation in 1866.[14] In truth, peace activists from "satisfied" nations, such as Britain, France, Belgium, and the Netherlands, were often stymied in the face of national issues. Henry Richard was persuaded that real social and political "modification" would come through "other means than physical force."[15]

The Seven Weeks' War of 1866 also frightened socialist members of the First International. A rash of articles, manifestos and open letters appeared in republican and socialist journals. Students in Paris pleaded with Italian and German colleagues "not to be duped by an absurd, antiquated policy which drives peoples to annihilate each other under the idiotic excuse of national interest or race differences."[16]

In April 1867, the Luxembourg crisis, which briefly threatened to become a Franco-Prussian war was the catalytic force that reinvigorated organized peace movements and international congresses. It led to the international network of peace activists that had eluded Potonié for a decade. Indeed, the war scare catalyzed the creation of three new peace associations. At first, the new initiatives ignored Potonié, although he and the group formed in Geneva, the Ligue internationale de la paix et de la liberté, spoke virtually the same language. The other two peace societies were founded in Imperial France, an inhospitable political climate for citizen-sponsored activity.

In Le Havre, the creation of L'Union de la paix under the leadership of Félix Santallier (1830–1885) quickly attracted over fifteen hundred supporters through Masonic lodges.[17] Almost as quickly, the French police insured that this initiative suffered restrictions, postal losses, and surveillance. (Peace activism led by Masonic groups eventually moved to Brussels, where the Loge des amis philanthropes under Charles Potvin was able to operate in a less-inhibiting environment.)[18] Santallier issued a public call to resist war over Luxembourg. He was not in contact with the other two peace initiatives—one in Paris and one in Geneva. His efforts were limited, partly because of his group's location in a provincial city.

In Paris, a well-to-do and well-connected group of entrepreneurs, economists, writers, and bankers succeeded in persuading dubious imperial officials that the creation of a peace society would not endanger public order. The formation of the Ligue internationale et permanente de la paix occurred after the influential newspapers, *Le Temps,* published three letters attacking government policies toward Luxembourg in April 1867.[19] The third letter, written by Frédéric Passy, invited the French to join a peace league. To the astonishment of Auguste Nefftzer, the editor of the paper, this letter elicited an enthusiastic response. Support and legitimacy came as the industrialist Jean Dollfus; the banker Arlès-Dufour; Isadore, grand rabbi of France; the Catholic activists Père Hyacinthe (Charles Loyson) and Alphonse Gratry; and a well-known Protestant pastor, Joseph Martin-Paschoud all added their names to those of Michel Chevalier and Gustave d'Eichthal, a Saint-Simonian mystic. From Belgium, Émile de Laveleye, Gustave de Molinari, and Auguste Couvreur sent support. Henry Richard (the secretary of the British Peace Society), while visiting Paris, urged the minister of the interior to grant permission for an international peace congress during the 1867 Paris Exposition. He was rejected with the admonition that "your people are accustomed to public meetings [but] with Frenchmen it is different. Where they have an opportunity of speaking in public—he ended the sentence with an eloquent shrug and grimace."[20] Police permission was denied for an international congress; the government finally permitted lectures on general principles, not on foreign policy. Audiences could ask no questions afterward. In Potonié's estimation, any society that received police permission to meet in Paris was suspect. Dryly, he commented, "peace can only spring from justice."[21]

After the Ligue internationale et permanente de la paix received permission to organize itself in May 1867, its animating spirit became Frédéric Passy, who was to become the dean of European peace activists.[22] By 1867, Passy had already developed a reputation as an economist but could not teach because he would not take the loyalty oath required by Napoléon III, whose regime he believed was illegitimate. He supported his large family by lectures, writings, and private income.

Potonié's allegations that the Parisian-based Ligue internationale et permanente de la paix was not a serious peace society were not entirely correct. Passy's group believed that only a legalistic vision of European peace had the slightest chance of converting skeptics and that Potonié's would lead to chaotic, not orderly, social change. A broad gulf divided Potonié's view of peace as a correlate of social justice from the view of Passy, Henry Richard, and Bastiat, namely, that peace was a condition in the national interest to be attained by established governments.[23] Passy firmly believed that real social change would evolve once the absurd costs of armaments were reduced. In the Paris ligue, he declared "war on war," because he foresaw that European civilization would destroy itself were it not to devise a system of international security that eliminated war.[24] Passy's approach differed from the earlier conservativism of Metternich's adviser, Friedrich von Gentz who, in 1818, wanted to avoid war because it might reproduce the French Revolutionary upheavals and turn the social order upside down. Passy honestly believed that liberal economic practice, uninhibited by drastic military expenses, would eventually raise the standard of living for everyone and solve the social question.

In France, Passy's group provoked reactionary protest. The liberal Catholic, Père Hyacinthe, who participated in the group, was denounced by his superiors and the right-wing Catholic journalist, Louis Veuillot, used the pages of L'Univers to insure that his coreligionists realized that the Ligue internationale et permanente de la paix was a "Protestant" front.[25] Efforts to gain Catholic support were largely in vain. The idea that war was divine, an argument developed by Joseph de Maistre after 1815, was refuted by a few liberal Catholics, but the hierarchy remained silent.[26] Only after a major struggle by well-connected businesspersons was the ligue allowed to hold a meeting in June 1868. Given the fact that membership fees were substantial—about one hundred francs for founders and five francs for associates—it was clear that Passy's organization never intended to be a mass, democratic-membership group. Generous donations from founders, such as Dollfuss, helped bring the ligue's treasury to about six thousand francs in 1868–1869 and about six hundred enrolled members.[27] The meeting of the ligue held in 1868 was tightly managed, thus prohibiting spontaneous discussion. Passy set the tone by noting that the Emperor himself as well as Pius IX on various occasions had excoriated war as antithetical to civilization. To crusade against war, Passy maintained, was a valid, respectable cause:

> We do not wish to ... overthrow anything, to transform anything but want the transformation that is occurring under our eyes to be accomplished much more rapidly. We want—now that the civilized world is becoming a single body,—a living network which can not be destroyed without ... damage for everyone; [we want] to push to the outer limits of this civilized world and then ... to the savage or barbarian world ... the circle beyond which the *unfortunate state of nature* still rules. We want ... *law and not force* used to decide ... not only the condition of individuals and cities but the *condition of nations.*[28]

Passy's emphatic repetition of the antirevolutionary aims of the Ligue international et permanente de la paix in Paris were also intended to distinguish his group from the "notorious" organization created in Geneva in 1867 with a confusingly similar name: Ligue international de la paix et de la liberté. The Paris group ignored the nature of repression in most of Europe and remained uninterested, publicly, in the question of human rights. Passy's *ligue* undertook a publication series, the Bibliothèque de la paix, directed at the educated public.[29] To demonstrate the respectability of the cause, the Paris *ligue* emphasized existing official commitments, especially the nonbinding *vœu*, Protocol 23, in the Peace of Paris (1856), where European governments promised to use "good offices" before declaring war.[30] Passy placed immense faith in educating elites about international peace. In a typical gesture, he approached Jules Simon in 1870 hoping for an introduction to the Société des gens de lettres so that he could explain Bastiat's ideas about arms reduction.[31]

The value of lobbying governments and elites was not entirely without foundation nor was it merely mindless conservatism. In 1862, an unknown Genevan business traveler, Henri Dunant,[32] miraculously persuaded a group of governments to meet; two years later, the Geneva Convention was signed, establishing the International Red Cross, which was to be awarded the Nobel Peace Prize in 1917. Although peace activists did not believe their cause was advanced by an international agreement to civilize warfare, the method of Dunant's success—a personal campaign waged by a citizen who had been tortured by the sight of the battlefield of Solferino—was unique. Dunant had persuaded Queen Augusta Victoria of Prussia to back his initiative.

Passy's Paris peace *ligue* also contacted the Prussian queen, urging her to support disarmament discussions between France and Prussia in 1869–1870. Henry Richard's European tour of 1869 promoted the introduction of arms-reduction resolutions in the French parliament (under Jules Simon's management), in the Prussian parliament (under Rudolf Virchow's charge), and in Saxony (under Edouard Löwenthal's leadership)—similar motions were also introduced in Italy, Spain, the Netherlands, and Sweden. The possibilities of collaborative international initiatives was cheering.[33] Peace activists prevailed on George Villiers, Lord Clarendon, to try to convince France and Prussia to reduce armaments, but the Prussian minister, Otto von Bismarck, would have none of it. Bismarck, the "realist," refused to discuss arms reductions, insisting that the discussion, itself, was dangerous. Clarendon was rejected as an honest broker.[34]

On the eve of the Franco-Prussian War, the proper, respectable and restrained methods of the genteel Parisian movement laid claim to modest success. Public lectures to select audiences and private overtures to sympathetic political figures characterized a discreet campaign—probably all that was possible under the Second Empire. The small international campaign for arms reduction was a heartening token.

The third peace society formed in 1867 following the Luxembourg crisis, the Ligue international de la paix et de la liberté, a group that lasted until 1939, was established in Geneva.[35] Its founders were a remarkable potpourri of European exiles, radicals, republicans, nationalists, moderate socialists, anarchists, liberals, and—after six months—women. Its program recognized the necessity of national independence as well as democratic participation. In the meetings of its congresses and the pages of its newspaper and brochures, the Genevan *ligue* made explicit its vision of peace as a function of social and national justice.

In September 1867, the founding congress of the Genevan *ligue* occurred after several months of organizing. The campaign started with calls published in the republican newspaper *Le Phare de la Loire* (beginning in May 1867) for a conference to be held in a neutral area in order to respond to the Luxembourg crisis. The call attracted activists associated with the First International; dissidents from a variety of political movements; German republicans living in exile after 1849; liberals such as John Stuart Mill; educators, such as Victor Cousins; and French exiles in Switzerland, such as Professor Jules Barni who organized support in his adopted nation.[36] As the organization of the September congress developed, a participant aptly labeled it "the great assize of European democracy."

Organizers clearly hoped to build a broad coalition on behalf of democracy and peace. The date of the opening meeting, September 1867, was intended to follow the congress of the First International so that delegates would incur no extra expense in traveling. Nonetheless, socialists were divided about whether they ought to participate. On Karl Marx's initiative, the General Council of the First International instructed its delegates "not to take any official part in the Peace Congress" and to oppose proposals at assemblies of the First International on its behalf.[37] Besides his profound differences with people who refused to admit that the labor–capital struggle was central to all political activity, Marx also believed that the peace-at-any-price group would dominate and that their proposals, if adopted, would leave Russia in a position to conquer Europe.[38] At the Lausanne meeting of the First International, however, this position was not supported, and a number of socialists chose to attend the Geneva meeting, which opened on 9 September, a day after the First International Congress closed.

Without doubt, the fact that Giuseppe Garibaldi presided at the Genevan peace congress launched this new organization with the largest audience ever mobilized in the peace cause. Besides the thousands who wanted to enter the meeting hall, the congress received support from over two thousand Swiss, sixteen hundred German, one thousand French, and hundreds of Italian, Russian, British, and Polish citizens. At least six thousand adherents in all were recorded. They included Victor Hugo, Edgar Quinet, Jules Favre, Élisée Reclus, Pierre Leroux, Mikhail Bakunin, Amand Goegg, Charles Longuet, César de Paepe, Charles Lemonnier, and a significant number of *garibaldini,* such as Timoteo Riboli. It was a distinguished roster of democrats, exiles, progressives, critics of the status quo. The program demanded:

1. The creation of a United States of Europe.

2. The establishment of all the rights and principles that revolutions called for—self-determination, freedom of conscience, abolition of standing armies, abolition of race prejudice, freedom of speech and assembly, the right to work, mass public education, and the "harmony of economic interests in freedom."

3. The establishment of a permanent international organization to struggle for the program's aims across boundaries.

For French exiles, the main attraction of the meeting was a chance to attack the despotism of Louis-Napoléon; for Italians, a chance to denounce papal politics and antinational positions; for Germans, a chance to attack the powers that had prevented democratic and constitutional unification in 1849. Conservative Swiss disliked the attacks on established authority and the brash participation of Swiss radicals and liberals, led by James Fazy in Geneva. Conservatives were even more disturbed in 1868 when the *ligue* added the emancipation of women to its program and supported public meetings around Switzerland to bring women out of their homes and into public spaces.

In the entire century, there was no peace congress as notorious as the meeting organized in Geneva in September 1867. Garibaldi's presidency assured coverage by journalists and police spies.[39] The congress was confused with the First International, despite the fact that worker support was ambivalent. Before the *ligue* was formed, the First International had recognized the work of "bourgeois congresses of peace, economists, statisticians, philanthropists and sociologists" in denouncing the "deleterious influence of large, permanent armies on the production processes."[40] Indeed, some First International activists, such as the Parisian worker Henri-Louis Tolain, were organizers of the Genevan congress, and the first British worker to be elected to the House of Commons, W. Randal Cremer (Nobel Peace Prize, 1903), was a founding member of the International and a founder of a Workman's Peace Association (originally League). Others, such as the German exile Johann Georg Eccarius shared Karl Marx's distrust of peace activists and advised socialists to preserve their distance and independence.[41] At the Lausanne meeting of the First International, which preceded the Genevan meeting of the peace congress, the resolution inviting socialists to support the congress and to work for the abolition of standing armies and a confederation of free states in Europe was subordinated to a statement insisting that the main cause of war was poverty, inequality, and injustice. First International socialists subordinated the struggle against armies to the struggle for the reconstitution of society.[42] Thus, arose a new critique of peace agitation from the Left in 1867.

Each group came to Geneva with its own agenda. Garibaldi's opening remarks attacking the papacy infuriated Catholics who threatened to invade the meeting.[43] Socialist speakers who followed Garibaldi entirely ignored his remarks, emphasizing their own message. On the second day, Garibaldi denounced despotism and called for the overthrow of the Papal States by violent methods. From the streets, Catholics threatened, once again, to break into the hall; papal denunciation of the meeting was issued the next month.[44] In their counterpoint, socialists insisted that the congress endorse the creation of a single class, producers, as a precondition of peace.[45] They denounced the idea that defensive militias were a guarantee of peace by pointing to the forces in the hands of the "bourgeoisie" that had mowed down workers in Chicago—that "El Dorado of work and freedom." An angry Gustave de Molinari registered his vigorous protest against any and all socialist resolutions. By the end of the second day, the meeting was assured its place in history as the most tumultuous and nearly violent peace congress in the entire history of the movement.

On day three, Geneva was covered with posters attacking Garibaldi, who had departed suddenly. (He returned to Italy to plan his final invasion of the Papal States, an affair that ended with his defeat at the Battle of Mentana.) Moderate voices, notably those of the Swiss politicians James Fazy and Pierre Jolissaint, tried to reestablish order, but angered citizens, armed with pikes, broke in. On the podium, a Neapolitan follower of Garibaldi stubbornly pursued the attacks on the papacy ("a scourge worse than monarchy"), and the Belgian socialist, César de Paepe, persisted in demanding that the congress denounce the bourgeoisie who funded warfare by refusing to distribute profits fairly among workers.[46]

German speakers, republican exiles from 1849, warned against enthusiasm for nationalism. Amand Goegg, who became an officer of the *ligue* created at Geneva, predicted that a Germany unified under Prussian leadership would threaten the peace of Europe. He called for a confederation of German states modeled on the Swiss or American type.[47] He, too, was repeatedly interrupted. The contrast with the Paris meetings of the Ligue internationale et permanente de la paix could not be more dramatic. One critic of the Geneva meeting observed wryly that the sort of peace the participants at Geneva wanted would require that "the 40 large and small rulers listed in the *Almanach de Gotha* . . . consent to their own abolition." Without a series of long and costly wars, how would this ever come about?[48] Still, delegates to the Geneva meeting in 1867 wanted peace based on the constitution of a republican German confederation; the removal of the papal authority from central Italy; the overthrow of Louis-Napoléon; the destruction of the Junkers, the Bourbons, and Hapsburgs; and the establishment of an independent Poland to buffer Europe from the tsar. This was a peace that might, indeed, require a last just crusade, such as the one Anacharsis Cloots had proposed during the First Republic of the French Revolution.

When the Genevan congress closed, participants agreed to establish a permanent organization. Considering the apparent chaos of the meeting, any decision was remarkable. The organization established after September 1867, the Ligue internationale de la paix et de la liberté, became a significant force in Continental pacifism. The nature of the organization prefigured twentieth-century peace organizations in its concern for domestic justice and human rights as the only basis for international peace and in its recognition that peace as a cause could not embrace everyone across the political spectrum—it was not neutral. Were peace to remain "neutral" it would defend autocratic, dictatorial states at the expense of their inhabitants.

The journal, *Les États-Unis d'Europe,* was a well-written, critical publication. In the early years of the organization, Charles Lemonnier, a French Saint-Simonian, along with Amand Goegg, a German pacifist, struggled to issue it in both languages.[49] With much volunteer help, especially from a young Swiss teacher, Élie Ducommun (Nobel Peace Prize, 1902), the organization began life in 1867–1868 with more energy and enthusiasm than any peace society had had in decades. It was not the project of a single ego; its international membership was substantial, and a spirit of hope in the dawning of something new enlivened its propaganda. Both Lemonnier and Goegg were married to activist women. Elisa Lemonnier was the founder of a system of schools designed to educate poor girls to support themselves.[50] Goegg's wife Marie turned to the founders of the Swiss-based *ligue* in the spring of 1868 and asked why women had not been included in the creation of the peace organization.[51] By the end of 1868, owing to Marie Goegg's exertions, the Genevan peace organization was the first to add women's emancipation to its list of demands. In addition to the well-known European radicals and progressives who supported the *ligue,* the best-known educated women, such as Clémence Royer (the noted French translator of Darwin's works) were involved.[52]

The energy liberated by the Geneva congress continued to resonate across Europe. Traveling through Germany and England, Amand Goegg spoke to numerous audiences; publicized the work of the congress; distributed subscriptions to the new journal, which published well over one thousand copies in its first year; and encouraged the creation of national societies. In England, the Reform League hosted Goegg and followed his appearance with a resolution:

> Surely the hour has arrived when the peoples of Europe should be . . . enlightened enough to unite in determined protest against being made the brute instruments of horrible mutual slaughter, . . . compelled to do the work of the demons at the bidding of dynasties, courts, cabinets, Kings or Emperors.[53]

In Italy, Timoteo Riboli worked from Turin to keep the connection alive between Garibaldi (who remained honorary president) and the Genevan *ligue.*[54] Edmond Potonié, who was initially quite piqued at being ignored, joined in December 1867, promising to share his own materials with the Swiss-based organization.[55]

Efforts to build a wide network in France were frustrated by the police and delivery of *Les États-Unis d'Europe* was nearly impossible. Lemonnier tried to publish news of the Swiss *ligue* in such papers as *Le Phare de la Loire.* In Lemonnier's view, the *ligue* was "the direct descendant of the European revolution of 1789; the daughter of Kant and the heiress of eighteenth-century philosophy."[56] Garibaldi's venture into the Papal States was applauded. Théodore Karcher, a frequent contributor to the paper, stated flatly:

> War is . . . legitimate and just against oppressors. Every armed struggle is a crime if it does not have the noble aim of attaining the eternal, immutable right of peoples and individuals for self-determination.[57]

The American Civil War was treated with sympathy, and when news arrived in September 1868 of the rising in Spain, the *ligue* greeted the antimonarchical forces of Emilio de Castelar with enthusiasm. "Let us hope that September 30 in Madrid can become the signal for Europe that February 24, 1848 in Paris once was," cried the peace league's manifesto.[58]

The Swiss *ligue* was not only a very different organization than its Paris counterpart, it resembled no earlier peace society in Europe. This difference was stated explicitly by Lemonnier:

> The International League of Peace and Liberty never follows the example of the [British] Peace Society; the chimera that the direct establishment of absolute and universal peace can be realized by the efforts of existing governments. The League labors for the establishment of peace by the constitution of a federation of European peoples. To expect good will from existing governments seems to be the mad hope of naive candor. The condition of Europe for three centuries has been a state of barely disguised war. Today Europe has a truce, not peace.[59]

The federation envisioned by the *ligue* required a code of international law based on the same principles as codes of national and domestic law. Quite simply, Barni argued that the same morality underpinning civil society bound the international community.[60]

The republican, the nationalist, and the Jacobin components of the ligue's peace program were woven into a whole cloth, but the integration of socialist and anarchist demands was an insuperable challenge. In 1868, the *ligue* planned its second congress at Berne. Socialists, who were assembled in Brussels for their own meeting, were warmly invited to come. The peace activists wanted to explore ways to integrate social and economic justice. Mikhail Bakunin, a member of the planning committee for the Berne meeting, was especially interested in this item. However, during the Brussels meeting of the First International, a resolution was passed that stated the workers group did not believe that the

> Ligue de la Paix has [any] reason to exist, given the work of the International, and invites that society to merge with the International and its members to join one or another section of the International.[61]

In the view of the influential Belgain socialist César de Paepe, workers had choices in the event of war—they could strike and they could refuse to serve.[62] In either case, they had no need of the Swiss peace *ligue*. Peace activists in Geneva were shocked at the open rejection. When asked for an explanation, Bakunin implied that "powerful influence intimidated them" and a "certain coterie" controlled the Brussels meeting—that is, Karl Marx, whose view of the peace society was clear in 1867. At the Berne meeting in 1868, Bakunin was as unwilling to compromise his position that "the existing economic system must be radically altered . . . for the liberation of the working classes" as the liberals were to entertain any collectivist social solutions. When Bakunin's propositions for redirecting the peace *ligue* in the direction of an anarcho-socialist position were defeated, he and his group walked out.[63] The left-center position of Lemonnier and the French exiles won. Warning the First International against organizing a sterile and pointless competition with the Genevan peace society, the latter group asserted its mission to "unite . . . certain forces which—while differing on some issues—share a unified sentiment on basic principles." One of these principles was the belief that personal liberty was the keystone of all reform, not collective ownership.[64] The peace group maintained that private ownership was a natural right. To Lemonnier, this meant a social order of small proprietors that would both guarantee and be guaranteed by republican institutions.[65] Republican institutions would protect a right to work and protect the work force. Lemonnier's social vision contrasted as starkly with the First International as the social vision of Potonié and Passy had contrasted earlier in the decade.

The rhetoric of the meeting was bitter, but the break was not absolute. Socialists came to peace congresses as individuals. The German socialists, August Bebel and Wilhelm Liebknecht, maintained that they needed to work with democrats and republicans just as Amand Goegg maintained his right to attend the 1869 Basel meeting of the First International. Potonié managed to belong to both groups, publishing much of his propaganda in workers' papers, such as *Le Mirabeau*.[66] Republican and socialist positions in the later 1860s were not so hard and fast that collaboration on peace issues was impossible.

Socialists might have been formally "lost" in 1868, but women were added. Marie Goegg published her call for the creation of a woman's association as part of the Swiss *ligue* in March 1868, and after a brief debate, including one anonymous male outburst against destroying the family as women left the home, the proposal was passed.[67] At the 1868 Berne congress of the peace *ligue,* Marie Goegg admonished the audience to recall the French Revolution that undermined its own objectives by proclaiming the rights of man and ignoring the "no less imprescriptible rights of women":

> Men have paid dearly for their mistake and their descendants still suffer. By denying women as their equal, arrogant men lowered their own stature. If women had been called from 1789 to develop their own abilities ... society ... would have progressed.[68]

Following the 1868 meeting, women's emancipation became an integral part of the *ligue's* agenda. Marie Goegg founded the first Continental feminist association concerned exclusively with women's rights and peace. The Association internationale des femmes—later named the Solidarité des femmes—became a network of women who corresponded over women's rights, access to education, the role of women in private and public places.[69] Marie Goegg's original motive, to involve women in the peace movement changed. She developed a feminist commitment to alter the social roles of women through a commitment to transform their consciousness. She observed, "The source of the majority of evils of the feminine sex stems from its dependence on the masculine sex."[70] The central committee of the peace *ligue* added Marie Goegg to its roster, but she insisted that the affiliated women's association be entirely run by women. Between 1868 and 1870, her association grew more concerned with women's education and training for public roles than with the peace congresses.

The Swiss *ligue* became the first peace society to campaign for mass, secular education. Among its early participants was a young French philosophy instructor living and working in exile in Neuchâtel, Ferdinand Buisson.[71] He led the move to engage the new league into a much greater activity among the masses by seizing the initiative to start a reform movement in public education in the different countries . . . [and] to become an international society for the universal organization of democratic education."[72]

Buisson was to have an opportunity to influence public education in ways that he surely would not have been able to envision in 1868. With the advent of the Third Republic, he became an architect of the French public school system.[73]

By 1869, the program of the Swiss peace *ligue* was the clearest statement connecting international peace with democracy. Victor Hugo left his Guernsey exile—now in its seventeenth year—to preside at the Lausanne meeting of 1869, a generation after he had run the famous Paris meeting. Here, he did not predict a United States of Europe based on the confederation of nations. Instead, in Lausanne, he states soberly:

> The first condition of peace is liberation. For this liberation, a revolution is needed which shall be a great one, and perhaps, alas a war which shall be the last one. Then, all will be accomplished. Peace . . . will be eternal; no more armies, no more kings. The past will vanish.[74]

So persuasive was Hugo that the French police spy present recorded that this congress was a meeting of revolutionaries, not pacifists.[75] Hugo ignored the ideological chasms that divided the radical democratic peace movement and the First International. He praised socialism for speaking to "the whole human condition," for its concern with

> the inviolability of the individual, the abolition of murder in all its forms, the elimination of backwardness by education, . . . free compulsory education; the rights of women equal to men. . . . It proclaims finally the sovereignty of the individual, identical to liberty.[76]

For Hugo, the opportunity to attack Louis-Napoléon from the podium of an international congress was as inviting as the chance to denounce the Roman Catholic Church had been to Garibaldi in 1867. Hugo, who had labeled Napoleon III, "the Little," delighted the Lausanne audience with "the enemy is he who reigns, governs and agonizes at this moment."[77] The congress had articulated a program for social democracy and international peace; its keynoter had issued a call to arms.

Suddenly, during the summer of 1870, the differences between the Paris and the Berne societies evaporated as a new Franco-Prussian crisis escalated toward war. Peace again became a truce that dynasts could rupture. The war, avoided in 1867, broke out, but not the war of liberation that Hugo and the Swiss *ligue* wanted. This was a war "not fought for the liberation of peoples but for the satisfaction of dynastic ambitions."[78] To activists in the Swiss-based *ligue,* the war proved everything they had prophesized. Had European nations been organized as republics, with popular control of government, this war would not have occurred, argued Jules Barni, Amand Goegg, and others. Marie Goegg saw the war as absolute proof of the need to transform the public roles of women by proper education.[79] Passy and Parisian peace activists wrote to the Swiss group, suggesting that the time had come to collaborate and bury differences. The Parisian peace community urged the Swiss to campaign for diplomatic intervention by their federal government offering itself as a mediator, but the battle of Sedan on 1 September 1870 made that suggestion pointless. The defeat and overthrow of the French emperor transformed the war.

Suddenly, the war resembled 1792. The French were fighting a war of national defense and liberation. French activists in the Genevan *ligue* went home to participate in the reconstruction of political life. In the peace community, Bismarck replaced Louis-Napoléon as the enemy and emerged as the sole culprit. The few Germans who protested the war, like the socialists Bebel and Liebknecht, were imprisoned. From Geneva, the peace *ligue* pleaded with German soldiers to go home, not to serve a royal paymaster against brothers.

With Paris surrounded by German soldiers in 1870–1871, peace activists ceased their debates. Caught in the city, Edmond Potonié tried to mail pleas to his German readership, reminding them that "cannon, the last resort of kings, can never be the first resort of peoples."[80] In the fall of 1870, having organized sympathizers into an active chapter of the Ligue du bien public, Potonié covered Paris with posters, called an open meeting (women were particularly invited), established an agenda in which the public would discuss the German peace proposals, and invited Parisians to consider making their own foreign policy. The moment was opportune because there was a real vacuum in government leadership. The meeting, held on 9 October, produced a resolution that was to be floated in balloons out of Paris in an effort to reach German soldiers. In part, it read:

> Do you want history to vilify you by a comparison with Attila's Huns? . . . Do you want to remain slaves? If so, then continue to make war on the French republic. . . . If not, return across the Rhine, break your chains and chase out your kings. Then history will pardon you for having dirtied yourselves since September 4 as William's accomplices. Your King has said that he made war on a government, not on a people. If he has forgotten that, then you should remember it and not sully the idea that peoples are honorable, even if kings and emperors are not.[81]

The French commander and now governor of Paris, Louis Trochu, refused permission for the plan. Potonié's attempt to reach out to German soldiers over the head of French authority—such as it was—violated protocol. Potonié's followers drifted away, some to die in the fighting; others joined the struggle for the Commune.

Passy, whose health was not good at this time, was not in Paris when the war broke out. After Sedan, in the name of his organization, Ligue internationale et permanente de la paix, he pleaded with the Prussian royal family to remember:

> You declared . . . that you only made war to defend yourself, not to attack [and] . . . that you were not struggling with the French nation but with the French government. . . . The government is no longer, yet you still attack; don't forget your promise.[82]

The mild and moderate Passy disappeared, replaced by a furious moralist. According to Passy, Bismarck reportedly ridiculed Louis-Napoléon in snide and arrogant language after the French defeat in September 1870. Passy retorted, "you are not . . . more than a narrow spirit, a molder of mindless policies and of false patriots which will be repudiated one day by the very land which produced you."[83] He returned to Paris, where he attempted to persuade the British ambassador to plead for neutral intervention, tried to reach the American embassy and even contemplated a trip to the Prussian king by balloon. Then Passy received word that his favorite brother-in-law had died in the Vosges. Discouraged, he left Paris, profoundly saddened that the *ligue* could do nothing.

The neutrality of the Swiss-based peace *ligue* disappeared when the Franco-Prussian War turned into a struggle for French survival. Marie Goegg entered into a polemic with one of her former German supporters, Henriette Goldschmidt, a woman who insisted that the French provisional government differed little from that of Napoléon and, therefore, that the war remained justified. Marie Goegg retorted by publishing a list of the members of the new French government who had been members or supporters of the Swiss-based peace group.[84]

Although the *ligue* lost many of its French members to government positions in the new Third Republic, German members of the Genevan *ligue* either melted away or went to jail. The coming of the Paris Commune and its brutal repression in the spring of 1871 further eroded the left-liberal base of the *ligue*. It was clear that the French were not going to produce a new *levée en masse* in 1871. Ligue activists were forced to support the initiatives of the provisional French government that urged the French to accept the Prussian peace terms. The reasoning that Amand Goegg, Charles Lemonnier, and Swiss members offered was the hope that if France set up a real republic, perhaps German soldiers might be persuaded to abandon their support of the reactionary state they had helped to create.[85] Amand Goegg's warnings about a German nation unified under Junker leadership came true all too quickly.

The war wrecked the spirited international life of the Ligue internationale de la paix et de la liberté. Remaining members denounced the massacre of the Communards, called the removal of Alsace-Lorraine from France a theft, welcomed escaped communards to a meeting in 1871, and demanded that August Bebel and Wilhelm Liebknecht be freed from prison.[86] As sympathetic as the *ligue* was to exiled communards, Lemonnier still rejected all calls for social ownership of property.[87]

Despite plummeting membership and revenues, Lemonnier and the central committee chose to republish its journal in 1872, after a hiatus of eighteen months. To raise money, Amand Goegg embarked on a fund-raising trip to England and the United States—from which he never returned. (His wife was left to raise three children). In 1872, when Lemmonier tried to reinvigorate the group, he again asked Hugo to preside. Hugo refused, "I cannot attend your congress. . . . In our time, war has created a sinister environment which jeopardizes civilization itself. An enormous hatred fills the future. The moment seems strange to talk of peace."[88]

The dream of the democratic peace activists—first formalized in the chaotic Genevan meeting of 1867 and then systematically developed in published works and congresses thereafter—was destroyed by the Franco-Prussian War. The bitter terms of the Treaty of Frankfurt—specifically, the loss of Alsace-Lorraine and, more generally, the insult to French pride—made peace activism in France a tenuous matter for the immediate future. German liberals were either silent or silenced in the face of Bismarck's achievement, a powerful united nation with the best army in Europe. German republicans were silenced. The new aggressive nationalism in Europe differed so thoroughly from Mazzini's generous vision of a European order built on the free association of nationalities that the content of the concept "nationalism" was totally altered. The women's peace society became involved in issues of women's education and emancipation.

During the 1870s, Lemonnier and Potonié took every opportunity to demand release of imprisoned and exiled communards. In his book *Les États-Unis d'Europe,* Lemonnier argued for European federation based on shared republican institutions, not the mere manipulation of juridical relations.[89] Political realities drove Lemonnier to argue in favor of a federation of Britain, France, Italy, Belgium, Switzerland, and (possibly) Austria and the Scandinavian states. His criteria for membership remained "republican governments [that] recognize the autonomy of the people."[90] The federation would coordinate a free trade zone in the Danube and Rhine valleys and contain a large demilitarized area among its members.[91] Uncompromising in his rejection of the status quo, Lemonnier denounced the work of the diplomats in 1874 at Brussels, where they further codified the laws of warfare:

> The peoples no longer consider the idea of substituting the rule of reason and law for the regime of force as utopian; the problem in their eyes is not to find ways to "civilize war" but to substitute . . . solid guarantees of peace.[92]

Passy continued to dispute Lemonnier's argument that democracy was the prerequisite for international peace. The new German Empire was not likely to become a democratic–republican state and the other European monarchs, including the Piedmontese ruler, Victor Emmanuel II, on the new Italian throne, were not about to create republics. Thus, Passy developed the strategy that required campaigning for international agreements, arbitration, and mediation, a methodology that largely meant lobbying among elites and leaders. Incremental change was the realpolitik for peace activists.

1871–1889: Peace Activism in the Age of Bismarckian Realpolitik

The rejuvenation of Continental peace activism after the Franco-Prussian War came from offshore. Britain and the United States, barely avoiding conflict during the American Civil War, agreed to settle several long-standing disputes through binding arbitration. During the Civil War, the British support of the Confederacy enabled the ship *Alabama* to wreak havoc on the Union side. For the arbitration hearing, a distinguished panel of jurists appointed by heads of state was convened in Geneva. At the end of its deliberations, it ordered the British to pay over fifteen million dollars in damages.[93] Although the British did not sign the Geneva arbitration award, they paid. From 1872 on, the *Alabama* decision provided fuel for peace and international law arguments that filled books, scholarly journals, tracts for peace propaganda, political speeches, and a library of academic literature. The Americans and British were hailed for having given the civilized world a working model of how a juridical order would function.[94] Its importance was perhaps exaggerated, as skeptics rushed to assert, but arbitration attracted serious attention.

On the Continent, both the war and the arbitration award stimulated the establishment of new peace societies. A Dutch group created by Daniël van Eyk, Philip Johannes Bachiene, and Samuel Baart de la Faille,[95] modeled on Passy's, not Lemonnier's, definition of a peace society, began life in 1871. In Belgium, besides the older activists from the midcentury congresses, Masonic lodges undertook peace projects. On the eve of the war, Charles Potvin had persuaded the Loge des amis philanthropes to urge brother groups on both sides of the Rhine to call for cease-fires and negotiations. Potvin wanted scholarly studies of the causes of war and peace.[96] When he discovered Louis Bara's prize-winning essay of 1849, it was republished.[97] Potvin's determination to make the study of peace as scientific as possible typified the "new realism" among peace activists. Essentially, it meant mobilizing scholarly studies that argued both from historical evidence and quantitative data.

In 1872, Passy ventured forth among his traumatized compatriots to ask if there were any who were willing to revive the Ligue internationale et permanente de la paix.[98] There were, Passy observed, two paths to the future. One was a fatalistic commitment to war and revenge to "redeem" Alsace and Lorraine. This path entailed permanent armaments, a standing army mimicking the Prussians, a world where young males grew up doomed to life in the barracks and a society devoted to narrow, ungenerous patriotism. The domestic results of this approach would be funereal for republicanism in France and for civilization in general. The economic costs would forever condemn a large part of the population to penury, poverty, disease, and hopelessness.

The second approach was positive: a long-term campaign to convince civilized states to accept a code of law. Such a code, once firmly established, would provide sufficient security to dismantle expensive military defenses. When arbitration became a habit among European states, a code of international law would evolve out of arbitral decisions. The creation of an organized international system would establish the conditions in the future for the peaceful return of the lost provinces through the use, for instance, of a plebiscite.[99] Passy had no illusions that these conditions would materialize in the near term. French people who shared his vision were asked to constitute a new peace society, the Société française des amis de la paix, an organization committed to the development of arbitration. Its name was carefully chosen; it carried no "international" connotations.

In the 1870s, arbitration became the centerpiece of moderate peace societies. The revival of serious interest in international law during the 1870s legitimatized this approach for peace societies, though Passy found it impossible to breach the gates of acceptance in the French intellectual elite. In his application for admission to the French Academy of Moral Sciences in 1875, he avoided using the word *peace* and noted:

My writings and lectures have been ceaselessly devoted to the study and explanations of the principal problems of public and private morality; that this . . . has been
carried out not without difficulty nor without sacrifices [but] I have been able to
exercise salutary influence on spirits and hearts, sometimes very decisively.[100]

Support for the development of international law was not widespread in
France. A new scholarly journal, the *Revue de droit international et de législation
comparée,* was launched by Gustave Rolin-Jacquemyns in Ghent; he also established the Institut de droit international in 1873 (the *institut* was awarded the
Nobel Peace Prize in 1904) which focused on the development of arbitration and
international law. The founding fathers of the *institut* were carefully selected by
Rolin-Jacquemyns to include respected scholars and public officials—not peace
propagandists. Among the original eleven founders, only Émile de Laveleye[101] had
been associated with private peace activism. The others, including such figures as
Italy's Pasquale S. Mancini, who became minister of foreign affairs; Johann Kas-
par Bluntschli (Heidelberg); Tobias M. C. Asser (Amsterdam); David Dudley
Field (New York); and James Lorimer (Edinburgh) were all scholars known for
their realism.[102] Lorimer had published a paper in 1867 that speculated over the
nature of an international court, a parliament, and an army to enforce decisions;[103] Bluntschli put fourth a modest proposal that described limited international organizations to preserve the essence of sovereignty.[104] The distance
between Bluntschli's notion and that of Lemonnier was immense. Lemonnier
opposed the Swiss professor's recommendations, which he called monarchical federalism, because they preserved the right to make war "as part of the fundamental
laws of nature."[105] Not all the founders of the *institut* were as conservative. Mancini believed that nationality had to be the basis of the existence of states. Thus,
no legitimate international law could be constructed on an irrational basis that
denied the fundamental human right of free national association.[106] De Laveleye—an eminent professor of political economy and a progressive Catholic who
converted to Protestantism in 1878—published *Des Causes actuelles de guerre en
Europe et de l'arbitrage* (1873), which achieved wide circulation and significant
influence. His expectation was that Europe would be wrecked by wars of nationalism for decades to come if the powers failed to create a system for defusing
tensions.

A second organization was also formed in 1873 in Brussels; it was called the
Association pour la réforme et le codification du droit des gens and in 1897 was
renamed the International Law Association. This group cast a wider net and
included leading peace activists with scholarly or political credentials, such as
Henry Richard, Passy, as well as interested American peace activists. It pledged
itself to concentrate on short-term practical problems. In the next decades, its
meetings increasingly resembled those of chambers of commerce or conventions
on such issues as weights, measures, postal charges, copyrights, shipping regulations, and credit exchanges.[107] It provided a forum where bankers, businesspersons, and some peace thinkers could meet on a practical footing and discuss possible ways to reduce friction among different national communities over the
practical problems involved in world-scale economies. To Passy and de Laveleye,

such exchanges were a significant method of enhancing the international culture that an international polity required. The repeated pleas of Henry Richard to the *association* as well as to the *institut* that each take up the study of arbitration went largely unheeded.[108]

The overarching desire of these post-1871 initiatives was to attain respectability and avoid the deadly label of *utopianism*. In France, moreover, respectability meant distinct separation from the taint of the Commune. Although Lemonnier in Geneva scorned such tactics—indeed, welcomed pro-Communards, such as "Mme. André Leo"[109] to the dais in 1872—the desire for realistic respectability even characterized the first attempt to establish a specifically working-class peace society in England, which was led by W. Randal Cremer.[110] Cremer's group, the Workman's Peace Association was run by laboring men who militated against increases in military spending, warned against intervention in the Franco-Prussian War, and who supported a "high court of nations," the use of arbitration, and the development of international law. Cremer asserted that "sooner or later, a substitute must and will be found for war" and declared that workers will play their part in moving that day along.[111] His group became financially solvent by 1872 owing to support from skilled workers, many of whom received the franchise in 1867. Convinced of the importance of transnational outreach, he tried to organize a meeting in Paris in 1872. The only group to contact there was Passy's. No remnants of the First International existed. Cremer sent a letter to "friends of peace in France," indicating,

> Nothing would give the Council greater pleasure than to enter into a peaceful and cordial alliance with the working men of France. . . . However divergent may be the interests of others, the interests of the working class are everywhere identical.[112]

When a meeting was finally held in 1875, most of the Parisian audience were the middle-class members of Passy's Société française des amis de la paix, but a few socialists, such as Auguste Desmoulins, son-in-law of Pierre Leroux, came.[113] The political situation of the Third Republic in 1875 was not conducive to a peace society.

The introduction of pro-arbitration resolutions into parliaments in the 1870s (briefly attempted before the Franco-Prussian War) was revived. To his astonishment, Henry Richard's motion actually passed the Commons in July 1873;[114] the initiative was copied by van Eck in the Netherlands, Mancini in Italy, Auguste Couvreur[115] in Belgium, and Charles Sumner[116] in the United States. Two resolutions were brought into the Austrian lower house; in Sweden, Denmark, and Canada, motions urging the foreign offices to organize an international conference for an arbitration treaty were debated.[117] Amid these initiatives, Adolf Fischhof, the eminent Viennese doctor, published two essays that defended arms' reduction and were widely translated.[118] Besides describing the well-known criticisms of bloated military budgets, he outlined the new political game played by war ministers, all of whom annually blamed their escalated requests on their neighbors. Obviously, this ritual would eventually bankrupt Europe. Fischhof proposed the only logical solution: a simultaneous reduction of arms arranged by all the states.

Fischhof, who earned his political credentials in the 1848 revolution, expected nothing from official quarters. Unlike cautious peace activists, he proposed that parliamentary deputies organize their own meeting to negotiate an end to the arms race. Members of parliaments would then return home to orchestrate a series of resolutions that favored negotiated arms reductions. Fischhof wrote to Garibaldi, asking for his endorsement on behalf of the "well-being of the world."[119]

Fischhof's project was echoed elsewhere. The Berlin editor, Edouard Löwenthal, who created the Deutscher Verein für internationale Friedenspropaganda proposed an all-European meeting of parliamentarians to discuss peaceful organization.[120] A similar proposal came from Edmond Thiaudière, a French journalist, who called for a convocation of members of parliaments to reach over the heads of recalcitrant executive authorities.[121] The notion that the governing heads of Europe were morally bankrupt and incapable of leading the way toward an organized peace led one French peace activist to dismiss them all as "barbarians," dominated only by "bellicose, ruinous and disastrous ideas . . . egotistical and inhuman."[122] Proof came in 1877 with the Russo-Turkish War that produced more converts to the peace cause. It inspired the debut of a Spanish senator, Arturo de Marcoartu, who began by throwing himself into the peace crusade with the publication of a book, *Internationalism*.[123] In 1878, he toured Central European capitals, uring the convocation of a meeting of parliamentarians. On a one-man crusade, Marcoartu traveled to a half-dozen capitals arguing for an organized peace. In the same year, fearing that the Russo-Turkish War would spread, Italian liberals in Milan formed the Lega di pace e fratellanza, which convened several large public gatherings that attracted an audience of both workers and the middle class to protest the possibility that their government might drag Italy into the war.[124]

Thus, although the Franco-Prussian War and the Treaty of Frankfurt dashed peace societies and initiatives from 1867 to 1870, those very events stimulated other initiatives. In 1878, determined to advertise the renewed vigor of their nation, the French government organized an exposition in Paris. The small, growing peace community decided to risk an international congress hosted by Passy's *société*.

The organizing committee took particular care to warn participants against raising "unpleasant" and provocative issues. The meeting paid formal respects to its predecessors from 1848 to 1851, but ignored the movements formed from 1867 to 1870. Thirteen nations were represented by 150 delegates, of which 95 were French. Adolphe Franck, a respected scholar, opened the proceedings and introduced a fixed agenda of seventeen resolutions. Franck rejected the criticism that peace activism was a waste of time with the comment that diplomatic meetings "seem to be instituted to consecrate past wars and prepare for future ones. Diplomats seem able only to send soldiers and cannon into the field."[125] Peace congresses could offer fresher ideas. Franck admitted that war once helped create communities, laws, culture, and (sometimes) even freedom, but the modern destruction and suffering that it also brought outweighed any positive purpose. Ignoring the rule that contemporary problems be left out, Franck attacked the abysmal record of Europe's two newest nations, Serbia and Rumania—recent products of warfare. Both persecuted their Jewish minorities. Franck insisted that the peace agenda include rights of minority populations.[126]

Lemonnier spoke next. He reviewed the contributions of peace movements in the nineteenth century.[127] Keenly aware of profound differences among peace societies, Lemonnier opposed a motion that urged the creation of a transnational organization, "In the current state of the peace party, I believe . . . it is impossible to establish a federation. We are not yet mature enough. Perhaps a loose network [. . . to exchange information]."[128] Delegates ignored his advice and passed the resolution, but his prediction was accurate. No formal international organization occurred until 1891.

The second arena of difference in 1878 arose when Passy objected to language in a resolution that charged war as "international brigandage" that "enthrones despotism and . . . aggravates the condition of the most numerous and poorest classes, both in the victorious and defeated nation."[129] Passy found any reference to class detestable—war was horrendous for the whole nation, for *all* its citizens. He maintained, moreover, that in republics there were no classes, for "civil liberty and political rights belong to everyone."[130] The vigorous debate that followed revealed the profound differences between peace activists over the legacy of the Commune. Those who defended the original language, including Lemonnier and a Parisian councillor, Gaston Morin, were finally outvoted. The conference sided with Passy's view. The majority refused to recognize class as a social reality.

Franck had challenged peace activists to come up with better ideas than diplomats did. The congress examined the possibilities of implementing arbitration among European nations that preserved national autonomy; it proposed ways to apply the codicil favoring mediation in the Peace of Paris (1856) in emergencies; and, for the first time, a peace congress demanded that governments consult with parliaments before declaring war.

The discussions about forms of international arbitration made Lemonnier nervous. He distrusted any Continental system that might involve the Russian tsar. Rather than arbitration, Lemonnier argued for federation, a "political contract . . . whose objective guarantees each member its own freedom, independence, and . . . autonomy."[131] Were the United States, France, Italy, and Great Britain to initiate a thirty-year treaty, Lemonnier maintained, a healthy future for an organized peace would emerge. This dispute between advocates of arbitration and advocates of federation was not trivial; it cloaked mutually exclusive views of social justice.

In the final days of the 1878 meeting, the French publicist Thiaudière attacked the congress for its timid refusal to create annual meetings of members of parliaments to sit in Switzerland. Elected representatives from constitutionally governed states, sitting together, could find the inspiration to undermine the militarists in all their nations. Another speaker urged the congress to assert *itself* as a permanent body, convene annual meetings, ignore governments, and pass binding resolutions in the manner of the Third Estate of 1789 in France. Arturo de Marcoartu, the only Spaniard to participate in European peace circles in the late nineteenth century, spoke in favor of an initiative from Great Britain, Italy, Switzerland, Austria, Belgium, and the United States to establish a European parliamentary system that would abolish war at least among signatories.[132] He, too, was impatient with modest objectives that called for arbitration because these seemed to be "realistic" and attainable demands by a movement that was doomed to function in an immensely hostile environment.

If Passy was displeased with talk of class differences at the opening of the meeting, the speeches calling on peace activists to constitute themselves as a "Citizens International" provoked rare sarcasm. The speakers, he charged, knew little about the problems facing peace movements. At best, peace activists might influence parliaments, friends, scholars, legal minds, and public speakers, insinuating their ideas on a wider public in the manner that the Enlightenment once had worked. Any other mode of action would bring derision and indifference. Militant members tried to interrupt, but Passy managed to carry the original resolutions unadorned with calls for direct action.

On the question of parliamentary control over declarations of war, this congress was firm. The Italian delegate, the Marquis de Pepoli, active in the newly organized Milanese Lega della pace e la fratellanza, bitterly attacked royal and ministerial manipulation of foreign policy as a way to encroach on parliamentary rights. The congress denounced conquests that ignored the popular will of peoples after hearing Alsatian Jean Dollfuss describe the "problems of policing resistant populations."[133] In addition, the 1878 conference passed a ringing denunciation of religious intolerance on behalf of the Jews who were persecuted in the new Romanian state.[134] A resolution supported Fischhof's call for arms' reduction was also passed, with the *rapporteur* observing that nations only need "an elite gendarmerie to preserve order and a less costly reserve army to assure security."[135] Few successor peace congresses cared so completely for human rights issues.

This international congress invited women to join the peace movement. In Great Britain, a woman's auxiliary of the venerable British Peace Society was headed by Mme. Henry Richard; in Switzerland, Valentine de Sellon attempted to preserve some of her father's work; and, of course, Marie Goegg, who had founded the Association internationale des femmes, had turned to work on women's emancipation after 1870–1871. Niboyet proposed that separate women's peace committees be created; this proposal passed—one of the few motions emanating from the floor without prior approval of the organizers.[136] The American Julia Ward Howe spoke on the significance of maternal influence in educating a generation of peace-loving children, but to do this, she noted, women themselves needed a decent education. Congress members were urged to support the emancipation of women if they wanted the peace agenda to go forward. The most direct assault on male attitudes toward women—as a barricade to the success of the peace movement—came from Léonie Rouzade, a Frenchwoman who was attending her first peace congress. She stated that women had an absolute right to participate in discussions on war and peace because war was fought by their children. Women are trivialized, she said, however they are

> considered by some to be an instrument of decadence; by others, as an instrument of civilization. . . . Whatever she tries to do, woman has always wanted positive

results. . . . Peace is the true right and interest of woman; having been prevented from participating in fighting, she can never be accused of cowardice.[137]

She was applauded vigorously. To Valentine de Sellon, the meeting was a vindication of her father's vision. A congress where "workers, women and even a former General" participated was a wondrous event—barely seven years after one of the most divisive wars ever fought.[138] (The general was Stefan Türr, a Hungarian who had fought with Garibaldi and who became a fixture at peace congresses in the 1890s.) Valentine de Sellon's enthusiasm was not shared by Lemonnier, who was bitter at the defeat of his vision of peace through a federation of nations concerned with human rights.

As serious as were the internal divisions among peace activists, the main reasons for the relatively limited impact of the movement were not the shortcomings of activists. Peace congresses, especially that in 1878, attracted progressive voices out of harmony with traditional, majoritarian values—few Catholics, numerous agnostics, Masons, Protestants, Jews, nonbelievers, and socialists. A new hurdle to the peace vision arose in the 1880s as nation after nation passed protectionist legislation to defend themselves against the advanced industrial economies of Great Britain and soon thereafter, the United States. Liberal economists and free traders, whose analyses underlay the positions of Passy, Richard, de Molinari, and de Laveleye were becoming passé. Moreover, the 1880s were a decade when European nations raced to occupy the remaining "free" territories of the globe—mostly in Africa, parts of southeast Asia, and islands anywhere. Peace activists, particularly in Great Britain, increasingly mounted campaigns against wars in Egypt and the Sudan.[139] In Great Britain, long the admired center of peace activism, peace campaigns faced the awful problem of attacking the policies of William Ewart Gladstone, whom they had just helped to elect on his famous platform of "Peace, Reform, Retrenchment." The Great Liberal, defeating his Tory enemy, Benjamin Disraeli, turned about and adopted the very imperial policies that he had bitterly attacked. It was not the last time that liberal politicians disappointed their peace supporters.

Passy's own *Société* did not flourish in the decade following the 1878 congress. One of its few new members, Charles Richet, Sorbonne professor of physiology, who became a leading peace activist in the next century, noted that sometimes the monthly meetings consisted

> only of Passy, Edmond Thiaudière and myself. Friends of peace imagined . . . that the noble cause would triumph without being trumpeted and that all that was needed to convert the masses were a few eloquent lectures in front of a restricted public.[140]

For Passy, the 1880s brought a welcome improvement in his personal fortunes. In 1881 at age fifty-nine, he was elected to the Chambre des députés from the *VIIIth arrondissement* (Paris), reelected in 1885, and defeated after a vicious campaign in 1889. During his tenure in the *chambre,* he followed a thoroughly independent political course; this persuaded police spies that he was a radical. (They had grudgingly admitted he was "honorable," though afflicted with an "indecisive character.")[141] He refused to support Jules Ferry's expansionist colonial policies and thus destroyed his chances for a senatorial seat. Passy denounced his fellow deputies for voting funds to conquer Tonkin China (Vietnam). In a speech to the *chambre* in December 1885, he challenged the French to face their hypocrisy about the proud and ancient Annamese peoples of southeast Asia, a people who they suddenly decided were "inferior," latecomers to civilization, in need of European tutelage. This instruction, of course, was insured by lethal weapons, "By flame and blood will you make your superiority known and yet you are the very same people who protest so strenuously . . . as French and Alsatians against the crime of conquest in Europe."[142] A public version of this speech delivered to a Parisian audience provoked a near riot and a standing ovation.[143] Passy struggled to remind his fellow citizens and parliamentarians of the fate of empires in the past, insisting that the decline of Spain was directly tied to overexpansion by conquest. Worse was the fate of the conquered natives, who were transformed from free individuals into slaves and instruments of labor. Passy realized that the population of Tonkin China was a sophisticated people with a well-developed culture, but his parliamentary colleagues did not wish to be inconvenienced by such facts.

Both Cremer and Passy discovered that the extension of the vote to a broader social base did not automatically produce sympathizers for peace agendas.[144] In England, an activist from the Rochdale cooperative movement, Hodgson Pratt chose to launch a brand new peace society in order to try to mobilize mass opinion.[145] Pratt set up the International Arbitration and Peace Association in London in 1877 and crossed the Channel to spread his message. The philosophy of this new group ignored the religious arguments of Richard and the older British Peace Society and strove to reach beyond the audience of the Workman's Peace Association.

Pratt came to peace organizing at fifty-six after a long career in the Indian Civil Service followed by years of work in the Rochdale collective movement. He had developed a respect for Hindu culture, established a press to translate Western classics into Hindi, and advocated a series of reform projects. After the Indian Mutiny (Sepoy Rebellion) of 1857–1858, he returned to England. There, he threw himself into organizing on behalf of workers' cooperatives and labor unions. When he took up the peace cause, Pratt possessed an independent income to help sustain the crusade. His background as an organizer and his impatience with euphemistic language gave a nonsense aura to the International Arbitration and Peace Association. In his view, arbitration was the most likely method of international conflict resolution that the sovereign states of Europe would accept with the least fuss. In order to persuade governments that this next step in world order had to be made, Pratt believed that peoples across Europe would have to be convinced. Using the new railway system, he traveled to Paris, Nîmes, Montpellier, Berlin, Stuttgart, Darmstedt, Frankfurt, Milan, Florence, Rome, Brussels, Vienna—with return trips to some of these cities from 1880 to 1883. Some visits were more fruitful than others. Following an appearance in Milan, a peace society was founded that attracted the energetic editor of *Il Secolo,* Ernesto T. Moneta. The Milanese organization, the Unione lombarda per la pace, developed into the most influential peace society in that country.[146] The affiliate group that Pratt inspired in Belgium evolved into the national peace society.

The International Arbitration and Peace Association benefited from the services of Lewis Appleton, who had been a member of Richard's group; editor George H. Perris, who produced *Concord,* one of the finest peace journals ever published; and Felix Moscheles, an artist named for his godfather, Felix Mendelssohn, who enjoyed wide connections in France and Italy.[147] Pratt developed close relationships with peace activists who had preceded him in the field. He was philosophically most comfortable with Lemonnier, but this did not prevent cordial relations with Passy.

In 1881, a meeting in Brussels attracted delegates from eighteen nations. There were positive letters from such eminent scholars as the Russian Frédéric [Fedor Fedorovich] de Martens as well as from some Germans. Among the new faces, were a few Scandinavians, including a Danish parliamentarian, Fredrik Bajer (co-winner with Klas B. Arnoldson of the Nobel Peace Prize, 1908). He was to become the leading peace activist in his country as well as one of the most important international leaders of the movement after 1891.[148] The Brussels conference turned out to be a serious and thoughtful affair, a logical follow-up to the meeting of 1878. Participants were aware of preceding peace congresses and the many efforts that had been made to influence diplomatic meetings. Peace activists meeting in Brussels understood contemporary realities, particularly the new order that stemmed from Bismarckian *raison d' état.*[149] A French participant, the Marquis Saint-Yves d'Alveydra challenged the audience to decide whether it wanted to confront the state system as the French had once confronted the Old Regime— that is by a long, costly, exhausting, but eventually, victorious struggle.[150] Or, he asked, were peace activists prepared to wage a long, patient campaign among the elites in the sciences, education, universities, governments, political parties, and similar quarters to set a process in motion that would transform public consciousness.

Delegates to the Brussels meeting were neither simplistic nor optimistic. Wary of virulent nationalism, they wondered whether a longer campaign on behalf of arbitration would produce results. A substantial number of speakers—including a newcomer, the French cooperative-socialist, Jean-Baptiste-André Godin;[151] the defrocked priest, Père Hyacinthe (Charles Loyson); the Spanish senator, Arturo de Marcoartu; an Italian international lawyer, Gaetano Meale (who wrote as "Umano"); a German professor, Max Müller, who was teaching at Oxford— argued for a Lemonnier tactic: a United States of Europe without German participation.[152] Marcoartu was particularly enraged that the old Congress of Europe routinely ignored Spain, Belgium, the Netherlands, Portugal, the Scandinavian nations, the Greek state, and Romania—over fifty million people. Proposals centering on a European confederation defended radical strategies. As in 1878, speakers in Brussels urged direct action and considered appointing themselves as missionary-diplomats. Some recommended that the peace movement pack parliaments with like-minded members, observing, "[The] peace party [already] exists in Europe. All social classes are represented in it; it will grow more powerful than the war party and will acquire parliamentary majorities."[153]

At Brussels, every possible shape for the organization of European peace was examined. Godin spoke for those who insisted that the extension of the franchise to workers must precede the achievement of pacific foreign policies. Only a democratic electorate would lead to a pacific foreign policy. But, he added, as long as twenty to fifty thousand francs are needed to run an election, the workers and the poor will never be represented in parliaments.[154] Godin maintained that French peace activists really had to struggle for the democratization of the Third Republic before a peace policy would develop. To "realize peace among nations . . . the conditions of civil and social peace" must exist. Otherwise, peace would remain an interlude between wars.[155] Though Pratt's new association emphasized arbitration, its supporters were closer to Lemonnier's Genevan *ligue* than to the positions of Passy, Richard, and Cremer.

To Passy and Cremer the connection of peace with a broader agenda of democracy, human rights, and republican institutions remained troublesome. Passy insisted, "Friends of peace have only one principle in which they can put their trust; it is arbitration. . . . Everything else [must be] subordinated to that single principle."[156]

Accepting this single principle meant ignoring protests against national oppression and social inequality (e.g.,—the sufferings of Poles under Russian control was not a peace issue). This single-minded tactic meant preserving silence about the Treaty of Frankfurt; it meant never using the word *class.* In Passy's experience, such neutrality was the only path to success and influence in the struggle for an organized peace. Following a speech at Reims, he reported, "I spoke of peace and international arbitration, [and] the mayor himself signed up as a member of our French Arbitration Society and then inscribed the entire city with a contribution of 100 francs."[157] To struggle for arbitration was to work to create a legal house in which the sovereign European nations would occupy independent and separate suites. They would develop certain commonly needed institutions, such as the Universal Postal Union that had begun to function. With time and the creation of international services, nations would trust each other sufficiently to pull down the dividing walls and enlarge the common rooms, knitting together a European community that had no need of war.

Lemonnier rejected this approach. He backed the rights of the Irish to their freedom and urged Greeks to take responsibility for freeing the Balkans from oppression.[158] When the German Kaiser was booed on a trip to Rome by crowds waving placards for Alsace-Lorraine and shouting "down with the Triple Alliance," Lemonnier was exhilarated.[159] With the organization of Pratt's group, the positions of the aging Lemonnier found new champions.

Cremer and Passy remained solidly committed to peace through arbitration. In the late 1880s, they launched parliamentary campaigns for bilateral arbitration treaties: binding, permanent commitments between the United States and Great Britain and between the United States and France to use arbitration no matter what the issue.[160] Obviously, there was little likelihood of war between these parties in 1888; the moderate peace activists chose to work for a plausible objective, more to validate their arguments than to prevent bloodshed. After a consultation with Andrew Carnegie, the American millionaire of Scots descent who had become interested in international peace, Cremer rounded up 232 signatures from members of Parliament and sent a petition to President Grover Cleveland and the U.S.

Congress urging a treaty. In November 1887, Cremer led a British "invasion of Washington" to lobby for the treaty.[161] At the same time, Louis Ruchonnet, president of the Swiss Federal Council (Bundesrat) opened negotiations with Washington.[162] Passy, simultaneously, secured 112 signatures from French parliamentarians that were sent to the French Foreign Office, much to the annoyance of professional diplomats.[163] Passy preceded his public call by careful preparation, enlisting support in the Chambre des députés that included Jules Simon and Georges Clemenceau.[164]

The campaigns to establish permanent treaties that required the use of arbitration among the most advanced, constitutionally organized nations eventually failed in their immediate objective. By 1896, the Foreign Offices in France and Great Britain and the U.S. Congress refused to sign treaties binding them in all contingencies for an indeterminate future. But the campaigns mobilized new energies and succeeded as publicity. They created a climate that finally gave life to Löwenthal and Thiaudière's recommendations in 1878—the establishment of annual meetings of parliamentarians to deal with issues of war and peace.

By the end of the 1880s, a permanent peace movement took shape in Italy when the Unione lombarda per la pace organized public meetings among workers, interpellated parliamentary candidates, and established rules for its own meetings.[165] In 1889, the *unione* sponsored a very successful national congress in Rome. Well-known intellectuals and politicians interested in discussing arbitration, militarism, the peaceful resolution of international conflict, and the reduction of arms expenditures all assembled.[166] At the same time, in Palermo, the Società per la pace was formed by Elvira Cimino. The Italian movement paralleled the successful creation of movements in Sweden[167] and Denmark during the same decade. In both northern and southern Europe, the newly organized movements were supported by writers, politicians, members of Parliament, journalists, lawyers, businesspersons, professors, and a few leaders of newly emerging working-class organizations, socialist parties and labor unions. The Milanese editor of the liberal daily *Il Secolo,* Ernesto Teodoro Moneta, wrote to Angelo de Gubernatis, an eminent orientalist, "I have become a peace missionary."[168] His definition of a peace activist was an individual who addressed both the long-range vision of international organization as well as immediate foreign policies.[169] The liberal political crusader in Denmark, Fredrik Bajer, who had organized the Society for the Promotion of Danish Neutrality in 1882, moved from his involvement in Scandinavian issues to a larger, European canvas in the late 1880s. Bajer, who had several careers—in the military, as a language teacher, as a member of Parliament—was familiar with the work of both Passy and Lemonnier.

In Sweden, the idea of permanent neutrality had also motivated the creation of a peace society. In 1883, Klas Arnoldson and others in Parliament, launched a group to agitate for neutral status and also established a peace and arbitration society that became quite involved in trying to resolve in a peaceful manner the disputes that emerged with Norway.[170] Arnoldson, a practitioner of applied Christianity, had been convinced by the wars for German unification that Sweden and Scandinavia in general must take the lead in developing pacific foreign policies and their own neutrality. His initiatives on behalf of private and legislative peace activism succeeded in getting him elected to the Swedish Parliament.

The multiplication of peace societies, of new faces across Europe who spoke out in favor of antiwar and antimilitarist postures were not numerous, but they were diverse, energetic, and willing to seek common ground for transnational action. Typical of this energy was the creation of a new organization in Nîmes by a group of mainly Protestant students in 1887, originally called the Association des jeunes amis de la paix (renamed Association de la paix par le Droit). The founder, Louis Barnier, had been impressed by the work of an English Quaker, Priscilla Hannah Peckover,[171] whom he had met as a student in England. Peckover, the animating and material inspiration of the Wisbech Local Peace Society, was a well-to-do Quaker firmly committed to absolute pacifism and nonviolence. The *lycéennes* Barnier assembled in Nîmes were also influenced by Godin's views of cooperation and Charles Gide's cooperative economics.[172] They launched their new organization with a dramatic denunciation of military service.[173] Peckover and Marie Goegg sent money and letters of support, but Passy published an admonition, warning young Frenchmen who wanted to see peace established not to back disarmament and antimilitarism. Eventually, the young members moved away from their radical pacifism, but Barnier left the country rather than serve in the armed forces. The group renamed itself the Association de la paix par le droit. Its members announced their intention was to "study and popularize the juridical solutions for international conflicts and particularly to gain the support for this position by the activity of young persons without distinction of sex."[174]

Peace societies grew in the French provinces. In the Aisne, Jean Godin's cooperative, the Familistère de Guise, created a subcommittee for peace and arbitration that prefigured the founding of a Société de paix et d'arbitrage international in 1886. *Le Devoir,* the cooperative's journal, published discussions of international problems in every issue from 1878 to 1906.[175] In 1885, the thirty individuals who established Les Amis de la paix in Puy-de-Dôme (Clermont-Ferrand) included artisans (bookbinders, carpenters, typographers, workers, road-crew members) and local notables (doctors, the mayor, and four councillors, three lawyers, a senator, and six members of the Chambre des députés). The group doubled its numbers by 1892, mainly by recruiting teachers. Their leader, Antoine Pardoux, regularly published accounts of the group's activities in *Le Petit Clermontois.*[176] Pardoux claimed a Jacobin legacy from the First Republic in 1792 for French pacifism:

> The year 1792 saw the power of a united people working in the service of Right . . . defeat despotism which was supported by the brutal and unthinking power of twenty other peoples. . . . At a century's distance, the year 1892, will see the right of all peoples, sustained by reason, compel the lingering remnants of barbarism within the compass of civilization, lay down their arms without a struggle.[177]

Thus Passy's Société française de l'arbitrage—the pioneers after 1871—was no longer the only organization in France. French peace activism was continued by Edmond Potonié-Pierre, who had settled near Paris and published occasional

papers on war and peace, "Petits Plaidoyers pour la paix." With his feminist comrade, Eugénie Potonié-Pierre, he was active in women's and labor causes. Both
Edmond and Eugénie worked to free exiled communards, to gain the vote for
women, to campaign against poverty, and to cut military expenses.[178]

During the 1880s, a young French notary, Émile Arnaud, came into contact
with Lemonnier's Ligue internationale de la paix et de la liberté. Arnaud[179] demonstrated superb organizational abilities and on Lemonnier's death in 1891, was
named president. The decade of the 1880s in France thus witnessed a new infu-
sion of energy into the peace cause.

Some of the founding members of the Geneva-based *ligue* had become prominent. Ferdinand Buisson shaped educational policy in the Third Republic and
became a Sorbonne professor of pedagogy. Élie Ducommun had become executive director of the Jura–Simplon Railway. Louis Ruchonnet was president of the
Swiss Federal Council (Bundesrat). Jules Simon, close to Passy, was a leading politician in France.[180] Other peace activists also developed public careers in the
1880s. Passy sat in the Chambre des députés for two terms, and Cremer occupied
a seat in the House of Commons. Moneta was a well-known editor in Milan as
was Klas Arnoldson in Stockholm. The Italian Minister of Education Ruggiero
Bonghi became interested in peace questions in 1888–1889 when he, too, became
frightened at the drift in foreign policy.[181] Similar considerations impelled a leading Neapolitan industrialist and member of the Italian lower house, Beniamino
Pandolfi as well as a Turinese entrepreneur and economist, Edoardo Giretti, to
become tireless supporters of international organization.[182]

Across the Atlantic in 1888, the National Council of Women was formed in
the United States. It created a permanent committee on peace and arbitration that
reached out to an international membership. By the mid-1890s, a transatlantic
network of women functioned as a pressure group to reorient the education of
children at home and in school. It was coordinated and organized by Mary E.
Wright Sewall, a feminist, school administrator and founder of the International
Council of Women.[183] Her interest was in creating curricula for schoolchildren
that would emphasize the peaceful solution of all disputes.

Thus, from 1871 to 1889, the mobilization of private citizens into peace societies in western, northern, and southern Europe belied the depressing months that
followed the Treaty of Frankfurt. Peace movements came of age. The aspiration
of the Congrès international des Sociétés des amis de la paix in Paris during the
Exposition of 1878 could be realized: an international organization coordinating
the diverse societies was an idea whose time had come.

In 1889, France celebrated the centennial of its Great Revolution with a major
international exposition in Paris. Alexandre-Gustave Eiffel displayed his tower; a
polyglot of languages filled the streets of Paris as celebrants and the curious came
to the wondrous exhibition. Everything was on display. Poster art at its most glorious celebrated the Great Revolution and "progress." The centennial inspired
interest groups to assemble. European socialists used the moment to create the
Second (Socialist) International, a counterpoint to the distinctly smug nature of

the offical celebration. Passy and Cremer persuaded parliamentary colleagues to meet and discuss peace and arbitration initiatives.

The 1889 meeting of British and French parliamentarians in Paris launched the Interparliamentary Conference (now Union), that still exists. In addition, Lemonnier, Passy, Pratt, and Cremer agreed to call a meeting of private peace activists. This assembly of the Universal Peace Congress, was the first of twenty-one held until 1914. In 1891, at the third meeting, held in Rome, the participants agreed to set up a headquarters in Berne; thus, the Bureau international de la paix was created. The parliamentarians also created a central headquarters in 1891 and they also convened meetings from 1889 to 1914.[184] In the quarter-century from 1889 to 1914, peace activists achieved a solid foundation of international organization among themselves. Lemonnier, once skeptical that peace activists could support an international association, helped to realize the dream in 1889. His death two years later deprived the newly established international movement of its most consistent democratic voice. By 1914, Lemonnier's linkage between domestic justice and international peace was so embedded in peace thinking that no one thought it remarkable, exceptional, or controversial.

3

Pacifism and Internationalism: The Creation of a Transnational Lobby 1889–1914

As both doctrine and movement, pacifism existed well before the word was coined. In 1901, Émile Arnaud, Lemonnier's successor as president of the Ligue internationale de la paix et de la liberté, first used the word *pacifism* to describe the ideology of the "friends of peace":

> Our great party needs a name; we have no name and this deficiency impedes our progress considerably. We are not passive types; we are not only peace makers; we are not just pacifiers. We are all those but also something more—we are pacifists . . . and our ideology is pacifism.[1]

From 1889 to 1914, this "great party" grew to include approximately three thousand European and North American activists coordinated in over one hundred national and regional peace societies. Most came from the nations between the Ural Mountains and the Rockies; in Japan, Australia, and Argentina a few activists organized societies.

During the same years, the generation of peace activists finally created a transnational network. The multiplication of peace societies occurred in nearly every European state (even tsarist Russia in 1910).[2] In France, Great Britain, Italy, Germany, Belgium, Denmark, Sweden, and Norway, national councils were created, some with paid directors. In 1892, peace societies established the International Peace Bureau in Berne to coordinate as unified a position as was possible among groups with widely differing philosophies. Membership surged in 1899–1900, partly in response to the First Hague Peace Conference of 1899 and to the enthusiasm that a new century inspired. Arnaud's characterization of the movement as a "great party" was not an exaggeration.

The internationally coordinated movement, composed of independent, often fractious members, directed its arguments to the public at large as well as to those in power. A small army of indefatigable workers—men and women—traveled lecture circuits, published and catalogued libraries of books and brochures, raised money from governments and private donors, confronted politicians, challenged military budgets, criticized history curricula, combated chauvinist and establishment media, lobbied diplomats, questioned candidates for office, telegraphed congress resolutions to foreign ministries, and held congresses nearly every year from 1889 to 1914 to thrash out common positions.

This new vitality did not mean that peace activists spoke with one voice. The word *pacifism* was (and has remained) one of the most difficult and contentious to define.[3] Pacifists were passionate, engaged activists with very independent personalities and vastly differing cultural, even political backgrounds.[4] The political milieu was hostile; attacked from Right and Left, pacifists struggled to create concensus among themselves as they simultaneously struggled to prevent a suicidal war. American and English delegates to international congresses learned to drop their requests for opening prayer services, which Europeans feared would make them the laughingstock of urbane constituencies.[5] Continental activists, usually agnostics, Masons, and the politically liberal or left-liberal found Christian apologetics a distinct embarrassment. For his part, Leo Tolstoy insisted "that the sole solution to the question [of war] is for the citizens to refuse to be soldiers. . . . The disappearance of war . . . [has] no need of conferences of peace societies."[6] He rejected the entire movement as irrelevant if not actually a hindrance to the achievement of permanent peace that, in his estimation, would come about from human agency, the refusal to serve.[7]

The task of negotiating among the many visions of pacifism to preserve public unanimity, was reluctantly undertaken by Élie Ducommun.[8] A longtime member of the Ligue internationale de la paix et de la liberté (Geneva), Ducommun was asked to serve as the first executive secretary of the Bureau international de la paix when it was founded in 1891 in Rome at the Third Universal Peace Congress. He retained the post until his death in 1906. The survival and growth of the Bureau, which began life in Ducommun's Berne home, was due substantially to his patience and genius at compromise. His counterpart, the executive director of the Interparliamentary Conference, was Albert Gobat,[9] a lawyer, superintendant of public education in Berne and a member of the Federal Council (Bundesrat). Gobat was devoted and hardworking but less willing to suffer fools in silence.

Uncertainty and fear of failure colored the early years of the international movement. Wary about nationalist invective, Cremer and Passy had insisted that the meetings of the parliamentary and private peace delegates in 1889 confine themselves to the Platonic virtues of arbitration. These two elder statesmen of private and parliamentary peace initiatives believed that the crucial goal was to persuade elites that arbitration was no threat to national freedom. In 1891, this strategy was reinforced when delegations of Austro-Hungarians and Germans came to the Universal Peace Congress and the Interparliamentary Conference in Rome for the first time—owing to the successful campaigning by Bertha von Suttner whose novel *Die Waffen nieder* had become a runaway best-seller.[10] The young peace movement, initiated mainly by British- and French-led groups, had to adjust to new arrivals from central Europe as well as the United States. To retain the involvement of peace delegates from the Hohenzollern and Hapsburg monarchies meant accepting the advice of a lone German delegate at the 1890 London meeting of the Universal Peace Congress:

> Our movement finds plenty of friends in Germany. If I might be allowed to give a few practical hints towards furthering our movement from the German point of view, I would recommend abstinence . . . from actual political questions which . . . lead to suspicions and injury to our cause. I would urge that we direct our action rather to inculcate ideas which would show to the middle and higher classes, the injustice and crime of waging war.[11]

Western Europeans and Americans were not familiar with the constitutional realities of central and eastern Europe. In the Hapsburg monarchy, even members of Parliament were proscribed from debating treaties; for private citizens, discussion of foreign policy might provoke charges of treason.[12] German citizen-activists were constrained by restrictive civil liberties legislation, laws against publication that could result in charges of *lèse-majesté,* strict regulations of public meetings other than church services, restrictions against women's participation in public meetings, all this coupled with broad public approval of the authoritarian constitution. The Italian politician, Ruggiero Bonghi,[13] had to relinquish the presidency of the Interparliamentary Conference in 1891 because of his article on Alsace-Lorraine, which blamed the German government for causing most European tensions. German delegates would have had to leave the Rome meeting had Bonghi remained in the chair.

In the early 1890s, the annual international meetings were exercises in compromise. Could or should Continental pacifists remain silent about the Bismarckian legacy in order to nurture the peace movement? Von Suttner, anxious to insure the continued presence of German and Austrian delegates, joined Passy and Cremer in insisting that arbitration remain the unifying denominator of international meetings.[14] Ducommun accepted the cautious approach.[15] This style of managing debate, infuriating to many pacifists, gave the young international movement time to survive its infancy.[16] But it was a strategy that did not last for the entire twenty-five-year period before the Great War.

By 1914, the international peace movement developed a far richer program. From 1889 to 1914, the Universal Peace Congress held twenty congresses and the Interparliamentary Conference met eighteen times in European and U.S. cities.[17] Both moved well beyond the arbitration agenda. Activists from fifteen European nations[18] struggled to transform the definition of *peace* from its traditional meaning, the absence of war, to a positive, organized process of interstate relations.

In those years, the growth of peace organizations across Europe continued without interruption. In the 1890s, the largest new constituency to join were women, reflecting the growing sophistication of feminists. Groups organized by Eugénie Potonié-Pierre, Sylvie Flammarion, Séverine (pseudonym of Carolyn Rémy), and Princess Gabrielle Wiesniewska in France; Ellen Robinson in Great Britain; Marie Rosseels and Claire Bauer in Belgium; Johanna Waszklewicz-van Schilfgaarde in the Netherlands, along with women's societies in Sweden and Norway brought in new energies. Although most of these groups spoke to middle-class women, the work of Flammarion and Séverine in the L'Association 'la paix et le désarmement par les femmes' was directed toward working-class women in marketplaces and poorer neighborhoods. In the next decade, Italian women, including Rosalia Gwis-Adami and alma dolens (pseudonym of Teresita Pasini dei Bonfatti), traveled the peninsula to spread peace arguments and establish women's committees. A group of French *institutrices* created the Société d'education pacifique, which contained nineteen branches on the eve of World War I. In the Auvergne (France), the leadership of La Paix par le droit fell to Jeanne Mélin— by 1910, an indefatigable worker for women's rights and peace causes.[19] From the International Council of Women under Mary E. Wright Sewall, peace literature addressed to educating children provided the movement with propaganda addressed to younger audiences. In countries where national women's councils were formed to militate for the vote, support came from such women as Margarethe Leonore Selenka in Germany and Mme. Jules Siegfried in France.[20] The best-known woman of the period involved in peace activism was Bertha von Suttner, who initially minimized any gender connection to the peace cause.[21]

The movement welcomed women's involvement. In 1892, the Berne *bureau* issued the first of many special appeals to women to support the movement and attend congresses. Women's organizations were urged to affiliate.[22] In one particularly purple piece of rhetoric, Henry La Fontaine (Nobel Peace Prize, 1913) appealed, "Oh ladies, it is to you that I speak, particularly; you, new Sabines, it is to you that the task belongs of saying 'NO' to the frightful monster which never swallows enough blood, pain, tears."[23] Women who had been active in earlier decades usually worked with eminent husbands (e.g., Mme. Henry Richard and Mme. Émile de Laveleye). The new women's membership came from those (often with their own careers) who adopted the cause on their own. One prominent example was Belva Lockwood—the first woman lawyer allowed to argue before the U.S. Supreme Court[24]—who served as the American correspondent of the Bureau international de la paix and sat on its governing council along with Bertha von Suttner and Ellen Robinson. Outreach to women's groups was supported by peace activists of all colors. By the opening of the twentieth century, many supported suffrage for women (including Passy, Novicow, Moneta, the Swiss leadership, and Pratt).

The international movement benefited from new theoretical studies devoted to the role of war and peace in history and modern society. Foremost among scholars was the sociologist, Jacques Novicow (Ivan Novikoff, 1849–1912) who brought a wide-ranging vision drawn from history, anthropology, economics, political theory, military strategy, and contemporary criticism to a dozen full-length studies.[25] Besides writing and lecturing, Novicow attended meetings of the Universal Peace Congress, served on subcommittees, and helped organize the International Sociological Association. His influence was most pronounced on Alfred Fried,[26] a journalist and founder of peace groups in Germany. The Polish railway magnate and financier, turned scholar, Jean de Bloch (Ivan Bliokh, 1836–1902)[27] produced an immensely influential six-volume study, *The Future of War in Its Technical, Economic and Political Relations,*[28] which provided the peace movement with arguments and information for over a decade. Norman Angell's best-seller of 1910, *The Great Illusion,* also served to popularize pacifist ideas, though Angell, originally, was unaware of the organized movement. His influence on political leaders was measurable on the eve of the war, as well. Indeed, a "new pacifism" was in the making as a result of his work.[29]

In France, the movement mushroomed. There, substantial centrist and center-left groupings—notably in the Radical, Radical–Socialist, and Socialist parties—provided a supportive political climate. Although the Foreign Office kept tight rein on colonial and foreign policies and although parliamentary challenges to foreign and military policy seemed to have little impact,[30] there were imperceptible changes. The Dreyfus affair, for instance, opened public debate. Vigorous feminist and socialist organizations whose programs intersected with peace concerns strengthened the French movement.

When the Third Universal Peace Congress sat in Rome in 1891, seventy-nine French societies were represented.[31] In the *fin de siècle,* Émile Arnaud delivered about a thousand lectures around the country in addition to his trips to Belgium and Spain. A surviving record book of 1897 indicates that the publication of the Berne *bureau, Correspondance bi-mensuelle,* went to 432 French subscribers, including sixty peace societies, one hundred popular universities, sixty cooperatives and *bourses de travail* (labor exchanges) as well as individuals.[32] The student founders of La Paix par le droit matured into lawyers, professors, public officials, judges, and writers. In 1902, about twelve hundred dues-paying members were counted; three hundred were university students. Its journal, *La Paix par le droit* had over three thousand subscribers and its annual, *Almanach de la paix,* over 10,000.[33]

With the Dreyfus affair, the creation of the Ligue des droits de l'homme, the oldest civil rights organization in the Western world, extended the reach of peace ideas. Its *Bulletin* supported peace arguments and publicized activities.[34] Arbitration resolutions were periodically voted by regional affiliates of the *ligue.*[35] In 1908, Victor Basch's report on arbitration, disarmament, and colonial policy adopted peace-movement analyses.[36] By 1910, the *ligue* shared and shaped peace positions.[37] Three of its earliest presidents were eminent peace crusaders: Ludovic Trarieux, Francis de Pressensé, and Ferdinand Buisson.[38]

In 1896–1897, French peace leaders established a national council—the Délégation permanente des sociétés françaises de la paix.[39] It held national congresses to develop unified positions and to provide a forum for peace activists who could not attend international meetings. The first meeting sat in Toulouse in 1902 and was organized by Théodore Ruyssen,[40] president of La Paix par le droit. Six more national congresses (in 1904, 1905, 1908, 1909, 1911, and 1913) met in France before the outbreak of the Great War, with an average attendance of about 250 to 300 delegates. French congresses attracted participants from teacher's societies, cooperative societies, Masons, labor unions, chambers of commerce, as well as *bourses de travail* and, occasionally, socialist organizations and women's groups. Meetings were deliberately held in provincial cities with special public sessions. In 1904 at Nîmes, for example, the public program attracted about one thousand people. In 1909, at Reims, over twelve hundred people came to the concluding public session. The Reims meeting was endorsed by historians Ernest Lavisse and Gabriel Monod, sociologist Émile Durkheim, as well as sixteen senators, twenty-four deputies, most of the local municipal council, and eminent political leaders, including Louis Barthou, Léon Bourgeois (Nobel Peace Prize, 1920), Émile Loubet, and Stephen Pichon, then minister of foreign affairs.[41] By 1910, France had the largest and most diversified peace movement on the Continent. The congress held in 1911 at Clermont-Ferrand was proud to list seven cabinet ministers on its letterhead, and it received powerful letters of support from a long list of intellectuals and politicians, led by Léon Bourgeois.[42]

In France, by 1910, thirty-six separate organizations—some of which had more branches than the whole international movement contained in 1890—were avowed peace societies.[43] A few of the new peace societies were founded by well-known professors of international law, such as the Société toulousaine de la paix led by A. Mérignhac. A Protestant society led by Paul Allégret (Limoges) and Henry Huchet, as well as a Catholic group, the Société Gratry, led by A. Vanderpol that grew to about twenty regional affiliates.[44] In addition, about sixty-five popular universities, fifteen *bourses de travail,* a dozen cooperative societies, five Masonic lodges, and over a dozen assorted other groups belonged to the national council. The council regularly prepared questionnaires for political candidates and electioneered. In the Chambre des députés, French pacifist positions were voiced by socialists, notably Jean Jaurès and Francis de Pressensé and by members of the Radical party, including Lucien Le Foyer and Ferdinand Buisson. In the sénat, the (usually lone) voice of Baron Paul Henri d'Estournelles de Constant (co-winner Nobel Peace Prize with Auguste Beernaert, 1909), articulated pacifist postures on foreign policy.[45] At teacher's congresses, Ferdinand Buisson argued for a revision of history texts to reduce militarist, chauvinist emphases. Horace Thivet opened an École pacifique in Paris in 1905, with the purpose of providing training for teachers and interested lay people in peace ideology in order to offer alternatives to the standard histories emphasizing traditional patriotism. L'École de la paix sponsored a number of public lectures at the Sorbonne, with eminent speakers covering a range of political views.[46]

The growth and transformation of the movement in France required a reconstitution of the National Council of French Peace Societies. Some of the founding societies had disappeared; others had grown to encompass nationwide networks of their own. La Paix par le droit had branches in Reims, the Ardennes, Bordeaux, Nîmes, and Paris that were larger than the entire movement had been in the 1890s. The occasional participation of eminent personages, such as Anatole France and Léon Bourgeois, required an honorary membership category, and the European situation required a means by which an emergency directorate could be rapidly assembled.[47] From 1911 on, the French peace movement debated ways to change their coordinating center into a council resembling the British National Peace Council, a process that was not completed when the Great War broke out.

At least one measure of French pacifist success was the increasing hostility of traditional conservatives as well as vicious campaigns waged by new rightists of the Action française and the Camelots du roi from 1905 to 1914.[48] The derisive hostility of tastemakers, such as Émile Faguet and Paul Deschanel was damag-

ing.[49] Passy was thrilled when Anatole Leroy-Beaulieu offered qualified backing to
the idea of a "United States of Europe" in his plenary address to the prestigious
Congrés des science politiques in 1900.[50] A set of widely publicized discussions,
which Émile Durkheim hosted on behalf of the Union de la verité deliberated on
internationalism in 1906, supported by Durkheim, Charles Gide, Yves Guyot,
Charles Andler, and Daniel Halévy.[51] But Faguet's book, Le Pacifisme left a significant misprint on the movement.

One estimate suggests that about three hundred thousand French men and
women were involved in the peace movement, not counting the members of the
Ligue des droits de l'homme.[52] On the Continent, it was the largest and most var-
iegated movement, thus exercising considerable authority at international
meetings.

In Italy, too, the movement grew impressively during the fin de siècle. An
attempt to form a national network of Italian peace activists was the object of a
congress in Rome in 1889, which Ruggiero Bonghi helped to organize. Bonghi
was worried that the united nation, which he had struggled to create, was aban-
doning its generous ideals, turning toward militarism, copying its German and
Austrian alliance partners, building a professional military instead of a healthy
economy, and planning to lunge into an imperial scramble. The congress in Rome
in 1889 was really more of an extraparliamentary caucus, with thirty-five of its
ninety participants drawn from the two houses of the legislature, determined critics of the government's foreign policies.[53] They listened to speeches from Vilfredo
Pareto (still a liberal), who proposed a European customs union; Ernesto T.
Moneta on arms reduction; Angelo Mazzoleni, who urged international arbitration; and Bonghi, who wanted the members to proselytize.[54] Bonghi and several
members of the planning committee followed up two years later by inviting both
the Universal Peace Congress and the Interparliamentary Conference to meet in
Rome, which they did. It was his hope that these groups would inspire broader
Italian interest.

In Milan, the Unione lombarda per la pace, organized in 1887, was led by
Moneta, who served as its president until his death in 1918.[55] Peace societies
inspired by Hodgson Pratt's international crusade were founded in Rome by two
academics—C. Facelli and Angelo de Gubernatis, the noted orientalist, and Victor Prestini, a journalist. In Palermo, the Società per la pace formed a woman's
peace society and briefly published a journal.[56] During the decade of the 1890s,
groups were founded across the Italian peninsula—in Perugia, Turin, Venice, Bar-
zano, Torre Pellice (Piedmont)—and from 1904 to 1910, another dozen local
associations were also formed, many of these were directed toward involving
women and teachers.[57]

In 1904, the Italian movement founded a national organization at its Turin
congress. Well over 150 delegates from twenty-five societies came, in addition to
representatives from Masonic lodges, veterans' organizations, popular universities, workers' associations, feminist groups, socialists, and "political circles."[58] The
social and political base of peace activism in Italy resembled France. The peace
societies created in Turin and the small Piedmontese town of Torre Pellice (a Waldensian center) were especially active. Edoardo Giretti's group drew much of his

support from that area. The spirit of the Italian movement reflected republican legacies of the Risorgimento.[59]

After the Turin meeting, the Italian pacifists tried to convene annual congresses. In 1906, Italian pacifism benefited when the Universal Peace Congress held a successful meeting in Milan and in 1907 when Ernesto T. Moneta became the first Italian to win the Nobel Peace Price (co-winner with Louis Renault of France). By 1907, at the Perugia conference, at least seventeen workers associations sent delegates along with the peace societies.[60] Two years later, teachers received permission to attend the Italian National Peace Conference in Rome.[61] The peace society in Rome, led by de Gubernatis and Victor Prestini claimed to have five hundred dues-paying members.[62] In 1910 at Como, alma dolens (pseudonym of Teresita Pasini dei Bonfatti)[63] urged pacifists to work harder to develop the potential in the feminist constituency. Whereas Irma Melany Skodnick and Paola Schiff, noted feminists, had participated in nearly every national congress since 1904, they did not attract women from the popular classes, as dolens urged. In 1908, she conducted a whirlwind campaign to set up women's peace societies across the north and center of Italy. This initiative was followed by Rosalia Gwis-Adami[64] and Adèle Alziator, who organized a peace society for women high school students and teachers in Milan in 1909. Gwis-Adami intended to make the society into the nucleus of an international student and teacher exchange program. Meanwhile, dolens—having organized a group of women's peace societies—had gone on to create a workers' peace society, the Associazione nazionale pro arbitrato e disarmo in Milan, which claimed over seven hundred members by 1910–1911.[65] The health of the Italian peace movement, by 1910, was flourishing. A successful national congress met in Como that year filled with enthusiastic speakers and reports of activity across the peninsula. Italian pacifists had succeeded in organizing a number of *feste della pace* on 22 February (Washington's birthday) that school and public officials encouraged.[66]

Without warning in 1911, the Italian movement collapsed. In September 1911, when the goverment declared war on Turkey over Lybia-Cyrenaica, Moneta, de Gubernatis, Gwis-Adami, and their supporters decided that the invasion was justified.[67] Other peace leaders, notably Edoardo Giretti, Victor Prestini, Elvira Cimino, and alma dolens urged that the Moneta faction be expelled from the international movement.[68] The fracas was bitter and even though there were attempts to heal the dispute after 1912, the Italian movement was permanently scarred.[69] Both peace internationals had planned to hold their 1911 congresses in Rome, in honor of the fiftieth anniversary of Italian unification. The meetings were canceled at the last minute.

When the Universal Peace Congress convened in Geneva in 1912, the confrontation between Italian delegates split the entire convocation. Giretti replaced Moneta as the Italian representative on the central committee. Arcangelo Ghisleri, who spoke against the Libyan war during the congress was brought up on charges in Italy and made to endure a nasty legal battle.[70] The Italian section of the Interparliamentary Union resigned.[71]

In German-speaking nations, peace societies were formed in 1891 and 1892. The Austrian Peace Society (Oesterreicher Friedensgesellschaft) began in 1890–

1891, following an invitation placed in the *Neue Freie Presse* by von Suttner.[72] In Berlin, her disciple, a young journalist named Alfred H. Fried, succeeded in organizing the Deutsche Friedensgesellschaft in 1892.[73] Its spread to the rest of German was slow but steady. Societies appeared in western Germany during the 1890s, the result of work by Adolf Richter (an industrialist), Franz Wirth (an engineer and member of the Frankfurt City Council), Richard Reuter (a lawyer), Otto Umfrid (an Evangelical pastor), and Richard Feldhaus (an actor).[74] Roger Chickering has suggested that the creation of peace societies in Germany was undertaken as much out of embarrassment as conviction by some of these campaigners.[75] In 1889, Adolf Richter was the only German who had remained in Lemonnier's society after 1871 and the only German to attend the Paris congress of 1889.[76] After 1899, he served as president of the National Federation of Peace Societies, but during most of the 1890s, Wirth was the most vocal German peace leader.[77] The question of how effective and how committed the German movement was became critical for the entire international movement. Whereas all Continental pacifists struggled to coordinate their patriotic impulses with an internationalist vision, German pacifists (in the main) remained most attached to values normally considered nationalist and militarist.[78]

The German movement, too, grew during the 1890s, drawing most members from western Germany, especially Württemberg, Baden, Rhineland-Hesse, and Alsace-Lorraine. The inspiration of evangelical Protestantism was stronger in Germany than in France or Italy.[79] By 1902, German peace leaders claimed about six thousand members who belonged to sixty sections; on the eve of World War I, there were about ten thousand members in ninety-eight sections of the Deutsche Friedensgesellschaft. As in most movements, only a few hundred were truly active.[80] In Germany, a single national peace society existed, not a constellation of different organizations as in France and Italy. National conferences were organized after 1908 when Ludwig Quidde succeeded Richter as president. About fifty delegates attended the first meeting in Jena. Meetings of the national organization occurred annually thereafter, offering German pacifists the chance to debate and prepare resolutions.[81]

Shortly before he retired as national president, Richter claimed that the German movement was composed of nearly ninety sections (in 1907), with a membership about four times that of France. Skeptically, Théodore Ruyssen questioned Richter's count, adding that the German "theoreticians [who] think and believe in the name of religion, philosophy and sociology, that war is holy, beneficial and inevitable" had affected its peace community.[82] German politics, Ruyssen complained "constitute for modern Europe, a permanent peril, the most dangerous of all for the preservation of peace—the normal development of civilization."[83] He could not believe Richter's claims. At the Wiesbaden annual meeting of 1910, thirty delegates represented sixty sections of the national organization; Ruyssen's assessment seemed plausible.

In Germany, women's participation in peace activities developed separately from the official movement itself, mainly organized by women active in feminist groups. At a meeting of the Federation of German Women's Associations in late 1898, Margarethe Leonore Selenka proposed a mass-petition campaign and public demonstrations to be organized by women in Germany and worldwide in support of the recently announced Rescript by Tsar Nicholas II that called for a meeting on behalf of arms reduction and arbitration (see app. C). The First Hague Conference, which convened in May of 1899, provided a major rallying point for women in a dozen countries. Selenka's initiative resulted in the collection of over a million signatures.[84] She also popularized the idea of making 18 May (originally the opening day of The Hague Conference) peace day—to be celebrated as a school and public holiday. A formal women's section of the Deutsche Friedensgesellschaft was charted in 1913, but German women joined the peace movement through their own organizations.[85] Feminist activists, such as Helene Stöcker,[86] Lina Morgenstern and Anna Eckstein attended national peace congresses. Eckstein, in particular, urged the Wiesbaden meeting of 1910 to address women's issues as a way of extending its pacifist program.[87] Eckstein, who moved to Boston, was also the force behind a world petition in 1910–1911 that urged the convocation of a third Hague conference expected in 1913 or 1915.

The struggle of German pacifists to attain respectability was a permanent problem.[88] Despite the fact that German pacifist leaders practiced the politics of moderation their influence remained confined, essentially, to those already convinced. To be a pacifist in the political culture of Wilhelmian Germany was akin to professing communism in Cold War America. In 1911, one of Fried's supporters, Otfried Nippold, decided to form a new group, the Verband für internationale Verständigung, which promised to recruit only from a select elite—the mayor of Nuremberg, the president of the Royal Bank, and a list of eminent professors and specialists in international law. Presumably, this membership would eliminate the utopian image of German pacifism and enable tough-minded realists to develop a "science of peace."[89] The insult to stalwart German peace activists was caught immediately by Albert Gobat, Ducommun's successor as executive director of the Berne Bureau international de la paix, who commented caustically, "There is no denying the fact that . . . in Germany, there still exists a dread of losing caste by making common cause with such an association as the Peace Society."[90] Privately, Gobat railed against Nippold's initiative. It would weaken German pacifism.[91] In fact, the *Verband* did not make significant inroads on public opinion in the time remaining before August 1914. As with most liberal causes before the Great War, the peace movement floundered in uncongenial political waters in the Wilhelmian state, where far too many middle-class leaders remained unconfident of their capacity to manage modern politics.[92]

In the Austro-Hungarian Empire the creation of a respectable peace movement was an equally thankless enterprise. The international success of Bertha von Suttner's novel provided a launching pad for the Austrian Peace Society in 1891 but to expand the group much beyond liberal Viennese circles was nearly hopeless.[93] Von Suttner was sensitive to nationalist charges that her movement was socialist, Jewish, liberal—words that were the kiss of death—and sometimes she reacted by minimizing these ties though both Bertha von Suttner and her husband openly opposed the anti-Semitic mayor of Vienna and his supporters. About two thousand members launched the Oesterreicher Friedensgesellschaft in 1891–1892, but its membership did not grow substantially in the succeeding decades.[94]

Branches in Prague, Budapest, and Trieste remained small in size as well. The forces arrayed against peace activism in official government circles were formidable.[95] Peace mongering was deliberately confused with socialism to discourage potential middle- and upper-middle-class membership. Government officials were horrified at the possibilities that private citizen groups—even one with an avowed humanitarian cast—might meddle in policy-making. This presumption, alone, seemed socialist.[96]

Elsewhere in the Austro-Hungarian Empire, peace societies were established in Moravia, Bohemia, and Budapest. In the last named, Count Albert Apponyi— a politician, parliamentarian, minister, and lawyer—became widely known because of his work in the Interparliamentary Union including service on its governing council.[97] The Hungarian Peace Society, founded in 1895, was also the creation of Anna Zipernowsky, a self-educated woman who devoted her life to the crusade, and Sándor Giesswein, who came to the movement through the inspiration of Christian socialism.[98] The brave struggle waged by Rosika Schwimmer on behalf of international peace was conducted in feminist organizations, mainly after the outbreak of World War I.[99]

At the opening of the twentieth century, the organized peace movement in Great Britain, nearing its centennial, was the largest and best organized in the Old World. In 1905, leaders of peace organizations created a central coordinating committee to serve as a British National Peace Council. Quaker and nonconformist membership remained significant, but secular activists, women's representatives, and labor activists (some self-defined socialists) made religious control of the cause problematical.[100] A vast array of affiliated and associated organizations supported peace planks—much as the Aborigines Protection Society had done over a half-century earlier. In Great Britain, a broader network of affiliated societies advocated pacifist ideas than elsewhere in Europe.[101] Frequently, complained the traditionalist Reverend Dr. Evans Darby, secretary of the British Peace Society, newcomers ignored the significance of the Gospel as the basis of antiwar thinking.

The British National Peace Council was composed of the original Peace Society, with twenty-nine branches in the British Isles and four in Australia as well as the International Arbitration and Peace Association, chaired by Felix Moscheles after Pratt's death in 1907, with ten home branches and with overseas affiliates in New Zealand, Belgium, and Italy. In addition, there were fifteen other independent peace societies.[102] British activism was invigorated by the energetic antimilitarist and anti-imperial campaigns conducted by the radical segment of the Liberal party and the emerging Lib-Lab alliance in the House of Commons. Peace activists in Great Britain were cheered by support from Sir Henry Campbell-Bannerman and David Lloyd George, despite the fact that ultimately, the ideals they championed were defeated.[103] The movement could depend on the support of a segment of the Independent Labour party and the trade unions but usually not of the Social Democratic Federation.[104]

In Belgium, peace activism was organized by the International Arbitration and Peace Association that Pratt had helped to found in 1889. Henri La Fontaine chaired both the private peace society and the Interparliamentary Union chapter.[105] The private peace society planned outreach to teachers, students, the mass of the population, and especially women, "our natural allies in the war which we are waging against war!" according to La Fontaine.[106] In the 1890s, membership averaged about 450 to 500 people, which disappointed La Fontaine. (In contrast, the Danish group had about three thousand members in a population of two million.) Membership increased after 1899, however.

After 1902, the association was joined by the Belgian section of the Alliance universelle des femmes pour la paix under Marie Rosseels and Claire Bauer. At one point, this society claimed about 1000 members. Its favorite tactic was to demand that the sums spent on the military be diverted to education. Along with the Belgian Peace Society, the *alliance* militated for a permanent treaty of arbitration among the Netherlands, Belgium, and Denmark, with a promise to use the court at The Hague (after 1900).

Belgium produced some of the most important international leaders—besides Henri La Fontaine, there was his collaborator, Paul Otlet, organizer of dozens of international cultural initiatives;[107] Edouard Descamps, a widely regarded specialist in international law, an active member of the Interparliamentary Union, and a delegate to The Hague Peace Conference of 1899;[108] and Auguste Beernaert, statesman, diplomat, and president of the Interparliamentary Union from 1909 to 1912.[109] La Fontaine convened the first national congress of Belgium pacifists in 1913, which was followed by a well-publicized national campaign to spread the movement.[110] Women's associations; teachers; freethinkers; cooperatives; union leaders; local socialist societies; chambers of commerce; university clubs; reform organizations, such as temperance societies; and even the Theosophic Society participated. In Belgium, the inviolability of neutrality during wartime was the issue of greatest concern to the movement.[111]

Belgians interested in the peace movement believed that their small nation could well serve as the center for international economic, agricultural, scientific, and cultural organizations—and conceivably for a distant European legislative or political unity. After the First Hague Peace Conference chose to locate the arbitration tribunal at The Hague, the Belgian reformer, Louis Frank,[112] launched a campaign to bring the headquarters of all international cultural, economic, and scientific organizations to Brussels, as a prelude to the day when a European federal district would be estabished. Frank actually designed the physical layout of buildings, parks, and new housing that would serve as a *cité internationale*.[113] Both La Fontaine and Otlet, in a related initiative, created The Mundanum, a center for documentation of all global projects—proof that modern, progressive forces operated beyond, above, and without reference to feuding, bitter national politics. Otlet and La Fontaine worked to set up a standard system of bibliographic reference to serve the information needs of an international culture. The peace movement in Belgium was probably more sensitive to internationalism as a cultural and economic phenomenon than was the case in other countries.[114] Peace activists wanted to persuade Brussels to host an international congress of international organizations to launch the vision of Belgium, although small in area, as the world headquarters of federations—but the foreign minister feared antagonizing the Dutch.

In Switzerland, organized peace activities had continued after the Franco-

Prussian War by the Ligue internationale de la paix et de la liberté, which Lemonnier ran until his death in 1891 with the essential support of Marie Goegg. The *ligue* held twenty-one congresses in Switzerland until 1889, continued to publish its journal as frequently as finances allowed, though with greatly diminished membership. When Arnaud took over, the effective center was moved to Luzarches (Seine-et-Oise), but the tradition of the *ligue* remained in the Swiss Romande, and a drive to revivify it resulted in recruitment of about 200 members by 1893. A specifically Swiss national organization was created between 1892 and 1908. Based in the Romande where the private funds and energy of Marc Bloch (Chauds-de-Fond) and Henri Monnier (Geneva and Lausanne) provided the core backing, the group expanded to include twenty-one regional societies with about 4500 members. Records for 1910 show about 4600 dues-paying members, with groups in Zurich, Geneva, Lausanne, Neufchâtel, and Berne.[115] Annual congresses, a journal (*La Paix,* edited by Eugene Rapin in Lausanne), and lively participation in the international meetings made the Swiss society an important part of the movement, and certainly one of the most significant delegations from smaller countries. The peace movement in Switzerland received considerable backing from the Social Democratic party. A Catholic peace society was formed in 1908; a Protestant youth association with over twenty branches participated in annual congresses, as did over twenty Masonic lodges.[116] A membership campaign in 1909 brought in 95 new members in Geneva and reorganized the Neuchâtel branch so that membership grew from 60 to 370. Deliberate efforts to recruit women resulted in a membership that was about one-third female.[117]

Besides the fact that two of the most important leaders of the international movement, Ducommun and Gobat were Swiss, a number of eminent politicians, such as Edouard Quartier-le-Tente, minister of public education, and Louis Ruchonnet backed the movement. Highly respected professionals—judges, pastors, professors, lawyers, bankers—were active, but local sections also included bakers, printers, farmers, confectioners, lumber merchants, court clerks, watchmakers, stonemasons, gardeners, innkeepers, shopkeepers, postal workers, notaries, teachers, and one sergeant in the gendarmerie.[118] The social base of the movement in Switzerland was unusual in Europe. In 1907, a proposed increase in military spending and the length of militia service was countered by a petition with 250,000 signatures mobilized by the peace movement—conservatives, of course, denounced them as traitors.[119]

The peace society in the Netherlands, founded in 1870, had become a genteel tea circle (in the words of a Dutch observer) by the *fin de siècle*.[120] Surprised in 1899 when the European governments decided to hold a peace conference at The Hague, peace crusaders in the Netherlands hastily awakened. New energy came from Johanna Waszklewicz-van Schilfgaarde and Cornelius van Vollenhoven, a professor of international law.[121] Waszklewicz-van Schilfgaarde turned her home into a meeting place for diplomats and peace crusaders and went on to devote several busy years to the cause. She also worked with a Parisian group, the Alliance universelle des femmes, and in 1901, decided to merge the Dutch woman's network with the older society, Vrede door Recht. Not content with discreet projects that spoke to those already committed to the cause, Waszklewicz-van Schilfgaarde campaigned energetically against the Boer War, even in Great Britain. She hoped to enlist the older peace activists but met with little success on the Continent.[122]

The movement in the Netherlands continued to function actively until 1914; its tea-sipping days were over.[123] P. J. Eijkman, editor of the *Revue de l'internationalisme,* campaigned vigorously to persuade diplomats to create a standing court at The Hague, which he saw as the nucleus of an international government. He was not pleased with the publication of Louis Frank's book *Les Belges et la paix,* which suggested Brussels for that position.[124] Van Vollenhoven argued for a special Dutch role in the development of modes of international peacekeeping, insisting that the legacies of Desiderius Erasmus and Hugo Grotius provided his compatriots with a special intellectual and political responsibility. He was one of the earliest proponents of an international peacekeeping police force.[125] At The Hague conferences, the expert Jacobus C. C. den Beer Poortugael was the only official military delegate who insisted that arms control was an attainable goal.[126]

In the Scandinavian nations, the peace crusade was associated with a movement to establish the permanent neutrality of northern Europe. Bajer's Association for the Neutralization of Denmark, founded in 1882, was the nucleus of the Danish peace movement. In 1907, it claimed six thousand dues-paying members in sixty-nine sections.[127] The association was fortunate in that Bajer was succeeded by the capable R. P. Rasmussen in 1906–1907.[128]

Neutralization was also significant in the creation of the Swedish Peace Society, founded and led by Klas P. Arnoldson, a member of Parliament.[129] Peace efforts in Scandinavia were aided immeasurably by the support from eminent novelist Björnstjerne Bjornson[130] as well as from Alfred Nobel's will of 1896 that established the famous peace prizes.[131]

The strength of the Swedish movement reflected the participation of women. A women's subsection, the Sveriges Kvinnliga Fredsförening organized by Fanny Petterson, was recruited among educated women. In addition, Petterson organized a society for peaceful education and an independent group, the Conféderation pacifique de la Suède, which operated in nine sections around the country.[132]

Growth of peace activism in Norway was retarded by the struggle for independence from Sweden, but with Nobel's will, membership grew modestly. Norway was the first nation to fund its parliamentary delegation to the Interparliamentary Conference (1890) and among the first to contribute to the central office of the conference. From the mid-1890s to 1912, the entire Storting belonged to the Interparliamentary Union. Private citizen activism gathered impetus after 1895 when the Norges Fredsforening was founded by Cornelius B. Nannsen, Didrikke Moller, and Halvdan Koht, who went on to a distinguished career in twentieth-century international organizations.

In Norway, religious influence was greater than in the other Scandinavian pacifist groups, and the peace movement campaigned successfully for relief from military service for religious conscientious objectors. In the tense political climate of the 1890s, with national passions at a near frenzy, the position taken by the Norwegian peace movement was not unanimously supported by its own members.[133]

Nonetheless, the government policy of jailing dissenters was halted by legislative action in 1902, despite objections by conservatives and military leaders—this, even amid the anti-Swedish uproar. When socialist antimilitarists demanded to be included, however, the peace movement grew cool, determined to defend conscientious objection for religious reasons only.[134]

Despite differences within the Norwegian movement over relations with Sweden during the struggle for independence, Norwegian and Swedish peace activists followed the remarkable practice of remaining in contact. One of the leading Swedes who defied public opinion was Edward Wavrinsky, who promised:

> Should our army be mobilized, we—I and my friends—intend to get up mass meetings against it and if possible, meet with our Norwegian brethern at the frontier in a great demonstration. If war breaks out, I am determined to go between the armies with a peace flag and I may fall from one of the first *Swedish* balls . . . my sacrifice for our cause.[135]

This personal commitment was unique among continental pacifists. A substantial segment of Swedish society was willing to dissolve the old union in recognition of Norwegian self-determination and Swedish peace activists confronted extremist nationalists in defense of Norwegian independence. Following the peaceful separation, the movement in Norway grew to eleven local branches and two vigorous women's societies.[136] The amazing example of the peaceful separation of Norway from Swedish control reached legendary proportions among pre-1915 Continental pacifists.

After 1907, the Danish, Swedish, and Norwegian delegations to the Interparliamentary Union formed their own, specific Scandinavian association concerned with regional issues.[137] Bajer's vision of a Scandinavian community of neutrals increasingly appealed to a broad public that feared involvement in an unwanted European war. Scandinavian peace activists, however, could not devise a method to insure that neutrality would be respected.

The constant struggle of the international movement to broaden its impact suggested that outreach to working-class organizations and socialist parties was crucial. Overtures from the pacifists, however, risked rupturing the unity of peace congresses as well as rebuff from socialists—not to speak of right-wing attacks.

During the 1890s, peace activists debated whether or not ties to socialists were worth pursuing. Moderates, such as Henri Babut, a founder of La Paix par le droit, pointed out that "we" work through education and juridical reform; "they" talk of revolution.[138] From the French economist Yves Guyot came the warning, "it would not be worth the trouble of suppressing international war if we want to replace it with social (class) war."[139] Fears that socialist organizations would take over peace congresses because of their numerical superiority were frankly expressed. No peace congress could ever meet on German soil, avowed one delegate, if socialists participated.[140] Passy continued to insist that class divisions did not exist and were irrelevant to peace activism.[141]

Nonetheless, the desire to reach a broader audience eroded the conservative and liberal concensus. By the mid-1890s, the Russian sociologist, Jacques Novicow admitted privately, "In a large number of cases, they [the socialists] are right.

I would have signed the Erfurt program with both hands."[142] A pragmatic peace activist realistically commented:

> The success of socialism in recent years has been so notable that even those who struggle against it with the greatest hostility are the first to admit it. The numbers of its supporters are counted in the hundreds of thousands in Germany where they submit to a remarkable discipline from leaders who have uncontested authority; in Belgium, they have found cooperation with an instrument of economic emancipation which makes them formidable; in France, even, although their divisions are a source of weakness for them. Socialism has entered Italy, Austria, Switzerland and if the purely corporative organizations of Trades Unions and American federations have—up to now—prevented English-speaking countries from giving themselves to it, certain indications suggest that this torpor—or wisdom—is only a passing stage. By the number of its followers, the organization of its forces, and also the impact it makes on the world, the Socialist party [offers] the Peace Party . . . a marvelous ally.[143]

Hodgson Pratt launched a campaign to attract working-class support. He repeatedly submitted memoranda to the Berne office and forced the issue onto congress agendas.[144] In 1896, the Universal Peace Congress in Budapest settled on a formula for representation of working-class and socialist organizational delegates that would permit a voice vote, but not a majority, vote.[145] Thereafter, the subject of working-class involvement became a regular feature of congresses.[146] In line with the shifting attitude of peace activists, Ducommun reached out to socialists through their own publications, sending news of the programs and platforms of the peace movement.[147]

Socialists were not necessarily responsive. In 1889 when the First Universal Peace Congress met in Paris, the German socialist leader Wilhelm Liebknecht sent restrained congratulations. A Belgian socialist federation sent a letter of congratulations to the 1892 Berne Universal peace Congress that was prefaced by a careful note that maintained the separate identity of the two groups.[148] The leading pacifist in Belgium, Henri La Fontaine, was a socialist who served in the Belgian senate for most years from 1895 to 1932. However, Filippo Turati, founder of the Italian Socialist party was furious that Moneta's group called *themselves* a "party." "They are not a party," Turati expostulated, "merely a handful of apostles. Everyone senses the insignificance of their doctrine."[149] Turati called them silly utopians; if militarism did not exist, it would have been invented by the middle class. Yet this ideological purism, which had appeared in the First International during the late 1860s, gave way to pragmatic agreements. In Italy, Claudio Treves recommended that socialists work with left liberals and republicans to reduce armaments, counter militarism, and oppose expansionist foreign policies.[150] In France, similar attitudes emerged from groups, such as the *bourses de travail,* that emphasized common ground shared with the peace movement—especially reductions of arms expenditures through creation of a defensive militia and, eventually, arbitration.[151] In 1900, the Universal Peace Congress met in Paris, where Alexandre Millerand, the first socialist to sit in a European cabinet, delivered the welcoming address. The audience included Enrico Ferri, a leading name in the Italian movement. It was a turning point.

Pratt continued to press the issue, incredibly disappointed at working-class participation in the international meetings as well as the workers' chauvinistic backing of the Boer War in 1900.[152] Ducommun managed to obtain endorsement from a growing list of workers' groups—or at least from their leaders, most of whom could not afford to attend the peace congresses.[153] National peace congresses in France and Italy in 1904 were relatively well attended by workers. In 1904 at Turin, Edoardo Giretti called for a collaborative alliance of workers and middle-class activists in favor of parliamentary control of foreign policy.[154] In France, as the new century progressed, a de facto collaboration between Socialist deputies in the legislature—notably Jean Jaurès, Francis de Pressensé, and Henry Hubbard—with centrist and Radical party deputies, including d'Estournelles de Constant, Ferdinand Buisson, and Ludovic Trarieux, made for a pragmatic collaboration that avoided issues of the social ownership of property. In 1907, Henri La Fontaine became president of the International Peace Bureau, a post he retained until his death in 1943.

Moderate socialist and centrist deputies also rejected the antipatriotic spirit of Gustave Hervé's antimilitarism. The socialist argument that workers would join a general strike in the event of a major war, carrying out military sabotage, strikes, and rank-and-file defection did not persuade middle-class peace activists. They did not believe that "workers . . . would [gain] more than the support of one-third of enlisted men" for such tactics.[155] Middle-class peace activists pleaded with socialists to recognize realistic arenas of potential cooperation—denunciation of the exploitation of women and children in the labor force and of native peoples in the Congo; an end to the use of armies to break strikes; appeals for Jews and Armenians; attacks on bank loans to belligerents; reduction in military service; reduction in arms expenses. Socialists, who repeatedly insisted that the abolition of class and private property had to precede all other questions, observed Jules Prudhommeaux, clouded the issue. Such an argument would not prevent Japanese forces from invading other nations to increase their territory.[156]

Pacifists remained disappointed at the level of working-class support.[157] But in 1908 at the London Universal Peace Congress, the movement was cheered by a jump in worker participation. Part of the reason for this was the involvement of the British socialist, G. H. Perris. Before the congress opened, two thousand participants including twenty-one labor organizations rallied in Trafalgar Square. During the meeting, workers took the rostrum to promise amazing antiwar measures: a French miners' representative reported that his group voted to cut off the coal supply in the event of war; an Italian pacifist surveyed workers in the Naples Armstrong armaments plant who maintained that they would rather be making some other product; worker delegates railed against military budgets and demanded that national spending be redirected toward education and public works projects.[158] For the first time, worker delegates to the meeting had been paid for by special subscriptions to enable them to attend a peace congress. Similarly, at the Stockholm meeting in 1910, the leading Swedish socialist, Karl Hjalmar Branting,[159] delivered an address on "the working class and peace" that offered a historic perspective (beginning with Marx) and concluded with the assertion that workers would never oppose *legitimate* patriotism.[160]

In 1907 at Stuttgart, the Second (Socialist) International debated and passed its famous resolution on the subject of war and workers. Its language, a compromise among contending visions, included an observation that ought to have made pacifists very happy:

> The Congress is convinced that pressure by the proletariat could achieve the blessings of international disarmament through serious use of courts of arbitration instead of the pitiful machinations of governments. This would make it possible to use the enormous expenditure of money and strength which is swallowed by military armaments and war, for cultural purposes.[161]

Peace activists seemed unaware that one of their most central arguments was adopted by the international socialist movement.[162]

Pacifists, great believers in the power of the idea, were prolific authors, journalists, editors, and sponsors of journals.[163] Some journals were simple propaganda tracts, especially the annual almanacs published in France and Italy each year; others, such as *Die Waffen nieder, Der Friedens-Warte, La Vita internazionale, Concord,* or *La Paix par le droit,* were serious journals of opinion, news, and criticism. In 1896, Émile Arnaud, Gaston Moch, and Charles Richet obtained controlling interest in a daily newspaper, *L'Indépendance belge,* in an effort to break the dreary antipacifist tone of most of the European press. In 1905–1906, when G. H. Perris became editor of the *Tribune* (London), the movement received reasonable coverage in a daily paper.[164] The pacifist press never broke the wall of unremitting hostility to the peace movement.

Media misrepresentation and trivialization remained an infuriating problem. The peace activists who joined together in 1897 to create the Association des journalistes amis de la paix were mainly journalists with commitments to the movement: Alfred Fried; Mihaelaes Lima (Lisbon); the English crusaders, William T. Stead and G. H. Perris; Séverine (Carolyn Rémy) and Angelo Crespi (Rome). Twelve years later, Fried proposed the creation of yet another such group, with no particular success.[165] Pratt, Fried, and Apponyi tried to establish societies of journalists who might report the realities of peace congresses, but they also failed.[166] Pacifists feared publicizing the reality that much of the press was "bought."[167] From an appeal launched by Franz Wirth in 1894 to a series of resolutions that occupied a 1913 Universal Peace Congress, the international movement could do little but plead with journalists for fair treatment.[168]

The 1892 congress at Berne, for instance, was described in a Berlin *Tageblatt* story as rowdy and uncontrollable, whereas the *Neue Freie Presse* stated that it had very poor attendance, barely fifty bored people in the audience (there were over three hundred), who yawned throughout the dull proceedings.[169] Von Suttner was unable to get either paper to publish a letter of correction. More serious was a full-scale attack on the peace movement and The Hague congress by the German military historian, Hans Delbrück[170] and the offhand remark of the famous historian Theodor Mommsen that the conference was a "misprint of History."[171] Similar denunciations became commonplace in Italy from the growing rightist nationalist movement led by Enrico Corradini, who denounced "pious bourgeois platitudes about universal peace and brotherhood" as dangerous invitations that would transform Italy into the "China of Europe."[172] The blatant lies of the London yellow press in September 1899—asserting that the British pacifists Pratt, Moscheles, Darby, and Robinson were on the Boer payroll—led to a riot in Trafalgar Square.[173] No major paper bothered to describe the chaos.

In 1913, the tense last year of peace, the Interparliamentary Union debated and passed a very serious resolution that criticized both German and British leadership as risking war (both Winston Churchill and Admiral Alfred von Tirpitz were named, a rare event in the history of that organization). Not one paper described it, to the utter amazement of Lord Weardale, president of the union.[174] That same year, Le Foyer argued that the vicious Balkan Wars might have been prevented had "we, pacifists from England, France, Germany sent authenticated information, news, documents to the newspapers . . . which the organizers of war were interested in concealing."[175] In May 1913, a conference of parliamentarians from France and Germany met in Basel to discuss ways to reduce tensions. The trivialization by leading journalists in their accounts was infuriating.[176]

Le Foyer's faith that the international movement would serve to correct chauvinist distortions, an old dream of Pratt's, seemed tired and pointless to Fried by 1913. After a quarter-century of disappointments, Fried wanted aggressive action: to publish a list of newspapers that invariably lied about the peace movement—a proposal that frightened British and French pacifists, who feared that the movement would be charged with attacking free speech. Instead, the Universal Peace Congress of 1913 accepted a compromise proposal by Jeanne Mélin to create a system for pacifists to monitor their national presses.[177] An international network of journalists would provide the Berne *bureau* with facts, and Berne would send out press releases.[178]

By the time the war broke out, La Fontaine observed that "the press in the hands of certain capitalists is a terrible force and there is little of consequence that can be done about it."[179] In twenty-five years, the movement made no major inroads on established national media.

Equally infuriating was the way that history was taught. Bertha von Suttner typified pacifist enthusiasm for the "new history" that emphasized cultural achievement over military domination. Her main character in *Die Waffen nieder,* the fictional Martha von Trilling, delivered an encomium to William Buckle's *History of Civilization* that clearly reflected the author's own awakening. Here was the first work of history that revealed:

> The history of mankind was not decided by, as the old theory taught, kings and statesmen, nor by the wars and treaties that were created by the greed of the former or the cunning of the latter, but by the gradual development of the intellect. . . . Buckle brings proof that the estimation in which the warrior class is held is in inverse ratio to the height of the culture which the nation has reached. . . . as society progresses . . . not only war itself, but the love of war will . . . diminish.[180]

The question became how to infuse this vision into school texts and how to encourage teachers, parents, and public authorities to bring this history to children. The movement wanted to reproduce Martha von Trilling's enlightenment, but not eliminate positive patriotic feelings.

During the 1890s, the teaching of history appeared repeatedly on agendas at international congresses.[181] Henri La Fontaine urged activists in 1894 to read *Histoire du peuple belqe et de sa civilisation* as a model of historical writing that emphasized cultural and democratic evolution.[182] The Peace and Arbitration Committee of the International Council of Women committed itself to "use its influence to modify the curriculum of the public schools to include training in citizenship and encouragement to a life of peace."[183] National committees studied fairy tales and children's literature, recommending against deleterious material and violent games. Their 1913 report argued in favor of history that described industry, labor and inventions, progress in commerce and the arts and that showed students where "existing social wrongs and miseries" prevailed. The council rejected "school history [that]eulogizes vanity and arrogance in the name of patriotism."[184] Their members ran for local school boards in countries where such was possible.[185] A frequent method used in the English-speaking world was the prize essay that the council sponsored.

French pacifists first turned toward the education of university students, who, in Jacques Dumas's view "were destined to carry the weight of public responsibility."[186] However, Passy wanted to encourage a textbook for nine-to-twelve-year-olds, so his group sponsored a prize essay in 1896. The issue of transforming the teaching of history in France became immeasurably more complicated for pacifists by the appearance of Gustave Hervé, a radical socialist prosecuted for his antipatriotism. Hervé's attack on the flag, the army, patriotism, and the entire mythology of national culture provided right-wingers with a convenient whipping post to denounce and confuse pacifism and socialism. A bitter split chararacterized a conference of teachers in 1905 at Lille. There, extreme right-wingers were hooted off the stage, but the audience divided bitterly between advocates of "scientific" history and those who believed that France—the most important Continental democracy—had a mission to fulfil. For Buisson, former director of elementary education, teaching youth meant instruction in

> the mutual interdependency of all human interests; to demonstrate the aim toward which civilization is developing . . . the establishment of international institutions destined to regulate by arbitration and not by war, the conflicts among nations.[187]

This did not mean, however, that students ought not be taught the importance of defending their nation against invasion.

With very limited resources, French pacifists struggled to reach out to the public at large, to in-service teachers, and to university students by public lectures, slide shows, and the creation of curricula materials. L'École de la paix ran a series of public lectures by eminent professors and peace activists at the Sorbonne or the Grands écoles.[188] Passy and d'Estournelles de Constant managed to publish a modestly successful work, *La Paix et l'enseignement pacifiste* in 1906, and in 1909, a total curriculum, *Cours d'enseignement pacifiste,* provided interested teachers with a structured approach.[189]

There is little evidence that peace activists worked for a revision of historical thinking and teaching in Germany, though Ludwig Quidde noted that the Baden authorities were willing to remove extreme jingoism from texts.[190] Italian pacifists wanted teachers of the classics to encompass the entire history of antiquity, not merely the triumphs of the Roman legions.[191]

Across Europe, the peace movement urged teachers to celebrate peace day— initially on 22 February (George Washington's birthday) and then (after 1901) on 18 May, to commemorate the opening of the First Hague Conference in 1899. By 1907, the Italian government agreed to a school day devoted to peace issues and pacifists from Palermo to Milan delivered lectures and met schoolchildren.[192] The Milanese peace activist Rosalia Gwis-Adami and a high school teacher at a prominent girls' school, Adèl Alziator, created in 1909 the Società delle giovenette italiane per la pace, which brought students and teachers together in after-school meetings. Discussion of the "new history" and different ways of organizing international relations provided the mainstay of these programs as well as celebrations of peace day. Gwis-Adami and Moneta also had plans to organize an international student exchange program that would ease the bureaucratic difficulties of obtaining credit for students who studied abroad and reduce restrictions on faculty exchanges.[193] Similar success occurred in Belgium regarding peace day celebrations, mainly because of the work of the women's peace group led by Bauer and Rosseels. By and large, peace activists had better luck with school curricula than with journalism.

The steady growth of national peace societies in central and western Europe, the creation of national peace councils that convened annual congresses, the near-annual convocation of international meetings of citizen and parliamentary peace groups, the establishment of modest lobbies to effect national policies, the struggle to transform school curricula—all testified to the health of the movement. As Passy noted in 1896, our beginnings "in modest halls where we were quite alone" stood in stark contrast to "how we are received in official palaces in capitals where governments . . . encourage our efforts."[194] That debut, in 1889, reinforced by the creation of the Bureau international de la paix changed Continental peace activism into a new phenomenon.

Chosen in 1891 as executive secretary, Élie Ducommun confided to Théodore Ruyssen that he wanted only to be an "honorary secretary," because he was concerned that the management of the Jura-Simplon Railway, his employer, might disapprove. Ruyssen, Pratt, and most of the Italian and Scandinavian leaders had wanted a paid central office staff and an activist leader in the *bureau*.[195] Ducommun's personal circumstances required that he follow the advice of von Suttner, Passy, Cremer, and moderates in launching the movement with a low profile.[196] So modest was this initial operation that it relied on Ducommun's family, pocketbook, and home. The Swiss pacifist hoped to be able to raise about 30,000 francs from peace societies by 1893–1894, but only 13,000 francs came in by 1892–1893.[197] Nonetheless, he sent out a handwritten newsletter cum newspaper, *La Correspondance autographiée,* twice a month.[198] The annual congress was organized on a 5000-franc budget. Ducommun managed to obtain a 1000-franc contribution from the Swiss National Council (Nationalrat) after organizing a petition campaign.[199] He hoped other small nations would contribute funds, but he was nervous about soliciting funds from France and Germany.[200] In the next decade monies did come from Scandinavian nations, with annual gifts ranging from 700 to 1000 francs. In 1912, the Danish government increased its sum to 3000 francs.[201] Government contributions remained small.

Larger financial contributions to the international headquarters as well as to national groups were raised from private individuals. Social reformer and peace activist Virginie Griess-Traut left a legacy to the *bureau* in the form of French bonds.[202] In France, legacies to the national movement came from Narcisse Thibault and Charles Brunet). But the most famous (albeit indirect) contribution came from Alfred Nobel, whose will in 1896 promised a sum of money to

> the person who shall have done the most or best work for fraternity among nations, for the abolition or reduction of standing armies and for the holding and promotion of peace congresses.[203]

To the leadership of the movement, there was no question that Nobel intended the money to be used by its activists.[204] Von Suttner's influence in interesting Nobel, briefly her employer, in the cause was well known. After four years of litigation, the first Nobel Peace Prize was awarded in 1901 to Frédéric Passy and Henri Dunant. (Dunant, the aged founder of the International Red Cross, was a problematical choice.) They were followed in 1902 by co-winners Élie Ducommun and Albert Gobat.[205] Thus, indirectly the two peace internationals were funded. For the most part, prewar winners of the Nobel Peace Prize were movement activists. Despite the fact that the award produced, in Passy's trenchant view, an "apple of discord" in the ranks of pacifists,[206] it helped the work of Passy, Ducommun, Gobat, Cremer, von Suttner, Moneta, Bajer, Arnoldson, d'Estournelles de Constant, Beernaert, the *bureau,* Fried, Asser, and La Fontaine. Until Ducommun received the prize, the average income of the *bureau* was so low— recently estimated at about twenty-five dollars per month—that the organization would not have survived without his extraordinary commitment.[207] A real boon to the *bureau* was the award of the Nobel Peace Prize in 1910 directly to the central headquarters of the organization. (In 1911 the co-winners of the Nobel Peace Prize were Tobias M. C. Asser and Alfred H. Fried.)

At Ducommun's death in 1906, Albert Gobat, then the executive director of the Interparliamentary Union, agreed to coordinate both groups.[208] This arrangement ended in two years when leaders of the Interparliamentary Union, uncomfortable with the close arrangements, moved the headquarters to Brussels. Auguste Beernaert became the chair and the energetic Christian Lange became the new director. Gobat kept his anger private but angry he was:

> The Interparliamentary Council has been sold to an Englishman who will never forgive me for the role which I played—instead of him—at the [U.S.] White House in 1904. Thus am I used and tossed aside after 18 years of absolutely unrecompensed services, thanks to which . . . the Interparliamentary Union was preserved.[209]

From 1909 until his death in 1914, Gobat remained in charge of the Bureau international de la paix in Berne, providing the organization with a more energetic, activist leadership.[210] Unfortunately, at the moment the Great War exploded, the central office of the movement was in the hands of an inexperienced, young employee, Henri Golay, and the president, Henri La Fontaine, was a Belgian war refugee.

Somewhat less dramatic was the support—moral and financial—that Albert I, prince of Monaco, offered to the movement. In 1902, he endowed L'Institut international de la paix in the principality, with Gaston Moch as president. The main purpose of this *institut* was educational, charged with preserving and publishing materials on law, peaceful solutions to international conflicts, the statistics of wars and arms rivalries, pacifist propaganda in general, and methods of encouraging international institutions.[211] It offered bibliographic services to the movement that the strained Berne office could not often provide. In Monaco, a museum and library were planned, but Moch moved its headquarters to Paris when he became chair of the National Council of French Peace Societies in 1904.

The well-to-do Polish railway magnate Jean de Bloch[212] contributed both wealth and analysis to the movement. His multivolume study of war and its probable impact,[213] brought instant celebrity to this self-made millionaire. Born in poverty, Bloch rose to great wealth and prominence. The tsar invited him to a private audience to discuss his ideas. Bloch used part of his fortune to endow a Museum of War and Peace at Lucerne, which opened before his death in June 1902, a venture he hoped would inspire others.[214] A legacy directly to the Berne *bureau* in the amount of fifty thousand rubles for a twelve-year period was administered by Swiss pacifists (Dr. Ludwig Stein, Henri Morel, and Élie Ducommun) so that funds went to peace societies, to the improvement of propaganda techniques (i.e., use of lantern slide lectures), to the support of publications and university competitions.[215]

Across the Atlantic, another self-made millionaire—also born in relative penury—endowed the European peace movement with his largesse. This was Andrew Carnegie[216] who gave millions of dollars to the cause by the construction of "temples of peace" (the Pan-American Union Building in Washington, D.C., the Peace Palace in The Hague, and the Central American Court of Justice in Costa Rica); by the establishment of trusts, especially the Carnegie Endowment for International Peace; and by a vast personal campaign against imperialism and for legal internationalism he waged among politicians. Carnegie, like Bloch, viewed war as "impossible," at least among civilized states.

In Europe, Carnegie's funding generated an even larger apple of discord than that of Nobel. Nicholas Murray Butler, head of the Carnegie Foundation, liaison to European peace movements, and future co-winner with Jane Addams of the Nobel Peace Prize (1931), decided to give d'Estournelles de Constant a large donation for Conciliation internationale, a group that met with his approval.[217] A $20,000 award to the Bureau international de la paix increased the budget to 98,000 francs per year. (It was 3000 francs when Ducommun began.) But the award in 1911 stirred trouble.

Initially, Butler hinted that the Carnegie Endowment wanted the Berne office moved to Brussels, for purposes of efficiency.[218] Gobat, already hurt from the move in 1909 of the Interparliamentary Union, reacted angrily and the request was rejected by Henri La Fontaine.[219] Delicate communications continued until finally, in the fall of 1911—amid the crisis in the peace movement engendered by the Libyan War—La Fontaine obtained the Carnegie contribution on his own terms.[220] The office stayed with Gobat. Gobat decided to replace the *bureau's* publication, *Correspondance bi-mensuelle,* with a new multilingual journal.[221] He projected an initial run of twenty thousand copies. French peace activists were furious, protesting both the decision and the way it was reached. Why launch yet another journal?[222] An angry Jules Prudhommeaux, new head of the European branch of the Carnegie Endowment (Dotation Carnegie) insisted "that in the future, peace societies all have the opportunity to influence the allocation of funds and the reasons for decisions."[223] Adding insult to injury, Gobat wanted the French National Peace Council to distribute six thousand copies—for which, Prudhommeaux noted bitterly, "we will get only 3600 francs."[224]

For his part, Gobat feared that Carnegie money would dictate the direction of the movement. The Carnegie Endowment wanted the *bureau* to "consolidate" the European peace societies, an injunction that hardly sat well with the proudly independent national groups. Butler had a low opinion of European peace organizations, apart from those directly managed by the Carnegie Endowment, that is, Conciliation internationale run by d'Estournelles de Constant and the Dotation, the Paris office of the Carnegie Endowment under Prudhommeaux.[225] The French movement coordinated by Gaston Moch found that the Carnegie Endowment leaders in Paris, many from La Paix par le droit, developed arrogant attitudes to their former confreres.[226]

Gobat's vigorous leadership distressed the devoted Mlle. F. Montaudon, secretary in the *bureau.* An individual accustomed to decision making, his method of shortcutting consultations made the devoted office secretary, hired by Ducommun, very nervous.[227] With no patience for hypocrisy and inconsistency, Gobat supported anti-Moneta factions in the Italian peace movement,[228] attacked Moneta and de Gubernatis for their support of the Libyan War; in turn, conservative activists criticized him.[229] Gobat also ridiculed the pretensions of German pacifists under Nippold who wanted to create a "respectable" peace movement and called French and German parliamentarians together in May 1913 to confront the probable outcome of their nations' continuous hostility. This vigorous leadership contrasted with Ducommun's lower-keyed style.

In March 1914, amid a meeting of the executive committee of the Berne *bureau,* Gobat collapsed and died, a disastrous loss. A young executive assistant, Henri Golay—recently hired in Berne—was left in charge. As La Fontaine observed, Gobat had "generously devoted about twenty years of his life to the peace movement before any adequate salary could be offered to him." However, now "no serious candidate consents to give up his actual profession in order to become the director of an institution whose future existence depends on an annual and changing subsidy."[230] La Fontaine pleaded with Carnegie Endowment officials to promise a three-year commitment, but they would not do more than offer an increase contingent on the ability of the movement to raise its income about seven thousand francs more per annum.[231] With the oubreak of the war, the subject became moot. The Carnegie Endowment cut all funding to Berne. The central office barely survived World War I and never was able to coordinate the new kind of peace societies formed during and after that war. In 1939, its papers were given to the Library of the League of Nations and the *bureau* closed its doors.[232]

In 1891, some of the founding members of the Bureau international de la paix had envisioned close ties with the Interparliamentary Conference. Angelo Mazzoleni[233] insisted:

> Members of parliaments would lose nothing of their authority by mingling with popular societies [and] governments . . . would be more readily obliged to alter . . . their international policies which actually [are] generalized anarchy.[234]

Mazzoleni, a founder of the Unione lombarda per le pace and a member of the Italian Camera dei deputati, believed that close ties would benefit delegates; a good deal of expense would be saved just in shipping and printing pamphlets, papers, and organizational materials for the meetings.[235] The collaboration of parliamentary and private activists was a sine qua non if militarism was to be confronted, argued a young German, Richard Reuter, who won a Swedish prize essay on organizing peace.[236] This collaboration, along with the idea that the peace internationals would organize vigorous citizen protests against war threats, was not to be.[237]

The relationship between the two peace internationals was checkered. From 1889 to 1892, the two groups often worked in tandem, only because of personal friendships and overlapping membership. In 1891 at Rome, the Interparliamentary Conference agreed to sit the next year in Berne. Albert Gobat, appointed to organize the sessions, worked closely with Ducommun since the Universal Peace Congress was also planned for Berne. But the English parliamentarian, W. Randal Cremer, who considered the Rome meeting of the parliamentarians a "failure" because of the time spent on the establishment of a central office, objected vociferously.[238] Though Gobat and Ducommun tried to work out a common program in 1892,[239] this arrangement could not continue. Cremer led the opposition; his secretary tartly let Gobat know:

> Mr. Cremer . . . thinks it right to inform you that the British Members take less interest in the proceedings of the Inter-Parliamentary Conference than they otherwise would because the promoters of the Peace Congress persist year after year in waiting until the date of the . . . Conference is fixed, and then placing their Congress immediately in front of what the Members of the Inter-Parliamentary Conference considers the most important because it is the most representative gathering. In this country, we have experienced a great deal of difficulty and confusion from the holding of these two gatherings so close together, and if it is continued, so far as the British Member's are concerned, it will—we fear—lead to the abandonment of the Inter-Parliamentary Conference.[240]

Precisely how widespread this attitude was among British parliamentarians, is not possible to know. It was not shared by such activists as Ellen Robinson, who struggled against British provincialism in support of international cooperation.[241] Cremer, thoroughly suspicious of non-English-speaking people, had become an irascible individual whom people began to fear and avoid.[242] (He seems to have been upset that many of the delegates to the Rome meetings in 1891 were "foreigners.")[243] German and English delegates complained about the expenses. Gob-

at's attempt to coordinate both groups was also opposed by Italian Senator Beniamino Pandolfi, who had sustained the Interparliamentary Conference from
1891–1892.[244] Pandolfi told Bertha von Suttner, Felix Moscheles, and others that
such an arrangement invited disaster. To Gobat he wrote:

> Co-existence is not discussable. Such a coincidence which no deputy would accept
> will only result in a permanent and disastrous conflict between the Conference and
> the Congress.
>
> You want peace and you are starting off by inviting war between the two orga-
> nizations whose objective is Peace. It would be more logical to suggest that the Con-
> ference would have no *raison d'être* and there only ought to be one Congress for
> all.
>
> If you want the Conference to occur, schedule it after the Congress.[245]

In 1892, Gobat was named secretary of the Interparliamentary Conference.
Two years later, a formal constitution was adopted and in 1899, the name was
changed to Interparliamentary Union. Auguste Beernaert was named president of
the new Interparliamentary Council in a revision of the governance structure.

Fredrik Bajer, active in both groups, was saddened but philosophical. In 1891,
he had hoped for close collaboration.[246] By the end of the decade, he observed:

> Diplomats look down upon interparliamentarians from high to low, just as the lat-
> ter have disdained congress participants. This pride of place is understandable.
> Nonetheless, the three movements are like converging lines; a day will come when
> they will meet at the same point.[247]

Bajer's comment came on the heels of Gobat's forced resignation from the executive committee of the Bureau international de la paix because the British parliamentarians, again led by Cremer, distrusted his dual roles.[248]

Despite these unpromising disputes, the Interparliamentary Conference made
more than modest strides in its first decade. The handful of delegates who assembled in 1889 had been politely received by the French government at a reception
but not taken seriously. At the end of the 1890s, a new reality existed. The Interparliamentary Union grew in self-confidence and public stature. Its members
included ministers, diplomats, professors of international law, and delegates to
The Hague Peace Conference of 1899.[249]

During the 1890s, the annual meetings of the Interparliamentary Conference
attracted between 200 and 250 members. Funding was erratic, and Gobat's free
services were crucial. Reliable income began when the Norwegian Storting voted
over twenty-eight hundred francs in 1895 and covered the costs of its delegation.[250]
Governments began to contribute thereafter but not sufficiently to save the publication that Gobat edited—*La Conférence interparlementaire,* suspended in 1897
because of financial shortfall, despite a membership of about eighteen hundred
current and former parliamentarians. Gobat laid most blame on the French "who
have deserted our enterprise."[251]

By 1903, when the union met in Vienna, about 300 delegates came. But in the
next year, when the Americans hosted the conference in St. Louis, a memorable
meeting topped by a White House session with Theodore Roosevelt, European

attendance fell—only 136 delegates traveled to the conference. This was followed by a drop in attendance again in 1905 at Brussels. A dramatic change occurred in 1906 when the meeting sat in the House of Lords in London. The first Russian delegation, a group from the newly formed Duma, was present. The excitement of their presence generated real coverage and publicity. Over six hundred parliamentarians attended, at least half from abroad, and the meeting was a great success. Sir Henry Campbell-Bannerman delivered a welcoming speech that assured wide coverage.[252] In 1908, the first meeting ever held in Germany occurred after Chancellor Bernhard von Bülow persuaded the kaiser that attempts to prevent a meeting would redound badly on his reputation.

In 1909, when the Interparliamentary Union hired Christian Lange, a salaried secretary, it also altered its constitution to create a tripartite governance: an executive committee, an enlarged council, and the annual (or almost-annual) conferences.[253] Lange worked to increase funding, essentially from government contributions. Lange managed to raise over 21,000 francs from nine nations, with the United States sending the largest contribution: $2500 (about 13,000 francs in 1910–1911).[254] Twenty parliamentary groups, with nearly twenty-nine hundred members, supported the union. Lange estimated that, on the *average,* about one-fourth of each parliament belonged to the organization. The biggest disappointment to the European organizers of the union was the disinterest of Latin Americans in the organization and the very low level of Iberian participation.[255] From Belgium, Denmark, France, the Netherlands, Norway, and Sweden, over 50 percent of the parliaments was inscribed. Lange's continued fund raising increased the income to over 60,000 francs from governments (including the Japanese and Russians) and in 1911–1912, the union raised a total of over 83,000 francs from all sources. His careful management produced a cash reserve of 78,000 francs, a tidy sum for an organization composed of parliamentarians from technically hostile states.[256] (Income declined slightly after 1911 with the resignation of the Italian delegation.)

Following Auguste Beernaert's death in 1912, Phillip Stanhope, Lord Weardale, became the president.[257] Lange remained in Brussels until 5–6 August 1914 when he had to flee the approaching German army. In the summer of 1914, as peace broke down, the distance between Lange and Weardale hampered communication.

Between 1891 and 1914, both peace internationals became firmly established with well-run central headquarters. Eminent political leaders endorsed the movement. In 1894, Leopold II, the Belgian king, gave the Universal Peace Congress in Antwerp a stunning reception; in 1900, at Paris, Alexandre Millerand, the first socialist ever to sit in a European cabinet, opened the congress. At The Hague Conference in 1899, diplomats mingled with peace activists who came to lobby the congress. Four years later in 1904, Theodore Roosevelt (who was to be awarded the Nobel Peace Prize in 1906) invited a delegation of parliamentarians to the White House at the conclusion of their meeting in Saint Louis. In 1906 in London, the Interparliamentary Union was addressed by Sir Henry Campbell-Bannerman. Two years later, the German chancellor, von Bülow greeted the parliamentarians in Berlin and Lloyd George delivered the opening address to the Universal Peace Congress in London, where suffragettes interrupted the proceedings repeatedly. By 1909, the political representation to the French National Congress meeting in Reims began with greetings from a former president of the republic; as well as Stéphen Pichon, the foreign minister; Aristide Briand, minister of justice; Léon Bourgeois, diplomat; and dozens of deputies and senators. In 1910, at Stockholm,the government provided funding, greetings, and hospitality to the private pacifist delegates at the Universal Peace Congress. Thus, Frédéric Passy, at the age of eighty-seven, completing his fifth decade of peace activism in 1909, could honestly comment, "The influence of these international [peace congresses] increases . . . from year to year; it becomes more and more evident that they are taken seriously in the highest quarters."[258] Even pacifists with far less experience than Passy's saw real change. The American Edwin D. Mead, a delegate in 1908 to the London pacifist congress, commented:

> If you had been told, ten years ago, that we should have an international tribunal, an international Parliament assured, sixty treaties of arbitration, and an international prize court, I say that the boldest of dreamers would not have believed it.[259]

Léon Bourgeois maintained that "a common conscience was forming among civilized nations," despite the continued litany of crises and wars that broke out—mainly on the peripheries of Europe.[260] The editors of the 1911 *Encyclopaedia Britannica* did not think it at all tendentious to invite a peace activist to write the entry "Peace."[261]

On the eve of the Great War, a survey of the movement counted 190 active peace societies, some with several thousand members, that published twenty-three journals or reviews in ten languages.[262] Some of these groups existed over twenty-five years. According to a claim voiced by Henri La Fontaine, the International Peace Bureau was supported by over six hundred groups who represented approximately one million members.[263] The Universal Peace Congress planned to hold its annual congress in Vienna in September 1914 to honor Bertha von Suttner (awarded the Nobel Peace Prize in 1905), where a film version of her novel was to be previewed.

Few pacifists held any illusions that their struggle would be over quickly. Most shared Bertha von Suttner's assessment (1905) when she accepted her Nobel Peace Prize:

> We must understand that two philosophies, two eras of civilization are wrestling with one another, and that a vigorous new spirit is supplanting . . . and threatening the old. . . . Quite apart from the peace movement, which is a symptom rather than a cause of actual change, there is taking place in the world a process of internationalization and unification. . . . The instinct of self-preservation in human society . . . is rebelling against the constantly refined methods of annihilation against the destruction of humanity.
>
> Complementing this subconscious striving toward an era free of war are people who are working deliberately toward this goal, . . . seeking methods which will accomplish our aim as soon as possible.[264]

II

THE APOGEE
OF EUROPEAN PEACE
MOVEMENTS
1889–1914

4

Arbitration: The Search
for Persuasive Propaganda

On the centennial of the French Revolution, the founding congresses of the Inter-parliamentary Conference and the Universal Peace Congress in Paris celebrated the promise of international arbitration. Frédéric Passy articulated the sentiment:

> Arbitration is on its way to becoming the custom of the world, either in the form of permanent and general treaties as we urge . . . or as limited specific treaties for particular cases.
>
> We say that it is the true sign of the superior civilization which has developed toward the end of the nineteenth century. . . . Civilization is peace; barbarism is war.[1]

His peroration derived from real experience mixed with a dash of hope. By 1889, peace activists and legal scholars counted ninety successful cases of arbitration during the century. From 1871 to 1890, despite rising tensions—the creation of the Triple Alliance, the intractable hostility between France and the German Empire, conflicts over imperial acquisitions—arbitration was used three times as frequently as in the preceding seven decades.[2] From 1890 to 1900, sixty-three more successful arbitration decisions were reached.[3] After two decades of meetings of the International Law Association and the Association for the Reform and Codification of International Law, more than half a dozen serious scholarly projects for systematizing international arbitration existed, all carefully couched to preserve national sovereignty. The prestigious *Revue de droit international et législation comparée* treated international law as if it were a reality in the process of becoming positive law—as medieval customary practice once became common law. Occasionally, a notable international legal specialist was named to an official position, such as Pasquale S. Mancini in Italy or Edouard Descamps in Belgium, to the complete satisfaction of peace activists.

French and British parliamentarians favoring permanent treaties of arbitration had established organized caucuses in the Houses of Parliament as well as in the Chambre des députés. To the press, Frédéric Passy was very cautious, fearing that negative coverage would frighten French support.[4] Lobbying in London, Paris, and Washington, parliamentarians sometimes went overboard, proposing that arbitration could solve every potential future dispute. W. Randal Cremer and Passy coordinated the campaign to persuade the world's three largest parliamentary states to sign a general treaty of arbitration and thus establish a model of enlightened behavior—as once Saint-Simon proposed at the end of the Napoleonic Wars. French and British parliamentarians took heart from the formation of the Pan American Union in 1889–1890. Perhaps it heralded a model for peaceful conflict resolution.

At its opening meeting, the Interparliamentary Conference resolved on a minimum program, "[to] publicize the principle that differences among states could be submitted to an arbitration tribunal to be resolved definitively."[5] This was to be the *raison d'être* of the organization. As this meeting occurred when Franco-British relations were not especially cordial, delegates were wary of grandiose claims and nervous about press treatment.

Private pacifists were also cautious at the First Universal Peace Congress. Charles Lemonnier, whose Ligue internationale de la paux et de la liberté was the more progressive and aggressive peace society since 1867, drew up a model treaty of arbitration that linked international and domestic justice. The aging Lemonnier, who died in 1891, did not press his argument in 1889. By then, most European nations had adopted some form of constitutional structure that included at least token respect for individual rights—male suffrage, freedom of expression, secular public education—thus signaling the erosion of the authoritarian state at least on paper. The central European monarchies had encased their militaristic societies in a constitutional shell. In the interests of preserving unity at the Universal Peace Congress, delegates from Lemonnier's wing of the pacifist movement avoided divisive positions, including women's rights. They agreed to emphasize arbitration—the highest common denominator among pacifists.

To Passy, arbitration, mediation, and good offices by neutral powers provided the international peace congresses with a sufficient agenda. There was no point in discussing human rights or the social question at peace congresses. Passy really did not believe that the state could solve the social question. Beyond providing public education, which he wholeheartedly embraced, state efforts to eliminate class differences, Passy feared, would ultimately prove self-defeating. What government could do was reduce its military spending, a change that would flow naturally from an international environment where security was ensured through legal arrangements—thus, his hope and faith in arbitration. Once a dependable international system would be established, nation-states would reduce military spending and, Passy insisted, capital would flow into productive investment, create jobs, and reduce the profound divide between haves and have nots.[6] His economic analysis, faithful to nineteenth-century liberal premises, anticipated the late twentieth-century trickle-down theory and strict separation of state power from economic life.

From 1889 to 1894, the international peace movement debated generic resolutions favoring the use of arbitration. What delegates actually meant by "arbitration" remained ill-defined until 1894. Initially, the congresses served as an educational forum.[7] Even when the American jurist David Dudley Field, an arbitration expert, presided over the London Universal Peace Congress in 1890, he offered no specific proposal.[8] But in Berne (1892) and Chicago (1893), when the first substantive discussions occurred, the differences among pacifists revealed problems that generic philosophic statements could not mask.

American and some British delegates endorsed the creation of a permanent international court of arbitration to be set up by a diplomatic congress. Continental delegates argued that this approach was unrealistic.[9] Some worried that a general agreement might require sanctions to enforce decisions against a recalcitrant state. If so, what sort of sanctions? Would pacifists find themselves in the position of defending military forms of enforcement? How would the costs of a court be apportioned? Would the tribunal be allowed to challenge national sovereignty in its deliberations? The German delegate, Max Kolben, flatly asserted that the American proposal—if advanced in his nation—would set the peace movement back twenty years.[10] The mention of a permanent court threatened sovereignty.

The discussion dramatized the levels of national and political differences separating peace activists. Hodgson Pratt was furious that pacifists, including his own compatriots, shied from a vision of European organization, and he attacked them as blinded by national demands for unbridled sovereignty. Nations should be led to understand that they must live within a code of law, Pratt asserted, "No man and no nation can judge its own cause. . . . an individual lives in a community, he is subject to its laws and his rights . . . can only be established in relationship to the rights of others."[11] The peace movement should not be content with reiterating the arguments of government ministers and backward-looking politicians; it must be the cutting edge of a new vision of international organization. Pratt wanted the movement to campaign for an international panel of judges and a diplomatic congress for a general treaty as a first step. Pacifists would establish their credentials as forward-looking actors rather than reactive, timid reformers of the status quo.[12]

At the Chicago congress in 1893, the domination by American delegates made the deliberations irrelevant to the Continental movement. As in the midcentury congresses, American enthusiasts insisted on the exportability of their federal constitution as the model for a European peace organization. Not until a British delegate insisted that his government would never abide by a decision reached by a Russian judge, did U.S. pacifists begin to grasp the irrelevance of their arguments.[13]

After the Chicago meeting, Élie Ducommun realized that the Continental movement would flounder without a common understanding on arbitration. Accordingly, he appointed a committee that included Henri La Fontaine (Belgium), Émile Arnaud (France), W. Marcusen (Switzerland) and Angelo Mazzoleni (Italy)—all specialists. (Mazzoleni, e.g., had written a comprehensive study on the subject that reviewed the history of successful arbitration.)[14] At the Sixth Universal Peace Congress of private peace activists in 1894 at Antwerp, the committee offered a model project of a general treaty. Its seventy-one articles incorporated parts of earlier projects, recommendations from legal experts and scholars,[15] and the spirit of Lemonnier's earlier project in which civil rights preceded states' rights in the international order. The Code of International Arbitration preserved the rights of independence, self-determination, and self-defense, and its framers designed it for bi- or multilateral adaptation. It passed after La Fontaine argued down objections from religious pacifists against the inclusion of sanctions.[16] In 1894, the international peace movement adapted a vision of arbitration that Continental progressives shaped.

Of course, adopting the code did not lead to any visible change in the European status quo. By the mid-1890s, peace activists became discouraged about the negotiations between Great Britain and the United States. The much-desired permanent treaty stalled, to the profound disappointment of its backers. Émile Arnaud urged pacifists to redirect their propaganda toward bilateral treaties. In their own nations, he asked that each peace society work for the conclusion of a treaty of arbitration with another state as well as for the inclusion of arbitration codicils in every treaty signed by their governments. Thus a network of agreements would be created crisscrossing the Continent and, perhaps, the globe. Pacifists, warned Arnaud, must be careful to exclude questions of national honor or vital interests from their advocacy of arbitration.[17] At the end of the decade, the Italian-Argentinian treaty, signed on 23 July 1898, lifted spirits. The parties agreed to adjudicate *all* differences; they did not omit matters of national honor or vital interests. Peace activists hailed the agreement as a "model for all to follow,"[18] but the disappointment about the Anglo-American failure lingered. The use of arbitration continued to be dependent on unpredicatable, capricious Foreign Office decision making on a case-by-case basis.

The slow progress of the international movement made new members impatient. Gaston Moch (1859–1935), who had left a successful military career to join the peace movement, favored arbitration clauses in all treaties, including military alliances.[19] Members of the French group, La Paix par le droit, enthusiastically embraced a proposal from Léon de Montluc (then a court official in Douai) that the movement proceed to design its own list of potential jurists for international panels of arbitrators, thereby challenging governments to act accordingly.[20] New, younger members of the French movement pressed to create a peace party.

In its first half-dozen years, the Interparliamentary Conference, too, trod very gently around the issue of arbitration. Not until its fifth meeting in 1894 at The Hague did the organization charge a committee to return with a report. Even this was not achieved easily. The British delegate Philip Stanhope originally invited all the parliamentarians present to coordinate a resolution in each of their legislatures on behalf of arbitration. His proposition encountered opposition from those who argued that the creation of a tribunal was premature in the absence of a system of international law. Stanhope argued the opposite: without a tribunal, no law would ever be codified. He convinced the group to let a subcommittee study the subject. An eminent scholar of international law from Louvain, Edouard Descamps, who was also a senator and counselor of state,[21] was appointed as chair of a truly international committee that included members from Austria, Belgium, Denmark, France, Germany, Great Britain, Hungary, Italy, Norway, the Netherlands, Romania, Sweden, and Switzerland.[22] A year later, the committee and the Interparliamentary Conference endorsed the report that Descamps prepared and later published as *Essai sur l'organisation de l'arbitrage international: Mémoire aux puissances.*[23]

Unlike the report that La Fontaine, Mazzoleni, and Arnaud delivered to the Universal Peace Congress, Descamps's *Essai* admitted the fundamental right of nations to go to war in the existing international system. For Descamps, international law differed in substance from domestic law; it accepted the use of violence in defense of its sovereign needs. There would only be an imperfect conciliation between the rights of the international community and the rights of the sovereign state. Given this tension, war was a justifiable form of "judicial procedure," but for the most part, Descamps believed that only in defense of national survival against aggression was this true.[24]

To him the right to go to war did not mean that arbitration was a chimera. To make arbitration work did not require an international government, a European federation, an articulated code of law, refined juridical procedures, or even progress toward reducing arms rivalries. Descamps's restricted vision of the value of arbitration placated conservatives. It would never solve challenges to sovereignty.

His positive recommendation amounted to creation of a College of Arbitrators, with members to be selected by sovereign states. These would be charged with creating a central office to preserve records, administer the work of a tribunal, and await invitations by governments for their services. No word of sanctions to enforce arbitral awards appeared in Descamps's fifteen articles—the "good faith" of governments would suffice. With the creation of such a board of arbitrators, the myth would be dispelled that

> the modern international world is somehow fatally committed to anarchy, except on the rare occasions when some form of fugitive justice appears on the earth . . . ; and that a long juridical conscience exists on the part of civilized peoples . . . [compatible] with the modern conception of the independence of states.[25]

The parliamentarians at the 1895 meeting in Brussels accepted his measured language.[26] Whereas La Fontaine's project voted by the Universal Peace Congress had called for the creation of a court, Descamps's project called for a tribunal to be available when willing parties wanted it. La Fontaine wanted a system launched that would establish international law firmly and, eventually, enmesh the big powers in its web. Descamps proposed a system that was a handmaiden to diplomacy. It would take up issues that did not challenge vital interests or national honor as a starting point for organizing international life. Both projects rested on the unstated hope that once nation-states became accustomed to arbitration, a habit would set in that would eliminate the resort to war, at least on the European continent, until one day when war became an anachronism. Descamps's proposal was the "realistic" position of moderate official voices.

Members of the Interparliamentary Conference were as disappointed as members of the citizens' peace international with the slow progress and eventual death of the Anglo-American arbitration treaty. In the Conference, speakers proposed a Belgian-British treaty or a treaty among Belgians, Dutch, and Swiss in place of the dying Anglo-American project.[27] Albert Gobat tried to revive interest in a Swiss-American treaty. The original suggestion of a Swiss-U.S. agreement had been made in 1882; when Gobat revived it, it was proposed, "with the aim of establishing for civilized states an example of a permanent international arbitration treaty ... from one republic to another."[28] Silence greeted his overtures. Swiss officials, fearing rebuff in Washington, D.C., did not pursue it. In 1897, the U.S. Senate effectively killed the Anglo-American project by insisting that in each case, a separate vote be taken to see if arbitration should be used. Gobat characterized the moment as a serious setback for arbitration. No mincer of words, he wondered how the flowery peace rhetoric of the American republic could be reconciled with actual policy.[29]

In a sense, the refusal of the U.S. Senate to ratify the treaty ended an era in the European peace movement. For several decades, particularly from the 1870s on, American institutions inspired European peace progressives. Lemonnier had urged his colleagues to study political practice and democratic rights in the United States and Marcoartu had argued that legislative control of foreign policy—not merely executive authority—functioned effectively there. The fact that peace activists in the late 1880s turned to the United States as the likely partner in a permanent bilateral arbitration treaty reflected the unexamined conviction that the Americans would lead the way into a new era of international peace.

The disappointment over the treaty in 1896–1897 was followed by a worse blow. In 1898, the United States went to war with Spain and another thread in the tapestry of the American "unicorn" unraveled. European peace activists were stunned. Francis de Pressensé—a Socialist deputy in the French *chambre* and a warm supporter of both the Interparliamentary Conference and the private peace movement—characterized Americans as intoxicated with "the new strong wine of warlike fury," on a path to

> militarism and Caesarism . . . , becoming unfaithful to the principles of its founders, to the precedents of its constitutional life, to the traditions which have made it free, glorious and prosperous. . . . The seductions of imperialism are drawing the United States toward the abyss where all the great democracies have found their end.[30]

Few delegates to peace congresses would have gone on record so baldly, but their disappointment was palpable. The enthusiasm for the movement that was so evident in 1889—and that drew in support from scholars and political analysts—diminished. The Italian writer Pasquale Fiore reminded pacifists that arbitration would never be used by governments except and only when it befit their interests. Nor would its use necessarily lead to reduction of armaments.[31] A similar argument came from Emanuel Besson, a French political analyst. Lacking a code of international law, Besson warned that arbitration would never amount to more than a rarely invoked tool, useful in cultural and commercial treaties but not as an umbrella of a general agreement.[32] Another French author warned that it would probably take centuries before arbitration would fulfil the promise it showed in 1872 with the historical *Alabama* case. The snail's pace of change in old Europe precluded a serious reorientation of the international system.[33] The position of Anatole Leroy-Beaulieu, the respected social scientist, was even less optimistic. He suspected that arbitration would never "be capable of application to all questions and particularly to the thorniest ones. It offers no recourse to oppressed peoples; . . . conquered provinces, divided and despoiled nations . . . ; it is a captive of the letter of treaties, it cannot repair the inequities of force."[34] Only the mildly optimistic English writer D. G. Ritchie reminded peace activists that the long, tedious path covered from "the first germs of representative governments" until the creation of parliamentary democracy could be measured in nearly a millennium.[35] Such assessments from intellectuals who were presumably "friends" of peace movements were not much encouragement.

Disappointed by the failure of the Anglo-American and Franco-American arbitration initiatives, committed activists nevertheless persevered. Arnaud undertook an exhausting lecture tour in the late 1890s, traveling across France, Belgium, and into Spain in an attempt to attract a broader public. Ducommun dutifully forwarded resolutions to all governments each time a peace congress so instructed him. Occasionally, the Berne office even received a perfunctory thank-you note from a government. But the main purpose of the movement, as stated in 1889, seemed far from realization. Then, in August 1898, a thunderclap revived the movement. The peace movement, profoundly discouraged by American behavior, was saved by a Russian.

Tsar Nicholas II published a Rescript that invited the nations to a conference that would discuss "the progressive development of the present armaments" and "the most effectual means of insuring to all peoples the benefits of a real and durable peace."[36] An unexpected and unwelcome missive among the diplomatic corps, the Rescript transformed the peace movement. Had all the resolutions and congresses, the journals and the lectures, the private meetings and the published books finally borne fruit?

Pacifists forgot that the tsar was not among their usual gallery of heroes. When she first read the Rescript, Bertha von Suttner thought that Frédéric Passy had written it; when she realized its provenance, she said "it was one of the loveliest hours of our lives."[37] The aging Henri Dunant wrote to her to say, "Whatever may happen, the world will not shriek 'utopia!' Disdain for our ideas is no longer possible, even if accomplishment does not immediately follow, . . . a beginning will have been made."[38] The Rescript recognized that no real security came from perpetually increased arms expenditures and that the misuse of capital and labor would eventually destroy European culture and economies. The document talked about justice and human rights, the welfare of peoples, and the security of states. It proposed the creation of a system for the peaceful resolution of conflict among the civilized nations. Von Suttner was right—it could have been written by Passy, Gaston Moch, Arnaud, or any number of peace leaders. Dunant was wrong—it did not stop the charges of utopianism. Pacifists, who would have routinely criticized the Russian state for its autocratic denial of basic human rights, sent congratulatory messages to the tsar.[39]

The peace movement mobilized to insure that governments would respond favorably. In England from January to February 1899, forty-six town meetings were held and 160,000 signatures collected on a memorial in support of the proposed agenda.[40] One Danish petition gathered almost 280,000 signatures on behalf of the agenda. Throughout the spring of 1899 the Société belge de l'arbitrage et de la paix organized petitions and sent memoranda on behalf of the coming Hague conference.

New energy poured into the movement. At the meeting of the Federation of German Women's Associations, Margarethe Leonore Selenka persuaded the group to support a worldwide women's petition campaign, adding "the propagation of peace" to the permanent agenda of the organization.[41] Selenka's initiative, along with a similar movement coordinated in Paris by the newly created Alliance des femmes pour la paix under Princess Gabrielle Wiesniewska, helped collect over one million women's signatures across the globe, ranging from a newly established school for girls in Tokyo to older Anglo-American organizations where women had several decades of experience as organizers. Women's participation brought the well-connected Dutch aristocrat Johanna Waszklewicz-van Schilfgaarde to the peace movement.[42] Her enthusiasm revived the sleepy Dutch movement, Vrede door Recht. When the actual Hague Peace Conference began in May 1899, she opened her home to pacifists from all over the world as well as to delegates attending the conference. Waszklewicz-van Schilfgaarde thus created a salon to provide space for peace lobbyists to mingle with diplomats.

For her part, Selenka engaged women from all over Germany and abroad to create a saner patriotism and inculcate "true love of country" by opposing "race hatred."[43] Most of the women activists took the same position; they backed arbitration not because it was the least common denominator possible in the world of egotistical nation-states but because it was the way to a future for their children. Even women with more radical biographies, such as Eugénie Potonié-Pierre publicly agitated for women's support based on their special role as mothers of the next generation. With Ellen Robinson, secretary of the British Peace Society, the French feminist Potonié-Pierre sponsored three public meetings in Paris designed to attract women's backing.[44] The tsar's Rescript tapped a well of sentiment among women active in general women's causes on behalf of peace. The well overflowed.

Peace societies responded everywhere in an effort to preserve the initial momentum of the call for an international conference. Léon Bourgeois, named to lead the French delegation to The Hague, received a citizen petition bearing four thousand signatures, pleading for the preservation of the original agenda proposed by the tsar;[45] a group of French scholars forwarded a memorial to all the diplomats bearing the same message—but also urging the conference to face the corrosive question of Alsace-Lorraine that threatened the peace.[46] Urging pacifists and their supporters not to lose the opportunity, the editors of La Paix par le droit noted that the Rescript "achieved what the least fantastic of us did not expect except in a distant future. A single gesture surpassed—and thus completed—the slow work developed by our congresses, lectures and daily propaganda."[47]

Among the more dramatic gestures undertaken on behalf of the tsar's call was the European trip by William T. Stead, the crusading English editor. Stead—a close friend of Cecil Rhodes, a supporter of the British Navy, a crusading journalist who had made his reputation with revelations about the demi-monde—became one of the most vigorous converts to the peace movement in 1898–1899—to the annoyance of more experienced pacifists as well as foreign office personnel. Stead launched his campaign to European capitals to insure that The Hague Conference would occur and to preserve the emphasis on arms reduction.[48] Hodgson Pratt attempted to persuade him that an arbitration agreement had a better chance of success, but the headstrong Stead refused to listen. Pratt wrote privately:

> The more I reflect on the matter, the more I feel convinced that those who have made the subject of international treaties *of arbitration* and of an international *permanent tribunal* . . . should . . . confer together previous to the Czar's Conference at The Hague; and . . . be at The Hague when that part of the Program . . . comes before the Envoys. This work seems to me of infinitely greater importance than any demonstration of "crusades" at St. Petersburgh. Several weeks ago, I wrote a letter to Mr. Stead for publication in his journal, *War Against War*, urging the pre-eminent importance of that part of the Programme which relates to mediation and arbitration, but he had previously written to me that public attention ought to be concentrated on armaments: and he did not insert the letter . . . in his Journal. I cannot but feel that while any agreement on the subject of armaments will be very difficult in view of the colonies and suspicions between the Powers—it may be possible to arrive at some agreement in reference to mediation and the judicial settlement of international disputes. And if there is any inclination . . . to accomplish something in that direction, surely jurists and other members of the "Interparliamentary Conference" may render most valuable service by private and unofficial conversations with the envoys.[49]

Pratt summarized the assessment of experienced pacifists, but Stead could not be deterred from his highly publicized voyage to European capitals. When The Hague Conference opened, however, he fully redeemed himself among pacifists. Stead along with Felix Moscheles and G. H. Perris published a daily chronicle that became indispensible to both diplomats and journalists.[50] For a brief moment, the peace movement attained its most cherished dream—a favorable press. (The official conference did not have a press office.)

Before the diplomats met at The Hague, their offices were deluged with technical papers, sent by Ducommun, that described arbitration processes and resolutions of Universal Peace Congresses.[51] Editors invited pacifist authors to discuss the implications of the tsar's Rescript. Gaston Moch, for instance, warned against expecting serious progress on arms reduction because (he predicted correctly) military experts would never agree on what constituted "equality" among disparate arms systems. What was possible, he argued, was an international treaty that bound Germany and France to observe the same rules of behavior and that would create a climate of respect based on proper juridical relationships.[52] Gaston Moch shared the commonly held assumption among pacifists that government leadership in Berlin and Paris could choose to cooperate in a legal arrangement and could choose to minimize the historic hostilities if they so wished. Peace activists all agreed that heads of state could decree a regime of organized peace if they were so inclined. Similarly, the Swiss professor of philosophy, Ludwig Stein, predicted that the very best that the meeting could produce would be an agreement to prevent peoples from capitulating

> impulsively and immediately to popular military passions [before subjecting themselves] to a juridical decision. . . . There is no better security than gaining time. If people were obliged to listen to judicial decisions before the definitive declaration of war . . . it would . . . reduce the possibilities of war.[53]

Stein expected even less than Gaston Moch did of the coming conference.

Pacifist authors tended to tread warily in public, asking for incremental changes from the diplomats. It was almost as if they did not want to taint the official proceedings with the odor of utopianism that haunted them. Established commentators writing for the mainstream press or on the side of military preparedness were constrained by no such inhibitions. The English journalist E. J. Dillon, a respected commentator on tsarist affairs, bluntly characterized the Rescript as a propaganda ploy inspired by the financial difficulties of the throne, by the struggle between westernizers and traditionalists in the Russian Empire, and by the tsar's own youthfulness, benevolence, optimism, and inexperience. Although he viewed the Rescript as a product of Russia's internal collapse, Dillon did not attack arbitration as a total fantasy.[54] On the other hand, the semiofficial spokesperson for the German Foreign Office, the journalist and historian Hans Delbrück, denounced the entire project as chimera—both the proposals for arms control and the suggestion favoring arbitration or international legal, machinery.[55] Delbrück wrote an influential article that appeared during the actual meeting in 1899. He scornfully characterized arbitration as a process that would never be applied in a serious issue. "No arbitration treaty would be of value in the Fashoda dispute between France and England," he wrote; nor, he continued, would it work on the question of Alsace-Lorraine.[56] The difference between Dillon's and Delbrück's reactions to the Rescript and conference presaged the differences that developed during the meeting between diplomats who were willing to consider some form of arbitral arrangement and the Germans, who refused.

Following the announcement of the Rescript in August, a flurry of diplomatic exchanges crisscrossed Europe. Governments wanted to know the *real* reason for the tsar's unexpected bombshell. France, a Russian ally since 1892, had not been forewarned that the Rescript was coming, an oversight that gossipy diplomats found more interesting than the content of the document.[57] The immediate skepticism that greeted the Rescript in government circles demonstrated that politicians were well aware of the issues it addressed and, perhaps, had even heard the arguments made in peace circles. Robert Cecil, Lord Salisbury, the British prime minister, quickly challenged the tsar's argument. On 30 August 1898, he asked the ambassador to St. Petersburg to determine if the Russians had actually thought through what they were proposing. Would the suggested meeting

> discuss existing causes which might lead to hostilities, e.g., Alsace-Lorraine, Constantinople, Afghanistan, Egypt? Are armaments to be fixed according to area, population, or wealth, or all three? Is the defensibility of a country or the reverse to be taken into account and if so, who is to be the judge of it? If any country refuses to disarm, are the others to go to war with her in the interests of peace?[58]

Salisbury's unconstrained sarcasm was not uniquely British. Diplomats in the French, Italian, and German service essentially considered the tsar's call to modify the international anarchy as unwise, fantastical, and an admission of Russian weakness. Nonetheless, it became clear that the conference would have to occur to avoid offense to the tsar's *amour-propre;* thus governments worked to transform the initial agenda into something acceptable. The private world of diplomatic correspondence that flew across the telegraph lines of 1898–1899 has been well plumbed.[59] Diplomats first wondered what the motivation behind the Rescript was; they then wondered how the entire project might be either dropped or carried forth innocuously. Between August 1898 and January 1899, a modified agenda was devised. Its focus was on arms reduction, on modification of codes of warfare but it retained a paragraph urging "acceptance, in principle of the use of good offices, mediation, and voluntary arbitration, in cases where they are available, with the purpose of preventing armed conflicts between nations."[60] Pratt and Gaston Moch's assessment had been largely correct. There was very little chance of any arms-reduction agreement, but there was some possibility for a limited arbitration arrangement. The Germans refused to concede even that much, insisting that no tribunal could ever be disinterested sufficiently to preserve the sovereignty of any state.[61] The German foreign policy adviser, Friedrich von Holstein, considered arbitration a "world historical mistake" and the aging ambassador, Count Georg Herbert Münster, appointed to head the German delegation to The Hague, viewed it as the toy of the boyish tsar.[62] The kaiser thought that the worst result of the meeting was that it "provided our Democrats and opposition with a fine excuse for agitation."[63]

The Hague Conference opened on 18 May 1899. In the subcommittee concerned with arbitration, most of the delegates were willing to develop a protocol that provided for a limited international arbitration scheme. The British ambassador to Washington, Sir Julian Pauncefote led the delegation, and, despite Lord Salisbury's initial sarcasm, Pauncefote carried instructions to negotiate a restricted arbitration agreement. Pauncefote had long experience on the subject, particularly with the aborted Anglo-American treaty.

Similarly, France and the United States appointed delegates capable of articulating an agreement consonant with sovereignty. Léon Bourgeois, Baron d'Estournelles de Constant, Louis Renault, Andrew White, William I. Hull, and Seth Low were favorably disposed. On the Belgian delegation, two active members of the Interparliamentary Conference, Descamps and Beernaert, provided expertise. Copies of Descamps's project were distributed. On the German delegation, only Dr. Philip Zorn understood that arbitration did not have to destroy state sovereignty, but he was ordered to oppose all schemes.

The German government seemed unable to grasp what other chancelleries had understood. Originally, official Europe did not want to insult the tsar; by May 1899, however, such popular enthusiasm had developed for the conference that it was unwise to flaunt sophisticated diplomatic sarcasm in public. Some form of public agreement had to emerge. Pacifists, suspecting that the conference would be a disappointment—von Suttner even predicted a kind of Red Cross result— nonetheless gathered at The Hague to lobby for their agendas.[64]

The subcommittee on arbitration began its discussions with a proposal by

Pauncefote—similar to that of Descamps—for a statement favoring voluntary (facultative) arbitration agreements and a panel (college) of individuals appointed by each government to serve when asked. By the end of May, Count Münster let it be known that there was no reason for Germans to participate in this subcommittee because no serious issue would ever come to such a tribunal and, for less important issues, diplomacy would suffice. No question that ever arose between France and Germany, he argued, would ever go to a tribunal. From von Bülow in Berlin, Münster was encouraged to stand his ground, "The establishment of a permanent arbitration process will have the inevitable consequence of legitimizing intervention in principle," echoed the foreign minister.[65] The conference stalemated, a blockage that only dissipated after members of the American delegation, White and Hull, took a trip to Berlin with Dr. Zorn. Simultaneously, the Austrian government decided to support the British-backed arbitration project and undertook to persuade its Berlin allies to do so, too.[66] The Italians also backed the proposal for an arbitration tribunal.[67]

While Münster continued to fulminate against the pack of rabble who had influenced the tsar—pacifists, socialists, Jews (Jean de Bloch), women[68]—and who congregated nightly to discuss the progress of the congress in private salons and public meetings, his superiors in Berlin reluctantly came round. Years later, in an apologia, Bülow asserted:

> We could accept and welcome everything that served the cause of world peace without jeopardizing our security, and that we must avoid taking up the position of setting ourself in the way of the pacific and liberal efforts of the other powers.[69]

This refashioning of the record, written after German defeat in World War I, in no way reflected policy in 1898–1899. What the Berlin government did learn was to project a subtler style of international intransigence after 1899.

The final language of the convention establishing arbitration procedures was a triumph of diplomatic linguistics. The signatories of The Hague conventions agreed, in principle, that peaceful ways to defuse conflict were preferable to war. They proceeded to hedge this innocuous admission with a plethora of loopholes that recognized that the right to fight was ultimately the essence of sovereignty. Between these two polar opposites, a timid program for peaceful solutions developed, the grandparent of the World Court of the twentieth century. The so-called Permanent Court of Arbitration was created as well as government-recommended lists of persons with competence to become arbiters if and when two potential disputants agreed to call on them.[70]

The signatories admitted that international commissions of inquiry to avert potential conflict were desirable, but they refused to create standing commissions that would actually be ready to act in a crisis. The signatories, likewise, admitted that an offer of mediation or good offices from a neutral power was a valuable means of preserving peace, a friendly overture.

The most significant agreement was the establishment of the Permanent Court at The Hague, essentially a college of arbitrators organized so that (theoretically) they did not have to be assembled for each crisis. The court was to be composed of distinguished individuals (not necessarily trained judges) appointed by the signatories. It would be funded in a manner similar to the Universal Postal Union by national contributions, and it would keep records and develop an administrative apparatus. Article 27 of the Convention on International Arbitration asserted that governments "consider it their duty, if a serious dispute threatens to break out between two or more of them, to remind these latter that the Permanent Court is open to them" and that this reminder "can only be regarded as a friendly action."[71]

Traditionally, diplomatic historians have dismissed The Hague Conference as "of no importance. It had no bearing on current political problems and it did not . . . affect the relations of the powers to each other. It was, in fact, distinctly a side show."[72] Following 1919, scholars who prepared the official British documents on the origins of World War I and most of the scholars who have debated the "war guilt question"[73] echo similar sentiments. These dismissals ignore another dimension altogether: The Hague agreements provided Continental pacifists with a new legitimacy to agitate for peaceful conflict resolution and to challenge the conventional wisdom of the European state system.

After the conference ended, the Italian delegate, Count Constantino Nigra, noted "we have sown a good seed at The Hague; now it is up to the peoples to do the rest."[74] Peace activists fully understood how tenuous the results might be. During the three months of the The Hague Conference, a handful of peace lobbyists found themselves in the center of political interest. Astonished, Felix Moscheles stated, "More than once, I have actually been treated with respect."[75] To the absolute amazement of Bertha von Suttner, the Austrian delegate to The Hague, Count Welsersheim "hitherto a stranger to me, made a call in order to secure facts relating to the peace movement."[76] Jean de Bloch conducted a series of public lectures while the meetings were in progress, and he was frequently consulted by diplomatic delegates during the conference meetings. The parliamentarians who attended the 1899 Interparliamentary Conference in Christiana (now Oslo) evaluated The Hague Convention as

> the acceptance in principle of a project adopted . . . at Brussels, 1895 . . . for the constitution of an international arbitration tribunal and [we are satisfied] that its labors have not been without usefulness for the decision of the Hague Conference.[77]

During the meetings, Stead's *Chronicle* focused attention on the work of the diplomats, making it difficult for the meeting to adjourn with no agreements. But hardly had the diplomats packed their bags when the established press exploded with laughter at the boring results of the conference, the inconsequential agreements and the "illusory" promises.[78]

Although peace activists could not know it, it was the vast public uproar in favor of the tsar's Rescript that made it impossible for the major powers either to ignore his call or depart from The Hague with absolutely no agreement. Passy correctly observed that the movement had no direct impact on the formulation of the Rescript, but "the thing was in the air." He understood that no regal proclamation could create the kind of world that pacifists wanted but only the "gradual growth of a spirit of peace, . . . of justice and mutual respect."[79] In some vague and inchoate way, The Hague Conference of 1899 hinted at an alternate path where citizen voices intruded into official international policy-making.

Knowledgeable pacifists understood how restricted the conventions were. A disappointed Auguste Beernaert, who had chaired a Hague subcommittee, openly reported that the arbitration agreements fell far short of what he had worked for and that the original Russian agenda had been "refined" by enemies of the entire process.[80] Fredrik Bajer of Denmark went further. He argued that the limited results reflected the limited abilities of many of the delegates. At future meetings, if politicians and "men of science" would be increased and technical advisers and military men decreased in numbers, Bajer promised more substantial results. In the subcommittee of international legal experts, he noted—where Louis Renault, d'Estournelles de Constant, Edouard Descamps, and Léon Bourgeois sat—measurable results emerged. In contrast, the results from the arms-reduction commissions, made up of "military experts," were nearly nil.[81] This was a meeting that blurred lines between diplomatic experts and an interested public.

The ink was still drying on The Hague conventions when the Boer War broke out. The exhilaration of peace activists following the conference gave way to defensiveness and despair as the British government refused to consider arbitration. After the British rejected President William McKinley's offer of mediation, Salisbury's government insisted that it was not bound by the convention because the Boers were not signatories. Her Majesty's Government maintained that "national honor" was involved, thereby obviating any requirement to abide by The Hague conventions.[82] British pacifists, risking immense unpopularity and some personal danger, denounced their government's decision. Cremer's peace group bluntly warned, "A war of aggression and annexation will excite in South Africa such fierce racial hatred as will create a second Ireland, will compel us to increase our standing army, and may end . . . in the severance of South Africa from the British Empire."[83] G. B. Clark, on behalf of the seventy-five-year-old British Peace Society, pleaded with the government to consider arbitration:

> The Transvaal government were willing to submit the differences . . . to a court of arbitration, consisting of four chief justices of South Africa, . . . [and] the Lord Chief Justice of England as umpire in the event that the two colonial and two republican chief justices [were] not able to agree.[84]

The British delegation to the Interparliamentary Union reminded Salisbury's government of the noble part played by Great Britain in the advancement of arbitration, in "the *Alabama* Treaty, the Venezuela Arbitration, and more recently in the strenuous support given by the representative of this country to the conclusions reached at The Hague."[85] British pacifists risked their lives in late September 1899 when they tried to hold a public rally in Trafalgar Square against the war. The "reptile" press announced that the pacifists were Boer agents and traitors, giving the time and place of the rally. Hodgson Pratt, Felix Moscheles, and the aging Darby were pelted with bricks, wooden posts, rotten food, verbal abuse— they were finally rescued by a desultory police. Most of the antagonistic crowd were workers and their hostility to the peace activists profoundly depressed Pratt.[86]

British insistence on pursuing the war was the second major blow suffered by the international movement. By the late 1890s, the world's two advanced constitutional governments, Great Britain and the United States, had refused to sign the bilateral arbitration treaty and had declared imperialist wars on smaller states.

"The war in the Transvaal follows the Peace Conference at The Hague without an interval," noted one observer. "England should have allowed some time to elapse between the Conference . . . and the war. . . . England has done violence to international decorum."[87]

Despite the immense disappointment with official Britain, the peace movement did not expire. Continental activists worked tirelessly to expose the plight of the Boers. In the Netherlands, Waszklewicz-van Shilfgaarde energized a campaign, raising funds for posters, lectures, and publications; delivering speeches; sending appeals to President McKinley; and mobilizing women. Could the agreements at The Hague not be invoked to stop the slaughter, she asked La Fontaine, urging the movement to propagate that approach.[88]

Over the longer run, the impact of The Hague Conference on the international peace movement was to alter its agenda, especially as regards forms and formalities of international organization. The movement took on a dual challenge: to improve and extend the reach of the agreements and to struggle to persuade governments to use the tribunal.

British refusal to use The Hague machinery was partly based on the weak argument that the Boers had not been signatories. The Universal Peace Congress convened in Glasgow in 1901 and voted a pointed resolution that demanded The Hague conventions be opened to any potential signatory and that the machinery of the court be available to any newcomer.[89] D'Estournelles de Constant campaigned in France to popularize The Hague agreements, urging that the tribunal be used so that it not die of inanition.[90] When the French government omitted any request for The Hague tribunal from its 1903 budget, he charged the inner circles of the French Foreign Office with engineering the demise of the protocols of 1899.[91] D'Estournelles de Constant then formed a parliamentary organization, the Groupe de l'arbitrage française, to lobby for utilization of The Hague services. This group worked in the Chambre des députés and Sénat on behalf of a nonmilitaristic foreign policy for years to come.

In 1904, when the French and British governments, two ancient rivals, signed the Entente Cordiale, they promised to use The Hague machinery for any future controversy not amenable to diplomacy. In the entente, any and all treaties between France and Great Britain were to be subject to diplomatic and then to international arbitral treatment as long as vital interest, independence, or national honor were not involved. For diplomatic historians, this agreement signaled a new stage in the prewar realignment of power. For pacifists and lobbyists favoring bilateral arbitration agreements, the Entente Cordiale was a triumph. Here was the permanent arbitration treaty so ardently desired by peace activists during the 1890s. In addition to this most significant arrangement between the two major constitutional powers of Europe, seventy-seven other arbitration agreements were signed between 1899 and 1908.[92] The apparently vapid *vœu* of The Hague diplomats in Article 19 that urged independent treaties of arbitration appeared to bear fruit.

Pacifists firmly believed that their role in the French-British Entente was catalytic. Shortly before the agreement was signed, parliamentarians from both nations had exchanged visits in a widely publicized set of meetings. Pacifists had also organized exchanges of members of chambers of commerce. D'Estournelles de Constant and his British counterpart, Thomas Barclay, proclaimed the central significance of their roles.[93] Parliamentarians from other European countries shared this view.[94] D'Estournelles de Constant was also pleased that a counter-weight to the Triple Alliance balanced the European equation—an added force for peace, he hoped.[95] The Anglo-French rivalries, most recently exemplified by the 1898 Fashoda crisis, slipped into memory. By 1903–1904, despite such crises as the Russo-Japanese War, the first Moroccan crisis, which threatened a Franco-German war and the ever-mounting arms expenses, which now included the growing German navy, it looked as if arbitration had a future.

The Hague Conference provided the international peace movement with a new direction. Universal Peace congresses heard reports from their subcommittees that analyzed and proposed improvements on the conventions signed in 1899. With the Russo-Japanese War, the tsar lost his privileged position as convener of The Hague Conference. The head of the Interparliamentary Union, Albert Gobat, called on American President Theodore Roosevelt to take the initiative as con-vener.[96] Although diplomats then went to work behind the scenes—either to orga-nize the next meeting or to prevent it—parliamentarians and private citizen pac-ifists devoted themselves to an energetic campaign to shape the coming meeting. Never before had a citizen movement been so consciously determined to mobilize on an international plane.

In the years from 1904 to 1907, the peace movement tried to achieve two changes. One was technical, to simplify and expand procedures hinted at in The Hague conventions and protocols; the second, more important, was to effect some form of obligatory arbitration.

To persuade governments that "obligatory arbitration" was not a violation of national security, d'Estournelles de Constant and moderate pacifists argued that it had already taken root. It existed, but it had not been named. A substantial list of conflicts was routinely arbitrated: disputes over borders and waterways, debt collection, customs, and a variety of property conflicts.[97] What parliamentary pac-ifists wanted was an international agreement that formalized actual practice. A new German recruit, Richard Eickhoff, thought Berlin would accept that argu-ment because his government, too, finally submitted a few cases of arbitration and even signed a limited treaty with the British. His view was supported by Austrian Ernst von Plener.[98] Official German support for obligatory arbitration was crucial at The Hague, so pacifists were heartened when German and Austrian parliamen-tarians seemed optimistic. In the discussions of the Interparliamentary Union put forth by moderate pacifists, the rights of overseas workers; rail and navigational disputes; patent questions; treatment of the infirm, widowed, and orphaned; inter-national sanitary and hygienic standards; copyrights on intellectual, cultural, and artistic properties; communications problems; and commercial issues were cited as the issues most amenable to "obligatory" arbitration.

The ideas of the moderate members of the Interparliamentary Union were encapsulated in a Model Treaty of Arbitration presented to their important Lon-don 1906 meeting, where over six hundred delegates from twenty-two parliaments assembled in the House of Lords. Among the newest members present at this historic meeting was the first delegation from the Russian Duma. The 1906 meeting was opened by Prime Minister Campbell-Bannerman, thus assuring wide publicity. The model treaty was clearly intended for the forth-coming conference in The Hague.

Given the initial program of the Interparliamentary Conference of 1889–1890, this model treaty was an immense leap forward. Governments were invited to use The Hague machinery for a vast array of issues that would largely accustom nations to a new routine. Such issues would automatically go to The Hague without specific government review. For Continental parliamentarians, this project reflected real changes in European politics.

American delegates, including William Jennings Bryan, however, came with a wholly different agenda that called for the creation of a European parliament, an international legislature, and a supreme court—a proposal Gobat dismissed as "chimerical . . . 50 to 100 years away."[99] Gobat, La Fontaine, and the majority adhered to their model project, which they hoped would be acceptable to Berlin and Vienna. It was not. An infuriated Austrian minister, Alois Lexa von Aehrenthal, complained that the Union, "constantly growing in size and significance [was] under the influence of strongly socialist tendencies."[100] To European reactionaries, the Model Treaty of Arbitration covered what was tantamount to *lèse-majesté*. That members of parliament appropriated the right to discuss issues of war, peace, and foreign policy was "socialist."

If the Austrian minister was apoplectic about the Union's existence, influence, and positions, had he heard of the proposal voted by the Universal Peace Congress in 1906 he might have developed the vapors. There, over three hundred delegates from the U.S. and European movements enthusiastically endorsed the creation of a real international judiciary. Arnaud, chairing a subcommittee, urged that The Hague Tribunal become a real court. Articles 20 to 29 of the 1899 Convention were to be altered so that the court would be composed of a set of permanent appointees sitting in regular sessions during the year, appointees who elected their own officers and created standing administrative offices. The pacifist proposals would then also empower the court to decide if an issue constituted a threat to national sovereignty, honor, or vital interests.[101] The reorganized court would be able to compel recalcitrant regimes to appear—a real challenge to sovereignty. Judges would have authority to draft arbitration treaties and recommend their adoption. Arnaud's report passed the 1906 Milan congress. National peace delegations were to use this issue as the basis of their lobbying efforts.

The 1906 Universal Peace Congress also asked the coming Hague conference to create permanent committees of its own in order to hammer out acceptable principles of international law. Were this done, it would be an admission by the powers of the inalienable rights of all peoples to obtain their independence. This evidently innocuous statement was no mere piece of rhetoric: it was an attack on the presumed right of conquest claimed by Europeans. The next Hague meeting was asked to simplify procedures for adding new participants to its conventions. Any state that so wished could add its signature to the agreements. Arnaud's committee proposed a maximum program, not a tepid common denominator. His report concluded with a request for a clear-cut statement of when the Third Hague Conference would sit.

Only the German delegate, Ludwig Quidde, demurred, fearing that it was "dangerous for our movement to demand immediate implementation of these ideas for which governments are not sufficiently prepared."[102] Nonetheless, the proposal was voted unanimously.

The issue of sanctions to compel recalcitrant losers in an arbitration process did not command unanimous support. French legal scholars and peace activists had developed a series of proposals for peaceful sanctions that would isolate a recalcitrant power. The jurist Jacques Dumas, the lawyer Léon de Montluc, and a new and younger voice, that of E. Duplessix, devised a variety of sanctions, ranging from economic isolation, boycott, and exclusion from international finance to sequestration of overseas investments, expulsion from international unions (such as the Postal Union), and (Duplessix's idea) an international armed force to blockade ports and disrupt commerce.[103] British delegates led by Dr. Darby wanted nothing to do with endorsing force. Because no nation had refused to abide by an arbitration decision, he argued, the issue was a diversion. Darby managed to deny the Dumas motion significant support. Sanctions passed only by a vote of eighty-one to forty-eight, with numerous abstentions, thus reflecting profound division among pacifists on this issue.[104]

Overall, the meeting in Milan was spirited, energetic, and optimistic. Delegates railed against government policies that mistreated native peoples and minorities. Peace activists fulfilled Hodgson Pratt's hope that the movement would become the vanguard of innovation, not an echo chamber for the status quo. But it was Quidde's caution that ultimately predicted the outcome of the Second Hague Conference.

Pacifists had some reason to expect glad tidings from the Second Hague Conference. To begin with, it was going to happen—an event that had not been assured in 1899 or even by 1906. Presumably, the leading nations of the world would not send diplomats and experts to a meeting with absolutely no expectations of success. Second, attendance increased dramatically: forty-four nations instead of the twenty-six present in 1899. Most of the new nations were Latin American. This change partly met pacifist desires for broad, inclusive participation in the arbitration networks.

The Second Hague Conference was scheduled from 15 June to 18 October 1907, nearly twice the length of the first meeting. As the names of delegates were published, pacifists were heartened at the absence of known skeptics and hostile figures. The German plenipotentiary in 1907, Marshall von Biberstein, was pleasant and charming, not like the vituperative Münster who detested concluding his career in 1899 at a "stupid" peace congress. Von Biberstein was so attractive that pacifists failed to see how similar his thinking was to that of his predecessor.[105] The delegates concerned with international law, arbitration, and related procedures seemed promising: Philip Zorn and Frédéric de Martens had both been present in 1899 and were highly regarded. They were joined by Tobias M. C. Asser (the Netherlands), Heinrich Lammasch (Austria), and James Brown Scott (United

States)—noted legal scholars and members of diplomatic services.[106] Auguste Beernaert again chaired a subcommittee as did Léon Bourgeois. The French delegation included d'Estournelles de Constant and the British plenipotentiary, Sir Edward Fry, was knowledgeable about arbitration. From Latin America came two diplomats with respected international law credentials, Ruy Barbosa and Luis Drago. Bajer's criticism of the 1899 conference regarding the quality of its professional personnel was less appropriate in 1907.

Again, pacifists swarmed to The Hague; W. T. Stead issued his *Chronicle* on a daily basis. Pacifists mingled with diplomats following the opening ceremonies that raised hopes. The committees set to work, but after a month, peace activists registered a sense of unease. Nothing seemed to be happening, even in Léon Bourgeois's committee. The French pacifist Jacques Dumas summed up pacifist concern in August when he wondered, "Would the Conference be abortive? After so much hope, will we be left only with the most somber disillusionment?"[107] Finally, a Portuguese diplomat—realizing that public opinion was becoming restless, skeptical, and critical—proposed that the model treaty designed by the Interparliamentary Union be considered, including the recommendations for obligatory arbitration in strictly defined cases.[108]

German hostility came out into the open. Their delegates insisted that the essence of sovereignty was threatened by any international institution that might develop a life of its own. Paradoxically, German officials also argued that the list of items proposed for obligatory arbitration was so inconsequential that it would do the cause more harm than good. After weeks of wrangling, the meeting voted a pious *vœu* admiring the potential virtues of obligatory arbitration. Even that minimal compromise received six negative votes, led by the charming von Biberstein.[109] The Sixteenth Universal Peace Congress, sitting in Munich in September, wired a plea "in the name of humanity" for "a general permanent and obligatory treaty of arbitration, as complete as possible, emerge from your deliberations."[110] It was ignored.

The diplomats did agree to restructuring the tribunal of 1899. An ambitious American proposal presented by Joseph Choate suggested that a real court with real people be appointed, to sit at The Hague and be prepared to hear cases.[111] Choate's idea would provide the court with a permanent administrative apparatus and thus would begin to develop an institutional "memory" of its own. In the Final Act of 1907, a draft convention creating a Judicial Arbitration Court—not to replace the 1899 tribunal, but to be coterminous—was drawn up and left open for signatures. Pacifists were left with the task of convincing governments to sign.

The only substantial promise made in 1907 conforming to pacifist requests was the commitment that the diplomats made to meet again—in six or seven years. Optimists among the peace community could argue that some embryonic form of international world order was taking shape.

Pacifist disappointment with the conference was evident before it ended. Embarrassed German pacifists hosting the Sixteenth Universal Peace Congress in Munich in September tried to argue that it was very difficult to expect a meeting of forty-four disparate states to agree on very much; the Baron Edward de Neufville claimed that a world court was taking shape, but Émile Arnaud could not see how if the German diplomats continued to bar its growth.[112] La Fontaine argued that much of the disastrous outcome occurred because the diplomats failed to work in small preparatory groups before their meeting. Arnaud attacked officials and diplomats who continued to ignore the serious work of concerned citizens. Italian pacifists pointed the finger of blame entirely on Berlin, "While England has signed ten treaties, Italy, six; The United States, ten; Switzerland, 19; Germany has signed only two. The facts speak for themselves."[113]

The anti-German mood among pacifists also erupted in 1908 during the first meeting the Interparliamentary Union had ever held in Germany—at Berlin. The conciliatory welcome address delivered by Bernhard von Bülow fooled no one. Bajer denounced the diplomats of 1907 for tossing a *bouton de rose*. La Fontaine proposed that the vast majority of nations that voted for obligatory arbitration go ahead and constitute a court.[114] Although the Austrians, von Plener and Lammasch, expressed reservations about the American project for reconstituting the arbitration tribunal into a court, they were far more annoyed at the Germans for derailing the consensus on obligatory arbitration.[115] German parliamentarians sat stonily, refusing to discuss obligatory arbitration. They defended their government. When the American Richard Bartholdt invited delegates to vote a resolution that accepted current national boundaries as inviolable, he was icily informed by Baron Conrad Haussman that freezing boundaries "was to assume that the evolution of nations is finished."[116]

In a tepid defense of the Second Hague Conference, d'Estournelles de Constant observed that diplomats had participated in sessions on topics utterly out of their usual experience but that after four months most had grown to respect and admire each other as they worked closely in a real international assembly. The laborious work of the conference provided a novel model of international behavior. Rarely were so many representatives of so many unique cultures engaged in mutual exchanges with each other in an atmosphere of apparent equality. Moreover, he noted, German opposition was less dogmatic and more guarded.[117] His compatriot, the head of the French delegation, Léon Bourgeois summarized the meeting as the germ of a "society of nations" that began the long task of recognizing the "acceptance of a common law for all, between great and small" and of "the codification of reciprocal obligations."[118] Most pacifists remained unconvinced. The hours of work parliamentarians and private citizen-activists had invested in devising modest, nonthreatening, and fairly balanced proposals to institutionalize international arbitration seemed to make no difference.

Following the reorganization of the Interparliamentary Union after the Second Hague Conference,[119] the focus on arbitration shifted. The Union turned to issues similar to what international law associations had discussed—trade, waterways, rights of neutrals, and the rights of private citizens in an international context. But the debate over German attitudes remained a subtext. Heinrich Lammasch hoped that further study would produce proposals that Germany could accept, but French specialists were cynical.[120] A stubborn Théodore Ruyssen refused to forget the twenty years of labor preceding The Hague Conference and insisted, "We must demand that governments prepare the work of the next conference with great care; and we must ourselves develop the code of nations."[121]

Alfred Fried responded differently. Determined to transform pacifism into a "scientific" movement, Fried proposed that arbitration had become an albatross and should be dropped. In a challenge to pacifist orthodoxy Fried wondered what nation would undertake arbitration if a real attack was imminent? What government dared risk losing every precious moment to mobilize in case of attack? In those real moments when wars broke out, the power of arbitration was nonexistent. Pacifists should stop wasting time advocating proposals that made them ridiculous. Their only logical work was to undertake a multifaceted campaign to educate elites and governments to what was patently clear: national egoism was an absurd, counterproductive atavism in an already internationalized economic and cultural world. The peace message must change to emphasize that Europe really existed as a civilization and not a geographic expression. Agendas of international congresses had to be thoroughly overhauled. The hours of debate refining small points about arbitration processes were wasted.[122] The resemblance between Fried's proposals and Novicow's recommendations that were made in his writings and in his reports to Universal Peace Congresses in 1900, 1901, and 1902 was not accidental.[123] The aging Passy responded. In 1908 at eighty-six, Passy had heard it all before. Wearily, he accused Fried of undermining pacifist energy and achievement. Nothing precluded the peace movement from focusing on arbitration as the mechanism for the global vision that Fried presented.[124] Fried's fulminations merely disguised the weakness of Austrian and German pacifists to effect their nation's militaristic values. Moreover, no matter how reasonable and logical were pacifist arguments on behalf of arbitration, no matter how restricted their recommendations to conform with existing government practice, the major powers did not want to sign protocols that would commit them to a course of action in advance of a crisis.

One criticism leveled at arbitration that pacifists admitted was justified was the absence of a system of international law. Lacking a common set of legal principles, arbitration was not likely to serve as the mechanism for international security that its advocates promised. The 1910 meeting of the Universal Peace Congress in Stockholm addressed this complaint. Ever-energetic, Émile Arnaud presented a Code de la paix of 145 articles that offered a statutory basis of arbitration or any other form of international conflict resolution. The project assembled all previous Universal Peace Congress resolutions and drew on recognized practices commonly used in western nations. Its philosophic bases descended from the Jacobin tradition of the French Revolution. It was the code that the pacifists in Milan in 1906 had hoped would emerge from the 1907 Hague Peace Conference. Arnaud observed:

> When the second Hague Conference met, we were saddened to watch the diplomats, meeting in a peace conference, busy themselves almost exclusively with the laws of war. . . . We want . . . the third peace conference which will meet at The Hague . . . not only to concern itself . . . with the laws of war . . . but to organize the peace, that is, the rapport which governs the relations of foreign peoples with . . . each other.[125]

Arnaud's report reminded the Stockholm audience of an 1891 resolution of the Third Universal Peace Congress, refined in Budapest in 1896. It stated, quite simply, that there was no universal, fundamental right to make war and to conquer others. It denied the claims of extreme nationalists and some social Darwinians as well as imperialists and expansionists that war was a historic and biological reality that could not be eliminated. It did not accept the "realism" of the Descamps position admitting the right to make war in the international arena. The pacifists were not saying that wars did not happen; they admitted conflicts existed between nations as they did between individuals. However, in civilized societies, civil law replaced the vendetta. So, it was time to begin organizing such solutions in the twentieth century across national boundaries as well as within them.

The resolutions of 1891 and 1896 contained four incontrovertible principles:

A nation's autonomy is inviolable.

Each nation possesses the right of self defense.

All nations are mutually dependent on each other.

In cases of disputes over nationality and national independence, the only acceptable solution was Kant's prescription—the right of self-determination.[126]

Under one circumstance only did the code admit the right to make war—that of self-defense.

The code incorporated principles traceable to the Enlightenment, the Revolution of 1789, the Republic of 1792, and most recently to the programs of the French Radicals and *solidaristes,* who considered human rights and freedom rooted in nature. Among the rights found in nature—beyond the oft-rehearsed rights to life, liberty, and happiness (or property)—was that of association, the right of peoples to live in a community governed by a regime of their own choosing. Unlike pragmatic, legalistic approaches to international peace, Arnaud's subcommittee insisted on national self-determination and, therefore, national justice as a basis for international peace.

Unlike earlier statements of principle, the Code of 1910 addressed the rights of native colonized peoples. It raised the nasty question of the horrendous costs of imperialism and proposed a few ideas to deal with the excesses. Besides the hideous scandals about the Belgian Congo, French pacifists were well informed about overseas abuse and mismanagement from the reports of François Nicol.[127] In 1910, the movement attempted to shape a set of procedures to deal with the overseas disaster that was in the making. Arnaud reminded his audience of the procedures created by the Berlin Congress of 1884 that were intended to regularize occupation of "disinherited" or presumably "uninhabited" lands. They had essentially provided a cover for a massive real estate landgrab resulting in the destruction of African independence. As repulsive as the imperial orgy was to pacifists, they shied from denouncing overseas expansion in principle. The Code of 1910 proposed the creation of a separate international court that would regulate any more so-called free lands and also create procedures by which native peoples might petition for redress, reclaiming both land and independence. The international court envisioned by the pacifist framers of this code would function in a way to prevent the stream of bloody revolutions that pacifists predicted would would come in the twentieth century, as native peoples sought to break intolerable yokes.

Continental pacifists, however, accepted the idea that numerous native peoples were unready to govern themselves. They admitted there was a "white man's burden" but viewed it as a solemn obligation. For such peoples, the colonial powers were enjoined to "preserve and educate the people, improve its moral and material condition and prepare it for autonomy."[128] Governments were urged to prevent and punish acts of cannibalism, human sacrifice, torture, mutilation, slavery, and prostitution. The tutelary role of European states on behalf of improving the human rights of subject peoples was accepted, but pacifists also addressed the violence of imperialism.[129] (A significant number of pacifists helped organize the first congress on behalf of subject races and peoples that was held in London the following year.)

The code addressed familiar issues: freedom of the seas, access to waterways for all commercial vessels, rights of foreigners, diplomatic immunity, extradition treaties, and ordinary freedom of movement. Tucked away was an endorsement of sanctions to be used against the nation that violated standard practices, refused to accept an arbitration award, or rejected the use of arbitration. Based largely on the work of Dumas, the code recommended embargoes; suspension of diplomatic relations; exclusion from international agreements on posts, waterways, telegrams, rails, patents, and copyrights; and finally, a joint statement declaring an offender to be an outlaw (*mise-en-interdit*).[130] The framers of the code left out more dramatic sanctions proposed by other pacifists—military or naval blockades and calls for general strikes against recalcitrant governments.[131] When religious delegates discovered that sanctions were buried in the code, they objected but were outvoted. The overwhelming position of pacifists present in 1910 was unanimously that the code should be passed intact. It was. The Code de la paix remained the last major testament before the Great War of the European peace movement for an organized peace that recognized individual and national rights.

The last significant arbitration debate in the peace movement before 1914 dealt with the question of sanctions and enforcement on the international arena. The most radical proposal for enforcement procedures ever presented to a prewar peace congress came to the floor of the Universal Peace Congress in 1913 at The Hague—the last meeting before World War I. Gathered there to partake in the festivities organized to celebrate the opening of the Peace Palace, the pacifists listened in silence to the Dutch professor of international law Cornelius van Vollenhoven, who argued for the creation of an international police force.[132] He had already shocked the Dutch peace community with his proposal, and the Berne *bureau* refused to schedule him as a regular part of their agenda. Van Vollenhoven thus delivered his proposal as a report, but he made no converts. Even Gaston Moch, normally willing to entertain defenses for the use of force, observed dryly that an international army or police sent into a nation like Germany would inevitably provoke precisely the major war it was supposed to prevent. Pacifist opinion was not ready to endorse a police force, even in the service of justice.

Van Vollenhoven, unaccustomed to pacifist congresses, was less interested in his peace army as a way to enforce arbitration decisions and more interested in preventing small nations from becoming unwilling battlefields. He believed that the Third Hague Conference—were it to occur—would probably be the last chance for any peace agenda and for small nations to have any impact. In his view, the small states in Europe desperately needed an international agreement, including an arbitration system and enforcement mechanism, more than the great powers did. War, once it broke out, would trample the rights of small nations if they happened to be in the way of a mechanized army. The truly uninvolved and innocent would suffer the worse casualties, thus the only chance for peoples such as the Danes and Dutch was an international force prepared to defend them.[133] Among pacifists, Gobat offered the only substantial support to van Vollenhoven. Gobat reminded pacifists that German Chancellor Theobald von Bethman-Hollweg had offhandedly remarked that international agreements "burn like tinder" if they must.[134]

If van Vollenhoven's recommendation for an international police force to ensure pacific conditions was too radical, most Continental pacifists had come round to believing in the necessity of sanctions. Despite British reservations, French peace leaders, such as Léon Bollack and Lucien Le Foyer, persuaded themselves and their colleagues that arbitration required realistic enforcement mechanisms. Le Foyer averred in 1913:

> Pacifist for twenty years, I have hesitated about choosing sanctions. I have reflected for a long time, and am no longer hesitant. Law must be accorded its force; the international tribunal must be given an international police. The United States of Europe must have an international army.[135]

Between 1911 and 1913, when Italy had gone to war against the Ottoman Empire for Tripoli (Libya-Cyrenaica), Gobat and Stead (the latter then went on to sail on the *Titanic*) proposed boycotts of Italian products

> since the Italian government made its treacherous attack on the property of others [and] the present state of anarchy in Europe puts nations in a state of legitimate defence against all who deliberately wrong them.[136]

Most Continental pacifists had become comfortable with the idea of sanctions and with lobbying actively and publicly for their use.

Pacifist preparations for the Third Hague Conference—delayed from 1913 to 1915—left general calls for arbitration treaties and tribunals behind. The movement wanted obligatory arbitration; a permanent court composed of judges who had full powers to deliberate, free of government pressure, and funded by an international system of contributions; sanctions to insure the enforcement of awards; and a code of human rights that would serve as the basis for decisions, judgments, and awards. Pacifists had incorporated Hodgson Pratt and Charles Lemonnier's two main demands: the assertion that no nation was a law unto itself and the proviso that the peace movement itself lead and sharpen international thought, not merely propose minimal programs in vain attempts to persuade conservative diplomats and politicians. Invited by the editors of the *Encyclopaedia Britannica* to write the entry for "peace," the British pacifist Thomas Barclay stated:

> Peace is an object in itself, an international political condition requiring its code of methods and laws just as much as the domestic political conditions of nations require their methods and laws.[137]

Peace, therefore, was not a period of silenced weapons punctuating periods of war and permitting the architects of national security the opportunity to construct vast arsenals.

The activists in both the Interparliamentary Union and the Universal Peace Congresses—although fully aware that a war could break out during any of the major crises that tested European polity—remained cautiously optimistic until August 1914. Over one hundred bilateral treaties incorporating arbitration were signed between 1903 and 1910. The palace constructed for The Hague Tribunal opened to great fanfare in 1913. Although international violence had not ended, cases of arbitration multiplied. Despite numerous well-known crises—Bosnia-Herzegovina in 1908; the second Moroccan crisis in 1911, followed by the Italian-Turkish war over Libya-Cyrenaica; the undiluted Anglo-German naval rivalry; wars in the Balkans in 1912 and 1913—membership in peace societies and participation in congresses did not diminish. The arguments and projects favoring international arbitration were not abandoned by a discouraged international peace community.

By 1914, the discussions and debates over the processes of international conflict resolution had engaged legal experts, politicians, diplomats, and ordinary citizens across Europe and the New World. Reluctantly, a few politicians agreed that national sovereignty could coexist with a formal prearrangement for limited prescriptive arbitration.[138] Among governing officials, especially those connected to foreign offices and war departments, the will to tolerate even a limited reign of law made very little headway.

Few of the prewar peace activists who had struggled to create arbitration mechanisms lived to see the creation of the Permanent Court of International Justice that opened at The Hague in 1922. The relative ease with which this court was established, following the war, was due, in no small measure, to the fact that most of the disputes that ordinarily attended such an undertaking had been addressed prior to the war. What the war did, at monumental cost, was to create the willingness absent before 1914. Thus, for instance, the French legal scholar A. G. de Lapradelle, who had urged all due caution in his analyses of international arbitration in 1899 and 1907, published a ringing denunciation of the original Hague Conferences in 1919. Their shortcomings, he noted, arose from their total failure to address questions of justice and human rights. They had ignored just longings for national self-determination. For analysts, such as de Lapradelle, it took hecatombs of dead to reach the conclusions known to pacifists for twenty-five years, at the very least.

5

Arms Control: The Dilemma of Patriotic Pacifism

In his Rescript of 24 August 1898, Tsar Nicholas II asserted that "a possible reduction of the excessive armaments which weigh upon all nations" was "an ideal towards which the endeavors of all governments should be directed." Using the household language of pacifism, the tsar's call to the powers for a conference that emphasized arms reduction admitted that the constant spiral of arms expenditure never bought security. Instead,

> the intellectual and physical strength of the nations, labor and capital, are for the major part diverted from their natural application, and unproductively consumed. Hundreds of millions are devoted to ... terrible engines of destruction, which, though to-day regarded as the last word of science, are destined to-morrow to lose all value. ...
>
> The economic crises, due ... to the system of armaments *à l'outrance* ... are transforming the armed peace of our days into a crushing burden, which the peoples have more and more difficulty in bearing. It appears evident, then, that if this state of things were prolonged, it would inevitably lead to the very cataclysm which it is desired to avert.[1]

The similarity between this proclamation and the widely publicized study of war in the modern world by Jean de Bloch was not sheer coincidence, merely an idea whose time had come into royal consciousness.[2] Nicholas had held discussions with Bloch, a Polish financier.[3] Moreover, the antimilitarist, promodernization coterie in the tsar's court, led by his finance minister Sergey Witte, had used similar arguments in an effort to redeploy Russian resources into nonmilitary projects, particularly the development of transport and industry. Anyone familiar with the arguments routinely presented by liberal economists would have recognized the spirit of the tsar's Rescript.

One year later, when The Hague Conventions were published, arms reduction was entombed in an innocuous *vœu,* a pious promise for future discussion. This toothless commitment—the product of months of diplomatic maneuvering that started a week after the Rescript was issued—hardly surprised peace activists. In some ways, it paralleled their own hesitations about arms reduction and the larger issue—the role of war. A loud pacifist silence greeted The Hague resolution on armaments in contrast to vocal criticism of arbitration conventions.[4]

During the 1890s, the issue of arms control stubbornly intruded into pacifist discussions, despite persistent attempts by the leadership to contain it. In 1892, for instance, the Swedish pacifist Klas Arnoldson spelled out the equation:

> Alongside the wild race for armaments [there is] a terrible struggle for existence, and discontent reigns in all lands. This condition . . . which fills the world with unrest and fear must in the near future have an end. It will either come in the form of a social revolution which will embrace our whole continent, or it may come by the introduction of an established condition of international law.[5]

If his prognosis was accurate—and four years later, Bloch's laboriously prepared charts and graphs gave it flesh and blood—peace propaganda ought to direct a frontal assault on this issue. But Bertha von Suttner, reflecting the movement's dead center, frankly admonished "friends of peace should not take up the armaments question: this can only follow from a preceding understanding and creation of a legal order."[6] Her friend and supporter, the writer Max Nordau, was even more discouraging. He considered the whole topic hopeless "until human nature changed."[7] Moderate and conservative peace activists were slightly more optimistic, assuming that arms reduction would follow the creation of a juridical order.[8] D'Estournelles de Constant insisted repeatedly that a general juridical accord had to precede any arms reduction. Passy, importuned by younger activists to attack militarism and support disarmament, insisted:

> While disarmament was obviously the distant aim of our efforts and our hopes, the moment had not come to ask for it. . . . to make what would appear to be an attack on the army or what could be interpreted as a weakening of discipline, was totally contrary to our method of seeing.[9]

Religious English pacifists refused to deal with arms questions as an unseemly subject for pacifists. Some pacifists tried to pass the issue to the Interparliamentary Union on the doubtful grounds that only it was competent to consider arms reductions. But, as Christian Lange (co-winner of the Nobel Peace Prize with Karl Hjalmar Branting in 1921) noted, "this burning and difficult issue was not discussed often . . . at conferences. [They] only rarely studied the problems of the possibility of a halt in the arms rivalry."[10] In fact, the language of the tsar's Rescript went well beyond the public discourse of the movement in the 1890s.

In France as the century concluded, the subject of arms reduction was immensely complicated by the passions around the Dreyfus affair, where patriotism and national security mixed with anti-Semitism and confronted human rights and antimilitarism. As noted earlier, the Alliance universelle des femmes pour le désarmement, established by the socially prominent Princess Gabrielle

Wiesniewska in 1896, initially campaigned with a direct focus on arms control.[11] Appeals to "sisters" in Austria, Germany, Italy, the Scandinavian countries, and elsewhere went forth on behalf of "the idea of international disarmament, to bring an end to fratricidal warfare and inaugurate the desired age of justice and harmony."[12] But three years after its debut, at the height of the Dreyfus uproar, the name was changed to the Alliance des femmes pour la paix. The controversial word, *désarmement* disappeared both from its title and discussions. International arbitration, education, and eventually, women's suffrage became its agenda. This slide toward respectability finally annoyed one of its founders—Sylvie Flammarion—who broke ranks in 1899 to create L'Association 'la paix et le désarmement par les femmes' to continue the commitment against weaponry as well as to reach out to working-class women.[13] In general, middle-of-the-road pacifists approved of the decision by the princess to drop direct mention of *désarmement*. The leading Portuguese feminist-pacifist observed:

> In the current state of the question [of world peace] it could be dangerous to suggest general immediate disarmament to an international congress. . . . War itself . . . might result from this well-intentioned initiative toward the ideal pacific state.[14]

In an effort to clarify her new position, Princess Wiesniewska insisted, "The aim of our society is not the disarmament of *la patrie*; [we oppose] the armed peace which will ruin and depopulate Europe before a war even breaks out—to the political and industrial benefit of America and the Asiatics."[15]

Rapporteurs at annual peace congresses in the 1890s dealt with the arms race by denouncing its unbelievable cost.[16] Everyone knew that six major powers were spending blindly, with no end in sight. One hope was that the recitation of the size of annual deficits would persuade intelligent political leaders to act before bankruptcy and social upheaval intervened. In 1894, the Universal Peace Congress urged the nations to adopt a "truce" (*trève*) on new expenditure in order to allow "the European powers to effect an indispensable reduction in their arms to balance their budgets."[17] (This innocuous, evenhanded proposal resembled a suggestion later placed before the military subcommittee of The Hague meeting in 1899 by the Russian delegate where it was rejected as a dangerous threat that would strangle scientific and technological innovation.) Nonetheless, for peace activists from rival nations, proposals for "truces" to freeze arms spending for a discreet time period—that is, five years—constituted the judicious approach to a tangled and tendentious problem.

In the Interparliamentary Union, the question of arms reduction was introduced in a sophisticated, indirect fashion by Edouard Descamps and Fredrik Bajer in the late 1890s. They devised a project for a "pacte de pacigérance" that urged the establishment of neutral zones for nonbelligerents. Were the smaller states of Europe—Belgium, the Netherlands, Luxembourg, Switzerland, perhaps the Scandinavian nations—to create a league of noncombatants and refuse to participate in European wars and remove their resources from the service of belligerents, they would, in effect, "assert the superiority of the laws of peace over those of warfare."[18] After The Hague Conference concluded, Bajer pursued the idea of a league of neutrals. Rejecting war as an instrument of national policy, the participants would use The Hague machinery to resolve all their own conflicts and would provide their good offices as peacemakers in the event of war around them.[19] The league would help realize Article 27 of The Hague agreement, binding the signatories to remind each other of the existence of the tribunal in the event of impending war.

If implemented, the proposal for a league of neutrals would remove six and possibly eight nations from the arms race, but it required Big Power recognition—first, of the right of a nation to declare itself neutral; second, of respect for the existence of neutral rights. Pacifists from major powers responded to the Danish and Belgian initiatives with skepticism. Could neutrality be self-asserted? Did it have to be condoned by international agreements, such as the 1830 London conference that guaranteed Belgian neutrality or the general willingness of most major nations to respect Swiss neutrality? Could groups of nations essentially "secede" from the Europe of the Big Powers and declare themselves as battle-free areas? Descamps and Bajer repeatedly urged pacifists to campaign for these rights, but the international movement never mobilized itself on behalf of the project. Finally, between 1911 and 1913, parliamentarians from Denmark, Sweden, and Norway created their own regional Interparliamentary Union meetings. From those sessions, Bajer carried a resolution promoting Scandinavian neutrality to the 1913 meeting of the whole Union. But the Union voted to send Bajer's proposal to a committee for "further study"—thus entombing an interesting move.[20] The brief life of the idea of neutralization as a way to delimit potential battlefield sites and control the cost of arms for smaller states was left to be recaptured by later generations.

The Dreyfus affair also unleashed a number of virulent attacks on barracks life, on military mores, and on the general effect of militarism on society. By the end of the century, middle-class pacifists could no longer avoid the social implications of militarism, though not all French peace activists believed in Dreyfus's innocence or supported Émile Zola's position in 1898 on behalf of the imprisoned victim.[21] Auguste Hamon, editor of *L'Humanité nouvelle,* in a study of the psychology of the professional soldier, detailed the common disorders associated with that career—delinquency, alcoholism, immorality, disorderly sexual behavior—and argued that the nonprofessional conscripted soldier was often ruined for civilian life by his two or three years of service.[22] Similar arguments presented in muckraking fashion by Urbain Gohier brought down the full force of the French government.

Gohier charged that French barracks were a breeding ground of decadence, vice, crime, and abuse of common men by officers of aristocratic background.[23] That he was brought to trial on charges of defaming the state enraged both center and left, producing a violent verbal confrontation in the Chambre des députés in November, wherein rightist delegates attacked Gohier, Jews, and other enemies of the state as traitors. Socialists led by Eugène Fournière responded that the case against Gohier was a step toward the destruction of democracy. The political climate in France worried Passy, who feared that the cautious and careful labors of years of pacifism would be destroyed in the uproar. When he heard that Austrian pacifists were planning a demonstration on Dreyfus's behalf, he quietly interceded to prevent it.[24]

The tsar's call in the atmosphere of the near civil war unleashed by the Dreyfus affair, created a quandary for organized pacifism. In the *chambre,* the eminent socialist deputy, Edouard Vaillant, insisted that the Foreign Office take up the Rescript, support international arbitration by the constitution of a tribunal, prepare proposals for arms reduction, recommend that European nations convert armies into defensive militias, introduce basic training into schools to create a trained people, and cut the length of service. Vaillant concluded with the recommendation that the European powers at The Hague agree to periodic meetings and that they create a permanent international office to handle the increasing problems of foreign workers.[25] It was a socialist who gave voice to the program that pacifists supported but feared would alienate the public. Foreign Minister Théophile Delcassé was furious. Discussion of any of these issues, he maintained, threatened national security and implied that France was weak. Despite Delcassé's energetic effort to defeat Vaillant's proposals, the first one—on arbitration—commanded a respectable tally even in defeat—228 in favor; 303 against. The proposals for national militias went down in a thundering rebuff—446 against; 76 in favor. D'Estournelles de Constant, though entirely unsympathetic to Delcassé's Fashoda policy and to all overseas adventures, nonetheless, did not believe that the legislature should vote on issues that would limit the freedom of the diplomats at The Hague. He abstained on the Vaillant proposal for a tribunal but stayed away for the rest of the votes.[26] D'Estournelles de Constant went to The Hague persuaded that a system of international security provided by legal mechanisms had to precede serious arms reductions. In effect, in the French legislature, only socialist voices backed the tsar's original call as if fulfilling Kaiser Wilhelm's warning that only socialists and anarchists would benefit from the Rescript.[27] Vaillant's recommendation, that the professional army be replaced by a popular militia, an argument made in the 1860s both by the First International and by Garibaldi republicans, was made famous by Jean Jaurès a decade later. In fact, it was the central focus of the pacifist project developed by Gaston Moch.

Along with E. T. Moneta, Moch was one of the few prominent pacifists with firsthand military experience; he had been an artillery captain. Impatient with vacuous propaganda—Anglo-American religious scruples, American recommendations to Continental pacifists that they agitate for a Continental adaptation of the U.S. federal constitution, and von Suttner's advocacy of caution—Moch wanted to articulate practical positions for French pacifists and, hopefully, for the international movement. His books, articles, speeches, and lectures were scholarly and scientific, appealing to reason and historical experience. He had not resigned his commission to produce airy rhetoric.

Moch realized that the arms race of the late nineteenth century, a race *à l'outrance,* was unique in history. Its costs were unprecedented. The adaptation of industrial technology to the battlefield had created weapons that promised to destroy more than enemy forces; the nature of warfare was transformed and civilization itself was threatened. It was a race that spared none: there were no neutral hiding places. The war fought with these new weapons would very likely eliminate Europe as a global force. No one could predict the probably long-term social and economic disaster that such a war or even such an arms race, would have.

The peace movement, however, would make no headway by campaigning for arms reduction in any one nation. Even a campaign coordinated across national boundaries, such as that Princess Wiesniewska had initially proposed, would evoke derision and charges of treason. Pacifists had to fashion specific, limited proposals that began with an axiomatic recognition of the right to self-defense.

Based on historical experience—notably the *levée en masse* of the French Revolution—Gaston Moch argued that a firm case existed for defensive militias, for arming and training a population to defend its territory, and for starting this process, nationally, in the school system.[28] A defensive militia eliminated the deleterious barracks existence and the social distance between officer and enlisted man. It reduced costs of training an army, did away with the lost years of productive labor that conscription entailed, and provided as good a force for defense as any professional military.[29] If politicians really meant that arms were only for defense, then the militia was the most appropriate force. Describing this book, *L'Armée d'une démocratie,* Moch wrote to a friend:

> I recommend nothing that will leave France open to combat without preparation and without an organized army. On the contrary, I have developed a project of organization, inspired by the Swiss force, which will give us at least as much defensive force as our current military and which . . . is economically and socially the equivalent of arms reduction.[30]

The Swiss system, an adaptation of the popular militia developed during the French Revolution, was democratic, effective, and inexpensive. "To prevent an attack," Gaston Moch noted, "a purely defensive organization was really all a nation needed. An organization similar to that of Switzerland is absolutely sufficient to confront all eventualities."[31] He anticipated Jaurès's *L'Organisation socialiste de la France: L'Armée nouvelle,* by a decade. Moch expected his proposals would obtain a hearing in France *only* if German socialists, simultaneously, would agitate for a similar project. August Bebel, the German socialist leader, published *Nicht stehendes Heer, sondern Volkswehr* in 1898.[32] Moch wanted a coordinated campaign by socialists and progressives.

Ever cautious about arms reductions, Moch saw a few places where carefully specified cuts might work. Using the case of Alsace and Lorraine, the tinderbox of Europe, he noted that nearly one-fifth of the military strength of both nations was concentrated in those few square miles. The area resembled a war zone with both sides in very close proximity set to explode. With the aid of charts and graphs, Moch—writing under a pseudonym, Patiens—pointed out that each side could make substantial reductions in their forces without undermining anyone's security. Indeed, security might be enhanced because the overconcentration was a dangerous provocation. In the mid-1890s, the existing ratio of one soldier per every ten citizens could be cut to one soldier per every two hundred citizens without endangering either French or German security. A number of forts could be dismantled and a good deal of money saved. Sarcastically, Gaston Moch pointed out that the Americans, not considered terribly civilized by many Europeans, managed to preserve peace on their continent with a ratio of one soldier per one thousand eight hundred inhabitants.[33]

If an arrangement for phased reduction of men and arms could work in those contested provinces, perhaps states would be more willing to entertain recommendations for limited projects elsewhere and still preserve national security. But a call as sweeping as the tsar's Rescript was destined to fail—a view shared by other "realistic" peace leaders and intellectuals.[34] When The Hague Conference blindsided arms reduction, they fulfilled his expectations:

> To ask the powers to disarm is to ask them to conciliate two contradictory ideas for such an agreement implies the absence of all suspicion and . . . as long as one suspects one's neighbors, one must remain in a condition to repel aggression . . . ; as long as the first obligation of a government [is responsibility] for the nation's existence, the largest military force that it can attain [must be maintained].
>
> Thus, the realization of a simultaneous agreement is materially impossible; for the problem poses itself differently from one nation to another—the configuration of the land, population density, wealth, the importance of the colonial empire,—produce very specific defensive conditions for each power.[35]

Were arms reduction to succeed, he argued, it might work in cases where two nations negotiated.[36] The establishment of national militias was the next logical move. In the final analysis, peoples would have to press their governments for basic changes, including a change as dramatic as French and German friendship.

On occasion, Moch campaigned at international peace congresses on behalf of his analyses. In 1902, at the Universal Peace Congress in Monaco, he recommended a resolution:

> A. that permanent armies . . . be replaced by the system of the armed nation, and
>
> B. that . . . in each nation, a constitutional law be passed stating that the army exists only for national defense.[37]

German delegates reacted with concern that any discussion of arms reduction would undermine their credibility at home and religious British delegates loftily observed that they represented a peace movement that had managed to exist nearly a century without treading on such controversial issues. In the next year's meeting, Gaston Moch exploded:

> We are told that people are speaking in the name of peace societies which have a century of history. Which are the wars which these societies have stopped during the last 100 years?
>
> If we dare to hope that people will follow us, that governments will obey peoples, . . . the peace movement must bid farewell to its purely rhetorical and sentimental character to become positive [scientific].
>
> I am astounded that these societies, so venerable, have allowed themselves to vote for the principles of national autonomy, . . . that nations are inviolable and that their territory is inviolable . . . [but refuse] to admit the right of self-defense of those very nations.[38]

By 1905, Moch, discouraged with fellow pacifists and with his hopes for a broad European accord, proposed a new Saint-Simonian vision of a western European model: "If only the current generation organizes peace in western, liberal Europe and establishes an agreement between itself and the United States of America, it will have accomplished its task."[39] The community would include France, Belgium, Italy, Britain, the Netherlands, and perhaps Scandinavia. Moch saw no hope of an international system of organized juridical and legal practice that would include the central European dynasts and the Russian autocracy, despite the best efforts of pacifists from those areas.

Among Continental pacifists, Moch's arguments most closely paralleled the analysis of the Italians, especially Ernesto T. Moneta. Founders of the peace movement in Italy in the 1880s usually came from the Garibaldi wing of the movement for Italian unification. One of Garibaldi's generals, the Hungarian-born Stefan Türr, who helped establish the international peace movement in 1889, was a longtime advocate of national, popular militias. In 1867, he had written to Garibaldi

> By the formation of national armies, there would be no more injust wars, enterprises undertaken by caprice, but only the supreme struggle for the defense of national independence and in war of this nature, no citizen must be exempt.
> ... The institution of national armies would end forever the awful division existing in many nations between the army and the people.[40]

Garibaldi, who shared this vision of a people's army, was disappointed when it was not incorporated into the conservative constitutional monarchy created by Camillo di Cavour and Victor Emmanuel II in 1860–1861. The creation of a professional army, with an aristocratic officer class atop a conscripted mass base angered progressives who had struggled with Garibaldi for unification. By the end of the 1880s, conservatives were obviously planning to use the army for overseas conquests. Moneta, editor of the liberal Milanese paper, *Il Secolo,* joined the peace movement in 1888 with a cohort of republicans who cherished the more democratic (Jacobin-style) traditions of the Risorgimento. He had fought against the Austrians in Milan in 1848 and in the wars for unification until 1866; he believed in the Mazzinian notion of the nation as the basic unit of European federalism. Moneta never abandoned the ideal that a just, free nation was the only basis for international peace and had no need of a stratified professional military.

In 1889, at the first congress of Italian pacifists held in Rome, Moneta observed that the costs of supporting four million men-in-arms paid by European nations, redounded only to the benefit of the young, dynamic transatlantic stepchild of Europe, the United States, a republic unburdened by military debts. Its products were running European goods out of markets. Its capital was invested in innovative new means of production. If European governments really meant that arms were only for defense, Moneta argued, they would support the creation of militias. "Let us demand disarmament," he urged, using the word to mean arms reduction and the transformation of professional standing armies into popular militias. National defense had to begin by training youth.

> If sharpshooting practice is made the keystone of civilian-military education, two-thirds of all soldiers can be sent home and, simultaneously, two million men would become adept in national defense.[41]

As early as 1889, the Milanese Unione lombarda per la pace had called for an international conference of the Powers to discuss the transformation of permanent armies into militias.[42] This point of view remained at the heart of the Italian peace movement. Moneta and Giretti both repeated it in Turin in 1904. At the Perugia meeting (1907) of Italian peace societies, a resolution easily passed calling for a "gradual transformation of the military into the armed nation."[43] The political culture that underlay the Italian movement, from center to left, was united in its opposition to professional armies, a position that Bertha von Suttner and her Austrian colleagues pleaded with Moneta not to pursue in the international arena.[44] Italian peace activists resonated to Gaston Moch's analyses in ways that neither British nor American pacifists understood. When Moch and Moneta argued for training youth in marksmanship at schools, British pacifists shuddered at the idea that military training would be brought into the educational system. British pacifists were nervous about Boy Scout organizations that were then forming.

Thus, when the tsar's call appeared in 1898, pacifists who remained cautious and skeptical about general reductions in armaments were fully attuned to nationalist sentiment and political realities. What the pacifist community could not know until after World War I, when the prewar diplomatic documents were published, was the full extent of diplomatic hostility to the tsar's proposal.

Within a week of the tsar's Rescript, Paul Cambon, a leading French diplomat, privately warned, "This disarmament proposal . . . has made everyone think that soon all will throw themselves at each other. . . . All projects for general peace always end up in conflict."[45] His assessment was typical. Nearly every diplomat, politician, statesman, journalist, and expert concluded that the Russian state was on the verge of bankruptcy or that the Russians were trying to buy time to prepare a major assault in the Far East.[46] That the tsar had behaved childishly went without question.

"How can anyone suggest general disarmament at the very moment when—in view of the danger of socialism and anarchy—Europe needs militarism more than ever to counteract dissolution?" observed the French editors of a prestigious review.[47] Unknowingly, they had echoed the precise sentiments of Kaiser Wilhelm. Angrily, he complained that his cousin in St. Petersburg "has placed a shining weapon in the hands of our democrats and opposition for agitation."[48] With bare control of his venom, Willy wrote dryly to his Russian cousin, Nicky:

> Could we, . . . a monarch holding personal command of his army, dissolve his regiments sacred with a hundred years of history and relegate their glorious colors to the walls of armories and museums (and hand over his towns to anarchists and Democracy). However, that is only *en passant*. The main point is the love of humanity which fills your warm heart and which prompts this proposal, the most interesting and surprising of the century. Honor will henceforth be lavished on you by the whole world, even should the practical part fail.[49]

Italian diplomats were less troubled by the proposal for arms reduction than they were by the possibility that the papacy might receive an independent invitation to attend an international conference and thus undermine the dignity of the Italian state, which panicked at the possibility that the Vatican would be recognized. Nonetheless, Italian officials were constrained to repeat that national defense was a sovereign arena and the war budget would "remain . . . independent of the existence or not, of an international commitment."[50]

The French were in a ticklish position. Allied to the Russian state since 1892, they could not openly demur about the tsar's call. Paul Cambon observed, "It is not possible for any government to reject outright the Emperor Nicholas' proposal . . . the Conference will meet; but it is unlikely that it will achieve a practical result."[51] French and Russian diplomats and politicians set about framing an agenda that would gently entomb the issue of arms reduction. In the Russian court, the struggle between the finance minister, Sergey Witte, and the traditionalists led by Count Mikhail Muraviev worked toward that end.[52] By the end of the year, the Russian legal expert Frédéric de Martens[53] was sent on a mission to European governments to create an acceptable agenda and a much weakened second manifesto was issued. The shift pleased the German ambassador, Count Münster, who was to be the plenipoteniary at The Hague. "It may be possible," he noted, "to get around the armaments question and suggest a few alterations in international law and the Statute of the Red Cross."[54] The second manifesto was transparent in its objective. Bertha von Suttner noted, with displeasure, that the "introduction of questions concerning military customs and the humanizing of war into the deliberations of the Peace Conference . . . [was] a wedge driven into it, calculated to rob it of its individual character."[55] She was correct.

The British government saw no hope for any international agreement on reductions. Among the myriad reasons that its naval and military experts produced was the argument that verification to enforce an agreement could never be devised without violating national sovereignty. Moreover, any attempt to freeze weapons at current levels risked favoring "the interests of savage nations." No agreement to curb new explosives was posssible without governments revealing current levels—a violation of national security. Overall, British experts concluded that proposals to "regulate the conduct of war . . . would be almost certain to lead to mutual recriminations."[56] The British further shrugged off the issue by noting that reductions in the sizes of land forces were essentially an issue for the Germans, "the military centre of gravity of Europe." British experts knew that Germans would never agree to discussion of the subject.[57] Hence, the British government did not have to refuse to discuss the issue because the Germans would reject that agenda item, incriminate themselves, and eliminate the issue.[58]

The British viewed arms reduction as a German problem; the United States decided it was a European, not a North American, issue. The American delegation was mainly interested in the rights of neutrals on the high seas and protection of private property during wartime, an issue where they shared some common ground with the Germans against the British.[59] Still, the American delegation contained the eminent Admiral Alfred Mahan, who believed in the principle that the more brutal a war, the more humane it would be—because it would be short.

The argument that the arms race threatened the future of civilization by undermining rational uses of economic resources—an old favorite among peace activists and liberal economists—had been a central theme of the first Rescript. This, too, was rejected by official Europe. Paul Cambon, for instance, noted:

> Without doubt the armed peace imposes . . . heavy budgetary charges, but at the same time, it supports . . . many factories of very diverse types and . . . thousands of workers. To stop or simply to restrain arms would be . . . to throw on the street hungry masses who would demand their right to a living with energy; to be free of the fear of external war is to expose oneself to internal social wars equally terrible and ruinous.[60]

Cambon's recognition that armaments also created work and that closed factories might cause social upheaval was a unique analysis among diplomats. During the conference itself, economic issues were not addressed. Few military and political experts saw connections between economic forces and national honor. A German technical expert, responding to the Russian proposal for a five-year truce in new weapons spending, sneered, "German public and private wealth is increasing; the general welfare and standard of living are rising from year to year; [Germans viewed military service] as a sacred and patriotic duty."[61] To official Germany, the idea that an economic crisis would ensue from arms expenditure was absurd. The German economy, a world leader, was edging out Great Britain.[62] The idea of a truce in military spending in order to restore economic health was perhaps something the Russians needed—but not the proud German nation. Only a maverick Dutch general, den Beer Portugael, supported the Russian idea.

At The Hague, there was some willingness to modify conventions regulating warfare: agreements about the wounded, prisoners, and spies; prohibitions against dumdum bullets and the launching of projectiles from air balloons were signed. Though The Hague Convention included the *vœu* urging future conferences to consider arms reductions, diplomats had no desire to repeat the exercise again.

The subject would not go away. Arms reduction—often called disarmament because the words were used interchangeably—became a ritual of dispute in the French *chambres* between right and center-left as well as between the center-left and the ministers. Prior to World War I, issues of foreign policy and military expenditure surfaced repeatedly in the French legislature. In the lower house, radicals attempted to establish parliamentary participation in the processes of foreign policy making.[63] Following The Hague Conference, d'Estournelles de Constant rather doggedly pursued the subject. He supported Jean Jaurès's powerful attacks on both French colonial disasters and squandered military resources, evoking the misery, unemployment, underdevelopment, and anguish of vast areas of France—in the Garonne, Loire, and Rhône valleys—which he attributed to national profligacy.[64] Henry Hubbard, also active in the antiexpenditure debates, noted that since the alliance was signed with Russia in 1892—presumably to enhance security—expenditures increased over fifty percent. Hubbard insisted that the government ignored the growing body of citizens, German as well as French, who believed international organization and not weapons had to be built up. He went so far as to read the names of peace groups into the official record, but the government, of course, had enough votes to silence this initiative.[65]

In the first decade of the new century, the campaign in parliament waged by d'Estournelles de Constant and Radical deputies along with eminent Socialist deputies—Jean Jaurès, Francis de Pressensé, François Fournier, and Maurice Allard—essentially built on the arguments of the liberal economists. Arms expenses were the chief source of "the social question." The main difference between the pacifist position of d'Estournelles de Constant and the socialists was an emphasis on juridical internationalism. But moderate as he was, the French senator was accused of advocating unilateral disarmament. He reacted:

> Disarmament is the last step of pacific organization. Before achieving disarmament, the reduction of arms must occur; and before that, the limitation of arms; and that limitation will have to be first preceded by a general accord among the powers.[66]

D'Estournelles de Constant's attempts to end the deliberate distortions of the pacifist argument by militarists failed. Between *disarmament* and the *reduction of armaments* lay a vast area of negotiation, but the common technique of promilitarist and so-called realist voices was to confuse the two. In 1904, he was elected to the Sénat, where there were far fewer supporters of his position.

After 1899, peace activists grew impatient to address arms issues. The limited (and immensely disappointing) *vœu* voted by the diplomats did not convince all pacifists that the subject was a dead end. Sylvie Flammarion, president of L'Association 'la paix et désarmement par les femmes,' campaigned in the stalls of Les Halles among the workers, men and women, where she denounced the arms race and urged common folk to agitate for real cuts in military expenses in order to meet the needs of people living in misery. Attacked by hecklers because of her sex and because of the German occupation of Alsace-Lorraine, she went on to characterize war as "useless carnage, imbecile massacre . . . the total fulfillment of masculine law."[67] With her friend and associate, the crusading journalist Séverine (Carolyn Rémy), Flammarion attacked the arms race as the pernicious source of evil oppressing the poor, women, and working-class men and as the cause of class dissension.[68] In a speech at Lille, she pleaded with women to stop supporting the military:

> Ladies, do you know the figures? Our taxes are higher than three milliards and the ministers of the army and navy devour a third themselves. . . . The household with six francs a day for expenses, for example, starts each day by throwing two francs away.[69]

One of her collaborators, Edward Spalikowski, tried to spread the message with a song, which included:

Women, if, occasionally, you could only tell men,
That it is cowardly and shameful to offer your children
As an offering to Moloch.[70]

Flammarion's direct attack signaled a change. After 1899, the movement could not avoid the issue of the arms race and the broader implications of militarism.

With the Boer War following upon the closure of The Hague Conference, British pacifists were forced to deal with the whole question of armaments and militarism.

Jean de Bloch provided ammunition. He noted that the British general staff

> unhesitatingly declared in June, 1899 that 10,000 men would be amply sufficient for the conquest of the Transvaal. . . . But shortly afterwards, 70,000 troops were found to be requisite. . . . They confessed that their first estimate was very incorrect; to err, however, is human. . . . But the results were as unfortunate as before. Thereupon, they increased their demands anew, until the troops dispatched amounted to about 300,000 in all, and like the two daughters of the leech in the Bible, the cry is still "give, give."
>
> The mistakes made as to the probable duration and cost of the war were correspondingly great.[71]

The war speeded up a process that ordinarily took several years to attain—a spiraling arms buildup that was simply never sufficient to attain the state of perfection demanded by the military. Bloch urged the peace movement to capitalize on the bungling errors of military leaders. For the more radical British pacifist George H. Perris, the Boer War encouraged absolute pacifist arguments against bearing arms. Perris urged the movement to rethink its rejection of Tolstoy and to reconsider support of resistors to conscription (such as the Russian Doukhobors). The "individual refusal to take up arms . . . and the organized strike against military service, as the ultimate weapon of democracy against militarism" were especially valuable in autocratic states, advised Perris.[72] If governments refused to find a formula to reduce the arms nightmare, then individual citizen refusal had to be considered.

Recommendations favoring conscientious objection, individual refusal to serve as a conscript or fight, usually a tool of religious peace groups, were introduced at the French National Peace Congress of 1904. The Protestant peace leader Paul Allégret wanted the national congress to campaign for the right to refuse to bear arms.[73] Allégret argued on religious grounds. However, the état-major of French pacifism closed ranks against this proposal. Charles Richet feared that both Perris's proposal and Allegrét's would invite attacks on the patriotism of pacifists, which quickly happened.[74] French pacifists could not endorse an individual's right of refusal if they intended to remain consistent in their definition of the obligations of citizenship. Individual refusals contradicted Gaston Moch's notion of the defensive militia, which would only fight in the holiest and most just of causes: to repel an invasion of la patrie. Pacifists dared not endorse such a position without inviting confusion with the unpatriotic antimilitarism represented by Gustave Hervé whose campaign against military service landed him in prison in 1905.[75] Privately, Passy complained that the dangerous ideas presented to the French peace congress only illustrated what happened when inexperienced raw recruits to the movement took the podium.[76] The idea that individual citizen refusals to bear arms might become part of the peace movement's philosophy was rejected by most Continental activists.

Bitter unremitting attacks on the arms race and its concomitant costs threaded through Italian pacifist propaganda more consistently than anywhere else on the Continent. In 1904, at a national congress, Edoardo Giretti connected the annual escalation of the arms budget with the parasitic behavior of the officer class in Italian society.[77] Not a socialist himself, nonetheless, Giretti urged pacifist colleagues to join forces with socialist organizations that were prepared to mount attacks on this rape of the public treasury. The editor of *Avanti,* Enrico Ferri, had charged the minister of the navy with corrupt practices, noting that each time Giuseppe Bettolo was appointed to the government post, the value of steel stocks in the Terni Corporation leaped on the market.[78] Bettolo resigned his post and charged Enrico Ferri with defamation of character; Giretti served as a witness for the socialist. The uproar was compounded in 1905 when the government spokesperson, Allesandro Fortis, head of the ministerial council, requested "millions to double the forces of the Italian navy and to improve the defense of our frontiers because I am a partisan of peace."[79] Despite mounting evidence that previous budgets were inflated, filled with waste, and invitations for corruption, the request passed.[80] An official inquiry conducted by largely conservative politicians admitted that "various ministers of the Navy always considered as managers of the Terni Corporation, took as good care of their interests as they did of the nation's defense."[81] Giretti crowed at the release of their five-volume report—but little changed. In Italy, the position of middle-class pacifists and most socialists differed little on the beneficiaries of the arms race.

D'Estournelles de Constant finally carried the issue of arms limitation to the Interparliamentary Union meeting in London in 1906, thus breaking its seventeen-year silence on the subject. This was the meeting that attracted considerable attention.[82] D'Estournelles de Constant wanted to persuade delegates to lobby their ministries on behalf of serious arms reduction at the coming 1907 Hague Conference. To demonstrate that arms limitation was an acceptable subject, he quoted an array of European leaders who favored it in principle. To demonstrate how self-defeating the arms race had become, he cited the Far East where a new competition blossomed between China and Japan, an obvious outcome of European policies. On the other side of the globe, Europeans had created the real "yellow peril" by the export of their model of national security. In Europe itself, from 1880 to 1905, the annual government requests for more and more money to stay abreast of new technologies led to staggering increases in spending that improved no one's sense of security. In France, spending had increased 245 million francs; in Germany—over 1 billion marks; in Great Britain—about 60 million pounds; in Italy—over 512 million lire. Also, Russia spent more than 1 billion rubles and U.S. spending increased by over 250 million dollars—even neutral Belgium added 252 million francs to its original base.[83] These expenditures were made when Europeans were not engaged in a major Continental war. In 1904, however, the Russo-Japanese War underscored pacifist warnings connecting arms expenditure, war, and revolution. The Russian Revolution of 1905 demonstrated that "henceforth, these two words, war and revolution, are inseparable."[84]

If war or its bloodless equivalent, the arms race, led to revolution, d'Estournelles de Constant invited Europe to consider the opposite situation. A decrease in costs would produce the reduction of hours of labor, . . . of the price of goods, the development of the country, the improvement of transport, of public instruction, of hygiene and the adoption of social reforms. People calculate what a country might do in the way of constructing railways, bridges, ports, machinery, schools and museums with merely a part of the money.[85]

Might it not be better to delay the Second Hague Conference, wondered d'Estournelles de Constant, so that serious public discussion on the "ascending march of war expenses" could take place?[86]

The delegates endorsed his analysis, but the Belgian representative, Goblet d'Alviella[87] insisted "let us recognize existing facts; the general arrest of armaments depends at this moment on one single power, i.e., Germany." Unless every power was willing to consider the issue, no progress would occur.

The campaign that d'Estournelles de Constant urged on parliamentarians did not succeed. In the French Sénat he pleaded:

I am not asking for disarmament; I am not even asking for a reduction in expenses, neither military nor naval. I am asking that we have the good sense to meet with those men from other countries who think as I do, to say: "All right, let us see if it is not possible to stop the increase of insane expenditure which will lead us to collapse, to revolution."[88]

The governments remained unmoved. Among peace activists in France, d'Estournelles de Constant's message produced mixed results. Maurice Bokanowski, active in the Paris section of La Paix par le droit, warned fellow pacifists not to devote too much energy to agitation for arms reduction:

Governments encourage this hope. It turns attention away from the real problems. Let us not become the dupes of the pseudohumanitarian comedy. . . . What the governments really want . . . is a total setback from the Second Hague Conference.[89]

Between the First and Second Hague Conferences, the arms control issue provoked a variety of pacifist responses. The most practical projects, transforming professional armies into national militias and managing reductions to create reasonably sized border defenses, appealed to radical, republican, and socialist activists. At international peace congresses, most delegates continued to denounce the dangers of the open-ended arms race; the threat of permanently bleeding European economies; and with the Boer War, the argument that professional armies were ineffective against determined popular defense of homelands. Under no circumstances would the international movement defend individual conscientious objection. In some communities, this position had a historic basis in peace churches; in early twentieth-century Europe, it had become the property of anarchists and radical socialist antimilitarists.[90] On the Continent, it seemed too close to the weapon of the general strike proposed by socialists as the antiwar antidote.

Prior to the Second Hague Conference, Earl Grey hinted that the British government would look favorably on an arms-reduction proposal (despite its massive new naval construction program). In the French parliament, Francis de Pressensé used the British suggestion to interpellate the French foreign minister, Stéphen

Pichon. De Pressensé, noting that France groaned under the highest per capita burden of the arms race in all Europe, urged the government to work out a proposal for a financial formula to cut armaments as the technical approach to reducing specific weaponry seemed so hard to attain. If The Hague could agree at least on a fiscal formula, argued de Pressensé, the onerous weight of armaments *à l'outrance* on the working classes might be lifted—and the potential civil war of rich and poor in France might be avoided.[91]

As foreign minister, Stéphen Pichon was shrewder than his predecessor, Delcassé. He did not denounce socialists and pacifists as *naïfs* or label them threats to French national security. He merely warned that the "absence of a concrete formula acceptable by [the Powers] makes chimerical for the moment, the limitation of military armaments."[92] Pichon did not bother to report that he had privately promised the Russians that the topic of armaments would be omitted. In the Sénat, d'Estournelles de Constant pursued it, usually with no support.[93] There, the naval minister urged prudence particularly because Great Britain and the Germans were constructing remarkable new ships—the Dreadnoughts and U-boats.[94] As the Second Hague Conference opened, Pichon promised that the French government would "continue to discuss the question with the United States, Great Britain, Spain, Italy and Japan" if no agreement came from The Hague.[95]

British and French politicians were quite safe in encouraging belief that they would honorably pursue arms reduction at the 1907 meeting—the kaiser had made it clear that Germany would not attend if that topic came up. The British ambassador in Berlin, Sir Frank Lascelles informed his London superiors that Kaiser Wilhelm

> definitely made up his mind, . . . if the question of disarmament were to be brought up . . . he should decline to be represented. . . . Each state must decide for itself the amount of military force which it considered necessary for the protection of its interests and the maintenance of its position, and no state could brook the interference of another in this respect.[96]

Thus, Earl Grey comfortably remarked "that the responsibility for the setback . . . will fall on the Emperor William and the moral impact would be considerable."[97] He encouraged the Americans to place arms reduction on The Hague agenda and told the British ambassador in Washington, "I want people here and in Germany . . . to realize that it is he [Kaiser Wilhelm] who has forced our hand in spite of our wish to limit expenditure."[98] The kaiser's fury at the possibility that arms reduction might be raised was a major reason that the Interparliamentary Union meeting planned for Berlin in 1907 was not held there until 1908.[99] The German government managed to bear the onus for an attitude shared widely among diplomats from all the major powers. In Great Britain, for instance, Eyre Crowe, the "German" expert of the Foreign Office, noted that the French would suffer most from a naval agreement at the moment. In general, he concluded, arms reduction would never be possible because there would always be "certain powers [that] do not consider themselves, at a given time, safe from serious attack."[100] In 1907, such a power was the Russian Empire, which needed to reconstruct its military and naval capacity destroyed in the war with Japan. Publicly, the apparent willingness of Great Britain to consider an arms agreement was a political ploy by which Earl Grey could handle the growing strenth of antiarmaments protest in the left-wing of the Liberal party and in the Independent Labour party at home.[101]

Central European leadership continued to confuse peace-movement pressure on arms reduction with international socialist plots.[102] Von Bülow, evidently tired of trying to put a good face on German refusal to accommodate liberal international opinion, wearily told the French diplomat, Jules Cambon, "it would be better to end [The Hague conferences] and no longer give opportunities to ideologues to periodically embarrass European cabinets with their disarmament projects."[103] In Vienna, the government planned to dispose of the limitation of armaments through another "Platonic declaration" as had occurred in 1899.[104] The Austrian government believed that any official consideration of the subject would feed antimilitarist propaganda even further.[105] Moreover, Austrian Foreign Minister Alois Lexa von Aehrenthal believed "the peace movement must be resolutely combatted for . . . [it] turns against heroism, without which a monarchical order is unthinkable."[106]

To an extent, he was correct. Liberal opinion in western Europe had been moving toward citizen-based defense if all the army was to do was *defend* territory. Von Aehrenthal's social peers, however, wanted a professional, disciplined force that might be needed for domestic police work as well as foreign struggle. His view was not substantially different from Ernest von Plener, head of the Interparliamentary Union in Austria.[107] Nor was the reactionary European view of armaments all that different than that of Theodore Roosevelt, the American president, so admired by peace activists for his role in ending the Russo-Japanese War and encouraging the Second Hague Conference. Privately, he sneered that arms reduction would merely benefit weaker, savage, or militaristic societies. The United States would have none of it.[108]

If the British were clever at avoiding the burden of rejecting discussion of arms limitation, they had no support for their position on the rights of neutrals during wartime. Both Washington and Berlin opposed the British view, which circumscribed neutral rights. Had the German diplomats been shrewder, they could have exploited this subject skillfully because peace activists and international lawyers had well-developed anti-British positions on it. Earl Grey refused to encourage the notion that "war can be made on limited liability."[109]

The minimal results of the Second Hague Conference enraged peace activists. The weakness of the moderate pacifist strategy urged by von Suttner, Passy, British religious peace activists, and Adolf Richter was transparent. Maurice Bokanowski had been correct. The diplomats did not even renew the agreed controls on battlefield etiquette passed in 1899—for example, prohibitions against launching projectiles from balloons (the airplane began to interest governments by 1907). Pacifists, who had distanced themselves from the diplomatic process of regulating warfare in order to make it "kinder," were nonetheless aware of the significance in 1907 of diplomatic silence. The French diplomat, Léon Bourgeois, knowing full well that arms reduction had been entombed again in a *vœu* (this time, of his own creation) covered the charade by asserting:

> The society of nations has been created. It is quite alive. A basis in law [is emerging from] the existing conditions of all nations and consequently [so is] international peace.[110]

The Sixth French National Peace Congress heard his words in silence.

Frustration with empty official rhetoric revived an antimilitarist mood in the resolutions and debates of international congresses. Socialist, radical, and anarchist assessments increasingly appealed to delegates at international congresses, but leaders of the French and Italian peace movements blocked this shift. Passy, Richet, Arnaud, Gaston Moch, Ruyssen, and Moneta all reiterated that "pacifists are not antimilitarists."[111] They refused to embrace a philosophy that undermined defense against invasion. Fried declared:

> Antimilitarism is not merely a danger for governments and states but also for pacifism. Antimilitarists do not merely pursue the same aim as us by different means . . . they only reject the symptoms; we attack the causes of militarism.[112]

Richet even moved to exclude all antimilitarist voices from meetings, but other delegates balked at "excommunications" of delegates.[113] (The same issue haunted the socialist and radical parties in France as well.)[114]

A different approach to arms reduction was introduced to the London Universal Peace Congress in 1908 by G. H. Perris, who recommended proposals relevant to the forthcoming London Naval Conference. Specifically, Perris urged that the British–German talks freeze naval expenditures at the amount spent in the last three previous years. Nervous German delegates at the pacifist congress amended the resolution to include the rights of neutrals during wartime, an issue that their government had thrown into the 1907 Hague Conference deliberations to undercut the British initiative about arms reductions. The pacifist discussion threatened to deteriorate into a parallel of the diplomatic exchanges and to be wrecked on the same shoals.[115] Perris sardonically commented:

> Personally, as a Socialist, I don't object to the manufacture of Socialists by the adhesion to antiquated institutions; but I believe that there is no sane man who wishes a social cataclysm to be precipitated by the refusal of those [in] power . . . to deal with the immense burden of . . . armaments. We have to face an absolute choice between the achievement of [arms reduction] and a social revolution . . . directed against the frightful hypocrisy of professions of peace whilst maintaining the weapons of war.[116]

A far-from-unanimous congress passed his proposition intended to influence the coming Anglo-German talks in a pacifist direction. The content of his proposal was less important than the fact that the delegates to the congress seemed willing to vote resolutions that lacked unanimous agreement on tendentious issues. The American delegate, Edwin D. Mead, admitted:

> The development of the machinery for the arbitration of differences by law in recent times has been very great but we cannot blind ourselves to the fact that the increase in the machinery of war has kept pace.[117]

In the last five years of peace, the subject of arms control appeared on every international peace congress agenda in some form. Perris had spearheaded a new direction in the movement.

The refusal of the diplomats in 1907 to renew their 1899 prohibition against launching projectiles from balloons assumed ominous proportions in view of the dramatic success of the Wright brothers, Wilbur and Orville. Word of the flying machine spread across Europe and its possibilities captured imaginations everywhere. The French peace community heard with astonishment that their favorite senator, d'Estournelles de Constant, argued for a one-hundred-thousand-franc appropriation for the Ministry of War to develop aviation.[118] Moreover, he wanted the government to construct *gares* (airports) in his impoverished home district (Sarthe) to create employment. By 1908, he had concluded that air power would provide better, cheaper defense for France than battleships and cruisers on the grounds that a plane cost between ten and twenty thousand francs, infinitely less than a ship and with far lower operating costs. D'Estournelles de Constant's enthusiasm was echoed by Charles Richet, who saw aviation as the solution to protectionism, a way to end customs rivalries, and thus a way to encourage international peace. Fleets of airplanes would make war so terrible, it would have to end because, Richet believed, no one would allow entire cities and sleepy villages to be incinerated.[119] Other pacifists were less certain. Charles Gide observed that governments would collect customs as easily at airports as at borders; Ruyssen remained skeptical that new inventions would make war technologically obsolete.[120] The debate continued among French pacifists with considerable passion. Richet, who was experienced with balloons, pointed out that the new airships would soon be able to carry heavy cargoes of chemicals, bombs, and dynamite; fly to one-thousand meters; and drop weapons on enemy arsenals—thus creating incendiary conditions unknown in European history. His revulsion over the possibilities of aerial annihilation led Richet to argue that the invention would have to be used for peace:

> We would prefer to see the advent of peace result from the victory of a superior morality. But what can be done! In the absence of this superior morality, there is the need to live and be happy. . . . The day when men . . . will be fully convinced that war means [complete] misery and ruin for them,—that day, war will end. It wont be from a high moral ground that they will learn the sweetness and value of human fraternity.[121]

He had no success. Delegates to the French National Peace Congress in 1909 refused to support Richet's claim that "this magnificent invention [would] be applied to destroying war."[122] Séverine summarized majority belief that "the results of all new inventions can be assessed more in destruction than benefit."[123] Similarly, in 1912 at the Genevan meeting of the Universal Peace Congress, the British delegate, Evans Darby, pleaded with fellow representatives to campaign against appropriations for airplanes and to appeal to their governments not to allow "the new horror [to be] incorporated into the domain of war."[124] Darby was especially bitter about French "progress," noting that by 1913–1914, their fleet would increase to about 500 planes, doubling the 1912 number of 230. Germany and Great Britain would soon catch up. The arms race would move from land and sea to the air. Albert Gobat supported Darby's plea by indicating how wrong Richet had been. In the 1911 war, the Italians had used a plane to bomb a Turkish hospital, a sign of the "murderous brigandage to come."[125] The congress voted to support Darby and Gobat, but it did not change the minds of those pacifists who saw the peaceful potential of airplanes. Many French pacifists were convinced that aviation promised cheaper defensive weaponry and speedier movement toward an all-European *zollverein*, a tariff-free common market.

The French position also severely divided the Interparliamentary Union. In 1912, d'Estournelles de Constant's enthusiasm for aviation as a pacific force clashed with the position of the aging president, Auguste Beernaert, who asked for a motion attacking air-launched missiles. D'Estournelles de Constant wanted to convince his fellow parliamentarians that air power offered the least expensive form of national defense, insisting, "I don't believe it will be used in war but that it will be used for peace. If it is the war minister who pays, so much the better."[126] The French failed to convince their fellow parliamentarians and Beernaert's rejection of air power and air-launched weaponry carried. However, the defeated French delegation warned that even if an arms agreement were developed at the coming Hague Conference, there would be "no right to prohibit one or another nation to choose the form of defense which best assures its security."[127] French pacifist attraction for air flight was not shared in the international movement.

Whatever shreds of caution that had characterized international peace congresses disappeared after 1911. The debate over aviation was one facet of the new "honesty." The runaway arms race, fueled to a new height of expenditure and chauvinism by German nationalists after the second Moroccan crisis of 1911, drove the absolute pacifist Benjamin Trueblood, president of the American Peace Society,[128] and the moderate patriotic French pacifist Gaston Moch into the same camp—to their mutual amazement. Both insisted that the movement launch massive lobbying efforts to persuade governments to prepare arms control projects for the coming Hague Conference.[129] Albert Gobat dropped all pretense of neutrality in an attack on nationalist Germans, whom he considered responsible for the recent round of arms escalations.[130] But the most original attack on the arms problem came from Perris in 1913 at the last prewar Universal Peace Congress assembled at The Hague.

At this meeting, the twentieth since 1889, Perris produced a report examining the nature of war industries, tying the manufacture of weaponry to the international economy as well as to national economic interests. At a congress of the middle-class peace movement, this approach was thoroughly novel. Perris drew on research carried out by the German socialist Karl Liebknecht, the Frenchman Francis Delaisi, and his own investigations in Great Britain. The links among the weapons producers, the Krupps, the Schneiders, and the Armstrongs were unraveled, as was their talent at manipulating public fear of "foreign" inventions. Perris reported on the interlocking directorates that assured profits would be shared across borders, and he listed ownership of stocks showing how the arms producers invested in each other's corporations. Sales of ships and weapons to the presumed "enemies" of the "other" nations characterized the business arrangements. The patriotism of sheer profiteering emerged as Perris described a British company, Armstrong:

> The chairman is one Sir Andrew Noble, and I beg you to note the impartiality of his patriotism. He is a Baronet and a Knight Commander of the Bath of Great Britain; a member of the Order of Jesus Christ of Portugal; and a Knight of the Order of Charles the Third of Spain. He is also a First Class of the Sacred Treasure of Japan, a Grand Cross of the Crown of Italy, and is decorated with Turkish and Chilean and Brazilian honours. His patriotism is truly a larger patriotism. *(laughter)*
>
> But, unlike our patriotism, it has a strict cash basis (applause). Messrs. Armstrong will build warships for any country in the world: they are quite impartial. They are constantly sending armor plate [everywhere] no matter what is the cause of the dispute. You will observe the double influence of these sales, for if they sell a battleship to a foreign country, it becomes an argument for increasing the British fleet in turn, and that means a new increase of orders for Armstrong, Whitworth and Coy!
>
> Some of you have, no doubt, looked down, as I have, on the chimneys of the Pozzuoli-Armstrong Company which pollute the Bay of Naples. Here Great Britain helps to maintain the fighting force of Germany's ally. There is also the Ansaldo-Armstrong Company of Genoa. These companies not only build for Italy but also for Turkey *(laughter)*. I do not know whether the warships of those two countries actually came in contact in the Tripolitan War, but if they did, they may both have been impartially built by Armstrong, Whitworth Companies.
>
> The Armstrong Company has its own ordinance and armor-plate works in Japan. It is always seeking orders for armaments in China. At the same time, in conjunction with two other British firms, Maxims and John Brown & Coy., and also in connection with Blohm and Voss of Hamburg and Messrs. Schneider, this triple alliance is building up a new fleet for Russia—at the cost of the famine-stricken peasantry.[131]

Defeated in 1902 and 1908 in his effort to introduce antimilitarist positions at peace congresses, Perris finally succeeded in convincing pacifist delegates of the baleful influence of arms merchants on governments and public opinion. The capacity of weapons producers and their economic and social allies to influence public policy had to be revealed to the public. Perris's presentation went well beyond the pleas of other peace activists who urged the movement to focus on the arms race. Whereas Bloch, Ducommun, and even Gaston Moch had warned against the frightful social and military results of using modern weaponry in a full-scale war, Perris persuaded an essentially middle-class peace movement to grasp the full implication of free trade in weapons and to support an analysis that had largely been the work of socialist critics. His success reflected a desperation by peace activists about the possibilities of failure of the next Hague Conference.

The congress also voted a stringent denunciation of war loans, urging that the free flow of capital be severed in order to make "the sinews of war . . . helpless." The peace congress agreed that "there can be no doubt that banks in London and financiers in Paris are *participes crimines* in the incitement to murder."[132] Such fury at international finance had not been aired since Richard Cobden's passionate speeches over half-a-century earlier. The anger of the congress was aroused by the experience of the Balkan Wars. Speaker after speaker argued that the poor nations of southeastern Europe would have been forced to find a diplomatic solution to their differences were they unable to borrow money to finance the military "solution." The financing of such conflict enraged the French delegate, Mlle. Jeanne Mélin. Women, she noted, "want money for the social works that concern them. They are always refused. They are always told that 'first the gaps [in defense] must be filled.'"[133] No previous international peace congress had heard that equation made by women peace activists so bluntly, though it certainly had been recognized before. The meeting in 1913 at The Hague spared no target in an attempt to preserve discretion and delicacy.

Perris drew his indictment of the international arms trade, in part, from the research of Francis Delaisi, who published a remarkable two-part article on the German and French arms industries, "The Patriotism of the Armoured Plates."[134] In the best muckraker style, Delaisi drew the parallels between the role of Krupp and Creusot in Germany and France, both energetically involved in bankrolling media campaigns to increase arms expenses, increase the years of military service, and heighten the trans-Rhine antagonism that served them so well. Delaisi wanted the public to realize that it was Hohenzollern wealth invested in the small Krupp (and other) plants that built the war matériel in 1867–1871 before sufficient German capital existed to finance such industries. In the French case, he provided the names of officers who moved into important positions in the arms industries on retiring.[135] He reported that the large military manufacturers and metallurgical suppliers had learned to control the distribution of their advertising budgets to journals and newspapers that maintained patriotic editorial policies. On the other hand, Delaisi named publications, such as *Le Petit Parisien,* that had absolutely insisted on their editorial independence. He concluded:

> On both sides of the Rhine the military metallurgical industry operates in an identical fashion. Strongly concentrated in a small number of tightly managed corporations, it attracts the chiefs of staff of the army to its boards of trustees, . . . inaugurates the programs for which they have a perpetual need, carries parliamentary victories through support by ministers and even heads of state associated to its interests, and shapes public opinion through the paid press which disseminates panic and hatred.[136]

By 1913, the peace movement had shed its timidity about arms issues. Delaisi's analysis of arms industries unified both middle-class and socialist peace analyses.

In 1913, the Interparliamentary Union also met at The Hague to celebrate the opening of the Peace Palace. To that meeting as well as to the Universal Peace Congress, Ludwig Quidde brought a "Model Project for an Arms Limitation Treaty."[137] The proposal began by admitting the realities of the international state system, the right of a nation to secure itself, and thus the right of a nation to determine its own defense needs. Annual expenses for national defense, Quidde noted, often included such items as costs of previous wars, debt service, replacement of lost or damaged equipment, colonial commitments—items that mounted up but did not impinge on immediate defense of the European homeland. Governments, he argued, legitimately could request funding for such matters, and these ought to be excluded from international discussion.

The heart of his proposal, encapsulated in a fifty-five-article proposed treaty, was a truce on spending and a freeze in all other categories. Nations could agree not to introduce new expenditures for a discreet period of time, perhaps five years. They could agree on a five-percent increase on expenditure to cover unexpected needs. Quidde's proposal was based on the assumption that all the expenditure that had accrued up to 1913 was enough. It did not consider radical departures from the status quo, such as transforming professional forces into national defense militias, letting colonies go, denying the "right of first occupation" and the obligation of Europeans to "tutor" less-developed peoples.[138] He never proposed that large and small states in Europe should eliminate the basic inequality of their relationships. Legal internationalism remained the "precondition for dealing with . . . universal disarmament"[139] But the European tension persuaded him that arms cuts could no longer wait. In 1912 at the fifth German National Peace Congress, it had been Quidde who presented the latest accounting of arms expenditure.[140] His proposal for a treaty on arms reduction presented in 1913 was part of the effort to mobilize official Europe to prepare arms-reduction proposals for the coming Hague Conference.

The frightening figures of the arms race of 1913 were framed in an imaginative chart by Charles Richet that demonstrated the costs of a war between the six Great Powers.[141] Its daily cost would range between 275 and 500 million francs. The likelihood of total European bankruptcy and collapse was assured. Even during the so-called peacetime of 1913, about twenty million Europeans were on a war footing, excluding those in smaller states outside the Triple Alliance and the Triple Entente. The costs were insupportable.

Thus, in the last years of peace, the leadership of the international movement had moved away from its original insistence on the primacy of legal institutions and began to propose methods by which governments, preparing for the next Hague Conference, could progress on arms reduction—without endangering national security. In 1912, La Fontaine challenged pacifists to line up their public rhetoric and private beliefs. Europe had become one world through the wireless, through stock markets, international insurance, standardized practices of all sorts—but Europe lived under political institutions fashioned in far more parochial centuries. Air travel would soon make "New York a suburb of London and Peking [now Beijing] a suburb of Paris," he observed. How can the antiquated politics of hatred continue in a global economy and culture?[142]

In a backhanded compliment to the potential success of pacifist attacks on arms control and reduction, the American admiral, Alfred Mahan unleashed a bitter attack. The danger of the movement, he asserted, was its "socialist" notion that greater and lesser states have the same interest and that arms reduction would benefit civilization. This, fumed the American admiral, would produce the inevitable decline and fall of Western civilization as cultural misfits would rise to take advantage of weakened superior peoples. Both arbitration and arms control, in his view, were sides of the same debased coinage.[143]

In 1914, the international pacifist community expected to convene in Vienna, to celebrate the twenty-fifth anniversary of the founding of both the Universal Peace

Congress and the Interparliamentary Union. The Universal Peace Congress was to be dedicated to Bertha von Suttner; its prime agenda item was to be Ludwig Quidde's "Model Project for an Arms Limitation Treaty." The meeting was planned for September but, of course, after the Great War began in August, it was canceled.

6

War: The Anatomy
of an Anachronism

When the war broke out in 1914, no Continental peace activist was taken by surprise. Never had the international pacifist community deluded itself. A year later in his Swiss exile, Alfred H. Fried wrote:

> *The present war is the logical outcome of the kind of "peace" which preceded it. . . .* Pacifism, which public opinion . . . has declared a failure . . . has in reality been fully justified by the war. Because we saw that war was bound to result from this condition of national isolation, we worked, warned and sought to develop the forces of organization as a preventative. We had no illusions; we were engaged in the struggle against a catastrophe which we clearly foresaw. . . . We never doubted that the opposing forces were stronger. . . . We saw the war coming.[1]

Pacifists and legal internationalists had denounced war as a lingering anachronism that threatened civilization; they never claimed that a specific war would never occur. They had characterized war among civilized nations as a flagrant contradiction of real international cultural and economic ties; they never claimed that rational forces controlled national policy decisions.

In 1914, rare was the pacifist in a belligerent nation who did not rally round the flag.[2] A quarter-century of transnational friendship among parliamentarians and private citizen activists was shelved. For most socialists in the Second International as well, a war of national defense took precedence over internationalist commitments. The rapid transformation of pacifist into soldier and patriot flowed logically from their analysis of war, peace, and justice.

One of the key elements of the prewar pacifist project had been a persistent campaign to unveil the nature of modern warfare. As prophets, pacifists were more successful than as propagandists or politicians. The human costs of modern war, the inevitable setback to economic progress, the moral decline of peoples infected by militarism, the danger to the political and social order that technologically advanced warfare entailed, and even the lethal standoff of trench warfare—all had been predicted. From the eloquent (some would say purple) prose of Bertha von Suttner's novel, *Lay Down Your Arms,* to the graphic calculations by French analysts who catalogued the misuse of European wealth—even to the use of the new medium, the moving picture, by 1913—peace activists presented war as a historic relic, an immense danger, an anachronism, a remainder from a militaristic and feudal past. Their argument has become a cliché: technological sophistication made war unwinnable and, therefore, victory impossible. When the costs of mounting a military endeavor outweighed any conceivable benefit and when victory was unattainable even after Herculean efforts were made, war as a means of policy belonged in a museum. Pacifist assessments of war derived from a few authors who sometimes took active part in congresses and on the lecture circuit. Their writings provided the intellectual underpinning that the movement craved.

The absolute rejection of war as state policy associated with British Quakers and with the Russian Leo Tolstoy had no resonance among Continental thinkers and activists.[3] Italian pacifists led the way in rejecting any hint of absolute pacifism. "Our [vision]," wrote one Milanese activist, "[was] political pacifism . . . to be achieved by political and even military means." Quakers, on the other hand, denounce all wars as "assassination . . . without understanding the difference between murder . . . for egoistical ends and killing for a nonprivate cause."[4]

Two of the main thinkers who provided wide-ranging analyses of warfare also came from tsarist Russia, where organized pacifism was hardly a feature of daily life. They were the sociologist Jacques Novicow and the Polish-born rail magnate, Jean de Bloch. Novicow and Bloch, both independently wealthy, used their leisure time to publish extensively on the history, economics, and sociology of warfare. Both spent considerable time either at peace congresses or in contact with movement leaders.

Novicow, born in Constantinople on 29 September 1849 to a Greek mother and Russian father, lived most of his life in Odessa, where he died in March 1912. Educated in Russia and Italy, he was trained in the classics and was fluent in the major European languages—Russian, German, Italian, and French with some knowledge of English. Almost all his works appeared in French, published by Félix Alcan. Heir to a family fortune, Novicow was able to devote himself to study. In his youth, he abandoned Orthodoxy to become a freethinker and an admirer of liberal Western ideals. In 1886, he attained international recognition with the publication of *La Politique internationale.*[5] It was the appearance of the massive two-volume work *Les Luttes entre sociétés humaines et leurs phases successives* that made Novicow the leading European authority on the sociology of warfare.[6] As a sociologist, he helped establish the International Institute of Sociology with René Worms in Paris, and his work *Conscience et volonté sociales* presaged arguments used by Gaetano Mosca and others on the role of elites in the formulation of ideas. Novicow's other contributions critiqued the application of Darwinism to human societies; rejected protectionism as a useful tool for developing nations; discussed poverty and its causes and cures; examined feminism and socialism; laid forth a plan for the federation of Europe based on Italian history from the Renaissance through the Risorgimento; analyzed the nature of justice; and rejected exaggerated claims for nationalism. In fifteen major books and numerous articles, Novicow established a solid reputation that disappeared after the war. On the occasion of his death, Charles Richet described him as:

> A true European, an internationalist among internationalists. Speaking French, Italian, Greek and Russian with the same ease, he knew the literature of these various countries and he extended his thinking beyond the borders of his own country.
> He described himself proudly and justly as a European and he used his impartiality admirably to fight prejudices of all Europeans.[7]

Novicow began with an organicist conception of sociology, which compared human society to a biological corpus—both collections of smaller parts. The body was a particular collection of cells, "fulfilling determined functions but laboring together for the benefit of the whole body." A society is "a collection of families grouped in a particular manner fulfilling determined functions but working together for the good of the social *corpus*."[8] Novicow argued that "the social organism is a direct extension of the biological organism and both share the same nature,"[9] a position he modified by integrating psychological material into the functioning of social groups. But the most significant result of this approach was the logical deduction that extreme individualistic and competitive behaviors did not favor "progress." To Novicow the cooperative activities of both biological and human organisms accounted for enhancement and achievement, not destructive, violent, and militaristic solutions. Misapplied and abusive usages of Darwinian biology along with wrongheaded protectionist legislation, presumably designed to enhance national economies, were the work of policy makers and scholars who misread the lessons of history and sociology. He tangled with such notables as Gabriel Tarde on issues of national policy and sociological analysis.[10] His sociological analyses paralleled the biological arguments of Pyotr Kropotkin in *Mutual Aid*.[11]

Sociologists and politicians confounded the meaning of struggle (*lutte*) and war (*guerre*), argued Novicow. Struggle existed throughout human history. In primitive eras, the struggle for food, goods, wealth, and comforts that characterized daily life, did not necessarily mean the elimination or annihilation of other humans.[12] In the four basic categories of social existence—physiological or biological, economic, political, and intellectual—forms of struggle occurred that ranged from simple or primitive to complex and interdependent variations. Most modern complex societies evolved through all the stages. In simpler social systems, in the distance past, some examples of direct extermination of enemies for food—as in cases of cannibalism—could be documented. But as complex societies developed, most peoples turned to farming to acquire food. Marauding tribes gave way to politically organized communities; in historic time, the conquest by one leader of another's territories became a system for changing the families at the top. The rank and file of humanity remained relatively untouched by most conquests. Over long periods of time, as political stability emerged, Novicow identified an evolutionary movement toward higher morality as brute force gave way to legal controls.

Novicow maintained that violence tended to be rationalized and displaced as societies advanced. By the fourteenth and fifteenth centuries when Renaissance Florence flourished, for instance, the population had developed such a detestation of violence and such a taste for peace that it preferred to hire mercenaries than to fight directly. Populations with skills and sophisticated training had little thirst for battlefield glory.[13] Florentines were in the vanguard of civilization in the fifteenth century, the center of an international trade, early capitalist practices, and banking and manufacturing. To Lorenzo de' Medici, glory consisted of being remembered in the future as a poet, patron of the arts, and ornament of a high civic culture.

Similarly, pacific forms of struggle—and not direct annihilation—characterizes modern economic relationships. Healthy competition among producers was to be prized, not direct theft of another's possessions. If modern economies were functioning properly, the contribution of each nation would also be respected and welcomed, not strangled by regulation. Older forms of confiscation lingered—protectionism was a case in point—but the worst atavism from the past was warfare. To Novicow it belonged in the same category as infanticide, murder, assassination, rape—all, presumably, repulsive to modern man.

Just as forms of violence were tamed and transformed into forms of socially acceptable struggle, Novicow argued that the nature and limits of human organizations also altered. From family and clan, through tribe and nation, modern society has produced the national state and multinational empire. No historical evidence, he observed, proved that any unit of human organization was its "final" form, and those authors who maintained that the modern nation-state, reflecting race or ethnic "purity" and greatness, were poor scholars. They were obviously either reflecting or manipulating popular prejudices.[14]

He argued that the forces altering history were always in struggle but that this struggle was not necessarily violent. Competitive struggle, particularly in intellectual and economic arenas, was the driving force of progress; but it did not require physical annihilation. So, Novicow concluded, government policies designed to obliterate national languages (i.e., German oppression of native Polish speakers; Russian policies toward German and Polish speakers) as a way toward creating a "higher" political unity were as wrongheaded as Turkish attempts to eliminate Armenian identity.[15] (This was his oblique way of criticizing tsarist repression of Polish, Finnish, and other cultures in the empire.) Healthy societies had nothing to fear from the exchange of ideas and the vitality of national cultures that they embraced. To Novicow the mark of a sophisticated and civilized nation was tolerance of debate and freedom of exchange. Competition of ideas "is the principal driving force of modern society." That was what he meant by struggle.[16]

An analysis of the numerous years of warfare in the Western world from 1500 B.C. to A.D. 1860—a total of 3360 years—revealed that there were only about 230 years of peace in over three millennia. In Europe alone, from the sixteenth through the nineteenth century, Novicow counted 286 wars. What had this bloody record achieved? In Novicow's view, precious little. Would yet another war produce any different outcome? Not likely.[17] Did this consistent pattern of warfare prove the contentions of writers such as Joseph de Maistre, that war was divine retribution for human folly? Did this record prove that war was part of the natural order, a position taken by numerous Hegelians and social Darwinists?

To Novicow such arguments revealed the stubborn persistence of antiquated mentalities, "diseased" centers of the social corpus. (He used the word *sensorium* to mean the intellectual and creative source, an elite brain trust, that generated the ideals that defined each society.) When a society became afflicted with an unhealthy set of "cells" in its intellectual center, its future became uncertain. Novicow sarcastically pointed to a substantial number of European nations burdened with aging elites from whom glory, honor, and pride were measurable in an "idolatry of square kilometers."[18] Such thinking preserved the absurd notion that conquest meant progress. The modern struggle was one that pitted this form of thinking against the new history and the new reality—internationalism. The healthy portions of the European sensoria were locked in a combat with an array of ministers, diplomats, parliamentarians, editors, writers, and scholars who threatened the future by their celebration of violence or, at least, their cynical acceptance of the inevitability of war. There are, observed Novicow:

> Celebrated historians who believe that their only mission is to recount the circumstances that influenced the territorial limits of States. Conquest hypnotizes us. The desire for aggrandizement has been foremost for so many centuries . . . that it relegates all other social preoccupations to the realm of the unconscious. Mechanical inventions . . . have revolutionized the human condition . . . [but] who knows the names of [their inventors]? In their own countries, perhaps, a few names are popularly known [but] who—in England, for example—does not know Wellington?[19]

There were eminent sociologists, such as Ludwig Gumplowicz, who believed in the inevitability of war between German and Slavic peoples, or popularizers, such as René Millet, who eulogized war as the ultimate psychological experience of humankind. To Millet, for instance, nothing in modern life compared to the exultation of Napoleon's triumph at Austerlitz. Novicow asked him how the spiritual value of Austerlitz could be of any use to Russian widows—or, alternately, if Millet was willing to write a companion piece describing the thrill that Sedan provided to the French.[20]

In Novicow's view, there was no question but that the real advances of civilization were the result of cooperative yet competitive human behavior, not annihilation. Capability, inventiveness, and creativity improved the human condition. From nomadic to industrialized society, from feudal hierarchy to parliamentary rule, brutality was replaced by lawful behavior and, were this process to continue, Novicow envisioned a day when women would be included in the political process.[21] But despite the powerful positive forces that shaped progress, the threat posed by the *Junkers* [to use Novicow's term for retrograde parts of the elites], "tied to archaic instincts of brutality . . . deeply rooted in . . . the immense majority of the human species," could break loose.[22] Seriously challenged, Novicow warned mournfully, they will let loose the horrific weapons of modern European industry and "the future battles of Europeans will be frightful holocausts."[23] Given the fragile ties that controlled this force, Novicow urged European liberals and progressives to collaborate wherever possible for the future. This staunch apostle of liberalism even went so far as to proclaim that "socialism, pacifism and feminism are the three great hopes of our times."[24]

Between 1896 and 1902, Novicow contributed his time to the organized peace movement, chairing its committees on the study of war and international organization. He published in pacifist journals, notably *La Vita internazionale,* and exercised an important influence on Alfred Fried, who saw in Novicow's work a scientific and scholarly basis for antiwar activism. Welcomed to the international movement, Novicow became a friendly critic. His complaint about the movement was directed at its central ideology, which (he argued) focused so totally on arbitration that it lost sight of the larger picture and drove away potential recruits because of boredom.

In his view, the movement failed to emphasize the probability that, even if a real war between the armed camps of Europe did not break out, the international anarchy would eventually have the same effect and undermine the civilized world. Novicow was astounded at the blindness of those liberal analysts who ignored the obvious tensions bred by class hostility, to him, a product of vastly misused resources. The immense inequality in the enjoyment of European wealth, exacerbated by spiraling arms expenses and protectionism, was the direct result of this anarchy. He calculated that ninety percent of European wealth sustained the top ten percent of its population in great comfort, a formula that promised social catastrophe.[25] Thus, he insisted, the logical route for pacifists was an attack on the international disorder itself, and concomitantly, a series of proposals that would promote alternate models of international federation and collaboration. Those who shied from this, he maintained, "demonstrate a mediocre understanding of the past."[26] This past was exemplified particularly in the history of Switzerland and Italy, two models of unification in Europe that provided orderly government for peoples once bitterly divided by wars, language or dialects, dynasties, and the accidents of history.[27] Novicow pleaded with European liberals and pacifists alike to energize their movements. They "could have a magnificent program," if they would focus on building "international security as they have established security within the state."[28] Were European liberals and pacifists to fail to address this challenge, probably the success of socialism would be assured. The Second (Socialist) International seemed to understand historical forces better than the liberals did. As a result, socialists will establish

> the liberty of nations . . . just as the freedom of the individual . . . was established by the bourgeosie. . . . The Third Estate will have had the glory of producing the rights of man; the Fourth Estate, the greater glory of creating the rights of nations.[29]

Pacifists avoided adopting Novicow's promptings to focus on federation and international organization as the key argument of their propaganda. Many worried that such a position would merely inspire more charges of utopianism. For his part, Novicow was fully persuaded that a European parliament—even constituted among a handful of willing nations—was likely to succeed and, if presented convincingly by pacifists, likely to persuade a broader public. The probable success of a permanent body to which parliamentary European nations sent delegates would provide powerful incentives for other nations to join. Novicow hinted that such an association would also serve as a powerful lever for the liberalization of conservative and reactionary regimes—though he carefully never named which ones he had in mind. Europeans, Novicow thought, had reached a sufficiently complex level of mutual interests to enable an embryonic legislature to work.[30] If pacifists were to continue their supremely cautious approach to peace propaganda, they would lose the golden argument that the war system gave them. "The peace party," urged Novicow, "must have a very advanced program because it has a special function to exercise in societies; that of opening new horizons, of showing the way which peoples and governments must follow."[31] Novicow based his view of pacifist propaganda on his fundamental belief that war had become absurd, useless, and unnecessary among Europeans, who had reached a stage of evolution where they were ready for new political institutions.

A few pacifists, notably in France and Italy, were not persuaded that all war was futile. Certainly the kind of massive upheavals unleashed by dynastic states in the seventeenth and eighteenth centuries or more recently by Napoléon were utterly pointless. But, for Théodore Ruyssen, one of Novicow's admirers, warfare occasionally produced unintended benefits:

> The colossal failure of the Crusades opened Christian ports to oriental civilization. The Italian wars, disastrous for our armies, expedited the maturation of the Renaissance in France; the Thirty Years War brought religious peace to Europe; Valmy and Jemappes opened Germany to the Revolution.[32]

Nonetheless, Ruyssen never believed that the positive by-products of warfare could only materialize after international violence. Nor did he accept the argument made by contemporaries in Germany that the immense prosperity of the new empire was the direct result of the Franco-Prussian War. Ruyssen insisted that much of Germany's economic miracle had been apparent before political unification in 1871. Ruyssen only intended to modify the absolute rejection of all warfare by Novicow.

Jean de Bloch, the second voice from the Russian Empire, also came to the peace movement as a friendly critic, having established his Europeanwide reputation with the publication of his six-volume study of war in St. Petersburg in 1898 in Russian, quickly followed by translations into German and French. Born in 1836 in Radom (Russian Poland), Bloch made a fortune in European Russia, largely through rail construction, military commissaries, and banking. During the 1880s he turned to studies of economic development and military modernization because the political atmosphere in St. Petersburg, after the assassination of Alexander II in 1881, became distinctly chilly for self-made millionaires. The result of these studies was the amazing collection of statistics and arguments that Bloch wove into his famous study of the economic, technical, and political impact of a future war between the Dual Alliance and the Triple Alliance.

Bloch's basic assumption was that both sides would enjoy such a terrible equality that only a stalemate of unimaginable horror would emerge. (This prediction was also made by the German general Colmar von der Goltz). Although no victory was possible, both sides would stubbornly persist—and a bloodbath unseen in Europe since the Mongol invasions would result.[33] After initial battles, Bloch predicted that the two sides would dig into the ground, shooting at each other from subsoil trenches:

> It is not unlikely that in future war on the battlefield, there will appear small trenches [*abris*] in the earth which resemble molehills, in which the enemy can be hidden from view and behind which, sharpshooters will fire at the opposing lines, as they wish. In that way, [soldiers] shall be protected both from rifle fire as well as artillery.[34]

In such warfare, "everybody will be entrenched," argued Bloch; "the spade will be as indispensable to a soldier as his rifle."[35] Behind and beneath their walls of earth, armies will be immobilized and officers will face the problem of getting their men to go out on offensives. But, once they attempt to overrun the top, enemy firepower will annihilate the first wave, soldiers will be encased behind hills of fallen comrades, and cavalry will be totally useless.[36] Because these armies would mainly be composed of conscripts, Bloch wondered how long they would be willing to endure indiscriminate slaughter. How long could ordinary soldiers watch their friends incinerated by melanite?

Months, perhaps years, of such attrition would enfeeble the modern economies that fed this future war; thus bankruptcy would follow. Civilian stamina would vary according to the ability of governments to supply daily needs, a problem that Bloch expected would rapidly test the abilities of all Europe. As an example, he studied the availability of selected foodstuffs (including oats) and concluded that after one year, no state could produce enough for men and beasts.[37] Using costs based on prices in the mid-1890s, Bloch estimated that a war in Europe would average about four million pounds a day, a figure that did not take into account the probable rise in commodity prices once war began.[38] After even one year of such expense, the debt that nations would assume could only be paid off by a generation of grinding poverty. An investment banker, Bloch could not understand the use of capital to create bankruptcy.

The next logical conclusion, promised Bloch, was revolution. The self-destruction of Europe by its military and political leaders, were they to unleash the war of equally horrible technological forces, would give credence to socialist and anarchist appeals. Hecatombs of young men would be dead and no victory possible. Battlefields would be filled with smoke and corpses—all for nothing. Modern technology applied to weaponry would produce such extraordinary butchery that war, itself, lost its rationale. Governments would lose whatever claim to legitimacy they had:

> The very development that has taken place in the mechanism of war has rendered war an impracticable operation. The dimensions of modern armaments and the organization of society have rendered its prosecution an economic impossibility and finally, if any attempt were made to demonstrate the inaccuracy of my assertions by putting the matter to a test on a grand scale, we should find the inevitable result in a catastrophe that would destroy all existing political civilization.[39]

Clearly the advent of a real war unleashed by the European alliances against each other was the death knell of old Europe. Bloch, however, went further. Even without a real war, the preparations that were under way would create the same result. The armed peace, with its ritualized annual escalations of arms budgets, would produce the same effect:

> The military expenses of Germany, England, Italy, France and Austria, constantly increasing, are leading to the ruin of Europe; agricultural and industrial output are already become the prey of America which—having no military budgets nor debts from former wars to pay, can use all its labor power . . . to produce everything at lower prices. There is no doubt that America will benefit from a European conflict to grab the world's markets from European industry.[40]

The armed peace "is nothing but a disguised war" taking place without bloodshed and more slowly.[41] Its costs can be measured by the constant growth of socialism, its new recruits, its parliamentary successes, its political publications, its journals, the size of crowds who come to hear speakers, its confidence in its future. Bloch, ever the quantifier, counted and catalogued socialist and anarchist publications, region by region, nation by nation, year by year.[42] He concluded that the increased size of socialist representation in European parliaments reflected the armed peace. As a result of unprofitable investments in military establishments, wages were artificially depressed, capital for investment was reduced, and the lives of the producing classes were perennially intolerable.[43] The maldistribution of wealth, in Bloch's assessment, was not the result of the capitalist system itself but a product of state expenditures in the economy on items that, themselves, did not reproduce wealth.

His expectations about the probable triumph of socialism turned out to be inaccurate only in its location. Bloch expected that the very backwardness of Russia would protect it against radical upheaval in a war and that the history and economy of France would make it the most likely candidate for revolution. Moreover, in France, he noted, authorities would have particular difficulties from women. There was a long tradition of activism among French women, from the Great Revolution to the *petroleuses* of the Commune to the ordinary outspokenness of shopwomen and the sophisticated organizations of suffrage feminists. Bloch considered French women to be immensely influential in domestic decision making and unsubmissive to husbands. In a long and grueling war, he fully expected them to organize to overthrow the government.[44] Other sources of internal discord were the ethnic tensions he expected would undermine the Austrian state and the probability of famine, which he fully expected to explode in Italy. Italians were his other possible revolutionaries during a prolonged war.

In his study, every conceivable detail about modern land and sea weaponry was charted, illustrated, evaluated, and plotted on graphs. Statistics summarizing the sizes of the major national military forces, the social and economic profiles of European nations, and changes in the sizes of military forces provided readers with an encyclopaedic understanding of the revolution in modern warfare that had occurred by the 1890s. Bloch realized that a future war would not replicate the relatively swift conflicts of 1866 and 1870–1871. He was one of the very few who foresaw the nature of "total war." For English-speaking readers, the main points were digested in a one-volume summary that became available after 1903.[45] Bloch's prestige was enhanced, of course, when word spread that he had helped persuade Tsar Nicholas II to issue the Rescript of 1898, which led to the First Hague Conference.[46]

In the late 1890s, Bloch developed a European and American following. During The Hague Conference itself, he was a familiar figure at receptions for diplomats and in lecture halls. By 1899, he was in regular contact with organized pacifism. Bloch gave the movement its most important scientific analysis of the probable outcome of modern war. No previous single work provided such a thorough examination, such detailed prognostication and stunning proof of ideas that pacifists held to be self-evident.

Bloch had not begun his researches with any awareness of peace literature. At the end of his book and throughout the few years left in his life (he died in 1902), he—like Novicow—also urged peace activists to reorient their argument. After his initial contact with organized pacifism, Bloch pleaded with movement activists to change their approach. As a participant in the 1900 (Paris) and 1901 (Glasgow) Universal Peace congresses, Bloch brought his message directly onto the floor.

Generally, he reminded pacifists that, despite the impressive growth in their numbers and their publications, the other side was winning. Arms budgets soared madly and global violence was uncontained. Battlefield behavior, as in the case of the Europeans in China after the Boxer Rebellion, was especially vicious. A few superrich citizens benefit from arms expenditures and overseas adventures. Popular opinion seemed either resigned to, or supportive of, the necessity of extending dominion over weaker peoples as a sign of greatness. Bloch feared that European moral fiber was already fatally compromised by militarism. Drawing on Tolstoy, he reminded peace activists:

> It would seem that the first duty incumbent on those who would wish to rid the nations of mutual slaughter and pillage is to reveal to the masses, the force that they are enslaved by.[47]

In Bloch's view, peace activists must focus on real events, such as the Boer War. Their literature and propaganda must drop its abstract language and emphasize the brutality of the present. The public must learn, argued Bloch, that modern technology could not overcome the resistance of a stubborn civilian population determined to prevent highly equipped professionals from driving them out of their lands. For a war to be pursued under such circumstances, a government risks destroying the morale of its own soldiers, encouraging acts of brutality against civilians, murdering innocent noncombatants, and wiping out the tools, farms, and villages where no actual fighting had occurred—just to punish. Bloch fully grasped the fact that the Boer War was different. Pacifists should leap at the opportunity to do more than deplore its horrendous bloodshed. The movement must teach a wider public that traditional victory could never be gained in modern warfare. Thus, war—even in Carl von Clausewitz's much admired definition: an extension of politics by other means—was a counterproductive tool. In the long run, it would guarantee the decline and degeneration of the victor.

Bloch wanted the movement to employ graphic, sensationalist images. Before his death, he planned a Museum of War and Peace which opened, in fact, in Lucerne to considerable fanfare. Unfortunately, the funding and management of the museum was not clearly established, and it did not last more than a few years.[48] But his most important contribution to the movement was the wide publicity given to his views. He provided the international movement with a vast amount of information to argue against technocrats and a broad vision incorporating data from various disciplines. Bloch's work followed by the tsar's Rescript provided the peace movement with an unexpected bonanza of publicity. Respectable European journals began to publish serious evaluations of the cost of the arms race.[49] From Bloch's work, committed peace activists drew inspiration for renewed campaigning. Even the aged Passy reconsidered the idea that only America would benefit economically in the long run from the disastrous European arms race, a position he had eschewed.[50] Lucien Le Foyer—a prominent Freemason, well-known Radical politician, and a new recruit to the French peace movement in the years before the war—dipped regularly into Bloch's cornucopia for his exhausting round of lectures and essays attacking the arms race.[51] Among his labors, Le Foyer organized a widely circulated petition that went to the diplomats at The Hague pleading with them to conclude more than a "face-saving" formula to protect the tsar's dignity.[52] In a short popularization of Bloch's thesis, Le Foyer postulated a modern war between two armies, eight million men each, charging from trenches under a deadly hail of bullets; fortified countrysides and besieged cities choking modern economic life; and the unpredictable nature of the financial needs of such a war destroying national solvency. Modern warfare was "a sphinx of whom none can pretend to unravel the mystery," declared Le Foyer.[53] If Bloch's guess was only half-right, it is clear that the pacifists were the ones with a solid grasp of reality in contrast to the architects who planned for Armaggedon on the grounds that arms would prevent a war from happening.[54]

Élie Ducommun, scrupulously neutral in his role as executive secretary of the International Peace Bureau, dropped his customary reticence under Bloch's influence and published another short popularization, *Les Conséquences qu'aurait une guerre européenne*[55] in order to give peace activists a pithy updated statement of Bloch's thesis. By 1906, Ducommun reported that the alliances were prepared to field twenty million men, not the sixteen million of Le Foyer's work. Moreover, the new European system involved six, not five, nations and the world's largest navy—the British. Perhaps, Ducommun argued dubiously, this new alliance system might actually brake a slide toward war, but if the brake failed, the actual war would probably cost about forty billion francs per annum, a figure that would exhaust the combined savings of all Europe in one year. Using the "lessons" of the Transvaal and the more recent Russo-Japanese War, Ducommun confessed he could not understand how Ludwig von Moltke's prediction—that a war was likely to last two years—was accurate. Ducommun predicted a holocaust on a shoestring.[56] Moreover, the Russo-Japanese War, concluding in the Russian Revolution of 1905, fulfilled Bloch's general prophecy tying war to revolution.

In an uncanny piece of prescience, Ducommun wondered what would happen to the small states were the big powers to undertake a general war:

It is not absolutely certain that the belligerents would resist—in the course of military operations—the temptation to cut a passage through neutral territory, following the requirements of attack . . . or retreat. Most likely, neutral populations will defend their own land from invasion, . . . increasing the scope of war fare.[57]

Finally, Ducommun reminded readers that in previous wars, at least ten percent of combattants were killed and about the same number left permanently maimed. Substantial civilian death rates from disease, poverty, famine, and general deprivation often followed major wars, as well. In a future war lasting two years, Ducommun conservatively estimated a death toll of about two million men. Drawn from the most vital, productive, and promising segment of the population, their loss was irreparable. He also demanded to know who were the dreamers and who were the realists.

The French physiologist, Charles Richet, following Bloch's method, noted that the rate of expenditure for armaments from 1870 to 1913 had increased at a geometric rate. In 1913, there was no evidence that this massive outlay had made anyone safer than their grandparents were in 1870. What was clear was that working families lived deprived lives and that scientific research was stymied for lack of laboratories, basic materials, and student scholarships. In 1913, he calculated that an all-out European war would cost about 275 million francs per day; if civilian costs were added, it would rise to 500 million. Were such figures even imaginable?[58] Richet also wondered what the meaning of utopian and the meaning of realist were.

In addition to Bloch, Richet also drew on Novicow's criticism of social policy based on social Darwinism. As a scientist, Richet had no patience with sloppy thinking. No analogy existed between the animal–plant kingdoms and human domains that offered the remotest basis for state policies and social ideals. Warfare, he insisted, was a uniquely human condition, a "social invention," and not a product of universal natural forces.[59] To those who argued for a *Machtstaat,* a vulgarized Hegelian entity that confused power, size, morality, and "destiny for greatness," Richet pointed to tiny Denmark. Would anybody reasonably argue that Danes were an inferior breed of humanity because of the size of their state? Did they seem foolish, backward, part of a lower order of evolution?[60] Clearly, the claims that warfare was essential to purge humanity of its lower, regressive, and inept members was a self-serving rationalization of militarists.

Besides Novicow and Bloch, the Belgian economist Gustave de Molinari, the Italian entrepreneur and economist Edoardo Giretti, and the Italian historical sociologist and journalist Guglielmo Ferrero contributed analyses of the role of war in history. All three agreed that warfare had played a significant, indeed, positive role in earlier periods. All three also agreed with Novicow and Bloch that advanced civilization would be destroyed by modern warfare and the military buildups that preceded it.

De Molinari (1819–1912), an established author by the time Novicow was born (1849), became the editor of *L'Économiste belge,* the *Journal des économistes,* and the *Journal des débats.* Over decades of writing, he propounded his analyses of the interconnection of war, peace, economic development, and social relationships. At the close of the nineteenth century, he published several works synthesizing his life's work on these topics.

For de Molinari, ancient warfare had played a positive role. Early agrarian communities had to defend themselves against marauding tribes. Only the existence of superior weaponry preserved the settled community from onslaughts of overwhelming numbers of hostile intruders, and without such settlements, civilization would not have developed.[61] Warfare, too, permitted the development of the state that de Molinari maintained, was crucial for the protection of early advances in production, trade, technology, and social stability. In a few cases, notably ancient Rome, the state was able to perform the task of civilizing other peoples after having served as a buffer against aggressors.

Warfare, however, changed. Once stability was established, the object became acquisition of wealth, power, profit, lands, and areas for investment of capital. In Europe, following the end of barbarian threats, from the eleventh to eighteenth centuries, the function of warfare became essentially economic. It provided the means by which Europeans developed a dynamic economy. In the nineteenth century, this function was globalized—in Asia, Africa, and the islands of the seven seas:

> The peoples belonging to our civilization have invaded the huge domain occupied by inferior or backward [sic] peoples; America, Oceania, the better part of Asia have fallen to their control and they divide up Africa today. The time is not far when they shall be the incontestable global masters.
>
> The ease with which they extend their conquests and totally obliterate resistance of the most bellicose peoples, proves that the danger of invasion has completely disappeared. . . . Civilization is fully assured against barbarism. War has achieved this assurance of security . . . and in ceasing to be useful, it has lost its reason for being.[62]

There was nothing sentimental or moralistic in de Molinari's "value-free" description of the conquest of backward peoples. Until relatively recent times, he assessed warfare as a generally beneficial means of the development of civilization and modern economic triumphs. War and conquest provided the basis for free enterprise, which he considered the only rational economic system. Warfare had assured the safety of the Continent from lesser hordes. Its day was done.

De Molinari moved to the next logical stage. If Europeans continued to prepare for warfare, they would endanger the very capital formation they had already secured. Advanced civilization did not need to stockpile weapons and continue strategic planning. Why, then, did they behave irrationally?

His answer was found in the very process by which states had evolved. A special class had been created in the evolution of the nation-state, a class concerned with its military and bureaucratic development. Their descendents survive intact and are ever anxious for their portion of state revenue. War and its preparation provided benefits to

> the military hierarchy by accelerating advancement in grade and pay; . . . to the politician by increasing his power and influence, and to a third class in the state, the officials, for it enlarges the scope of their activity.[63]

Despite the fact that these elites play no useful function, they remain entrenched. From his viewpoint, since the French Revolution, they have been superfluous because "throughout the civilized world, pacific interests in number and importance outweigh . . . [warfare]," but

> the control of State affairs continues—despite all the revolutions and political reforms,—to belong to a class whose professional interest . . . [is] in immediate opposition with those of the interest whom they govern. There lies the real cause of wars which now, more than ever, undermine the world, for warfare has no more purpose.[64]

De Molinari was as critical of parliamentary states as he was of autocratic regimes; he was as cynical about the "free press" as he was of government mouthpieces. The press was run by the same groups that benefited by the perpetuation of the military–political bureaucracy. Clearly, the solution for the preservation of warfare in a world where it was superfluous, was by eliminating the elites whom it sustained, but de Molinari would not countenance revolution. His solution was in the creation of an international order.

In line with Novicow's pessimism, de Molinari expected that liberals would fail to achieve that rational solution, and thus only socialists would benefit from the likely collapse of Europe.

The Italian economist, industrialist, and member of parliament Edoardo Giretti (1864–1940)[65] also developed an analysis of war and militarism similar to that of de Molinari. Giretti, raised in the Waldensian creed of pre-Reformation Protestantism that survived in the mountain valleys of the Piedmont area around Turin, became an exponent of free trade liberalism in Italy and a well-known critic of the protectionist craze that blossomed during the 1880s and 1890s. Acerbic, Giretti denounced the large industries that needed protection in order to cover their deficiencies. He was a successful entrepreneur and an advocate of small and medium-size companies to help develop his nation, which was poor compared to Great Britain, France, Germany, Belgium, and the United States. Aware of the lag between Italy and the others, Giretti was furious at the capital wasted in Italy in the vain effort to remain a leader in the arms race. He saw no advantage to naval and land armaments when most of the nation needed roads and schools.

In 1896 and 1911, when the Italian government undertook foreign military adventures in East Africa that cost blood and money, Giretti led the opposition. Remarkably, he withstood horrendous denunciations as a traitor, especially in 1911 when he denounced the Italian attack on Libya-Cyrenaica. For Giretti, this sort of war, undertaken for the usual imperialist reasons, was no more justified than an attack on a European neighbor. As a consistent critic of overseas conquest, Giretti parted company with de Molinari and many other social scientists who supported peace activism *and* imperialism.

Given the particular needs of the Italian economy and the obvious misuse of limited wealth to support a military establishment, Giretti argued that the annual escalation of arms expenditure only occurred to underwrite a parasite class. A meeting of Italian peace organizations in 1904 heard Giretti charge:

> The careers of military commanders and of the administrative and colonial bureaucracy, once reserved only for the cadets of ancient, feudal and noble families, today

have become a comfortable sinecure for the enervated bourgeosie, which—lacking initiative and the will to work, but anxious for secure income—is willing to take from the State . . . for the maintenance and education of its offspring to which it regularly gives birth.[66]

The power of these social classes to distort development and hamper progressive improvement was such that Giretti (no fan of socialist solutions), nonetheless, insisted that middle-class peace activists had to build ties to socialist organizations. Only in a coalition would strength be found to counter the power of those who have access to state wealth.

In the analysis developed by Guglielmo Ferrero (1871–1942), the past, examined through case studies, offered insights into the role of war played in social evolution. Ferrero's interest in the subject was evident as early as high school, when he won a contest sponsored by the Milanese Peace Society on the causes of war. His reputation was established in 1898 when *Il Militarismo* was published, a work that reflected on the distant past with a perspective fashioned by events surrounding him. These events included a brutal military repression of uprisings, sparked by food shortages, which General Bava Beccaris carried out. The domestic nature of militarism was made very clear to Milanese liberals, radicals, socialists, pacifists, and even Catholics as the heavy-handed general used cannon against— among others—homeless people lined up at a monastery for food. Military tribunals dispensed justice thereafter and numerous eminent socialist and Radical leaders received lengthy jail terms. The domestic ramifications of militarism to Ferrero was not a theoretical issue—it was as real as a walk down the street.

Ferrero emphasized the emotional, psychological, and impulsive sources of war and violence. Using the whirling dervishes in the Sudan as a case, he examined "primitive" experience where warfare was an unbridled opportunity to plunder, to exult, and to break the routines of struggle for bare survival. Their enthusiasm reflected "the instinct for destruction inherent in man" and the childlike belief "that happiness could be found in destruction."[67] In precivilized societies, communities in states of nature, observed Ferrero, little self-control was exercised over impulse. Self-control, patience, and wisdom were conditions that characterized higher forms of social evolution.

Ferrero did not explain the processes by which ancient civilizations grew from primitive communities. But even as the capacity for philosophy, the arts, complex economic arrangements, and sophisticated legal systems arose, warfare did not disappear. Given its frequency, Ferrero observed, it served some useful purpose, essentially economic, "[It reflected] the difficulty that they had in finding new employment for accumulated capital, a condition . . . partly the cause and partly the effect of the unlaborious habits of the population."[68] In ancient society, Ferrero explained, warfare was a source of employment and a means of capital formation among peoples with limited inventiveness and labor patterns. Such conditions have disappeared. The main characteristic of modern society are the classes who

occupy themselves in putting accumulated capital to good use, directing work, perfecting and multiplying instruments and machinery, not from any noble sentiments of social duty but for the same reasons that aristocracies of the past went to war so frequently—for the accumulation of great and superfluous wealth, the chief cause of the creation of modern commerce and industry.[69]

Consequently, modern Europe attained a level of development (especially after the German and Italian unifications) that not only made war unnecessary but an atavistic catastrophe. For a place such as the Ottoman Empire, a paralyzed society, Ferrero saw some value in violence to abolish the "oligarchy in power" and substitute another "more desirous of progress and civilization, . . . [willing to remedy] the present evils and rehabilitate that portion of Asia."[70]

Far more relativistic in his appraisal of warfare than other writers of the prewar generation, Ferrero was also less convinced that a federation of Europe or an international security system were plausible or even a logical answer to the problem of war. As an Italian, he was not able to overlook the differences between the advanced economies of England, France, and Germany vis-à-vis the backward, debt-burdened nations—Italy and Russia. The former three enjoyed civilization; the latter two, only a superficial appearance.[71] There was far greater reason for poorer nations to work for reductions of armaments, to fear war and to struggle against it. Elaborate military arsenals in countries where the peasants could not even afford the food they grew (a favored example of his was Sicilians exporting their oranges to London dockworkers) were patently absurd, but this kind of reasoning would have no effect on the political authorities in the larger states. The answer—if there was one—for Ferrero was to persist in a struggle to educate a sufficient part of the population to grasp the realities of modern international economic life and to understand that militarism was a crushing mental burden from the past that threatened to foreclose the future. Never once did Ferrero believe the argument that improved armaments would better preserve the peace; he was convinced that they would be tried out on battlefields one day.

Bloch, de Molinari, and Novicow all died before World War I. Ferrero lived to see World War II, exiled from Italy in 1930 after enduring years of house arrest under the Fascists. It was his unreconstructed refusal to abandon his principles, especially his insistence on freedom of speech and expression, that persuaded Benito Mussolini to spend hundreds of dollars a day on his incarceration—until international pressure embarrassed the regime to allow Ferrero to go to Geneva in order to take up a post as professor of international relations.[72]

Contemporary writers who shared some of the outlook of peace activists attacked the claims made by Darwinian vulgarizers who persisted in defining war as "survival of the fittest." Using the evidence from China, where a joint European expedition was sent after the Boxer Rebellion (1898–1900), the English writer J. M. Robertson pointed to gruesome evidence of pure race hatred that exploded. Thin bonds tying humans together evaporated as soldiers in frenzy, unrestrained by their officers, dragged civilians by their queues to drown them in the Amur River.[73] European soldiers sent overseas seemed to lose all sense of proportion, their officers either unable or unwilling to contain them, agreed Richet. Bestiality, rape, pillage, and unconstrained egotism replaced civilized veneers worn in Europe.[74] Brutalized abroad, how would these troops behave if ever pitted against each other on the Rhine frontier? Alfred Fouillée, a French social scientist with an interest in psychology, was convinced that if French and German troops confronted each other, both sides persuaded that theirs was a mission for the survival of a superior race or civilization, the outcome would be the rebarbarization of Europe. War would no longer be "duels among professional soldiers," but the "risings of entire peoples against others . . . in the name of some supposedly endemic or hereditary hostility."[75] Evidence from overseas combined with the "improvement" in weaponry in Europe persuaded pacifists and their supporters that war could never achieve a rational and justifiable objective. The sense that slaughter, based on race hatred, was possible horrified European peace activists.

A few years before the outbreak of the war, Norman Angell's immensely successful book, *The Great Illusion,* was published, a work, like von Suttner's, often criticized by scholars for superficiality but universally understood as influential. Angell, who was not an activist in peace circles prior to 1909 when an early version of this work appeared, absorbed the arguments of antiwar writers half-consciously and transformed them into a best-seller.[76] His work was also infused with the passion of an individual whose direct observation and experience impelled him to warn as wide an audience as possible of the coming collapse from the arms race. Among other careers, Angell had worked as a journalist in Paris for a decade, from the days of the Dreyfus affair, watching the spiraling escalation of arms expenditure and international crises. By the time the third edition of his book appeared, he recognized both Pyotr Kropotkin's and Novicow's preexisting work.[77]

Angell's arguments combined the older Cobdenite liberal tradition with arguments offered by Novicow, Bloch, de Molinari, Ferrero, John A. Hobson, and others. The explosive Anglo-German rivalry that was growing out of control provided the immediate grist for his well-known thesis:

> The wealth, prosperity and well-being of a nation depend in no way upon its political power. . . . We are told by all the experts that great navies and great armies are necessary to protect our wealth against the aggression of powerful neighbours, whose cupidity and voracity can be controlled by force alone; that treaties avail nothing, and that in international politics might makes right. Yet when the financial genius of Europe . . . has to decide between the great States with all their imposing paraphernalia of colossal armies and fabulously costly navies, and the little States . . . possessing relatively no military power whatever, such genius plumps solidly, . . . in favour of the small and helpless.[78]

He insisted that modern states could not be conquered and that a theoretical occupation of London by the German army would not enrich the Germans—they would have to spend far more in occupation and policing. They could not plunder the Bank of London without undermining their own economy because stocks and bonds were owned internationally. A global economy had altered the processes by which wealth accrued among capitalist nations with sophisticated financial instruments. Investments were transnational; capital operated across all boundaries. The national obsession with increasing armaments reflects the fundamental illusion, fostered by political and military leaders, "that national power means national wealth; that expanding territory means increased opportunity for industry; that the strong nation can guarantee opportunities for its citizens that the weak cannot."[79]

Angell's success (editions of the work appeared in French, German, Danish, Spanish, Finnish, Dutch, Japanese, the Scandinavian languages, and Russian by 1913—plus four British editions and several in the United States) amplified the arguments of the peace movement. Indeed, a movement called "Norman Angellism" developed, supported from California (David Starr Jordan's sponsorship at Stanford University) and even, briefly, entered the German Empire.[80] It affected upper echelons of British policy-making.[81] Until 1914, the antiwar analysis of Angell—another cannon shot against the argument of the universal necessity of warfare—seemed like an idea whose time had come. For the international peace movement, it provided a significant reinforcement from a fresh new voice. (Norman Angell was awarded the Nobel Peace Prize in 1933.)

The justification for warfare in the distant past asserted by de Molinari and Ferrero and the evolutionary displacement of warfare by competitive struggle identified by Novicow, became the gospel of peace activism. Where there was less unanimity was (1) the issue of a justifiable use of war and (2) whether or not peace congresses should even consider the subject.

If war was a dangerous anachronism to European civilization, under what circumstances—if any—was a nation or a people entitled to fight? The question was so divisive that organizers of congresses strove to prevent it from appearing on agendas, but to substantial numbers of French and Italian activists it was crucial. The major voices of the movement in Italy—E. T. Moneta; the linguist and scholar Angelo de Gubernatis, who headed a society in Rome; and Rosalia Gwis-Adami, daughter of a Risorgimento patriot, novelist, and acolyte of Moneta—insisted on the centrality of national independence as a sine qua non of internationalism. Independence in Italy's case came after several short but bloody wars. In the view of one Italian pacifist, an antiwar position "did not mean the renunciation of independence, the right of self-defense which is as sacred for nations as for individuals."[82] The vast majority of Italian pacifists insisted that the enduring legacy of the French Revolution was the inalienable right of peoples to govern themselves. Inseparable, was the requirement that peoples respect the civil rights and liberties of each other—domestically and internationally. This truth was more important than arguments of *raison d'état* and provided the basis for international security. Thus, Moneta could assert with no sense of inconstancy or contradiction to pacifist principles:

> "Friends of peace" who belong to the Lombard Union would fight to the last man against anyone threatening the nation's integrity; that many [members] had demanded that the entire Italian population be called out to reinforce the army in 1867 to throw those French *chassepots* sent by Napoleon III into the sea [in support of Garibaldi's] call for the liberation of Rome.[83]

Moneta never doubted the justice of the right to fight to the last bullet on behalf of national liberation from oppressive, foreign rule. A half-century after his own debut on the Milanese rooftops against the Austrians, he considered the war to create a united Italy as the only option, realistic and just.[84] Overall, Italian pacifists (including Ferrero) believed that war could be condemned selectively. For some, it was an affliction, likely to be present for decades. This meant that armies would also continue to exist and Italian pacifists devoted much energy to attempting to introduce democratic forces and controls into the military.

At international meetings, Moneta's belief—"If there is one thing more horrible than war, it is the oppression of one people by another, slavery"[85]—was shared by most Continental pacifists, especially the former artillery captain in the French army, Gaston Moch. Indeed, Moneta spoke these words amid a rare and nasty debate at an international peace congress, which was occasioned by Moch's persistent demands that the movement clarify itself on "the rights of legitimate defense." In 1897 at Hamburg during the Universal Peace Congress and in 1902 during the first French National Peace Congress, Moch pushed resolutions onto the floor, over the reluctance of the congress organizers, who wanted to avoid dispute.

To Moch three contingencies still justified war: (1) response to aggressive invasion; (2) refusal of a nation to abide by an arbitration decision; and (3) refusal by a nation to try arbitration before rushing to war.[86] Moch argued vigorously in support of this position, insisting that the movement could not expect to make converts if it refused to admit the legitimacy of defensive war. But those who chose to avoid confrontation won out by garnering enough votes to support the proposition that the subject was inappropriate to a peace congress. Moch became angry at von Suttner and the moderates who feared controversy. He continued to study and press the subject, returning in 1910 to the international meeting in Stockholm with essentially the same resolution.

There, in 1910, the congress considered a lengthy, important document prepared by Émile Arnaud, the Code de la paix, designed to help the (hoped for) future Hague Conference of 1913 agree on common precepts of international behavior. Arnaud, a close associate of Moch, had included the rights of self-defense and self-determination in the code. The congress endorsed the code, with little discussion. Moch assumed that the delegates then would pass a separate, clear-cut resolution backing the right of self-defense. He was wrong.

Again, the opposition—Anglo-American pacifists backed by Ludwig Quidde—argued that the Moch approach would destroy the movement. A furious Moch rejoined that he would never have left the army to join a movement that was incapable of simple declarations of the unequivocal right of citizens to defend themselves. No movement advocating nonresistance—whether it be Quaker or Tolstoyan in inspiration—would make any headway in Europe and "outsiders" (Americans and Britons), whose political conditions were totally different, had no right to impose their views. Finally, Moch caustically observed:

> I am astonished to see the emotion generated by this proposal. I believed that the majority of congress participants . . . bothered to investigate what they were supporting when they attend a peace congress. . . . The principles of the pacifist movement adopted in Rome, 1891 and confirmed in Budapest in 1896 . . . have always been enthusiastically applauded. . . . One of our fundamental principles is the right of national defense.

> If these principles are not clearly stated by peace congresses, we can say goodbye
> to pacifist propaganda. Even [in Switzerland] the good bourgeoisie would not . . .
> host the Berne peace bureau . . . to defend a Tolstoian principle of non-resistance.[87]

Moch did not prevail. The Stockholm congress refused to vote a specific endorsement of the right of legitimate defense. Pacifists from Great Britain and the United
States, representing nonresistance constituencies, were able to prevent passage of
resolutions on self-defense and just war.[88]

Bloch's message about modern warfare, however, permeated peace propaganda of all types. Delegates to the Universal Peace Congress in 1908 protested
"the use of the great invention of the airship as a new means of carrying on war."
Further, they condemned the twenty-one nations that refused to renew the 1899
convention prohibiting projectiles from balloons during the more recent 1908
Hague Conference.[89] (Von Suttner's plea that pacifists avoided issues, such as
weapons and military equipment, where they had no competence provoked a
weary Alfred Fried to observe that pacifists "might not prevent inventions but
they might try to regulate the use of them.")[90]

By 1910, new faces and voices appearing at international peace congresses
assumed that war was so obviously an absurdity that there was no point in stating
the obvious. The former Finnish political official Leo Mechelen wanted the Stockholm congress of 1910 to create a committee to investigate the historic explanations for nineteenth-century wars in order to refocus peace propaganda
on those forces. His motion presupposed that a group of scholars, chosen for
competence and scientific objectivity, might identify causes that would then be
studied as guides for war avoidance. The Stockholm congress did not endorse
the project;[91] however, in two years, the newly created Carnegie Endowment
for International Peace planned to fund an international team of over one hundred scholars to produce a definitive study of warfare—to update, in effect,
the work of Bloch and Novicow.[92] The report was another casualty of the Great
War.

An understanding of modern war emboldened the movement in its attacks on
actual wars, most of which were fought on the periphery or in the colonies. With
each war or crisis—from the Boer War, the Russo-Japanese War, and the Moroccan confrontation of 1904–1906 through the Libyan War, the second Moroccan
crisis, the Balkan Wars, and the failure to convene a Third Hague Conference
(1911–1913)—pacifists ceaselessly hammered away at the catastrophic implications of modern war. In 1913, the second Balkan war and the bitter social confrontation in France, occasioned by a new three-year conscription law, exemplified the international and domestic impact of militarism on both sides of the
Continent. A sense of impending explosion inspired German and French socialists
and middle-class peace-minded parliamentarians to meet at Basle to open a dia-
logue.[93] It was supposed to be the first of many future meetings.

Pacifists were offered a new propaganda weapon in 1913 that promised to
engrave indelible images of battlefield realities on European audiences—a moving
picture. A German filmmaker, Robert Schwobthaler, having received permission
from the Greek government, moved a crew onto the fields to document the second

Balkan war as the Greeks drove the Bulgarians from Salonika back to the border. His film, carrying a title in three languages, was offered to the peace movement.[94]

> After working for several long months, exposed to hunger, thirst, cholera and the machine gun, I was able to create this work ... which shows in *living images* what war has achieved: the gloomy, ravaged country of Macedonia; the devastation caused by battles and the bombardment in cities—Salonika, Serres, etc.; the starving Turkish and Greek refugees; Bulgarian prisoners of war; the long marches of armies under a tropical sun ...; destroyed bridges, bloody combat as far as the Bulgarian border, cavalry charges, infantry assaults from cannon and bayonet, soldiers falling on the field of battle only 70 meters from the camera, artillery duels with shrapnel and shell explosions in the closest proximity; dead and wounded in the battle lines; transport of the wounded to ambulances followed by the immensely moving work of the Red Cross; demonstration of the different kinds of wounds between regular and dumdum bullets.
>
> In a word, the *impression* which this film leaves on the spectator is such that no one *who has seen it can forget it.*
>
> My principal reason for undertaking this perilous enterprise was to show *for the first time ... what war really is* and to carry out a campaign against this revolting, insane butchery among civilized peoples.[95]

In the filmmaker's opinion, the movie was "a means of propaganda unlike any that has existed ... recognized by only a handful of people up to now." After a private showing in London, several reviewers agreed with Schwobthaler's assessment. One reporter urged the British Peace Society to show the movie across the country.[96] Publicity about the film began to make the rounds of peace societies in 1914 to take advantage of its graphic message. But this new technique for peace propaganda was also stillborn by the events of August 1914.

The kind of war that broke out in 1914, at least the kind of war that governments insisted they were fighting—a defensive war—silenced pacifists in France and Germany at once. When Belgian neutrality was violated a few days after the war broke out, British pacifists supported their government's decision, portrayed as reluctant, to aid the Belgian victim. Italian pacifists could have remained neutral but many chose to voice sympathy with the entente long before their own government chose to enter the war. In other neutral nations, pacifists transformed their organizations into centers for the study of why the war broke out and how a permanent, durable peace could be insured. The international movement was unable to issue a unified denunciation of the war from its Berne headquarters because the council of the movement was split between pro-French and pro-German groupings.[97] The position of pacifists when actual war broke out clearly reflected the fact that Gaston Moch and Moneta, although they never carried resolutions through international peace congresses on defensive war, had been correct. European pacifists accepted self-defense against attack as a legitimate justification for war; they accepted official explanations for taking up arms. Every government asserted that it made war only to preserve its national integrity against outrageous aggression. Each government persuaded a sufficient portion of its population that a neighbor had been the aggressor and that the war was just. Thus, at least initially, the Great War was supported by Continental pacifists in belligerent nations on the grounds that it was essential to save national independence.

7

Pacifism and Contemporary Crises

In the last decade of the nineteenth century, the rival alliance system that defined the formal structure of European international life unceremoniously buried the remnant congress system. The collective security of the post-Napoleonic era, shaped at Vienna, was replaced by the classic balance of power following the Franco-Prussian War and the Treaty of Frankfurt. After 1892, the Dual Alliance composed of the French Republic and tsarist Russia faced the Triple Alliance of Hohenzollern Germany, the Hapsburg Austro-Hungarian Empire, and the conservative constitutional monarchy in Italy led by the House of Savoy. British participation in the first was formalized in 1904 and 1907. Political leaders from both sides along with "realist" scholars and publicists routinely stated that the purposes of the agreements were purely defensive: to preserve peace through strength, deter aggression, and insure national security.

Rare was the year that passed without a crisis capable of dissolving this peace into its opposite. It was not an abstraction called the alliance system or the balance of power, but rather it was the calculations of political leaders that kept—or ruptured—the peace. The repeated renewals of the Triple Alliance; the chronic Eastern Question; the creation of the Dual Alliance; the Fashoda affair; the Boer War; the bitter British-German naval and economic rivalry that ushered in the twentieth century; the alliances between Britain and Japan (1902), between Britain and France (the 1904 entente), and between Britain and Russia (1907); the two Moroccan crises (1904 and 1911); the Austro-Russian crises following Austrian annexation of Bosnia-Herzogovina (1908); the continued upheavals in the Ottoman Empire; the Italian invasion of Tripoli (1911); and the Balkan Wars (1912–1913) all strained the fragile "peace" that finally was destroyed by the assassination of the heir to the Hapsburg throne and his wife at Sarajevo on 28 June 1914.

In the month following the assassination, the alliance system, the only formal "order" in the European international anarchy, collapsed as had the congress system. International anarchy prevailed again. Pacifist apprehensions were justified. Alfred Fried observed:

> Peace [as] the non-existence of war is by no means a pacifist peace, which only comes about when, following an organized agreement between the different States, war is regarded as something extraordinary and not as a regular political instrument. The pacifist conduct of peace does not exclude the employment of force, but this too would be used in the service of right. It would be an instrument of organization and . . . would no longer oppress peoples.[1]

In the prewar atmosphere of constant tension, pacifists knew very well that the growing usages of peaceful forms of conflict resolution, especially arbitration, were the happy exceptions and not sufficient to prevent a catastrophic war. By 1913, a sense of foreboding among pacifist leaders replaced their traditional optimism.[2] This shift in outlook reflected the movement's awareness that its rational arguments about the interdependency of European peoples had reached the limit of effectiveness. From 1871, over four decades of crises and hostilities vacillating between peace and threats of war had tested pacifist creativity and ingenuity. Pacifists were often as divided as the wider public on solutions to lingering tensions.

As the twentieth century opened, a new, aggressive integral nationalism exploded in Europe, frank and arrogant in its adulation of war and violence. Charles Richet detested the amoral values—influenced by Friedrich Nietzsche and Maurice Barrès—that enthroned violence as end and means, calling their acolytes, "les apaches."[3] The escalation of nationalist conflicts, of *affaires* provoked by extremists on both sides of the Rhine, led a French activist, Père Hyacinthe (Charles Loyson) to comment that a new "street" politics had shaped a dangerous climate of "latent war" that needed only the smallest spark to explode.[4] The sense of violence pervading modern life, threatening the civilized order, became a subject of sociological and journalistic speculation.[5] The pacifist struggle had been conducted carefully to respect state sovereignty and rational patriotism; it could not match the emotional appeal of "les apaches" among many students and intellectual hangers-on in Paris. Thus, the conundrum of contemporary realities and crises challenged the ingenuity of the peace movement at every turn.

Should formal congresses debate contemporary threats to peace or concentrate on long-range solutions to the structural issues of European order? In the early 1890s, leaders of the newly organized Universal Peace Congress and Interparliamentary Conference responded very cautiously to pacifist militants who wanted peace congresses to speak and act aggressively on contemporary injustices and crises. Anxious to attract responsible membership, pacifist leaders insisted—as they had done in the 1840s—that contemporary politics were off-limits. Such delicacy bored younger recruits.

The newly mobilized membership of L'Association de la paix par le droit militated for a crusading posture: "Devenir un parti" ("Become a party"), they cried.[6] To Charles Brunet, Jacques Dumas, and the others in the first generation of the French student group, there was no choice but to fashion a partisan pacifist platform and become a political force.[7] No subject should be taboo. Not only were young pacifists so inclined, the energetic English Quaker Priscilla Hannah Peckover, founder of the Wisbech Local Peace Society, privately funded the young French activists and backed their strategy. The former Italian minister of public education, Ruggiero Bonghi, was sixty-five years old when he urged that the Universal Peace Congress and the Interparliamentary Conference take up the question of Alsace-Lorraine and demand that France and Germany heal the breach that threatened world peace. Otherwise, he observed, the whole attempt at an international movement was doomed to fail.[8] Hodgson Pratt also wanted an energetic, politically involved movement, and he disagreed profoundly with the approach urged on Élie Ducommun by W. R. Cremer, Passy, von Suttner, and the German pacifists and their allies. Pratt hoped that the central headquarters of the movement would not only provide intellectual leadership for constituent societies, but it would also act forcefully in the name of the movement between congresses.[9] Similarly, Gaston Moch warned that peace congresses had become dull academic exercises of little interest to people who wanted to take a stand on current issues.[10] But traditional peace activists resisted as long as they could. "The peace congress is not a socialist congress," warned a British delegate, J. B. Clark.[11]

Despite Ducommun's best efforts, the Universal Peace Congress was challenged in 1892 by a problem that Sellon, Cobden, Hugo, and Potonié had also faced: What posture should the peace movement adopt toward Europeans seeking support for their national liberation? A delegate favoring Polish freedom pleaded in 1892 at Berne that "friends of peace" champion their independence. Passy, though sympathetic, demurred, "We are hardly a diplomatic congress charged with redesigning . . . the map of Europe."[12] Felix Moscheles feared:

> If we want to take a stand supporting all the world's oppressed, twenty meetings would not be enough. After the Finns and Arabs, . . . we must concern ourselves with Poles, Alsatians, Lorrainians, Irish, Hindus, Danes in Schleswig-Holstein, and so on.[13]

But to the Italian delegation, this argument was specious. Moneta could not understand how any international group could discuss peace and ignore "the just claims of a people."[14]

Attempts to avoid contemporary issues collapsed in the mid-1890s when peace congresses could not ignore the reports of Ottoman Turkish atrocities against subject Christian peoples—Armenians and Greeks. Because European diplomats had frequently denounced these abuses, pacifists could take a stand and remind governments to invoke international covenants signed after 1878 (the Russo-Turkish War) that allowed intervention.[15] Peace activists petitioned Great Britain, France, and Russia to interfere and stop the massacres. However, when Young Turk exiles, led by Ahmed Riza, asked peace congresses to support the overthrow of the Sultan's regime, the pacifists demurred.

Revulsion at Turkish atrocities opened the way. In 1894, the congress at Antwerp militated for European intervention to stop the Sino-Japanese War.[16] An oblique statement of support for oppressed Poles even emerged. It noted, "[The] work of peace is inseparable from that of liberty" and hoped that Russians would soon have "a representative and constitutional government . . . [compatible] with liberty [and] civilization."[17]

In the Interparliamentary Conference, the prohibition against involvement in contemporary crises evaporated suddenly when Franco-Italian relations began to deteriorate in 1893. The French and Italian senators, Ludovic Trarieux and Beniamino Pandolfi, founding members, vigorously lobbied their colleagues to help diffuse the crisis that promised to become war.[18] French and Italian parliamentarians met, held public dinners, and celebrated the community of interest binding their nations. Italians remembered French help in their wars for unification in 1859-1860 and French pacifists spoke of an ancient Latin bond. In general, although the group avoided contemporary issues—"not to compromise its activity and efficacy itself . . . ; not to alienate the sympathies of one or another party in conflict"—the possibility of a real war changed the equations.[19]

Thus, by the mid 1890s, the initial commitment to omit contemporary issues was undermined in both peace internationals. In place of prayer, annual congresses routinely opened with reports on political *actualités*. Threats to the peace arose from specific overseas crises and wars or from long-term Continental tensions. Congresses had an easier time condemning distant clashes than confronting stubborn European questions, particularly those involving the rights of nationalities.[20]

Pacifism and Alsace-Lorraine

Without question, the subject of Alsace-Lorraine threatened the survival and cohesion of international pacifism more than any other long-term problem. Widely perceived as the probable cause of the next Continental war, a solution to the legacy of 1871, when the victorious new German Reich annexed the two French provinces, was highest on the list of pacifist desiderata. It was an American who broke the taboo against raising the subject. During the meeting of the Universal Peace Congress in 1893 at the Chicago Exposition, a U.S. delegate denounced "the bitter hostility of France and Germany":

> The peace of the world demands that Alsace and Lorraine be neutralized by universal consent and that, then and thereafter, France and Germany cease their hatred and preparation for war with a neutral zone between their boundaries.[21]

From the other end of Europe, Jacques Novicow offered a slightly different approach:

> The only solution for the question of Alsace-Lorraine is this: Let the population vote and from this side of the Vosges to the other side of the Rhine, respect the decision that will emerge from its plebiscite.[22]

Neutralization of the provinces was urged by the British Peace Society, the Società per la pace in Palermo, Lega italiana per la pace in Turin, and the Association for the Neutralization of Denmark. In 1889, Moneta pleaded with the young, new occupant of the German throne, Kaiser Wilhelm II, to seek a revision of the Treaty of Frankfurt regarding Alsace and Lorraine. Real glory, Moneta lectured, consisted in farseeing statesmanship to preserve the European community—not in the flags and banners of combat troops.[23] Reluctantly, French and German pacifists took up the issue. All of Passy's forebodings were fulfilled.

On the French side, during the 1890s, Jean Heimweh, a crusading journalist, and Gaston Moch challenged the generation-old caveat of Léon Gambetta, the revered republican leader of 1871, who had urged, *pensons-y toujours mais n'en parlons jamais* (always remember but never talk about them). Heimweh proposed, instead, *pensons-y* et *parlons-en* (think *and* talk about them) because silence and denial would never resolve the "only apple of discord that impeded the achievement of a durable peace between the two great civilized nations of the continent."[24] Moch pleaded for public discussion in the press, pointing out that the two provinces were not stolen by the German people but by the Prussian military and political leadership.[25] Because the question of Alsace-Lorraine was uniquely capable of destroying the peace of Europe, Heimweh and Moch argued, the issue deserved a higher priority than the question of other oppressed nationalities.[26] Moch, whose family had originated in Alsace, understood that the provinces also symbolized a place where two very different conceptions of human rights struggled.

The elder statesman of the German peace movement, Franz Wirth,[27] responded by attacking the very idea that there was an "issue" to be discussed by pacifists at all. In *La Paix par le droit,* Wirth scathingly warned French pacifists to forget Alsace-Lorraine. The French would never be able to retake the provinces by force from the better-trained German army, he taunted. Pacifists had no right even to discuss the provinces—they were German. And Wirth added, they were more prosperous under German rule and the people were happy to be part of the kaiser's Reich.[28]

In the ensuing war of words (which lasted until Wirth's death in 1897), the French pacifists cited the numbers of emigrants leaving the provinces; the numbers who crossed to France to celebrate patriotic holidays; the oppression experienced by second-class citizens who lacked legal rights in the German state. Gaston Moch attacked Wirth for not supporting Bertha von Suttner and urged that Wirth quit the peace movement.[29] Wirth demanded that the French recognize the historic decision at Frankfurt or drop any pretense of an international peace movement. Moch, Heimweh, and Moneta followed by insisting that the international movement condemn conquest and recognize that among civilized peoples, nationality was a voluntary, not a forced, association.[30] A resolution voted in 1896 at the Budapest congress sustained this position; it defended the inalienable right of peoples to national self-determination.[31] There was little sympathy for the position of German peace activists. Privately, Novicow wrote to Alfred Fried:

> You are right. Had the French won in 1870, they would have done precisely as the Germans. . . . [But] I regret that Alsace was taken, not because France lost a province, but because the principle of collective servitude was again applied by a great nation such as Germany . . . just after the Italians escaped this disastrous practice with such success.[32]

Novicow sympathized with Fried's desire to work for the future and not rehash the past, but that strategy was undermined by the reality of enduring protest by oppressed populations. Moch complained:

> Peace societies of the German spirit . . . seem to want to concern themselves only with causes of eventual conflict which could threaten peace in the future. . . . The theory of the status quo which they accept as a given . . . neglects the permanent causes of conflict which are . . . the most serious of all.[33]

The debate opened by Heimweh and Moch did not alter German pacifist positions, but it undermined the attempt of movement moderates to steer the international congresses away from controversial subjects. A public debate ensued over just compensation for the return of the provinces (exchange of African colonies was the usual idea); over the use of plebiscites as a measure of democratic decision making and for ways to create a neutralized band of territory between France and Germany.[34] Novicow, convinced that the establishment of a European federation was the precondition for peaceful solution to *all* problems, including Alsace-Lorraine, seized the opportunity to insist on a league of neutral small states, including Belgium, Switzerland, and the two provinces.[35] This wedge would buffer the two hostile larger powers and serve as a modern re-creation of the old middle kingdom of Charlemagne's grandsons. It included some of the richest, most productive territories and populations in Europe.

One unforeseen outcome of the discussion was that French progressives learned that Alsatians might want to remain within the German Empire, were they accorded autonomy and civil rights.[36] After a decade of debate, the Parisian peace activist Jules Prudhommeaux noted, with exasperation:

> France is armed to the teeth in preparation for a revenge which will never come and which, in reality, no one wants. Were it truly wanted or were it wanted in the past, there would have been many ways to make the occasion happen. . . . The majority of the country does not want war because there is not a family without a son, brother or husband in the army.[37]

Novicow raised the question of Alsace-Lorraine at the Twelfth Universal Peace Congress in 1903 held in Rouen. In an attempt to accentuate the positive, he proposed that the meeting congratulate Dr. H. Molenaar and his newly founded group, the Ligue franco-allemand in Munich.[38] Molenaar, not a known peace activist, was the only German who had indicated some willingness to discuss the issue of the provinces. Novicow proposed that this wonderful augury be the first stage in a public discussion of Franco-German tensions. His motion passed. The Berne *bureau* was required to plan for a discussion that it had skirted for fourteen years.[39] Resigned to an uproar, Ducommun in 1903 invited the French and German delegations to submit statements for a future congress.

The peace leadership debated its position at the Second French National Congress in 1904.[40] French pacifists legitimatized their enterprise by citing a roster of distinguished Europeans, starting in 1872 with the Spanish republican, Emilio de Castelar, who had pleaded for a renegotiation of the Treaty of Frankfurt for the good of Europe. The leaders of the French movement alleged that international law had been violated by the seizure of the provinces but quickly added that another war would not solve anything. The only fair solution was a plebiscite insuring the "right of peoples to dispose of themselves." Were the Germans to be voted out, their investments could be compensated. The French pacifist community concluded by appealing to the fatherland of Kant to recognize right and justice.[41] One French pacifist proposed that France might abandon *revanche* if Germany would accept obligatory arbitration and begin to negotiate serious means to reduce armaments.[42]

There was no parallel German debate. Dr. Molenaar's group issued a set of proposals for discussion:

1. Lorraine might be returned to its linguistic border and the fortress at Metz be dismantled.

2. German indemnification either through acquisition of Luxembourg or an unspecified colonial transfer.

3. Autonomy for Alsace within the German Empire.[43]

Molenaar (who may have been the only member of the Munich league)[44] was ignored by German activists. Alfred Fried was so furious that he would not publish a hint of Molenaar's suggestions in *Die Friedens-Warte,* and the dispute between Fried and Molenaar was conducted in French journals.[45]

For his part, Fried attacked French pacifists for asserting that the Germans should have recognized international law in 1871 that not only did not exist, but was the main objective of the peace movement![46] Ludwig Quidde, successor of Adolf Richter as head of the German peace movement, warned French readers that it would be best for the growth of pacifism in his country if the results of Sedan were left undiscussed and undisturbed.[47]

Unfortunately, these rather one-sided exchanges occurred as Franco-German tensions over the first Moroccan crisis inspired an explosion of jingoism. French conservatives "discovered" the peace movement amid its discussion over the "lost" provinces. From the nasty pen of the eminent editor of *Revue des deux mondes,* Ferdinand Brunetière, came a denunciation characterizing the movement as a tissue of lies, spiritually related to Gustave Hervé's antipatriotism, and potentially treasonous.[48] Pacifist visions of a Europe with interests that transcended the nation-state were naive. Passy and d'Estournelles de Constant were allowed to publish responses, but the attack continued in *Le Temps*[49] and in the Chambre de députés, Paul Deschanel charged French pacifism with abetting anarchism.[50] In the Chambre de députés, Ferdinand Buisson disputed Deschanel—to no avail.[51] Exasperated, the editors of *La Paix par le droit* asserted "our motto is 'peace through law,' . . . not 'peace at any price.'"[52]

Amid these inauspicious auguries, the subject reached the Universal Peace Congress at Lucerne in 1905. The Berne office of the Universal Peace Congress crafted a careful resolution asking France and Germany to seek an equitable compromise to preserve peace and law "in their interest and in that of the civilized world." Although the resolution admitted the right of nationalities to determine their own destinies, it stressed the possibility that oppressed nationalities would find justice—without a bloodbath—under the umbrella of a lawfully organized Europe.[53] The peace congress resolution in 1905 shifted the emphasis from a discussion of Alsace-Lorraine to the question of Franco-German rapprochement. This was not mere opportunism. The Moroccan crisis revived genuine fear of impending war. At the Lucerne congress, Passy and Quidde defused tensions by crossing the platform and shaking hands, to the thunderous applause of the meeting.

Handshakes did not mean that German pacifists would or could consider a revision of the Treaty of Frankfurt. The German press pounced on Quidde's handshake in Lucerne and distorted his few words on Alsace-Lorraine into unrecognizable lies.[54] Even speculation about the future (e.g., the transformation of Strasbourg (Alsace) into the headquarters of a future European federation) could barely get a hearing. To internationalize—not neutralize—the city and to make it the center for international cultural, health, research, technical, and scholarly networks would be to recognize Strasbourg as the heartland of a multicultural community.[55] At most, the German pacifist Wilhelm Forster, a noted Berlin astronomer, described a distant future when scientists and scholars would set the tone, not nationalist, religious, or ethnic hatreds.[56] Novicow concluded that the political consciousness of Germany was controlled by a "small clique of *hobereaux*" who acted as if they were on their own planet but who threatened the peace of the globe on a daily basis. "Were it not for the violent annexation of Alsace, the union of Europe might have almost been a *fait accompli*," he complained.[57]

French pacifists and their Continental supporters could derive little comfort from the proposals of Molenaar. Besides the fact that the German movement evidently ignored him, his recommendations became unseemly. In 1905, he made clear that his major concern was German global hegemony, for he observed that the less numerous French posed little threat to Germany, but that British economic prowess had taken over the globe. It was his object to alert both Germany and France to their futures as third-rate powers: "Shall English become the universal tongue of our planet?" he asked. "Shall other nations fall into the role of vassals?"[58] For good measure, he worried that the other global threat came from Russia.

The international peace movement survived its relatively unsuccessful effort to deal with Alsace-Lorraine. French pacifists essentially concluded that the German peace movement was too weak to be effective at home, though every one remained polite to delegates at congresses.[59] The centricity of Franco-German tensions to European peace remained the core problem. "There is still a long way to go to reach a true and solid peace in Europe," wrote Moneta to La Fontaine in 1913. "It depends entirely—as you well know—on the improvement of German and French relationships and to attain this, I assure you that we will spare no effort."[60]

Italian Pacifists and *Italia irredenta*

Among Italian pacifists, the issue of captive peoples was central to their entire program. It raised immediate issues about foreign policy, alliances, friends and enemies, and the arms race. An essay contest sponsored by the peace society of

Milan in 1889 was won by a teacher, Ignazio Scarabelli, who argued the Mazzinian position, that international peace would remain a distant goal attainable only after all ethnic groups were freed—Poles, Irish, Slavic peoples, and the "unredeemed" Italians under Hapsburg rule.[61] Scarabelli was optimistic, predicting that political oppression would not last much longer. Rulers, such as the tsar, who "have millions of slaves [but} are themselves enslaved" would soon pass into history.[62]

For Italian pacifists, the parallel issue to Alsace-Lorraine was *Italia irredenta,* the Hapsburg governed provinces of Trento (south Tyrol) and Trieste—the unredeemed Italian territories still separated from *la patria.* There were, of course, major differences between this and the French situation. Hapsburg rule was long established in those areas. Moreover, the Italian government was tied to the Hapsburgs in the Triple Alliance, the very oppressers of Italian-speaking people. Each time Rome renewed the alliance, a crisis brewed among pacifists. To Moneta, the "lost" Italian compatriots could not be abandoned. Were the dividends that Italy derived from the alliance worth the costs? Would the peace of Europe benefit if Italy was to change sides? Could the Italian government ameliorate the condition of the Hapsburg Italians through negotiations with Vienna? For Italian pacifists, the debate about foreign alliances was far more fundamental than a program encouraging arbitration or federation.

In 1901, as the alliance came up for renewal, Moneta's group sent out a questionnaire to survey politicians and intellectuals. Could the secret treaties with Vienna and Berlin be replaced with a series of binding arbitration treaties such as the one signed with Argentina? (Such treaties would require obligatory use of The Hague Tribunal.) What point was there for Italians to remain in an alliance that protected them against France and Russia, wondered Moneta, countries that were no threat? Were Rome to sign separate agreements with Paris and London, there would be no reason to remain in the Triple Alliance.[63] The questionnaire launched a thoughtful debate.

Cesare Lombroso, the eminent criminologist, noted slyly that the Dutch and Swiss "live very well without alliances and are happier and richer than we are."[64] On the other hand, Enrico Catellani admonished pacifists against exaggerating the results of arbitration. He pointed to the failure of its leading practitioners, the British and Americans, to consummate a binding treaty. Nor were the British willing to use arbitration when the Boer War broke out. Catellani, nonetheless, recommended that Italy sign agreements with Great Britain and France and drop the *Triplice,* a recommendation also backed by Gaetano Mosca.[65]

By far, the most unequivocal attack on Italian participation in the *Triplice* came from the international law specialist Edoardo Cimbali, who called the connection a "disaster for Italy and a shameful disaster for Europe."[66] In his view, the only purpose of the Italian peace movement should be the cancellation of the Triple Alliance:

> The highest and most vital interests of Italy as of any honest and sensible nation are not [to be found] in equilibria which are formed by tearing populations to pieces and stealing their territories . . . [in any part of the globe.][67]

Cimbali saw little difference between the oppression of Italians in the Alpine regions of Europe and the mistreatment of natives in Africa or Asia. If the modern state derived its legitimacy from the just consent of the governed, then the entire international system had to be overhauled—it could not preserve the institutions appropriate to dynastic rule.[68] Cimbali charged that the peace movement had merely tinkered with the international order, it dallied with the practitioners of realpolitik.

Should Italian pacifists campaign to dislodge their nation from its alliance with militarist monarchies? Jacques Novicow thought so. In a series of letters, articles, and a book, *La Missione dell'Italia*,[69] Novicow urged Italians to work for an end to the alliance and use Italy's unique position in Europe as a lever toward a federation. Just as he insisted that the ultimate solution to Franco-German tensions over the "lost" provinces was a European federation (and plebiscites for the peoples), Novicow pleaded with Italians to follow a similar course. From Italian history, Novicow, of course, saw a model for the European confederacy.[70]

Italy was in the best position to lead a move away from the alliance system. Italian interests coincided with British and French (he ignored their North African rivalry) and were compatible with Russian interests in the Balkans (both anti-Austrian).[71] Italy had the least to gain from the arms race and economically the most to lose. In Novicow's view, the mission of Italy was to point toward the future.[72]

The outbreak of demonstrations and street clashes in May 1903 between students of Italian- and German-speaking backgrounds in Innsbruck gave the debate a new urgency. An explosion of irredentist sympathy in Italy placed the Roman government in a very uncomfortable position.[73] Hapsburg authorities issued a vague promise that a program in Italian legal studies would be established at Innsbruck, but it was never started.[74] To complicate matters, the Italian dominion over commerce in Trieste was under attack from an influx of Slavs who moved in and were protected by Vienna.[75]

The pacifist community rediscovered how nasty an issue nationalism was. In the politics of the new century, the cry to liberate the oppressed Italians living under Hapsburg rule—once a Garibaldian and Mazzinian ideal—was appropriated by the new radical right of reactionary nationalists who attacked the liberal state relentlessly. They, too, wanted to rupture the Triple Alliance and free their compatriots by force, at least they said they wanted to do so. Italian pacifists found themselves in a stunning quandary. Once they had never doubted the Mazzinian ideal of the gathering of a people into one nation, such was the faith by which Moneta's generation had lived. But the new rightist agitation for military action against the Hapsburgs violated both pacifist desiderata for peaceful change and political reality. Strident rightist nationalism forced pacifists to reconsider the Triple Alliance as the only practical route for a peaceful solution.

In 1904 at the national congress of Italian peace activists, the irredentist question and the issue of the Triple Alliance dominated the proceedings. Guglielmo Ferrero lectured on nationalism and irredentism, fashioning a moderate pacifist position.

Should Italians launch a war on behalf of *Italia irredenta?* Were Italians willing to die to change the borders of their state? What support would other governments offer Rome for such a war? How long should Italians expect a war would have to be fought to regain the lands? The more questions that Ferrero asked, the more absurd the violent solution seemed. It was clear that Italians were not ready to fight their Triple Alliance brethern—Austria and Germany. Thus, what rational action could they take?

Thoughtless rhetoric and demonstrations (piazza politics) achieved nothing, warned Ferrero. Italians must struggle for the creation of a significant center of culture and learning at Trieste, a place where the great Western heritage embodied in Italy could be disseminated to Balkan peoples. The Roman government could initiate official overtures to create and support such a center; Italian scholars could teach there and Italian-speaking subjects of the Hapsburg monarchy would have a place to explore their own culture. Ferrero separated cultural nationalism from political irredentism. The audience was far from convinced.[76]

The power of nationalist sentiment infected the debates. Dr. Giovanni Quarelli, representing the international university student group Corda Fratres, wanted the congress to assert its primary commitment to national liberation everywhere in Europe.[77] (Quarelli's interest was not only the oppressed Italians; his organization was in the forefront of defending the rights of Jews in Romania to citizenship and university admission.) Congress organizers were nervous about language that committed the peace movement to unattainable transnational undertakings. Giretti, for instance, warned against undertaking the role of "knight errant of nationalism in Europe" and wondered what the meaning of national liberation would be in the Ottoman Empire.[78] The congress eventually endorsed both Ferrero's position as well as that of Quarelli. Italian pacifists were unable to speak with a single voice on the irredentist issue. Some demanded constant vigilance and militant statements; others wanted to persuade their government to work for Ferrero's vision. The issue of support or opposition to the Triple Alliance continued to fester. Then in 1908, the Austrian government annexed Bosnia and Herzegovina, nearly provoking a major war with Russia. It acted without bothering to inform its Italian ally of its plans, a distinct humiliation.[79] Anti-Austrian sentiment pulsed across the peninsula. Here was another example of high-handed indifference to the rights of ethnic minorities, a violation of the Treaty of Berlin (1878) with no pretense of a new diplomatic congress to reorder its contents. Peace activists insisted that Rome vigorously defend the rights of ethnic minorities with their Viennese ally.[80] Italian pacifists asked their Austrian colleagues to organize protests but soon discovered that von Suttner's group was as reluctant to deal with the issue as Quidde's group was to address the question of Alsace-Lorraine. Alfred Fried nervously argued that the "annexation" was consonant with previous treaties and that Bosnia-Herzogovina did not lose any freedom. Although he agreed that the Viennese might have been more subtle—organizing a diplomatic meeting in advance to approve the changes—he maintained that nothing really occurred to contravene the larger principles binding pacifists.[81] In response to the request for Austrian pacifist criticism of its government, Bertha von Suttner promised Moneta to do all in her power to counteract anti-Italian chauvinism. But, she warned, the most efficacious campaign would have to be indirect, that is, by organizing evenings to celebrate Italian culture and achievements, such as art shows or operatic performances. Anything more directly political and critical would boomerang.[82] Fried also assured Italian pacifists that the crisis was not likely to lead to a general war and that the growing democratic forces in Austria would not support a war of expansion.[83]

To Italian pacifists, these fainthearted responses severely undermined their new-won credibility based on Moneta's 1907 Nobel Peace Prize. The Italian peace movement as well as the government in Rome were humiliated: the first by its ties with Austrian pacifists, the second by a ridiculous foreign policy in which Italians remained loyal to an ally who could not remember their address. Bosnia-Herzegovina did not lead to a war, but it led to a peace that only benefited militarism, Moneta concluded.[84]

The failure of the Italian peace community to denounce the Triple Alliance aroused the ire of the respected commentator, Gaetano Salvemini who—like Cimbali—also charged Moneta with indirectly abetting militarism.[85] The peace community, fuming privately at the behavior of its eminent Austrian colleagues, continued to plead with Rome for vigorous prosecution of minority rights in the Hapsburg territories. Rome, they held, should not renegotiate the Triple Alliance without firm assurances that such rights would be respected.[86] But at its congresses, pacifists voted against renewal.

Ironically, the Italian movement born in the 1880s, with an unwavering commitment to the link between peace and national self-determination, began to retreat a generation later. In 1910, a last effort at a reasonable approach to irredentism was made by Arcangelo Ghisleri at the national congress in Como.

Ghisleri rejected warfare as a solution to *Italia irredenta.* He asked rhetorically, should thirty-two million Italians spill blood to free eight hundred thousand conationals? He noted that Italians who lived in Ticino (Switzerland) never dreamed of rejoining Italy—there, an accommodation among ethnic groups had been created and the relative contentment of Italian-Swiss citizens suggested that multicultural political systems could be established. On the other hand, the leadership of the Italian communities living in the Tyrol were clerical, conservative, and pro-Austrian who maintained close ties to ruling circles in Vienna. Only when Italian communities in the Hapsburg lands shed these leaders and associated themselves with the popular Slavic groups would a solution to the mistreatment of all minorities become feasible.[87] The congress endorsed Ghisleri's argument. Reluctantly, pacifists accepted the idea that the Italian population under Austrian rule might well have to remain there. Short of a major European war, which might again redraw the map of Europe, Italians in the Hapsburg Empire had to struggle for a future of autonomy within a multinational state. Changes in their status, argued one Italian pacifist, must be made in the same way that the Swedish-Norwegian crisis was settled—by negotiation.[88]

To Cimbali, the resolutions voted by Italian peace congresses, particularly the flabby statements on the Triple Alliance, illustrated the political inanity of the movement.[89] On the other hand, Ghisleri and Moneta had an eye on new right-wing gangster rogues who abused nationalism by preaching wild-cat violence for its own sake. Moneta, the former Garibaldian, observed that a new era had come into being in which "national claims could be satisfied by means . . . not as tragic as war. Europe is tired of ruins and blood and wants peace."[90]

Pacifism Confronts Imperialism

In 1911, the question of irredentism suddenly disappeared from the Italian pacifist agenda. To the amazement of European pacifists, Moneta actively campaigned in favor of the invasion of Libya-Cyrenaica and the war against Turkey.[91] For two decades Italian pacifists had insisted that national independence and human rights preceded pacifism and that aggressive war was not an option. In September 1911, the Unione lombarda shifted, defending Italy's rights to a North African Empire.[92] When some Italian pacifists joined the international peace movement in an angry attack, Moneta denounced them as unpatriotic.

Moneta, Angelo de Gubernatis, and Rosalia Gwis-Adami argued that the war against Turkey was entirely justified. They repeated the official rationale: Italians were entitled to the fruits of their labors; they brought their "industry, their intelligence and their labor" into the backward Muslim world and were often murdered for their attempts to introduce progressive change.[93] Were Italy to control territory in North Africa, close to its mainland, immigrants would not be lost to distant transatlantic lands, where they were disconnected from their *italianità*.[94] Gwis-Adami's tortured defense of the invasion destroyed her organization of teachers.[95] She maintained that hers was a "patriotic pacifism" that placed the interests of Italy above all else.

Italian pacifists who disagreed were vilified. Privately alma dolens asked Albert Gobat in Berne to support the "true" movement—led by Giretti in Turin, Domenico Maggiore in Naples, Arturo Dolara in Como, Milanese worker groups, and feminist organizations.[96] Victor Prestini sent private appeals to Gobat and to Henri La Fontaine in which he indicated who the true Italian pacifists were.[97] In 1912, at the Universal Peace Congress in Geneva, a nasty confrontation exploded between the two wings of the Italian peace movement with Giretti, Ghisleri, Gwis-Adami, and Agnelli denouncing each other.[98] Convinced that she would be ejected from the meeting just as Leonida Bissolati had been ejected from the socialist groups, Gwis-Adami left hurriedly.[99] She and Giretti repeated their shouting match at an organizational meeting of the Carnegie Endowment in Paris. Afterwards she wrote, "Giretti . . . makes me die of fury. To see contradicted everything that I have said in honor of my country by an Italian![100] The two sides of the Italian peace movement could not be mended. Attempts began in 1912 to create a new movement, which opposed the intervention, centered around the work of alma dolens, Pasquale Ricciotti, Victor Prestini, Domenico Maggiore, and Giretti.[101] Moneta went too far when he described Italian action against Turkey as the requisite catalyst to earn respect for Italy in the Triple Alliance. Perhaps, he argued, pacifists should abandon their visions of an alliance with France and England as the start of a European federation.[102] Giretti saw little hope for Italian pacifism unless it broadened its outreach, thus invigorating a movement for free trade and, perhaps, ties with moderate socialists.[103] The war also affected the Interparliamentary Union. Italian members, who had resigned in the fall of 1911 in a fury at the organization's criticism of Rome's aggression, never returned.[104]

The crisis of 1911 spilled over into the international movement as Gobat vigorously denounced Moneta's apostasy. Gobat went further—funding the groups that dolens and Prestini named, and he carried on a public correspondence attacking so-called patriotic pacifism. In addition, the Italian war against Turkey so enraged the pacifist community that leaders such as Gobat and W. T. Stead seriously talked about organizing boycotts of Italian products.[105] Alma dolens may have funneled some of the money from Gobat (who had it from Carnegie) to anarchist direct-action groups that stopped trains of soldiers going to the front.[106]

A few pacifists were unhappy at Gobat's vigorous campaign against Moneta, de Gubernatis, and Gwis-Adami, although it was the logical product of a new militancy in the movement.[107] From the mid-1890s, the international movement—influenced by the arguments of Moneta, Moch, and Pratt—had insisted on self-determination as a precondition to peace. The Stockholm meeting of 1910 had passed the Code de la paix, intended as a guide for the next Hague Conference. In the code, international law was anchored to human rights. The justification of the 1911 Libyan War offered by Moneta's party contradicted over twenty years of his own argument. Clearly, when he spoke of human rights, he meant only Europeans. By 1911, a number of activists in the peace movement moved beyond that position to embrace the rights of non-European peoples. At the very time when Moneta's faction of the Italian peace community decided to defend imperialism, the international movement was dallying with its first anti-imperialist resolutions and precepts.

The peace movement underwent a complete change in its positions on extra-European adventurism. Initially, pacifists had urged European governments to intervene in the Ottoman Empire when massacres against Armenians and Greeks occurred. If the powers did not take steps, argued peace activists, Europeans would be "accomplices to one of the most horrible massacres that history would [record]."[108] The minimal European intervention in Crete in 1896–1897 won pacifist approval.[109] Pacifists initially approved the joint European expedition to China following the outbreak of the Boxer Rebellion (1898) to "insure respect for international law."[110] On these occasions, the peace community celebrated the positive possibilities of the congress system to preserve life and law.

Then, reports of European atrocities against Chinese traveled back to Europe; pacifist support crumbled. Moneta commented that "the crimes of the Boxers are obscured by the indescribable scenes of the new order which is put forth by iron and fire in the name of civilization."[111] His journal published hideous illustrations of European soldiers drowning Chinese civilians en masse. One commentator observed—as had Sellon six decades earlier—that blood-soaked expeditions were hardly effective propaganda for extolling the benefits of Western culture.[112] European pacifists reexamined the recent history of contacts with China, concluding that from the Opium Wars to 1900 missionaries, traders, naval officers, entrepreneurs, and diplomats had done nothing but destroy a venerable civilization. It was time to leave China to the Chinese.[113] The Paris Universal Peace Congress in 1900 listened to Paul Boell, a longtime resident of Chinese cities, soberly analyze the causes of the Boxer Rebellion, which he laid at the doorstep of Western arrogance.

The congress passed a ringing denunciation of Western conduct in China, the first salvo of organized pacifism against European imperialism.[114]

What could the peace movement suggest to protect the dignity of the Chinese state as it crumbled before European assaults? Perhaps China should be recognized as a neutral, protected by a joint allied commission to counteract foreign invasion and manipulation. Perhaps nothing. If a government of four hundred million people was so inept, perhaps it should be left to fall into history on its own. Pacifists were profoundly troubled by the problem China presented in 1900 and equally troubled by their own inability to do more than protest nauseating military behavior by the very joint expedition they had initially hailed.[115]

The normally discrete Interparliamentary Union that met in 1900 also found the China disaster a compelling enough issue to abandon its usual reticence about contemporary politics. D'Estournelles de Constant, a foe of imperial adventurism and an experienced diplomat, attacked European behavior as murder, pillage, and a wholesale violation of human rights.[116]

Pacifists also confronted the widespread fear of so-called yellow peril—a terror that governments from Washington, D.C., to St. Petersburg encouraged as a justification for increases in military budgets. Passy observed that if a race war should break out, it would be the result of European provocation. He noted:

> We, under the pretext of civilizing them, entering those distant regions with our vices and violence, disrespectful of their way of life and principles, . . . condemning them to labor in their own lands, often murderously; persecuting them and finally inflicting all sorts of moral and material tortures on them . . . [have created] by our own hands, the yellow and black peril.[117]

When the independence of peoples was sacrificed to European control, argued G. Sergi, then such explosions as the Russo-Japanese War, which a number of pacifists saw as a response of the yellow peoples against the whites, became understandable.[118]

Even attitudes toward the Ottoman Empire became more subtle. Armenians had petitioned the international headquarters in Berne for help, and Novicow argued their case in 1900. But one of the Young Turks, Ahmed Riza, objected, insisting that pacifists recognize a more complex reality: the government that had exiled him oppressed numerous minorities, including Muslims; the entire government had to be replaced. It was not enough to ask the sultan to stop killing Christians. Riza wanted peace activists to endorse his removal through revolution; most would not. Pacifists found themselves drawn once again into the dilemmas of opposing ethnic, racial, and religious oppression without any real solutions that did not entail force. After 1900, the peace movement ceased calling on European governments to enforce human rights abroad by joint intervention.[119]

The heart of the peace movement was nearly broken with the British declaration of war against the Boer republics of South Africa. For Europeans, this was a worse disappointment than the American War against Spain. The refusal of the British government to accept the Boer offer of arbitration made by Paul Kruger was a depressing way to begin the twentieth century. Besides China, the Boer War

dominated the congresses of 1900 and 1901. Although moderate pacifists, led by
Passy, did not want to attack the British government directly, few others shared
his scruples. Novicow demanded that the congress single out the "party which . . .
refused arbitration, that is, the British government." La Fontaine wanted the congress to organize relief for the Boers, who were being decimated. The British journalist W. T. Stead exploded in 1901:

> We don't want namby pamby resolutions affirming things . . . when nations go
> against the sentiment of the civilized world, there should be an explosion of pacific
> sentiment. I see precious little explosion here and if a Peace Congress will not
> explode, how do you think the general public will do?[120]

Stead called his nation an "excommunicant of humanity" and pleaded with every
clergyman in Britain to begin church services with a denunciation of the government.[121] The Dutch pacifist Johanna Waszklewicz-van Schilfgaarde traveled to
Britain to publicize the destruction of family life in the Boer communities. In the
Netherlands, she had already organized relief efforts.[122] An attempt by the British
peace movement to protest the war led to the "battle of Trafalgar Square," where
pacifist speakers had to be removed by a phalanx of police after forty to fifty thousand furious British citizens had massed against them, enraged by newspaper mis-
information that peace activists were Boer agents.[123]

The official British excuses precluding the use of arbitration forced the Interparliamentary Union to discuss the Boer War, despite their immense reluctance
to handle a current controversy. Because The Hague Conventions were particularly precious to the parliamentarians, the Belgian senator Lorand was able to
bring the issue to the floor of the 1900 meeting in Paris, where he asserted that
the British-Boer dispute had been an absolutely perfect example of the kind of
issue that arbitration could solve.[124] Lorand persevered, despite the fact that British delegates had privately pleaded that discussion of the war be avoided so that
they would not have to walk out.[125] British parliamentarians who opposed the war
struggled at home against government propaganda with great courage.[126] They did
not want to return home to be denounced as traitors. The particular bravery of
the British parliamentarians against the war was singled out by the Union for a
standing ovation and resolution of support, but the delegates made clear their disappointment with the decisions of Lord Salisbury's government.

For Jean de Bloch, the Boer War was a tailormade event, ready for pacifist
propaganda. First, it demonstrated the futility of professional soldiers confronting
a determined guerrilla band, an argument that paralleled Moneta and Moch's
insistence on the superiority of national defensive militias. "Stout hearted yeoman
who can ride and shoot well serve the purpose quite well as soldiers trained in
Germany," he noted.[127] Second, the British were in for an unpleasant surprise
when the costs of these "skirmishes" would quickly devour the 1900 budget.[128]
Bloch envisioned the government, hat in hand, pleading with Commons for
increasingly larger appropriations, year after year. Coincidentally, the British analyst John Hobson published a list of the prowar interest groups for whom taxpayers were footing the bill.[129] Hobson's major work, a study of imperialism, provided
the movement with a powerful arsenal. The young, not-yet-famous historian, G.

P. Gooch, also emphasized the narrow economic advantages of the war to small groups.[130] The Boer War forced antiwar groups to understand the class benefits of imperialism.

As the British fought on, the Continental press bristled with denunciations. The British were lawbreakers; the Boers were brave and beleaguered. Arthur Desjardins, a French authority widely quoted by pacifists, examined the damage to international law wrought by the wars of the century's end.[131] Although he was able to find some justification for the Chinese intervention, Desjardins characterized British policy as a total departure from the rational pursuit of national interests. Another French author, Paul Fauchille, asserted that the Anglo-Saxon peril far exceeded the yellow peril as a world threat.[132] In Italy, the view was echoed by a journalist, Mario Borsa, who observed that "a grand illusion" about British behavior was destroyed as the great liberal nation "put itself also in the first ranks of militarized nations, [a condition that] seemed to be the sad privilege of the continent until now."[133] In Giretti's assessment, the war arose from the "egoistic interest of the ruling classes" who want to persuade peoples to believe "in the deception of the utility of war."[134] Even if Great Britain won a "victory" of sorts, it would rule over a sullen population that would resist anglicization as thoroughly as the French Canadians.[135] Ferrero went further. The war revealed the powerful, lingering influence of a feudal, reactionary spirit in a nation advertised as the quintessential model of liberalism and modernity.[136] In Britain itself, a vigorous antiwar campaign continued—despite its unpopularity—by peace, anti-imperialist, and pro-native societies, notably the Aborigines Protection Society and the British Peace Society. Often, ironically, these were the same people who had been agitating against Boer behavior toward native peoples in South Africa and attacking Kruger and his followers for their vicious exploitation of African natives.[137] Pacifists did not delude themselves. Ever realistic, Pratt admitted that the vast majority of working-class people—except for a few trade unions and cooperative societies, the Independent Labour party, and the Social Democratic Federation—did not much care about the war. A large portion did not vote in the national elections, with over two million out of four million eligible abstaining; many other workers supported the war. The peace groups had a tough task cut out for themselves.[138]

Pacifists abandoned any pretense of neutrality and indifference about contemporary issues. Evidently, this situation made the Austrian official, Count Agenor Goluchowski, sufficiently nervous so that he attempted to derail the Interparliamentary Union meeting planned for Vienna in 1903.[139]

The wars that concluded the nineteenth century forced the international peace movement, finally, to recognize that European treatment of native peoples could no longer be rationalized as a temporary accompaniment of global progress.[140] The issue of colonialism was as difficult for peace activists to confront as it was for socialists, but in the end, the peace movement devised a principled position.[141]

In the congresses of the peace movement, a consensus against abuse of native peoples took shape after 1900. Marie Pognon wanted pacifists to recognize the rights "of organized tribes in Africa and Asia," but she was politely ignored in 1894.[142] Ellen Robinson returned the subject to pacifist consideration at the Paris congress of 1900 when she offered a detailed description of gross humiliations and violations of human rights when Europeans introduced their notions of "progress" into Africa. Rail construction, for instance, depriving peoples of lands where they had traditionally lived effectively destroyed their communities, she argued. Supported by Lucien Le Foyer, Robinson urged that a statement recognizing the rights of native peoples be voted. The 1900 meeting agreed.[143] Ahmed Riza went further, demanding that Europeans cease their efforts to impose Christian values and education on native peoples, a proposal that outraged the religious delegates, mainly those from Great Britain.[144]

Pacifist anger at imperial treatment of non-European peoples became unalloyed fury when the news of Belgian massacres in the Congo spread. It was infinitely worse than China. The litany of horrors reported out of equatorial Africa were reproduced in the pacifist press with some of the earliest usages of photographic evidence. Reports sent by E. D. Morel, the English reformer, appeared with illustrations—one of a black father named Nsala de Wala sitting on a porch staring at a hand and foot, all that remained of his five-year-old daughter. Others depicted mutilated children and adults whose limbs had been cut off because they did not deliver sufficient quantities of rubber to agents of the Congo development company.[145] This time there was no rationalization such as unfortunately excessive military zeal; these atrocities resulted from unalloyed greed and racism. In 1906, the international congress meeting in Milan issued an angry denunciation and a demand for reform of administration of territories as well as punishment of European murderers of native peoples. Pacifists who tried to argue that European imperialism could bring benefits were nearly laughed out of the meeting.[146] The same congress denounced massacres of Armenians and Jews, despite the fact that such language offended governments in Constantinople and St. Petersburg.

A faint attempt at defending European imperialism as a form of beneficent progress was rejected. François Nicol, executive director of the Comité d'action républicaine aux colonies françaises, argued that French colonies—Indochina, Algeria, and Madagascar—were reasonably well governed. To curtail abuses an international code for colonization was needed, and he asked for pacifist support.[147] Nicol also tried to enlist pacifist backing with the appeal that Europeans had little reason to fight each other over overseas expansion because "the dogma of the solidarity of the white race, confronting other hostile races, must outweigh all else."[148] Pacifists supported his call for a congress to regulate abuses, but they were uncomfortable with his language in 1908.

By 1911, Nicol returned, admitting that colonial regimes would not create a rational process for handling grievances. He urged that pacifists back the creation of representative assemblies where native peoples could vote and make law. The Hague Tribunal was to be used to resolve colonial conflict between nation-states and to award independence to a colony. Nicol detailed areas of abuse and shame: slavery in the Sudan, black troops against Algerian populations, complete ignorance of Muslim values in the Colonial Office. But most prophetic was his observation that Europeans did not appreciate what the real result of the Russo-Japanese War had been: a victory by a nonwhite nation over a major European power, which thus served as a model and inspiration for native peoples "where you might have thought nationalist ideas non-existent."[149] He was thinking of Annam (now part of Vietnam), where the Japanese victory combined with the Chinese revolution of 1911 that drove out the last emperor stiffened resistance against French occupation. The French peace congresses adopted Nicol's proposals, many of which were merged into the Code de la paix by Émile Arnaud.[150]

In 1908, the Universal Peace Congress in London applauded a newcomer, Mrs. Drysdale, representing the Subject Races International Commission, which was made up of the Aborigines Protection Society, the British and Foreign Anti-Slavery Society, the Egyptian Committee, the Friends of Russian Freedom, the Georgian Relief Committee, the International Arbitration and Peace Association, the National Council of Ireland, and the Positivist Society. She asked the peace congress to back a proposal enabling subject peoples to use the International Court of Arbitration at the Hague for justice.[151] Her request followed upon a description of horrendous human rights abuses that she had seen or could document.

In the pacifist congresses held in 1912 and 1913, the subject of native rights, of violation of human rights, and of civil justice became a normal agenda item. Delegates to the 1912 Geneva congress strongly rebuked the Italians for their North African invasion; the Russian government for its mistreatment of Finns (a subject already raised in 1910); and the British for their indifference to Egyptian rights. The Egyptian resolution was particularly remarkable:

> The Congress, which has been addressed for many years with protests from many Egyptian delegates on the subject of the current political situation in their country, created by the British occupation;
>
> Considering that the British government itself has always regarded the military occupation of Egypt as a provisional measure;
>
> Considering the numerous occasions that this Government, notably in 1882 and 1884 from the mouths of its ministers, Gladstone and Lord Granville solemnly undertook the promise not to prolong the occupation of Egypt indefinitely;
>
> Considering . . . that the Egyptian delegates have put themselves entirely on the side of law and have rebuffed all violent means to make their demands succeed;
>
> Addresses a pressing appeal to the honor of the English nation and . . . the promises of its government . . . that the military evacuation of Egypt take place with the least possible delay, and that an autonomous government, offering efficacious guarantees to all legitimate national and international interests, be reestablished in Egypt.[152]

The resolution on Egypt provoked serious debate; opponents complained that the British side was not presented. Others wondered how a movement that refused to take a stand on Poland could take one on Egypt. In rebuttal, a young Egyptian nationalist, Farid Bey, argued that Great Britain had repeatedly promised to leave his country, whereas the Russians had made no such promises about Poland. Several speakers admired the Egyptian movement for its absence of violence and bloodshed and its use of lawful, peaceful forms of protest. The resolution passed with a few abstentions. To Ghisleri it meant that the movement had adopted "our Garibaldinian, Mazzinian, Italian tradition" of associating freedom, justice, and peace.[153] The difference was that this tradition was adapted for a non-European peoples, a people Evelyn Baring, Lord Cromer, the British governor, considered permanently incapable of self-rule.

The Rupture of the "Peace"

The nature of the crises of the last four years of peace before 1914 was not lost on the peace movement's leadership. When the second Moroccan crisis, another French-German confrontation, exploded in 1911, the secretary of the Berne office, Albert Gobat, pointed a finger at chauvinist agitators in both nations (making clear that he believed the Germans more responsible). In 1912, the Universal Peace Congress firmly denounced warmongers in the two nations for manipulating a crisis. In France, the second Moroccan crisis inspired proposals for a new three-year conscription law and for dramatic escalations of the arms budget (including that for airplanes). French pacifists opposed the militaristic responses, but the radical groups of syndicalists, socialists, and workers organized noisy street protests against the conscription law. Working-class women in the Comité féminine contre toutes les iniquités sociales harangued at street corners, threatening strikes against conscription and urging sabotage.[154] Although these groups had nothing in common with the older peace societies, they illustrated just the kind of social uproar pacifists had promised would come, someday, if militarist policies dominated the political processes of Europe.

The French senator and former diplomat d'Estournelles de Constant tended to exaggerate the importance of small victories. When the second Moroccan crisis was settled through arbitration, he thought it might signal "nothing less than German recognition of obligatory arbitration" and the probable demise of chauvinistic, adventurous ministers in both nations.[155] The agreement, he added, could become a model for solving European friction throughout Africa, rationalizing imperial policy.[156] By and large, pacifists were far less optimistic. Gobat and d'Estournelles de Constant, truly worried about the weakness of the German movement and the power of Franco-German hatred, tried a new approach in 1913.

Gobat persuaded the Swiss National Council (Nationalrat) to issue a formal invitation to members of the French and German parliamentary delegations, especially members of the Interparliamentary Union, to convene in Switzerland in order to discuss ways in which they might reduce international tensions. Gobat was desperate to try anything to avoid the war he believed was coming.

When the meeting assembled, of the 400 members of the German Reichstag, only 34 came to Basel, and only 4—Baron Conrad Haussman, Ludwig Haas, Franz von Liszt, and Friedrich Naumann—were not members of the Socialist party.[157] Over 180 French delegates came, representing the Center and the Left. Their agenda addressed broad issues—ways to reduce the arms race and tensions in general. Probably, the most significant result was that they agreed to meet again. German parliamentarians promised to come in larger numbers in future if the meeting was not held during elections.[158] Ferdinand Buisson, disappointed at the ratio of participants, concluded that it was better that the meeting had occurred than not, for peoples as well as governments had to find ways to deal with questions of war and peace.[159] The imbalanced attendance was rationalized by another French pacifist who noted that German politicians and intellectuals were "far less accustomed" to exercising initiatives than were their French counterparts![160] That the Germans came at all, according to one commentator, was notable.[161] An optimistic postscript came when Conrad Haussman and d'Estournelles de Constant published a joint article calling the Berne meeting the first step toward a new "entente cordiale."[162] Conceivably the meeting had some impact because it generated more than the usual nasty press attention.[163]

Pacifists attempted to increase French and German understanding through educational and cultural exchanges. Initiatives aimed at forging bonds between teacher–student and professional groups were launched with increasing frequency after 1911. Père Hyacinthe (Charles Loyson), a French peace activist, organized Pour Mieux se connaître in 1912, which planned an array of citizen activities: language courses, theater and art exchanges, joint literary publications, and a journal, *France et Allemagne*. One issue of *Cahiers franco-allemands* appeared in August 1912.[164] From the German side, a call for the creation of the Institut franco-allemand de la réconciliation appeared in June 1913 under the sponsorship of Ernest Haeckel (in Jena) and Henriette Meyer (in Paris).[165] This organization wanted to develop understanding of French and German history and culture among ordinary citizens. Youngsters from each country would meet in summer camps and adults would attend cultural events designed to illustrate the history and civilization of each country. The attempt to accelerate citizen contacts in 1913 took on a frenzied quality, reflecting real anxiety about the shrill levels of nationalistic rhetoric.[166] The editor of a French cultural magazine published in Berlin observed that his group had brought nearly three thousand French visitors into Germany in 1912–1913 alone, and he had great hopes for the impact of these trips.[167]

Amid the crisis-ridden years of 1911 to 1913, there was little to celebrate apart from the formal opening of the Peace Palace at The Hague in 1913. The expected Third Hague Peace Conference did not occur. Lord Weardale, president of the Interparliamentary Union, agreed with Earl Grey, the British prime minister, that the Third Hague Conference was not likely to take place for three to four years.[168] The outbreak of the Balkan Wars generated the predictable ridicule from "realists" of all types, which Norman Angell valiantly tried to counter.[169] But the headlines favored the ideas of the rising young British politician Winston Spencer Churchill: "Who is the man bold enough to say that force is never a remedy? . . . that martial virtues do not play a vital part in the health and honor of every people?"[170] No wonder that J. de Louter, the Dutch president of the Universal Peace Congress in 1913 at The Hague, urged the delegates to hold onto their faith and recognize that a rational world order would not appear overnight and that the struggle to transform the ancient habits of European public leaders would take many years to win.[171] Similarly, Lord Weardale urged Christian Lange not to schedule a discussion of Anglo-German rivalry for the 1913 Interparliamentary Union meeting because only "our captious critics" would benefit from it. He compared the public mood with that in France in 1870; in England, after years of resistance, there was a good chance that Lord Roberts's military preparedness scheme would pass parliament. With irony and bitterness, Weardale concluded:

> There is no doubt that the really sincere and enthusiastic peace people are the socialists. There is no surrender to spurious influences among them and their fidelity to principle can be confidently depended upon.[172]

Amid the tense atmosphere of the last year of peace, Lucien Le Foyer campaigned for a proposal that had been briefly discussed in the Ligue des droits de l'homme. Le Foyer recommended that the entire process of treaty making be transferred to legislative authority in parliamentary states (beginning with France). Foreign policy had to be removed from the exclusive control and secret machinations of executive circles, a vestige from monarchical centuries. If peace were to become a reality, secret diplomacy had to end.[173] "All treaties should be submitted . . . to the Chambers for ratification," asserted Le Foyer.[174] Secret treaties ultimately violated individual and community rights.

> [In 1911, as Italy invaded Tripoli] Italy left France a "free hand"—I am not saying a clean hand—in Morocco because France left them the right to act . . . in Libya. An entire network of tacit agreements was extended across North Africa and Europe. France had admitted English rights in Egypt; English agreed to French occupation in Morocco on April 8, 1904. The precedents had their logic: Italy claimed Tripoli in 1911. The example . . . inspired . . . the Balkan state, in 1912, to decide that the Italian-Turkish War gave them the right to attack Turkey in Europe. The Slavs wait to emulate this initiative, if it succeeds. Germany is . . . nervous. And all Europe imprisoned in these funereal rituals, arms and trembles.[175]

Le Foyer proposed to exempt existing agreements but demanded that all future ones be arrived at "openly"—a proposal initially offered by the Spanish peace crusader, Arturo de Marcoartu, in 1878 but which had been forgotten. Le Foyer planned to campaign in 1914 for his idea, which would have required a fundamental amendment to the French constitution.

The apprehensions of Gobat and French pacifists about Franco-German hostility in 1913 were also shared by Alsatian activists. At the invitation of the German branch of Conciliation internationale, Théodore Ruyssen undertook a lecture tour in Alsace in February 1913. He described the various resolutions of the international peace congresses, emphasizing the inviolability of national autonomy, the right to legitimate defense against conquest, and the efforts made by French pacifists to defuse the legacy of Alsace-Lorraine. Ruyssen emphasized the positive role that the two provinces could play as a bridge between cultures. Insisting that the dead should not rule the living, Ruyssen talked of a series of future possibilities for reducing tensions.[176] His lecture on the comparative ethical similarities of all European cultures at Mulhouse was picked up by a French rightwing nationalist journalist who described it as a case of a French pan-Germanist "offering Alsatians the spectacle of a slave voluntarily preaching slavery to the conquered."[177]

In the charged atmosphere of 1913, this slander produced nasty consequences.

When Ruyssen returned home, the Camelots du roi and the Action française launched a campaign against him, threatening him personally and denouncing him publicly. Burglaries were attempted in the middle of the night at his home; urine was poured into his mailbox; his family and housekeeper were menaced, and posters were hung in the streets of Bordeaux vilifying him as a traitor. Ruyssen could only answer in formal lectures and in print, media that hardly matched the direct methods of the Action française. This polite professor of philosophy noted:

> Alsace wants to make its own life in between the two great German and French cultures, in a mixed culture of a double language, . . . from which comes the marvelous growth of its own theatre, literature, humor, press, etc., . . . a new personality.
>
> For Alsatians and Lorrainians, to realize this dream of building an Alsatian-Lorrainian life today, one essential thing . . . is necessary: peace, confidence and security.[178]

Over and again, he repeated the point that Alsatians do not want another war; they want civil rights in Germany. War with France would endanger the lives of many of their relatives serving in the French army. In France, his lectures were applauded by supporters of his point of view; the attacks from the rightists continued.[179]

The French peace community understood that four decades after Alsace and Lorraine had been removed from France, most of the new generation did not want war. Other French progressives began to deliver this message to their compatriots. "The most faithful friends of the lost provinces must submerge their own preferences to the wishes of the Alsatians and Lorrainians," observed Félicien Challaye.[180] Alsatian wishes for peace and autonomy had to take pride of place in the dreams and plans of German and French peace activists, warned E. Riquiez, during a lecture series sponsored by the Carnegie Endowment.[181] French pacifists took up the argument that Alsatians wanted autonomy, not war.[182] This awareness of a new reality about the "lost provinces" among French activists became another casualty of the war.

French pacifists finally realized that their attempts—through lectures, resolutions, letters, exchanges, articles, questionnaires—to combat dreams of military revenge would not be matched by a similar campaign in Germany. Most German pacifists did not think there was a problem. A despairing Ruyssen wrote, after the war finally came, that French pacifists had waited in vain for any significant gesture from Germany that might have been used to calm anti-German hysteria in France. None ever came.[183]

In the gloomy environment of the last years of peace, peace activists continued to struggle. The movement lost a number of its major leaders between 1912 and 1914—Passy, Beernaert, Novicow, de Gubernatis, von Suttner, and Gobat, among others. Nonetheless, peace militants labored down to the last hour of peace to persuade Europeans that war was not merely "barbaric, costly and often useless but . . . the scandal of reason."[184] But, as Bertha von Suttner admitted in 1912:

We have been mistaken—not as to our principles but in our estimate of the level of civilization to which the world in general had attained. We thought there was a far more widespread desire for justice . . . and a far deeper abhorrence of despotism than appears to be the case. But that war is at present being waged . . . does not prove the falsity of beliefs held by the peace party. It merely proves that the truths of these beliefs has been insufficiently realised either by the nations themselves, or by their leaders, or by both; and that the peace movement is not yet powerful enough . . . to overthrow the deep-seated forces of ancient despotism.[185]

Von Suttner's comment emphasizing the lingering power of ancient authoritarianism never achieved the fame of a similar observation made by Joseph Schumpeter, whose study of imperialism is a classic. "Aggressive nationalism," wrote Schumpeter, "the instincts of dominance and war derived from the distant past and alive down to the present—such things do not die overnight." Elsewhere he noted:

Whoever seeks to understand Europe must not overlook that even today its life, its ideology, its politics are greatly under the influence of the feudal "substance," that while the bourgeosie can assert its interests everywhere, it "rules" only in exceptional circumstances, and then only briefly.[186]

8

The Collapse

Sarcastically, Norman Angell pointed to the apparent success of the peace movement in 1913:

> I have spoken of Pacifists and Bellicists but, of course, we are all Pacifists now. Lord Roberts, Lord Charles Beresford, Lord Fisher, Mr. Winston Churchill, the Navy League, the Universal Military Service Leagues, the German Emperor, the editor of the *Spectator,* all the Chancelleries of Europe alike declare that their one object is the maintenance of peace. Never were such Pacifists.
>
> The German Emperor speaking to his army invariably points out that they stand for the peace of Europe. Does a first Lord want more ships? It is because a strong British Navy is the best guarantee of peace. Lord Roberts wants conscription because that is the only way to preserve peace, and the editor of the *Spectator* tells us that Turkey's great crime is that she has not paid enough attention to soldiering and armament, that if only she had been strong, all would have been well. All alike are quite persuaded that indeed the one way to peace is to get more armament.[1]

Angell's pithy characterization captured a familiar public relations ploy—pacifist language to civilize militaristic policy. That European politicians occasionally clothed the politics of muscle in the language of sweet reason was a backhanded tribute to the success of peace arguments, a technique that became routine politics in the twentieth century.[2] In the summer of 1914, the euphemisms ended. The men and matériel, presumably the inoculation against war, set to their fatalistic finale. A few months after the bloodshedding began, Henri La Fontaine wrote in anguish "never for twenty centuries of Christianity has a war been carried on with such an accumulation of horrors, and such a disregard of every law, human or divine."[3]

From 28 June, when the assassination at Sarajevo occurred, through most of July 1914, peace activists kept an eye on the brewing crises but shared the general opinion that some settlement would emerge. Rumors of mediation leading to a peaceful outcome continued to the third week of July. Perceiving no threat to their annual meetings planned for September—the Universal Peace Congress in Vienna, the Interparliamentary Union in Stockholm—pacifists printed agendas that emphasized the 1915 Third Hague Conference, the contributions of Bertha von Suttner, and Quidde's model arms-reduction treaty. The movie based on Bertha von Suttner's novel was completed, ready to be shown at the Universal Peace Congress in Vienna.[4] Travel plans were in place. Some American delegates to the Stockholm meeting were already in Europe, touring before the conference opened. As late as 31 July, Philip Stanhope, Lord Weardale, president of the Interparliamentary Union, commented, "The prevailing nervousness is natural but I hope and believe, exaggerated. Neither France or Germany desire war, I do not think that Court circles in Russia desire it either." Weardale expected the crisis would be resolved with a formula to "teach Servia [sic] a lesson." He wanted the Interparliamentary Union to use its Stockholm meeting as an opportunity for the neutral states to issue a declaration on behalf of settling the latest Balkan issue.[5] Had peace leaders paid attention to the Viennese press, including the liberal dailies that had occasionally befriended the peace cause, they would have been less sanguine. The assassination of Archduke Franz Ferdinand and his wife, Sophie von Hohenberg, transformed even the relatively liberal *Neue Freie Presse* and the *Neues Wiener Tagblatt* into an incantation for blood vengeance against Serbia.[6]

By 31 July, confusion and uncertainty gave way to unmistakable reality. The Austrian declaration of war was delivered to Belgrade on 28 July, despite efforts by British, French, and some Russian diplomats to find a formula for mediation.[7] Invasion followed swiftly. Continental peace activists were alarmed, angry, and resigned; they made a heroic last effort to prevent the catastrophe. From Paris, L'Association de la paix par le droit sent frantic wires to European chancelleries, reiterating their obligations under The Hague Conventions to use arbitration before arms. They placarded the walls of Paris with posters that pleaded for peaceful solutions and invoked the use of The Hague machinery. The Franco-Russian Treaty placed obligations on France, noted Théodore Ruyssen, "The Hague conventions are also treaties. Why do these not bind us equally?"[8] In Belgium, the national council of the movement published a call to the small powers for a joint *démarche* in the capitals of the Great Powers "to avoid the menacing catastrophe" and to insure their participation in a conference to resolve the crisis.[9] In Torre Pellice (Piedmont), a public meeting of the peace society voted in favor of Italian neutrality if Austria attacked Serbia. Five hundred people endorsed the words of Edoardo Giretti, who urged the Italian government

> to undertake any action that is one of peaceful mediation among the peoples being sucked into the whirlwind of a struggle which is the utter negation of civilization and humanity.[10]

La Fontaine convened an emergency meeting of the leadership of the Bureau international de la paix in Brussels on 31 July. About fifty people came, repre-

senting the major national societies—except for Austria. Jong van Beek en Donk
came from the Netherlands; Evans Darby, J. G. Alexander, Frederick Green, and
G. H. Perris came across the Channel; Ludwig Quidde and Edward de Neufville
arrived from Germany; the Italian movement was represented by Rosalia Gwis-
Adami and alma dolens; the American Edwin Mead was there; from France came
Jeanne Mélin, Théodore Ruyssen, Lucien Le Foyer, A. Vanderpol, Gaston Moch,
and Émile Arnaud. A substantial Belgian delegation, including Paul Otlet, Mme.
de Laveleye, Marie Rosseels, and Jacques Housa, chair of the Catholic Peace Society, attended. Lange came from the Interparliamentary Union. When they assembled in the Palace-Hotel, they only knew about a localized war in the Balkans.

The pacifists demanded immediate emergency sessions of the parliaments of
Europe. (This demand was taken up by Christian Lange, who wired the heads of
national parliamentary groups urging that they convene to help avoid the crisis.
Lord Weardale sent a special plea to Ernst von Plener, head of the Austrian group,
but there was no response.)[11] At the Palace-Hotel, the last assize of Continental
pacifism assessed the public response to the Austrian ultimatum and declaration
of war against Serbia. Ludwig Quidde assured them that the Austrian declaration
of war was regarded with anger in Germany; naturally, he continued, if Russia
supported the Serbs by attacking Austria, the Germans would defend their Viennese ally, but no one expected that this would spill over into a war with France.
Nor, stated Quidde, was there a desire for a war with France.[12] The meeting concluded with an agreement that a round of telegrams would be fired off at once to
governments pleading for restraint.[13] When the assembly broke up at 4:30 P.M.,
they learned that the Germans had cut rail lines on the Luxembourg and Alsace-
Lorraine borders; the German delegation caught the last train from Brussels that
departed before the violation of Belgian neutrality. On the next day, the mobilization of the Belgian army was ordered.

A group of French pacifists meeting on 1 August in Paris considered a march
to the Foreign Office but decided, instead, to send urgent wires to Nicholas Murray Butler and Edoardo Giretti, pleading for neutral intervention. When the pacifist contingent left its meeting at the Institut de la paix, they passed groups of
young men singing "La Marseillaise," but there were no fanatic howls to "get"
Berlin. There was a quiet resignation in the streets. On the kiosks, Ruyssen saw
the official notice of general mobilization hung next to the posters of La Paix par
le droit with their motto: "guerre à la guerre."[14]

By 2 August, Lord Weardale and Lange realized that the Interparliamentary
Union meeting had to be canceled and that few of its national sections would be
able to meet. They oriented their efforts toward public statements on behalf of
Belgian neutrality; this, too, slid away. Houzeau de Lehaie, long active in the Belgian movement and profoundly troubled by his government's decision to resist
the German ultimatum, commented sardonically "The Americans, the Chinese
and the Japanese are preparing to profit from the ruination of Europe."[15] Soon,
Lange and La Fontaine would have to flee Belgium. The British section of the
Interparliamentary Union issued a statement insisting on the validity of European
treaties, including the neutrality of Belgium, but simultaneously, they admitted
that war with Germany was probably unavoidable.[16] The Balkan War began on

28 July 1914, escalated to a Continental, then to a world war in a week. The National Council of the British Peace Movement, representing forty-four societies, pronounced its "utter detestation" of the use of war; condemned the "grouping of Powers in hostile combinations and . . . the balance of Power . . . [supposedly] an instrument for insuring the peace of Europe, has involved the whole of the Continent in a bloody and fratricidal war"; attacked the government for its secret engagements to France; denounced the German violation of Belgian neutrality; and urged that any and every measure be taken to restore peace as soon as possible. The council created an emergency committee for the duration and voted a memorial condemning the murder of Jean Jaurès (assassinated in Paris).[17]

On 4 August, as the German infantry entered Belgium, the British dropped their neutrality and entered the war on the side of the French and Russians. These events fractured any possibilities of continued international cooperation among pacifists and internationally minded Europeans. Belgian neutrality, guaranteed by the Treaty of London since 1830, played a significant role in international peace activity, particularly since 1889. It was regarded as a solid feature of European international life and law by legal internationalists and pacifists. The German invasion traumatized and sundered the peace movement more than the Austrian ultimatum to Serbia, the Russian mobilization on Serbian behalf, the German support of its Austrian ally, France's support of its Russian ally. Lord Weardale, who had held out hope to the very last, accepted the need for war to insure that democratic states would not be governed by "vainglorious despots or unscrupulous statesmen" in the future. After the invasion of Belgium, he observed:

> If Germanic ambitions pursued with such ruthless disregard of treaties, solemn obligations or humanitarian considerations should, as I hope, fail, the Throne of the Hapsburgs and the Hohenzollerns will be swept away. Europe will have learnt a lesson and those who have the primary share in all this misery will properly be the first to suffer.[18]

Ludwig Quidde did not grasp the stunning effect of the aggression against Belgium. Somewhat innocently, he wrote to the new executive director of the Berne peace office, Henri Golay, requesting, "in view of the current situation," that a provisional executive committee be created to direct the Berne office including La Fontaine, Arnaud, an Englishman (perhaps Green), Fried, and himself." Golay, considering the disruption of post, transport, and the general anguish, viewed this request with skepticism but transmitted it to La Fontaine in London.[19] Quidde followed his overture with a promise to travel to Stuttgart to see what the peace community there might wish to do. He did not immediately clarify his objectives for a renewed peace effort.

La Fontaine saw no reason for a meeting, and he quickly understood that both Quidde and Alfred Fried, who also wanted the meeting, evidently believed the German military rationalization for the Belgian invasion. (The German position, of course, was that the French were planning to invade Germany through Belgium and that their own move was essentially a preemptive strike; that they had no intentions to annex Belgian territory and would compensate for any damage caused by their troops "passing through.") Neither Quidde nor Fried, observed La

Fontaine, grasped that the violation of treaties and the vicious sack of Louvain cut the heart out of the movement's unwavering insistence on peace through law. La Fontaine also believed that the Germans were determined to annex all neutral neighbors as well as the colonies of other nations. The Balkans were to be added to Hapsburg lands, controlled by the Austrians. It was definitely not the time for a meeting.[20]

In London, Frederick Green agreed there was no point to a meeting:

> I do not think that any good purpose would be served by some of us going to Berne. . . . It is no use to talk of peace till Prussian militarism has been crushed. When the time for settlement comes, then we must try to make our voices heard.
>
> The invasion of Belgium by the Germans was an outrage and everybody must admire the brave defense of the Belgian troops. . . . Our people feel that they have taken the sword in a righteous cause, to defend Belgium and to help France from being crushed.[21]

Gaston Moch was vehement. In a remarkable letter to Quidde, he placed the entire blame for the war on Prussian and Austrian militarists but promised that their day was over—their stupid brutality guaranteed the "uprising of the peoples."

> We live in a period that can only be compared to the great days of the Revolution. August 4th (funeral for Jaurès and a meeting of the Chamber) and 21 and 22 (sign-up of foreign volunteers) are the noblest and most uplifting days which I have seen. More than 40000 foreigners from everywhere . . . arrived in good order, . . . on the Invalides Esplanade to sign up—Italians, Russians, Czechs, Spaniards, English, Americans, Swedes, Swiss, Romanians, Russian Jews, Poles, etc. (I am only describing the ones I saw) marching in regular columns, with French flags alongside their own flags. . . . It is like the volunteers of 1792 but not because "the nation is in danger" . . . it is humanity in danger because of the Prussian regime and the two military-feudal camarillas.[22]

He described the tears of a forty-year-old Russian father of three, rejected for service because of physical problems. He reported that France's leading pacifists entered national service: Arnaud in a territorial infantry troop; his son, Maxime, the likely successor as head of the Ligue internationale de la paix et de la liberté, on the front; Le Foyer had become an official in the hospital administration; Maurice Bokanowski was at the front; Gabriel Chavet, for poor health, was in the auxiliary services. Gaston Moch asked to be sent to the Belgian front and resumed his artillery commission. (Charles Richet and André Weiss toured Italy, lecturing on the achievements of The Hague conferences to underscore German intransigence against arbitration and German responsibility for the destruction of Louvain, Soissons, and Malines [Mechlin]. Italian pacifists cheered and wished Richet's two sons, in the infantry, a safe return.)[23] Clearly, Moch was in no mood for a meeting of the Berne executive committee.

In Italy, the shock of Germany's invasion of Belgium silenced talk of a mediated settlement. At first, leaders of Italian pacifism applauded their government's neutrality. Rosalia Gwis-Adami advised "private citizens not to think . . . war inevitable nor near," and she prayed that the government "would not let itself be drawn into using the army except for the defense of national integrity."[24] The blind, eighty-three-year-old Moneta announced:

> To the comfort of us, Italians, there is the knowledge that in the war against France and Russia, essentially unleashed by Germany, Italy has not the slightest obligation to take part.
> As Italians, we may congratulate ourselves with confidence that neutrality will be preserved to the very end whatever may be the direction that the war will take.[25]

By the end of September, however, Italian pacifists began to wonder at the wisdom of neutrality. As one writer asked, How long could Italy remain neutral in the battle for civilization that the French and English were waging?[26] Giretti became convinced that the government—still neutral—had already decided to enter the war. Convinced that Italy could not sustain a war, neither militarily nor economically, Giretti expected a social disaster. But what fully revolted him was the "sale" of Italy's participation to the highest bidder. "I would have preferred the declaration of war on Austria and Germany to protest the violation of Belgian neutrality," he wrote.[27] The mood among Italian pacifists was shifting toward a pro-entente position, which they formally adopted in November 1914.[28] Italian pacifists abandoned their neutrality even before Mussolini launched his prowar campaign and broke with the Socialist party.

Ludwig Quidde, convinced that Germany had been attacked, also argued the just-war position: everyone had a primary duty to defend his fatherland. In a pamphlet widely attributed to his authorship, he wrote:

> Since the question of war or peace has now been removed from the realm of what we want, and our nation, threatened in the East, North and West, is engaged in a fateful struggle, every German friend of peace will have to fulfill his duty toward the fatherland as any other German. He will not be outdone in patriotic devotion by those who had nothing but derision and scorn for the idea of peace when it was still time. We share the general duties with all our compatriots.[29]

Toward the end of August, Quidde went to the Netherlands, where he remained for a month as a new peace society, the Anti-Oorlog Raad, was being formed. There, he evidently was persuaded that peace societies had to forget both past and present to concentrate on a campaign to shape both the future peace and the future political organization of the globe. With Alfred Fried, he concluded that an analysis of the causes and responsibilities of the current war was a fruitless task, certainly not one that pacifists could pursue with any hope of success.[30]

In Berne, the *bureau* found itself the center of painful requests by parents and relatives of people who had been studying or living abroad when the war broke out to help locate their lost or interned families. Golay and Mlle. Montaudon in Berne worked ceaselessly to put people in touch, and pacifists in enemy nations continued to help.[31] "The Peace Bureau," wrote Montaudon, "slowly has been transformed into an agency for repatriation of poor children placed in foreign countries or as a way of obtaining news for anguished parents. Today we must adopt to new conditions and help war victims."[32]

By September and October, Belgium was occupied and France was invaded with German troops advancing on most fronts. (Continental pacifists seemed completely unaware of the Eastern front.) To French pacifists, talk of a mediated peace or a truce prior to the withdrawal of German troops from Belgium and France was tantamount to treason and a betrayal of the principles of the movement that rejected conquest and occupation. Charles Richet described German behavior in Belgium:

> German soldiers finish off the wounded, shoot civilians for nothing, assassinate children, put women and the aged in the front of their troops, bombard undefended towns without cease, brutalize and terrorize villages where they march, . . . fly white flags to mask their attacks, shoot members of the government, use dumdum bullets and generally act like savages, Huns. . . . Shall we behave like them? . . .
> Shall we dishonor ourselves like them? . . .
> The only reprisals worthy of us are to redouble our efforts for humanity and justice. . . . When the struggle will end, [we must act] with great sympathy for the unfortunate victims of two sinister rulers. . . . In this colossal struggle, we stand for the freedom of peoples, liberty, the future and the definitive pacification of the world.[33]

Similarly, Ruyssen published a pointed "Letter to a German Pacifist" when the war began: "In 1792, the Legislative Assembly declared that the Revolution would wage war not against Peoples but against Kings. A similar feeling animates us today," he wrote.[34] There could be no permanent peace until the kaiser and empire were removed; peace needed a democratic base in all nations. This was hardly the spirit of conciliation that a meeting in Berne would require.

La Fontaine, who reached Great Britain in September, substantially agreed that nothing of significance would arise from a meeting. In November, La Fontaine published a powerful manifesto, "What Pacifists Ought to Say," which denounced the lies and calumnies that preceded the war. His presentation of the events between 31 July and 4 August affirmed his view that the Germans bore the brunt of blame for triggering the war potential of the alliance system, a system that pacifists had long regarded as provocative, not pacific. In three months of fighting, involving eighteen million combatants, spending over eight million pounds a day, the threat to civilization that the pacifists had predicted had become a daily reality. La Fontaine urged pacifists to band together in order to agitate for the kind of peace that would be as unbreakable as humankind could forge. His manifesto anticipated a democratically run peace conference that agreed to abolish the armaments industries; that transformed armies into militias; that established mechanisms to punish those who advocated race or ethnic hatreds; that created courts to try violations of human rights; that recognized the universal right of national self-determination; that created open diplomacy and parliamentary control of foreign policy. "Less developed peoples" might need the "collective protection" of the advanced states, he argued, but peaceful ways to bring about independence must be pursued. When the slaughter ended, La Fontaine envisioned an entente cordiale among the peoples.[35] The immediate task for pacifists, he urged, was to try to stop the bloodbath and to influence the nature of the peace that would follow. For his part, he planned to go to the United States in order to crusade for neutral intervention to stop the war.

The British peace movement initially welcomed an offer of mediation from President Woodrow Wilson.[36] But soon the National Peace Council also began to reevaluate neutral intervention as the occupation of Belgium and France altered realities. The National Peace Council turned to less controversial discussions of a lasting peace instead of specific proposals to stop the current war.[37] Military training in schools, once a standard object of criticism by British pacifists, was dropped from public discussion and taken up discreetly with the head of the school system. In November, the Council came forth with a general statement that resembled La Fontaine's. Denouncing the international system that produced the war, the Council insisted on a peace that reflected a new public law: self-determination for the rights of nationalities; the repudiation of militarism; and the establishment of a system of law to replace the system of alliances.[38] These broad guidelines reflected prewar aspirations for an organized peace.

In France, d'Estournelles de Constant succinctly summarized the pacifist position against a negotiated truce, "The world can now measure what Prussian militarism cost: peace can only be re-established by war to the finish."[39] For pacifists who had waged the war against war in an effort to prevent the horrendous reality, there is no choice, continued d'Estournelles, "Better to die, better to lose everything, than to let ignoble German militarism win." He rejected any idea of a meeting on neutral territory of peace internationals. Such would only produce sterile discussions on violations of human rights. Now, he argued, is the time to act; later to talk. D'Estournelles de Constant agreed that neutrals might meet but not in the spirit of the "neutral" Pontius Pilate; a valuable meeting would be a denunciation of the violation of international law.[40] He circulated the text of a speech delivered at Columbia University by Nicholas Murray Butler, who proclaimed:

> We are a neutral nation . . . ; but neutrality is not indifference. We cannot, we must not refrain from judging the conduct of men, individuals or nations. First, we are unanimous in deploring this unprecedented war. . . . Then we insist, all of us, that this war was declared by kings and their governments and was not wanted by peoples.[41]

For d'Estournelles de Constant "the world was divided into two camps; on the one hand, that of the past, of violence and domination, detested by everyone . . . ; on the other hand, that of the future, that is, of peace."[42] He kept up a lively correspondence with American peace leaders to prevent them from working for a cease-fire or neutral intervention before a battlefield victory.

Among French peace activists, Jeanne Mélin voiced doubts about the causes of the war, despite the fact that she was a refugee from her hometown in the Ardennes, which was occupied.[43] Although she did not question the responsibility of Austria and Germany for starting the war, she wondered privately if it were not the product of a male mentality that "violated the laws of equity that require both sexes to collaborate in the oversight of security and not allow one to dominate public affairs."[44]

By the fall of 1914, reassessments of neutrality filled the columns of Italian peace journals. One writer asked: What kind of future would Italy enjoy if it had no place at the peace conference table?[45] Another posed the rhetorical question: What kind of world would exist if German militaristic values predominated in Europe?[46] By the end of 1914, after nearly four months of war, Moneta compared German militarism to a cancerous growth that impeded the natural evolution of the United States of Europe. The cure was radical surgery.[47]

In fact, Henri Golay, director of the peace office in Berne, fully shared La Fontaine's assessment of the causes of the war and privately supported the entente with all his heart. He, too, did not want the executive committee of the Bureau international de la paix to convene in Berne. To Jeanne Mélin, he wrote:

> The cause of France is, in my eyes, the same as the cause of right and law, without which, the peace is worthless. I am entirely in communion with the pacifist ideals of our French friends . . . Ruyssen, Richet and the others.[48]

Ruyssen voiced his opinion in a brutal attack on German pacifism. The president of La Paix par le droit compared the different right-wing nationalisms of the two adversaries to demonstrate that German pacifists, themselves, were influenced, fatally, by militarism. Moreover, they had completely failed to educate their compatriots about the horrors of war. In addition, they never had the courage to take on the extreme nationalists who dominated the public political discourse.[49]

In Berne, the peace office was in severe difficulty. The Carnegie Foundation suspended its support, willing only to subsidize *La Paix par le droit* and *Die Friedens-Warte*.[50] The office received about thirty thousand pieces of mail after the war broke out. A decision about its role and future had to be made, and its governance required a meeting of its council. German members of the executive committee, supported by Dutch, Austrian, and some Swiss, pressed throughout the autumn 1914 for a meeting. French and most Italian pacifists totally refused to come to Berne, but the English agreed to send a delegate. La Fontaine finally assented to the meeting because a petition signed by eight council members asked for one (under Article 10 of the statutes),[51] but he expected very little of it. In January 1915, they assembled: delegates came from Germany, the Netherlands, Switzerland, Austria, Italy, Britain, and Hungary. La Fontaine chaired. The absent delegations, notably the French, gave proxies.

The two days of meetings, 6 and 7 January 1915 were the obsequies for the prewar international peace movement. Apart from grieving the death of Bertha von Suttner (which occurred in June along with Sarajevo) and Adolph Richter (August 1914), the participants agreed on nothing of substance except to preserve an unpublished stenographic record of the meeting in the archives of the *bureau*. Gaston Moch forwarded an impassioned document attacking the meeting, analyzing what went wrong with Europe and proposing the grounds for a reconstituted peace movement after the war.[52]

Edoardo Giretti objected to the decision to preserve the record of the meeting in secrecy and to require unanimous support in order to publicize resolutions.

Pacifists should have nothing to hide and silence was cowardice in his estimation. But the group refused to go public with divisive and divided opinions.[53]

The financial problems of the *bureau* required radical changes. *Mouvement pacifiste* was to be reduced to a short, bimonthly in French. La Fontaine, planning to travel to the United States, offered to try to raise money but was not optimistic.

Although Quidde and Fried wanted to discuss the general direction that the *bureau* should pursue during the crisis and to explore principles of a lasting peace, Giretti wanted the meeting to start with an unequivocal denunciation of the violation of the neutrality of Belgium and Luxembourg. In his view, that statement was the main purpose of meeting. His proposed resolutions flatly blamed the Triple Alliance for the war, a position that Quidde vigorously disputed:

> The question of the responsibility for the great European war is much too complicated to be resolved here. It is not in accordance with the attitude that pacifists, representatives of international justice and fairness and of careful judgment, should take in such matters by [simply stating] in one word: the war was caused by Germany or by Austria.[54]

Quidde contended that no one had sufficient information or objectivity to determine causation. Given the nature of the war—where the survival of entire peoples and nations was at stake, wherein political parties from left to right had agreed to suspend debate and shelve their disputes—Quidde insisted that it was absolutely inappropriate for pacifists to challenge the probity of any government's assertions. This war was not like the Boer War or the Tripoli adventure, which pacifists had criticized; in those cases, the fate of millions did not hang in the balance.[55] Quidde wanted "all of the belligerent powers" accused of "regrettable violations against international law," and he insisted that the meeting:

> Restrict our negotiations to the formulation of the tasks which are to be recommended to the pacifist organizations for their further propaganda and which ones are to be recommended to the Peace Bureau for its future peace resolutions.[56]

The struggle was joined. Giretti spoke on behalf of the Italian and French peace community and was backed by La Fontaine, the British, and the Swiss Romande delegates. The Dutch delegate waffled between Quidde and Giretti, finally landing on Quidde's side. He wanted the "responsibility of the war [placed] in the governments' policies . . . all of them guilty."[57]

Giretti was furious. As an individual, he had withstood denunciations and opprobrium in 1911–1912 when he attacked the government and the pacifists who supported the war against Tripoli. He had no patience with the argument that it was dangerous to criticize a nation at war. It was the council's duty

> to reaffirm the principles proclaimed by all the peace congresses and to protest energetically against all offenses committed against International Law in the course of the current war, notably against the aggressive and inexcusable character of the Ultimatum addressed to Serbia . . . and the brutal violation of the treaties which required the German and Austro-Hungarian Empires to respect and guarantee the neutrality of Belgium and Luxembourg.[58]

Joseph Alexander from Britain supported Giretti, adding his detestation of the alliance system, its secret protocols, and the concomitant arms race. He wanted both the long-term and immediate causes named. On Quidde's side, the Dutch delegate actually questioned whether there was a violation of Belgian neutrality—a point that forced La Fontaine to drop his neutrality. Astonished, La Fontaine reminded him that it was the German chancellor, Bethman-Hollweg himself, who stated bluntly in the Reichstag that Belgian neutrality, unfortunately, had to be sacrificed. To pretend otherwise was to play ostrich. The final vote, counting proxies, was divided evenly: ten for and ten against the Giretti resolution blaming the Triple Alliance for egregious violations of international law and custom. In this last meeting of the leaders of organized international pacifism, the postwar debate on the origins of the war and the war guilt clause was prefigured.

As the discussion developed during the afternoon of 6 January, Quidde reiterated his position that "when this war will end, the great moment of pacifism will arise" and that "the German organizations will be in a position to influence public opinion." Currently, however, Germans believe that British violations of international law, the rights of neutrals, and their domination of world trade are justifiable reasons to fight.[59] If the meeting insisted on voting a resolution that attacked German and Austrian decisions about the war, the German pacifists would have to resign from the council. It would make their work at home impossible.

The discussion on 7 January, replete with parliamentary maneuvers and procedural disputes, centered on whether the *bureau* ought to encourage neutral nations to seek a negotiated peace. Joseph Alexander pointed to the stalemate on the western front and to the earlier example of the long South African War, which bedeviled everyone's estimations of its probable length. Fearing the total destruction of Belgium, Alsace-Lorraine, northern France, and the other battlefields in "this terrible war," Alexander argued against a war to the finish. He confided that his compatriots were not thrilled with the task of fighting the tsar's cause. A joint intervention by the United States and European neutrals, organized by the Swiss government—at least to probe what terms the belligerents would accept—was absolutely appropriate.[60] Alexander raised an altogether new reason for trying to shorten the war, the fact that a move was developing among university youth at Oxford and Cambridge that blamed "our generation and the generation that preceded it" for forcing them to march off. "The stupidity which afflicted our generation" was turning our children against us, he observed, citing friends of his own son.[61]

Swiss delegates reported on their attempts to persuade their government to undertake diplomatic inquiries preliminary to a cease-fire, but the outcome was disappointing. The president of the Swiss National Council (Nationalrat) had insisted that the present moment was infelicitous.

La Fontaine was also skeptical, convinced that neither side would reveal the acceptable conditions for a cease-fire. The French would only discuss peace when German soldiers were back over the Rhine and the sense that victory was imminent, held by both sides, made peace overtures impossible in January 1915. Giretti opposed a call for peace that ignored the violation and occupation of Belgium and Luxembourg. Were neutral nations to initiate a peace overture without a concomitant and simultaneous withdrawal of forces, they would be actually supporting the German side. With most of Belgium and a large part of France occupied, Giretti commented, "As much as I am a pacifist, I do not want peace under such conditions."[62]

La Fontaine concluded that the only reasonable step for the *bureau* to take was to issue an appeal to intellectuals. The time was ripe to call educated people to their senses in the hope that they could begin to influence their fellow men to consider open diplomacy, a general peace conference and some form of restriction on armaments.[63]

On the final afternoon of the meeting, the principles of a lasting peace were debated. Postwar organization, in La Fontaine's view, must include an obligatory system of international jurisdiction, a major role for neutrals, and the formation of an embryonic United States of Europe. Minority rights and national minorities must be respected, the right to preserve culture and language in a majoritarian culture was fundamental. Giretti added that the postwar world would have to organize an international police force to protect small nations, such as Belgium, a remark that provoked Quidde. Finally, the role of the press in inciting peoples was briefly raised. There was no agreement about how to prevent this "terrible power" as La Fontaine called it, from doing evil.[64] When the session closed, La Fontaine's farewell fell like a bombshell:

> What we can hope for, as we separate, is that these sad circumstances will soon change. As much as I am . . . an internationalist, I am also . . . Belgian. But here, permit me to express the hope that our friends from German and Austrian nations will acknowledge the wrong that they have done to us.[65]

The result of the meeting of January 1915 was to commit the *bureau* to public neutrality during the war. Although that outcome was preferred by French pacifists, in the long run, it undermined the remaining prestige and moral presence of the Bureau international de la paix as a force in peace circles.

La Fontaine and Golay issued an appeal to intellectuals around the globe to preserve civilization.

> Yours is a sacred duty. . . . Peoples face one another full of hatred and bitterness, intent on mutual destruction. . . . Incapable of seeing that they have anything to do with one another. . . . You, . . . the priests of science and art, seekers of truth . . . are aware of the interdependence of nations and you know that when the delirium of war is over, an iron law will compel [the combatants] to seek out each other again.[66]

The two authors did not expect the world's thinkers and artists to stop the war but pleaded that they remain "aloof from the slough of hate" so that "your words and your deeds can help heal the wounds."[66] The group separated. Quidde returned home, to become the object of close police surveillance.[67] La Fontaine soon embarked for the United States. Giretti in Italy became persuaded that his country would have to enter the war.[68] Golay remained in Berne, struggling to keep the organization intact and to collect information from the belligerent nations about the state of mind of peoples.

In France, Ruyssen, still fond of survey questionnaires, wanted the surviving peace community to investigate the attitudes of a select sample on the future of small-power neutrality in Europe. What, specifically, should be done in the postwar world to preserve the freedom of small states and what role would they have at the expected peace congress?[69] Jeanne Mélin, however, wanted French pacifists to break their patriotic silence, issue a statement regarding the type of peace that they wanted, or, at least, hold a meeting to consider a strategy. She was rebuffed by Charles Richet, who warned her, early in 1915, "At this moment . . . there is no place nor point in writing or speaking. We must act and fight."[70] When she approached Ruyssen a year later, he vaguely proposed a meeting in Paris but asked her to keep the idea to herself because he was under police surveillance.[71] From the Ligue des droits de l'homme, a little more activity was forthcoming. Late in 1914, it urged its surviving sections to preserve records of human rights violations in occupied areas. The war "was characterized by an imaginable number of acts which the civilized world would never have believed possible" and their memory must not be lost.[72] Victor Basch undertook an analysis of all the variously colored books issued by all the governments defending their actions in 1914 and rejected the German position. He insisted that France was fighting for the ideal articulated by Immanuel Kant: "a rule of law equally for all States as for individuals; the establishment of a society of nations governed by justice. . . . The final aim of this war will be a step in the direction of realizing this aim."[73] Elsewhere, he wrote that the *ligue* always defended a pacifism that was rooted in the right to life, "a primordial right of individuals and nations."[74] French pacifists who had led the prewar movement felt thoroughly justified in supporting their government, for "this war is exactly a war of defense and from it will come the future society of nations."[75]

The Italian pacifist position, in support of the entente well before their nation entered the war on that side (23 May 1915, after months of negotiations with Great Britain and France for territorial concessions after the war), was a logical extension of the "patriotic pacifism" that characterized their movement. That pacifism and "sacred national rights" were compatible and that these rights included "building a greater country" was an unchallenged truism.[76] Italian pacifists heated up their prowar campaign by persistent attacks on Germany (a nation gripped by "a mad dream of . . . dominating the world, one in which German intellectuals desire to be heralds)."[77] Women activists promised to "organize women's work in the event of mobilization or war . . . to substitute for those absent in offices . . . so as not to impede the economic and social life of the nation."[78] Edoardo Giretti, who had never been a captive of the virulent nationalism of 1911–1912, reluctantly and sadly concluded that military intervention on the entente side was inevitable and just. "I remain an intractable enemy of . . . conquest and militarism," he wrote in May 1915, "but I . . . hope that Italy does not delay [in] accepting and undertaking a terrible obligation which will destroy the fortunes and happiness of thousands of Italian families."[79] Italian pacifists greeted Pope Benedict XV's repeated calls for ending the war and for preserving Italian neutrality with silence.

Moneta, not content with Italy's entry into the war, also declared war against

German pacifists. When he learned that Ludwig Quidde had attacked Italy's "perfidious" entry in an article in the *Berliner Tageblatt* (2 June 1915), Moneta let flow a stream of invective in an open letter, "Dear Ex-Friend." Moneta began by analyzing the differences between the kind of national movements that had unified Italy and Germany. In Italy, all social classes had been engaged in an honorable struggle to drive out an oppressive foreign occupation, whereas in Germany, the Prussians had led a unification movement that ended by humiliating others—Alsatians, Lorrainians, Poles, French, and Danes—with no grasp of human or national rights. Germany learned "duplicity" under Bismarck, continued Moneta, and its liberal and progressive citizens had all become infected. For the world to enjoy peace, German militarism had to be eradicated. Moneta expressed joy that Italians had fought in Libya-Cyrenaica in recent years, thus providing them with fresh experience to use in Europe against tyrants. It was a comprehensive attack.[80] It added decoration to the well-nailed coffin interring international pacifism.

The position of the Italian and French pacifists opposed neutral intervention, a truce, a negotiated peace, or any attempt to stop the war that fell short of eliminating Hohenzollern and Hapsburg authority. British pacifists, too, dropped talk of negotiated peace and neutral intervention to stop the war. Although the National Peace Council had been willing to send J. G. Alexander to the Berne meeting in January, it voted against any similar activity in the future. Vague commitments to attend another meeting of the *bureau* in the spring of 1915 were dropped.[81]

By the end of 1915, a discouraged Carl Heath, now head of the British National Peace Council, commented:

> I cannot help thinking that not much will come from America in the way of solutions for the problems that are strangling Europe. For one thing, I doubt if Americans widely understand the situation.[82]

Attempts by neutrals to help shape a peace congress in 1915 were not successful, and Heath saw this as further reason for gloom.

Heath's assessment of the United States was accurate. La Fontaine was unable to persuade American peace societies to band together to create a large, coordinated antiwar campaign. They insisted on pursuing their own agendas, and the results were disappointing. His arguments to the Carnegie Endowment obtained a tiny contribution in 1915 for the Berne office but not willingness to speak out on the war.[83] In the United States, La Fontaine lectured, taught at various universities, wrote and argued, and conducted a wide private correspondence in an effort to reach influential Americans. He reiterated the principles of the peace movement to describe the contours of a future peace:

> 1. Peoples have the inalienable right to dispose of themselves freely; backward peoples must be placed under the tutelage of the states. There is no right of conquest.
>
> 2. All disputes between States must be settled by conciliatory or judicial procedures (mediation, commissions of inquiry, councils of conciliation, arbitration, international court of justice.) There is no right of self-redress.

3. The maintenance of order . . . is to be intrusted [sic] to the combined moral, political, economic or military forces of the States. There is no right of war.[84]

La Fontaine's campaign in the United States did not turn out as he had wished. But when word came of the Russian Revolution in 1917, followed by the Russian decision to leave the war, he was overjoyed that the United States decided to enter:

If our Russian comrades had said to the German soldiers, either form a Republic and peace or fight till the Hohenzollerns are dethroned or exiled, that would have been one thing. There is no other solution; blessed was the day that the United States entered the war. The U.S. . . . will save the world whatever it may cost. The socialists who cannot understand that are the blind tools of the worst reactionaries. May our Russian comrades not be misled.[85]

The general weakness of the international peace movement was particularly galling to Golay, who recognized that the organization and the central office would lose all credibility by its silence. He had wanted to speak out on behalf of the forces fighting for a democratically based peace, a determination that was reinforced when the Russian Revolution in March 1917 rid the entente of its embarrassing ally. The executive committee of the Berne office had been split throughout the war—those wanting to speak out on the shape of the postwar peace (essentially, the German and German-Swiss position) and those wanting to speak out for a democratic-based peace (the French-Italian position, which required the elimination of Central European monarchies).[86] A Swiss journalist captured the fundamental problem of the movement in 1917:

It is easy to abuse pacifists but was it not clear that once war broke out, despite all their preventative efforts, they were honor bound to embrace their national causes and serve loyally? Have they not always insisted on their uncompromising patriotism?

Truthfully, pacifism never could disengage itself from the ties of nationalism. . . . The war has revealed the weakness of pacifist opportunism and the half-measures through which it operated. A radical pacifism which knows how to separate itself from nationalism and which will be the antithesis of nationalism must be developed for the future.[87]

That radical and different pacifism was born in the course of World War I, drawing on people who had little to do with the prewar movement or who moved away toward new premises. In 1915, Gaston Moch had predicted that the postwar peace movement could

not maintain the appearance of unity in a party with principles that some adherents did not dare defend and others did not recognize. . . . Democratic pacifists will become the peace party: simple humanitarians and mystics will revert to what they never stopped being—friends of peace.[88]

Besides the organizations that grew up in the Netherlands (e.g., the Anti-Oorlag Raad), to consider the shape of a durable peace, a strikingly new initiative occurred at The Hague in the spring of 1915. There, a group of about twelve hundred courageous women, called together by Dr. Aletta Jacobs (chair of the Dutch

Suffrage Society), came from a dozen nations—including belligerents—to consider how to stop the present killing as well as how to shape the future peace. From Hull House in Chicago, the noted American reformer Jane Addams was asked to chair. The most important long-range outcome was the formation of the Women's International League for Peace and Freedom (WILPF) which adopted that name in 1919.[89] What was significant about this organization—in contrast to prewar groups—was its willingness to meet during wartime, to demand an immediate halt to the carnage, and to insist that the rights of women (including suffrage) were a crucial part of the future society of nations.[90] (The tie between women's rights and peace had been forged earlier by Eugénie Potonié-Pierre, Séverine, Flammarion, and Wiesniewska, but it had not been central to male-run peace societies.) Its participants were unanimous in wanting to stop the war, and they ardently hoped that Jane Addams (later co-winner with Nicholas Murray Butler of the Nobel Peace Prize in 1931) could mount a successful campaign in the United States to that end. Energized by their success in holding the meeting at all, one English organizer claimed that women would conduct superior antiwar activism in contrast to the "passive and negative" peace movement that predated the war.[91]

A close analysis of the meeting reveals that, at least in 1915, the reality of politics and the war intruded on the best ideals of the organizers. For one, French women did not come—and it was not entirely a result of official refusal to let them travel. Jeanne Mélin, the most-likely French feminist and pacifist to attend, was cajoled repeatedly by Jacobs and Chrystal Macmillan, "Without you, France will not be represented," they wrote, and added that German women had agreed to come.[92] Mélin would not go, despite her growing belief that the absence of women from serious participation in public life was a major force for war. Traditional French women, such as Mme. Jules Siegfried, chair of the French women's suffrage alliance, was outraged that a meeting was held. No Serbian women came either.

As the meeting progressed, despite commitments to avoid divisive issues and hold debate on the future of the peace, neither Jane Addams nor Aletta Jacobs could eliminate disruptive problems much better than any earlier peace congress. Did respect for nationalities mean that Belgium would have to be broken into its linguistic parts? The Belgian women present feared discussion of that topic on the grounds that it might preclude their return home! Did respect for nationalities mean that the Irish were to be free of the British, and if that was what the women's meeting was proposing, were they also proposing violent revolution to attain it? If the meeting agreed that Poles should have their own nation (which it did), did that mean that Italy should take Trieste or the Tyrol?[93] These questions of national interest found no more satisfying answers among the women at The Hague than they had earlier. (The Swedish feminist and pacifist Ellen Key responded to the problem by denouncing chauvinism but defending patriotism as consonant with internationalism.)[94]

In terms of the final resolutions that the women voted at The Hague, except for the demands for women's rights and a place at the peace table, the structures for a peaceful world resembled those proposed by liberal internationalists: juridical tribunals, a society of nations, collective security, disarmament, control of arms manufacturing, and the sort of education that trained world citizens.

A less-known women's initiative was attempted in Switzerland, coordinated by Marguerite Gobat, daughter of the deceased Albert Gobat. In February 1915, L'Union mondiale de la femme was formed, dedicated to attaining and preserving peace. The founding members were related to male activists in the Swiss or international peace movement.[95] Women, called "the creative half of humanity," were continuing their "work of construction, while man, despite his most earnest desires and skillful diplomacy, has been drawn against his will, into the work of destruction," announced the group's brochure.[96] One of the founders wrote to La Fontaine that modern woman, "highly educated, privileged . . . and nearly emancipated, should be capable of coping. . . . Her field is greater . . . than the battlefields of Europe . . . [she has] the power of Universal mobilization." Evidently, the author imagined that women—despite the war—would be able to continue their clubs—such as the Red Cross and the International Suffrage Alliance—and the volunteer activities that they undertook. The membership of this women's group did not spread beyond Swiss borders.

Besides women's peace organizations, the war inspired other new societies, entirely unaffiliated with the Berne office and prewar groups. In England, the Union of Democratic Control became prominent; in the United States, the eventual emergence of the American Union Against Militarism altered the landscape. In France, amid the war when it was highly unpatriotic and suspect, Séverine was the first of the prewar pacifists to adopt a more militant antiwar posture. She joined the Société d'études documentaires et critiques sur la guerre (Society for Critical and Documentary Studies of the War) in 1916 with Mathias Morhardt and Georges Demartial. This group pioneered the revision of patriotic self-congratulation about France's purity at the outbreak of the war. Amid the war, threatened with censorship and worse, she challenged the sacrosanct fantasy about France's strictly defensive behavior in 1914. At the end of the war, Séverine became one of the first Continental members of the War Resisters International— another new pacifist group founded in the conflict. Jeanne Mélin, dissatisfied with the reluctance of her former pacifist colleagues, moved toward the Communist party.

The war provided a great shakeout of the movement. Antimilitarism such as that Bart de Ligt preached in the Netherlands banned him from publication and public life in 1915.[97] Antimilitarism defended by Karl Liebknecht and Rosa Luxemburg sent them to prison during World War I. Although middle-class Continental pacifism had always shunned antistate, anarchistic, and individualistic behavior, this form of action proved more powerful and compelling during wartime than the discrete silence of patriotic pacifists or the anger of Rosalia Gwis-Adami, who denounced Romain Rolland, the eminent French writer, for choosing Swiss exile, "above the fray," instead of defending his nation.[98] And, of course, the initiative associated with the socialist parties, particularly the Zimmerwald Conference, were entirely separated from the remains of the prewar peace movement.

The war exercised a profound transformation on religious-based pacifism. The Fellowship of Reconciliation, launched by Protestant groups, spread from Great Britain across the United States and into Europe during the 1920s; Quaker activism revived; the emergence of Christian socialism among Dutch and Swiss activists, such as Jules Humbert-Droz[99] provided the basis for a host of pacifist initiatives from democratic schoolrooms to communal living arrangements to resistance to the draft. Catholic pacifist groups formed, drawing on Pope Leo XIII's warning (1894) against the arms race and the militarization of youth and Pope Benedict XV's denunciation of war in World War I.[100] During the 1920s, advocacy of draft resistance spread among youth as well as veterans groups. Mahatma Gandhi's methods of opposing British rule in India provided a major model for the application of nonviolent resistance to European groups hungry for alternatives.

The end of the war also brought forth groups that resembled prewar societies in their commitment to democracy, national self-determination, and the formation of a systematic international order. Typical were the associations for the League of Nations founded in France and Italy. The French group included Léon Bourgeois, Ferdinand Buisson, Charles Richet, Jules Prudhommeaux, Théodore Ruyssen, d'Estournelles de Constant as well as leading socialists—Alexandre Millerand, Albert Thomas, and the historian, Alphonse Aulard. The Italian group attracted Arcangelo Ghisleri and Giuseppe Riccieri from prewar organizations as well as Leonida Bissolati, Gaetano Salvemini, and a number of Milanese liberals associated with *Il Secolo*.[101] The Dutch society, the Central Committee for a Durable Peace, wanted to organize a meeting of citizens from all the belligerents, but French activists feared meeting Germans in the winter of 1919. Women from all nations assembled, however, in February 1919 in Berne, invited by Swiss women, to consider joint demands from the peace congress.

In the spring of 1919, when the negotiations were under way for the Treaty of Versailles, Carl Heath issued a memorandum regarding the changed situation of the peace movement. Recognizing that altogether new groups had appeared during the war and that many of the older constituents of the International Peace Office had disappeared, he called for a census to be taken, nation by nation, of the new groups and for the kind of reorganization that would attract the support of feminist and socialist societies.[102] Heath hinted that a professional director had to be hired, replacing Golay, and that a much more vigorous international campaign had to be launched. His suggestions appear to have been ignored. In 1921, two years after the Treaty of Versailles, the Berne *bureau,* led by La Fontaine and Golay, chanced another Universal Peace Congress. Despite the fact that annual meetings were reinstituted[103] and that some prewar friendships were mended, the élan was never recaptured. Marguerite Gobat and Henri Golay fell out, and she took her considerable talents to WILPF.[104] Attempts by a few French and German peace activists to build bridges between their peoples, notably efforts by Buisson and Quidde to defuse national hatreds, won both the Nobel Peace Prize in 1927 but did not succeed in reconstituting a serious international peace movement. By 1924, La Fontaine was aware that the prewar movement could not be reconstituted: "You know as well as I do that the old pacifist movement in every nation is in a condition of profound somnolence."[105]

Just before her death, Marguerite Gobat mused that

> at the beginning of our century, pacifism seemed to have won the day. By the force of things and because of the goodwill of its partisans, it had become a party defending a doctrine that uplifted our old world, tired of injustice and barbarism.[106]

By the mid-1930s, when she wrote those words, Marguerite Gobat fully realized that the pacifist vision for the twentieth century was far from realization. Those prewar pacifists, such as the members of La Paix par le droit who became ardent Wilsonians or organizers of societies to support the League of Nations, had held great hopes for collective security through the 1920s that evaporated with the 1930s. With the coming of World War II, the International Peace Bureau closed its offices and the Swiss government assumed control of its assets.[107] Henri Golay wrote sadly to La Fontaine:

> I have taken advantage of my leisure . . . to put a bit of order into the archives which remained more or less in the condition that they were in when they arrived in Geneva. It is a work which evokes overwhelmingly melancholy memories. The past is past; it is towards the future that we must turn. . . . One has the feeling of having made such useless efforts.[108]

La Fontaine, caught in occupied Brussels with a dying wife and strict rationing, watched his world catch fire for a second time. This time there was no escape to the United States. He could only hope that a new generation would rise from the ashes and do a better job in the future. In 1941, Golay wrote to report that Quidde, de Neufville, and Ferrero all died, two of them in exile—the last voices of the movement formed in 1889. "All this work, all these efforts may bear fruit some day," commented a depressed Golay. "Candidates for doctorates will doubtless find precious materials for their theses."[109]

World War I also transformed the Interparliamentary Union, but this organization, suspending activities during the two global conflicts of the twentieth century, reorganized and reappeared after each. As a forum for members of parliaments from every continent, the Union continues to hold annual meetings and serves as a network for those interested in a global rule of law. As such, it has fulfilled a small part of the vision which Marcoartu, Passy, Cremer, and others had a century ago.

9

Conclusion

During the course of the nineteenth century, citizen activists on the European continent launched repeated campaigns to discredit the fatalistic assumption that international peace could never be more than a tense vacuum, the interludes between wars. In place, they proposed a positive definition that construed peace as the normal routine of international relations protected by juridical and political institutions. By waging war on war, peace activists ineluctably, often unwillingly, challenged royal, ministerial, and diplomatic control of international processes. They introduced the voices of a wider public, initially drawn from the progressive sectors of the *pays legal,* into the political discourse of the nineteenth century. Peace became the focus of movements sustained by self-selected, interested volunteers in private, unofficial societies who developed the habits of speaking unpopular truths to power. Citizen campaigners moved questions of peace from the precincts of philosophers and legal scholars onto the reform agendas of Europeans, frequently the same people who celebrated the new technological and industrial accomplishments of their day. Often, classical liberal and socialist thinkers shared a broad consensus that rejected war and militarism as irrational, wasteful impediments to development *and* a major source of social misery. With her Saint-Simonian colleagues, Eugénie Niboyet argued forcefully that the thirty years of peace from 1815 to 1845 produced more progress than the preceding two decades of warfare. Battlefield glory was a meaningless bauble to a society that needed railways laid, canals dug, and roads paved—not an increase in taxes to cover escalating barracks expenses.

Continental political realities were inhospitable to the peace positions articulated by religious pacifists. Religious pacifism enjoyed its main support in British and North American circles and, at the end of the century, in the work of Leo

Tolstoy. Its absolute message tolerated no exceptions. Warfare was never legitimate; to Tolstoy it was premeditated organized murder. On the Continent, "practical" and secular peace activism developed differently. Among the complex of antiwar reasons argued by Jean-Jacques, comte de Sellon, was the possibility that European war might unleash the social class war inherent in the Jacobin enterprise of 1792–1795. Sellon was well aware that the injustices of modern life might revive the mentality that once mobilized ordinary people to wage "war on the castles and peace to the villages."[1] Similarly, at the end of the century, Jean de Bloch repeatedly warned that the probable consequences of a major European war would be the overthrow of thrones and social revolution, a prediction that seemed prescient when the Russian Revolution of 1905 burst forth amid the Russo-Japanese War. In 1913, the newest European peace society established in Saint Petersburg heard a roster of speakers describe a "compelling tableaux" of the destruction "in men, money, commercial interruption, the suspension of industrial life, rail traffic, etc."—in short, the end to civilization—that a European war would induce.[2] The threat that war posed to the social order and to advanced civilization, a fear of diplomats assembled at the Congress of Vienna, continued to worry middle-class and conservative peace advocates throughout the nineteenth century.

Sellon was equally adamant against the use of violence as a tool for opening new markets. His denunciation of the French invasion of Algeria in 1830 launched a tradition of peace activists' attacks on bloody imperial adventures. At the first general peace congresses during the 1840s, English and American voices criticized the British government's wars in China (over opium) and in Afghanistan as well as for its attacks on South African natives; English peace activists including Henry Richard and W. Randal Cremer attacked British bombardment of Alexandria (1882); Frédéric Passy characterized the French destruction of Vietnamese culture as a historic catastrophe (1884–1885); the entire European peace community joined in denouncing European military atrocities in China and British warfare against the Boers (1900). The arguments used by anticolonial and antiimperial peace campaigners combined humanitarian and practical elements. Sellon, for instance, wondered how the French invasion in North Africa would ever persuade the local population to buy European products or, more significantly, to accept the presumed superiority of Christian civilization. Anticolonial and antiimperialist arguments led peace activists to doubt the legitimacy of European adventurism. French and British peace congresses began to pass resolutions that projected peaceful routes to independence for overseas territories. In 1911, the international peace movement, including its relatively conservative arm, the Interparliamentary Union, did not hesitate to denounce the Italian invasion of Libya and criticize those Italian pacifists who backed their government. The plea by a young Egyptian nationalist in 1912 at the Universal Peace Congress elicited a near-unanimous vote, whereas earlier meetings would never have scheduled such a topic on agendas. (In 1892, a Polish patriot had been rebuffed in his attempt to garner pacifist support for national independence at a Universal Peace Congress.) Attacks on the abuse of native peoples had been a fundamental platform of religious-based peace societies, such as the London Peace Society, whose membership overlapped with the Aborigines Protection Society. By 1914, the international movement, led by the French and Belgian peace communities, added the rights of native peoples to their platforms and began to consider methods for peaceful decolonialization.

In the middle of the nineteenth century, the peace movement confronted a major crisis when revolutionary protests sustained by oppressed nationalities in Hungary, the Italies, and the Germanies were destroyed by the superior military forces controlled by kings, aristocrats, and conservatives in general with the aid of the French president (later emperor), Louis-Napoléon. Whereas Richard Cobden, widely admired for his political success as head of the Anti-Corn-Law League, wrung his hands over the fate of Kossuth's Hungary and Mazzini's Rome during the 1849 Paris Peace Congress, a new generation of continental pacifists flatly asserted that some struggles justified the use of violent means. The fundamental rights of oppressed peoples to their freedom—whether these were Russian serfs, nationalities, or slaves in the United States—claimed the allegiance of a new generation of realistic peace activists who redefined the idea of just war. Edmond Potonié-Pierre's Ligue du bien public insisted that its democratic program had to precede international peace, a position given greater currency by the Ligue internationale de la paix et de la liberté. Sellon's nephew, Camillo di Cavour, the chief minister of the Kingdom of Sardinia who orchestrated the political and military stages of Italian unification in 1859–1860, obviously rejected his uncle's advice that warfare could never attain any justifiable end. In the 1860s, republican voices were joined by the first internationally organized socialist movement, which militantly proclaimed that total domestic reorganization through revolution must precede peace. By 1910, when Moneta observed, "the pacifist idea is the product of free nations," he voiced an opinion that had become unremarkable in European peace circles.[3]

Moderate and conservative pacifists, such as Frédéric Passy and Henry Richard, who doubted the significance of national liberation and unification through warfare, directed their energies toward the development of instruments of international law after 1871. In their estimation, the evolutionary processes of history would eventually resolve the problems of unfree peoples. They totally rejected the widely admired Mazzinian view that before permanent peace could be organized, the map of Europe had to be redrawn.

Pacifists were adamant that peace was not the quiet time between battles. "Europe is in a state of latent war," Lemonnier asserted in 1868. That men were currently not shooting at each other did not mean peace existed; nations were preparing for the next bloodletting. Peace activists proposed a wide, rich variety of new possibilities—periodic diplomatic congresses, bilateral or general arbitration treaties, agreements stipulating mediation or good offices to precede mobilizations, formalized methods for neutral intervention, a standing court with trained jurists prepared to hear disputes, the possibility of an all-European congress, extensions of international agreements to cover topics as diverse as waterways and the rights of widows, orphans, and migrant workers who might be stranded abroad. War, an atavism in modern civilization, permitted militarism to survive and to provide a source of unearned income for the parasitic offspring of old elites in the officer corps. Militarism also justified generous taxpayers subvention of a few powerful monopoly industrialists who produced weaponry and to their dependent, well-paid fraction of the working classes. Pacifist analyses of peace, war, and militarism grew increasingly impatient and militant as the century wore on and the costs of national security seemed to become a threat to national survival.

Conservative and progressive pacifist voices shared this point of view. For Passy, military expenses were the main explanation for the social question. For the heirs to Lemonnier's point of view, especially Moch, Émile Arnaud, Auguste Hamon, Moneta, and most women peace activists, military expenditure was the single most deleterious chokehold on social and cultural progress.

By the end of the century, peace activists realized that Europeans, though hobbled by the most expensive arms race in history, had created a new economic and cultural order that contradicted the international political system of two hostile alliances. This vital economic and cultural internationalism cried out for complementary political and legal structures. In Brussels, Henri La Fontaine and Paul Otlet opened the Mundanum to serve as a center to coordinate the rash of new international organizations—official and private, from postal unions to libraries—that mushroomed around the globe. So powerful was his faith in the new internationalism that the German Alfred Fried vigorously defended its existence even in exile during the Great War itself.

> In the last century the world has completely changed. Something that stands above and between the nations has been evolved. The State is no longer an independent organism. The rapid development of science and industry has begun to weld the states into a complex organism . . . parts of a higher whole. I know how sceptical some people are today in regard to this so-called internationalism. . . . [but] we are dealing with facts. . . . Men and nations are at each other's doors. All the peoples of the earth have become interdependent. He who does not see this . . . when the war has upset the entire life of the world, must be blind. There is interdependence in material and in spiritual life, in production and exchange, in ideas. . . . A tendency toward "symbiosis" has asserted itself with the force of a natural law.
>
> Meanwhile the political relations of nations and the spirit in which they are conducted have not kept pace with this mighty force.[4]

Fried's description was the quintessential statement of liberal internationalism.

The dichotomy between the positions developed by Frédéric Passy, on the one hand, and Edmond Potonié-Pierre and Charles Lemonnier, on the other hand, during the late 1860s continued in transformed fashion for the rest of the century. For Potonié-Pierre and Lemonnier, an organized peace was the final product of republican democracy. Although he rejected Marxian socialism and Bakunian anarchism, Lemonnier insisted that Jacobin principles, broadened to include women's rights, provided the only just foundation for international peace. Moreover, the United States of Europe envisioned by Lemonnier would be fortified with the right to intervene within member states to protect human rights. Heirs to Lemonnier's vision of international peace after 1889 included moderate socialists, most continental feminists, and the left-wing of the international peace movement led by Moneta, Moch, Arnaud, Albert Gobat, Pratt, alma dolens, Séverine, the Potonié-Pierres, Sylvie Flammarion, Jeanne Mélin, and most of the members of La Paix par le droit. By 1889, many of Lemonnier's basic demands had become constitutional rights in Western Europe—universal male suffrage (he had supported universal suffrage), the right to compete for public office, separation of church and state, secular state-supported elementary education, a reasonably uncensored press. Intellectually, the most significant legacy of Lemonnier's position was the articulation of a just war position among continental pacifists, the heart of patriotic pacifism. The vast majority of delegates to Universal Peace Congresses before the Great War essentially approved of the use of force on behalf of self-defense or national liberation as a last resort.

From the position argued by Frédéric Passy and his many supporters, the peace movement developed its thoroughgoing examination of the tools and methods of peacekeeping—arbitration, international law, international tribunals, mediation, the rights of neutrals, the possibility of a league of neutrals, treaties stipulating peaceful resolution of differences. For problems where sufficient international agreement already existed—the rights of foreign visitors, joint access to waterways, settlement of territorial disputes—the peace movement lobbied for formalized treaties to codify these accepted situations into law as part of the strategy to narrow and eventually eliminate casus belli. Standing treaties that provided mechanisms for conflict resolution *in advance* of conflicts were rejected by most foreign offices as violations of sovereignty and national interest. The peace movement waged a persistent, but ultimately unsuccessful, struggle against that mentality.

Well into his eighties, Passy was indefatigable in his willingness to campaign on the lecture circuit on behalf of the movement, but he believed that only behind-the-scenes discussion with influential elites would succeed. In 1889—when he helped create both the Universal Peace Congress and Interparliamentary Conference—Passy envisioned the private citizen groups as a supportive constituency for the parliamentarians, who would have the task of shaping policy at home with the private activists serving as a loyal backdrop. When the tsar's Rescript of 1898 appeared calling for a conference of the powers to discuss a peace agenda, Passy believed that his preferred strategy had been vindicated. By keeping peace arguments as apolitical as possible, Passy believed that they could become respectable, that heads of state would see the folly of an infinite arms race and realize that their own interests would be secured through collective security.

It is not clear that Passy and his colleagues fully grasped the depth of hostility to their ideas that permeated official quarters. The depth of the backlash that formal discussions of arbitration, such as occurred at The Hague in 1899 and 1907, unleashed in executive mansions, palaces, and foreign offices was not fully revealed until after World War I when the documents on the origins of the war were published. Nonetheless, powerful hints of those attitudes were widely communicated by intellectuals who shared established points of view before the war. Hans Delbrück's assaults on arbitration before The Hague Conference met in 1899 and Ferdinand Brunetière's vitriolic trivialization of pacifism were two examples. After 1900, a common tactic of antipacifists was to red-bait the movement as socialist, an approach that crossed the Atlantic to be used by Admiral Alfred Mahan.

Official attitudes toward the 1899 conventions from The Hague meetings were manifest almost immediately as governments simply signed and then ignored their commitments—beginning with Great Britain and the Boer War. But the peace movement refused to accept this blatant tactic. In 1906, both the Interparliamentary Union and the Universal Peace Congress voted model projects that the next Hague Conference could use to create a system involving limited obligatory arbitration. In 1910, the Universal Peace Congress in Stockholm voted the Code de la paix in response to the criticism that an international tribunal could not operate without a code of law. By the eve of World War I, the private citizens peace movement in Europe had designed a series of model instruments, obtained backing from a cross-section of parliamentarians and produced a variety of proposals to contain the Great Power rivalries. The creation of the World Court in 1921 did not occur without significant prewar familiarity with the idea of such an institution.

Passy's legalistic approach was popular with religious and secular peace activists in Great Britain and with most central European pacifists. It avoided dangerous subjects, such as nationalism, Alsace-Lorraine, the right of self-defense, reduction of arms expenditure, and revision of the Treaty of Frankfurt, and it looked forward to a more-positive future when new generations would not be detained by the hostilities of the nineteenth century. Still, though he had urged pacifists to avoid contemporary issues, his last recorded memory on his deathbed was the moment at the Universal Peace Congress in 1905 at Lucerne when he and Quidde crossed the platform to shake hands at the end of the fractious debate over Alsace-Lorraine.[5]

With the new century, pacifist reluctance to confront the arms race eroded. The annual ritual of war ministers demanding increases in their budgets to protect national security by buying weapons, which they all claimed they would never be the first to use, was too dangerous a game to continue. In addition to older economic arguments against arms costs, the Dreyfus affair underscored the threat of a military caste to republican institutions; studies of barracks' life correlated social degeneracy with the draft; studies of military history suggested that defensive militias of trained citizens probably would surpass professional forces at a fraction of the cost. Pacifists joined with socialists to reveal the secret international connivances of the "merchants of death" and illustrations in the popular press of hideous European atrocities in China, the Congo, the Sahara, and South Africa emboldened voices to speak out vigorously. The fact that the German pacifist, Ludwig Quidde presented the 1913 Universal Peace Congress and Interparliamentary Union with a Model Treaty for Arms Reduction was an amazing change. By that year, the movement began to realize the potential of film, particularly with the Swiss produced film on the Balkan Wars.

The argument that European global preeminence was at risk made some headway in official circles before the war. Economists, journalists, and scholars increasingly argued that the European arms race was only of benefit to the United States, where the government supported barely 25,000 soldiers in peace time. Others portrayed a future Asian (Japanese) development that would outstrip the Old Continent, quite a different Yellow Peril than the image conjured up periodically by the German kaiser as an excuse for more weaponry. The fact that Norman Angell's analysis exercised even a limited impact on political circles testifies to the gnawing apprehension that Europe's global hegemony might be undermined.[6] Conceivably, Winston Churchill's public offer to drop construction of four new ships in 1913 if the German government was willing to eliminate two planned vessels can be seen in that context. Angell, of course, argued nothing substantially different than the peace movement had done for decades before him. The wild success of his book *The Great Illusion* between 1910 and 1914 demonstrated that a prepared public was willing to hear these claims.

The militant postures increasingly adopted by peace activists after 1900 demonstrated both the maturation of the movement and the gnawing terror that events would outstrip the slow evolution of public awareness and the self-control of government officials to prevent war. The belief that Time in her fullness would bring victory to the peace cause[7] had little appeal for younger recruits. From the Boer War down through the Italian invasion of North Africa in 1911, voices of angry peace activists mobilized wider and wider segments of the public. A few pacifists who engaged in direct action or confrontation with nationalist policies were attacked physically—the British protesters against the Boer War in Trafalgar Square in 1900 and the campaign against Ruyssen by the Action française in Bordeaux in 1913 are the two best examples. Antipacifism took on some of the shape of postwar fascist street politics.

The new militancy after 1900 was evident in the willingness of Ducommun, Pratt, Giretti, Prudhommeaux, Novicow, and Ruyssen to reach to the one group that might have exercised mass influence—the socialists. Ideological antipathies slid away as middle-class pacifists and moderate socialists created coalition politics, particularly in the Chambre des députés. There, Jean Jaurès, Francis de Pressensé, and Henry Hubbard routinely voted with the Radicals, Radical-Socialists, and centrists. A similar membership belonged to the Ligue des droits de l'homme where de Pressensé presided and Ferdinand Buisson served as vice president. Pragmatic considerations that developed after the Dreyfus and Fashoda affairs encouraged the political liaison. In Italy, during the 1904 Turin peace societies congress, Eduardo Giretti urged similar collaboration to the movement and to the working-class organizations represented there. Novicow, increasingly disenchanted with the shortsighted and selfish politics of liberals, eventually concluded that the future belonged to socialists, pacifists, and feminists.[8] Their collaboration, he urged, was the key to future progress.

The desired articulation between working-class and middle-class peace forces appeared to make some headway at the 1908 London Universal Peace Congress where substantial contingents of continental and British delegates shared the platform. Socialists, assembled in Stuttgart a year earlier for their annual meeting, had voted their famous resolution threatening a general strike in case of war and voicing support for arbitration as a form of peaceful conflict resolution. The hope of moderates among the middle-class peace movement for joint action against the headlong rush toward war or bankruptcy seemed to be growing. In 1912, Ruyssen urged La Fontaine, both a socialist and president of the International Peace Bureau, to ask the International Socialist Bureau if the two groups could not convene a joint conference on European peace. Ruyssen considered the threat to the preservation of peace so palpable that it overrode all other considerations.[9] The meeting never occurred but a conference of parliamentarians from France and Germany did sit a year later in Basel, the result of Gobat's labors, inspired by similar apprehensions.

In the decade before the Great War, the impact of women—as individual participants in peace societies or organized in their own separate groups—on peace thinking and activism emerged as a distinct force. Although most women participants did not dispute the general direction of the Universal Peace Congress—and, of course, Bertha von Suttner was on its executive committee—neither a specifically feminine nor feminist direction to peace propaganda was of much significance in the 1890s when the international movement was struggling to survive. After 1900, however, women's distinct tones were heard. Before her death, the Princess Wiesniewska concluded that peace projects would go nowhere unless the suffrage was given to women; she had not begun with a feminist agenda. Marguerite L. Selenka emerged from the ranks of middle-class German feminism to connect the civil rights aims of her associates to a transformed international climate that would undermine militarism. Flammarion addressed working-class people—women in particular—connecting their problems with military budgets. Jeanne Mélin, among others, demanded to know when the movement would support a reduction in military spending in order to provide for the needs of the socially excluded, especially underfed children and their exhausted mothers. Anna Eckstein, who moved from Germany to the United States, organized a bicontinental crusade for a world petition on behalf of a third Hague Conference that she presented to the 1910–1913 peace congresses. Outraged at the war against Turkey, alma dolens—prohibited from public-speaking engagements in Italy in 1911–1912—described the conditions in the Agro Romano (Rome), Milanese, and Neapolitan slums:

> Malaria is rampant. . . . The worker is forced to live in ancient hovels in degrading promiscuity with convicts, social misfits, surrounded by tuberculosis, the center of every and any vice . . . where young girls early lose their ability to smile. Such misery is not only characteristic of Italy.[10]

On a lecture tour in Belgium after the end of the Libyan War, she insisted that the majority of Italian women remained silent but furious about the war. They learned

> that the enemy is not at the border; it is all around us: it is poverty, tuberculosis, unemployment. The cure for these diseases is the end of formidable and costly weaponry.[11]

Thus, dolens spoke the language of the crusading women reformers for whom the idea that state and society had a social obligation to all members, especially the weak and defenseless, was sacrosanct. On both sides of the Atlantic before 1914, the consciousness of women crusaders concerned with peaceful social change eventually collided with the military state. For women activists, militarism blocked social amelioration and manufactured social misfits. For Moneta, it inspired immigration to distant lands where his compatriots lost their *italianità* and were bleached into Anglo-Saxons; for Richet, it starved sophisticated scientific research in Sorbonne laboratories. Only a major reduction in arms expenditure would avoid the derailment of civilization.

The fear of appearing unpatriotic eroded, and pacifists began to formulate a new language of patriotism on the eve of World War I. Everyone recognized how tenuous it was. Charles Richet observed

> The madness of the mob is nearly universal and we are only a tiny minority, we who hope for peace. . . . What weapon do we have to counter the impenetrable ignorance of personages on all social levels who refuse to entertain any suggestion of international justice? . . . All those acolytes of militarism only grasp hard facts— actual carnage, real rivers of human blood. . . . A general disaster will have more impact than rational argument.[12]

When the war broke out, of course, most pacifists, including Richet, along with most socialists including those who had supported the Stuttgart resolution, accepted their government's assertions that they had been attacked. Patriotic pacifism demanded that defensive war be waged. The War of August 1914 was a "just war."

Pacifists lost sight of their long-range vision in the midsummer madness of 1914. Their ideas, projects, and propaganda, however, have been flattered by imitation for most of the twentieth century. The legacy of nineteenth-century pacifism is modern liberal internationalism, most recently adapted in the new European Community, with headquarters in Brussels and Strasbourg.

Appendix A
Peace Societies, 1815–1914

Great Britain

1816 Society for the Promotion of Permanent and Universal Peace, London and numerous branches (Wisbech, Liverpool, York, Dublin, and Manchester–Birkenhead). Name changed to British Peace Society. (Twenty-eight branches in 1895.)

1868 Workman's Peace Association (also called Workman's League of Peace and Liberty and International Arbitration League). Sections in London, Birmingham, Liverpool, and Birkenhead.

1877 International Arbitration and Peace 'Association. Sections in Britain, Brussels, Milan, and Rome.

1882 The Women's Auxiliary of the Peace Society. Renamed (1888) Central Association of Local Peace Associations; renamed again (1895) Peace Union.

1886 Liverpool and Birkenhead Women's Peace and Arbitration Association.

1888 Peace Committee, Society of Friends.

1889 Christian Union for Promoting International Concord.

1890 British and Foreign Association (London).

France

1821 Société de la morale chrétienne. (Peace was not a primary interest of the organization, though occasionally, the group took up the issue.)

1858 Ligue du bien public (actually, a Belgian organization founded by a Frenchman, Edmond Potonié).

1867 Union de la paix (Le Havre), founded by Félix Santallier.

Ligue internationale de la paix, founded by Frédéric Passy. Name changed to Société française des amis de la paix (1872) and later to Société française pour l'arbitrage entre nations (ca. 1892).

Ligue internationale de la paix et de la liberté, founded originally in Geneva; headquarters moved to France in 1891. Founders included Jules Barni, Charles Lemmonier, Armand Goegg, and Pierre Jolissaint.

1880   Société de la paix par la justice internationale, founded by Hippolyte Destrem.

1884   Groupe des amis de la paix du Puy-de-Dôme, founded by Antoine Pardoux.

1886   Société de la paix du familistère du Guise, founded by Jean-Baptiste Godin.

1887   Association des jeunes amis de la paix, founded in Nîmes by students, including Charles Brunet and Jacques Dumas. Renamed Association de la paix par le droit (1889); merged with Société française d'arbitrage entre nations in 1910. Lasted until 1948.

1891   Union de la paix—Bergerac (Dordogne), founded by Auguste Desmoulins.

1892   Alliance des savants et des philanthropes.

Société de la paix d'Abbeville et du Ponthieu, founded by Jules Tripier.

1893   Société de la paix à Felletin et Aubusson.

Ligue française pour la paix, Sainte Colombe.

1895   Union internationale des femmes, founded by Eugénie Potonié-Pierre and Ellen Robinson, Paris and London.

Internationalis Condordia, founded by Emile Lombard.

1896   Alliance universelle des femmes pour la paix et pour le désarmement, founded by Princess Gabrielle Wiesniewska, Paris. Name changed to Alliance universelle des femmes pour la paix par l'éducation (1899).

1899   Comité de défense et de protection des indigènes.

Société Gratry de la paix.

Association internationale des journalistes amis de la paix.

L'Association 'la paix et le désarmement par les femmes,' founded by Sylvie Flammarion and Séverine.

Société chrétienne des amis de la paix.

1900	Association toulousaine de la paix.
1901	Association montalbanaise de la paix par le droit.
	Société de l'éducation pacifique, numerous sections throughout France and Belgium.
	Société castraise de la paix.
1905	Association marseillaise de la paix.
1905–1906	Conciliation internationale, founded by d'Estournelles de Constant in Paris.

Switzerland

1830   Société de la paix, founded by Jean-Jacques, comte de Sellon, Geneva.

1867   Ligue internationale de la paix et de la liberté, founded in Geneva (1867) by Pierre Jolissaint, Jules Barni, Charles Lemmonier, and Amand Goegg. (See 1867 in French listing.)

1889   Section suisse, Ligue internationale de la paix et de la liberté, created at Neuchâtel, merged with

1889   Société suisse de la paix. (Grew to twenty-two sections.)

1894   Société chrétienne pour la propagande de la paix.

Belgium

1858   Ligue universelle du bien public (Antwerp), founded by Edmond Potonié.

1867   Association internationale des amis de la paix, founded by Albert Picard. Renamed Ligue internationale de la paix et de la liberté. Belgian section of the Genevan society.

1889   Fédération internationale de l'arbitrage et de la paix, founded in Brussels, a branch of Hodgson Pratt's International Arbitration and Peace Federation founded by Émile de Lavaleye and Henri La Fontaine.

1898–1899   Alliance des femmes pour la paix par l'education, founded by Marie Popelin. A branch of the Parisian organization.

Italy

1868   Lega di libertà, fratellanza e pace, founded in Turin by Timoteo Riboli in connection with the Genevan Ligue internationale de la paix et de la liberté.

1878–1880   Congresso per la pace, founded in Milan.

1887   Unione lombarda per la pace e l'arbitrato internazionale, founded by Carlo Romussi and E. T. Moneta. Name changed to Unione lombarda: Società internazionale per la pace in 1891.

            Associazione per l'arbitrato e per la pace internazionale, Rome, founded by Ruggiero Bonghi, Beniamino Pandolfi, and Victor Prestini.

1889   Società della pace, founded in Florence.

1890   Società della pace, Palermo, founded by Giuseppe D'Aguanno.

            Comitato delle signore per la pace et l'arbitrato internazionale, founded by Elvira Cimino.

1891   Società della pace ed arbitrato (Perugia), founded by Lepoldo Tiberi.

            Società della pace (Venezia), founded by Beniamino Pandolfi.

1893   Comité franco-italien, founded by Ruggiero Bonghi and numerous members of the Italian parliament.

1894   Pionieri della pace e l'arbitrato (Turin).

            Società per la pace (Borgosesia, Barzano, Missaglia, and Voghera).

            Società per la pace e l'arbitrato internazionale (Turin).

1896   Comitato di Torre Pellice, led by Edoardo Giretti.

1899   Lega italiana per la pace et per la difesa degli emigranti.

1904   Comitato per la pace (Gallarate, Firenze, Spezia, Terni, Pistoia, Bari, and Bologna).

1908–1909   Società per la pace femminile, founded by alma dolens in various Italian cities.

1909   Giovine Europa, founded by Rosalia Gwis-Adami and Adèle Alziator in Milan.

The Netherlands

1871   Algemeen Nederlandsche Vredebond, founded in Amsterdam with sections in other cities. Renamed Vrede door Recht (1899).

1884   Pax humanitate, société de la paix.

1894   Société des étudiants (Fredensvereinging), founded in Groningen.

1899   Alliance des femmes pour la paix, section founded by Johanna Waszklewicz-van Schilfgaarde; merged with Vrede door Recht in 1900–1902.

German Empire

1874   Deutscher Verein für internationale Friedenspropaganda; reconstituted in Berlin (1895).

1886   Frankfurter Friedensverein.

1892   Wiesbadener Gesellschaft der Friedensfreunde.

Deutscher Friedensverein. Renamed Deutsche Friedensgesellschaft.

    1893   Branches in Breslau, Constance, Ulm, Königsberg, and Heidenheim.

    1894   Branches in Leipzig, Stuttgart, Pforzheim, Offenburg, Neustadt, Insterburg, Görliz, Munich, Hanau, Siegen, Königstein, and Alzey.

    1895   Branches in Löwenberg, Blaubeuren, Erbach, Hamburg, Sölfingen, and Schwab.

    1910   The German society claimed eighty-eight branches.

Denmark

1882   Dansk Fredsforening, founded in Copenhagen by Fredrik Bajer (also called Association pour la neutralisation de Danemark). (Seventy-three branches by 1905.)

Sweden

1883   Svenska freds och skiljedoms-föreningen (Swedish Society for Peace and Arbitration). Thirty-three branches by 1905.

1899   Association des femmes de Suède pour la paix.

Norway

1892   Norges Fredsforening (Norwegian Peace Society). Thirty-three branches by 1905.

1897   Alliance universelle des femmes pour la paix, section norvégienne de la société à Paris.

Austria

1891   Oesterreicher Friedensgesellschaft, founded in Vienna by Bertha von Suttner.

Wiener akademischer Friedensverein.

1894   Società triestina degli amici della pace.

Litterarisch-künstlerischer Verein für Verbreitung der Friedensidee

Hungary

1895   Société hongroise de la paix.

Portugal

1899   Ligue portugaise de la paix.

Romania

1902   Ligue de la paix.

Russian Empire

1910   Société de la paix (Moscow), founded by Prince Paul Dolgouroukoff; in St. Petersburg, E. Séménoff.

Peace Organizations with International Membership

1867   Ligue international de la paix par la justice (Paris and Brussels).

Ligue international de la paix et de la liberté (Geneva, France, Italy, Belgium, and the Netherlands).

1880   International Arbitration and Peace Association (Great Britain, Belgium, Italy, and Switzerland).

1889   Congrès universel de la paix (Paris), led to creation of Bureau international de la paix (Berne and Geneva, 1891–1939).

Conférence interparlementaire (Paris), led to creation of Bureau interparlementaire (Berne and Geneva, 1893 to present). Name changed to Interparliamentary Union (Union interparlementaire) in 1899. Headquarters currently in Geneva.

1898   Corda fratres (International Student Federation).

Appendix B
International Congresses, 1889–1914

Universal Peace Congresses, 1889–1914

1889	Paris	President: Frédéric Passy*
1890	London	President: David Dudley Field
1891	Rome	President: Ruggiero Bonghi
1892	Berne	President: Louis Ruchonnet
1893	Chicago	President: Josiah Quincy
1894	Anvers (Antwerp)	President: A. Houzeau de Lehaie
1896	Budapest	President: General S. Türr
1897	Hamburg	President: Adolf Richter
†1898	Turin	Assemblée Générale: President, Hippolyte Luzzati
†1899	Berne	Assemblée Générale: President, Fredrik Bajer
1900	Paris	President: Charles Richet
1901	Glasgow	President: Robert Spence Watson
1902	Monaco	President: Gaston Moch
1903	Rouen and Le Havre	President: Edward Spalikowski
1904	Boston	President: Robert Treat-Paine
1905	Lucerne	President: Élie Ducommun
1906	Milan	President: Ernesto T. Moneta
1907	Munich	President: Heinrich Harburger
1908	London	President: Lawrence Courtney, Earl of Penwith
†1909	Brussels	Assemblée Générale: President, Henri La Fontaine
1910	Stockholm	President: Carl Carlson Bonde
1911	Rome	(Canceled at last minute.)
1912	Geneva	President: Louis Favre
1913	The Hague	President: J. de Louter*

*First congress, 310 participants; twentieth congress, 950 members.
†General Assembly meeting of congress.

Sept. 1914   Vienna   (Canceled July 31; emergency meeting in Brussels of
                        Executive Committee.)

Interparliamentary Union Meetings

1889	Paris	Presiding officers:	Jules Simon, Frédéric Passy; Philip Stanhope Lord Weardale; W. Randal Cremer	96 delegates from 9 nations
1890	London	Presiding officers:	Philip Stanhope, Lord Weardale	118 delegates from 11 nations
1891	Rome	Presiding officer:	Giuseppe Biancheri	192 delegates from 17 nations
1892	Berne	Presiding officer:	Albert Gobat	113 delegates from 12 nations
1894	The Hague	Presiding officer:	E. H. Rahusen	152 delegates from 15 nations
1895	Brussels	Presiding officer:	Edouard Descamps	84 delegates from 15 nations
1896	Budapest	Presiding officer:	Dezider Szilàgyi	441 delegates from 15 nations
1897	Brussels	Presiding officer:	Auguste Beernaert	200 delegates from 12 nations
1899	Christiana (now Oslo)	Presiding officer:	John Lund	468 delegates from 18 nations
1900	Paris	Presiding officer:	Armand Fallières	275 delegates from 19 nations
1903	Vienna	Presiding officer:	Ernst von Plener	294 delegates from 16 nations
1904	St. Louis	Presiding officer:	Richard Bartholdt	197 delegates from 15 nations
1905	Brussels	Presiding officer:	Auguste Beernaert	264 delegates from 17 nations
1906	London	Presiding officer:	Philip Stanhope, Lord Weardale	617 delegates from 14 nations
1908	Berlin	Presiding officer:	Prince Heinrich von Schönaich-Carolath	610 delegates from 18 nations
1910	Brussels	Presiding officer:	Auguste Beernaert	393 delegates from 19 nations
1911	Rome	(Canceled at last minute.)		
1912	Geneva	Presiding officer:	Albert Gobat	170 delegates from 18 nations
1913	The Hague	Presiding officer:	Dr. Meinard Tydeman	282 delegates from 19 nations

(Next meeting occurred in 1921.)

Appendix C
Rescript of Tsar Nicholas II, 24 August 1898 to Representatives of the Powers Accredited to Saint Petersburg

The maintenance of general peace, and a possible reduction of the excessive armaments which weigh upon all nations, present themselves in the existing condition of the whole world, as the ideal towards which the endeavors of all governments should be directed.

The humanitarian and magnanimous ideas of His Majesty the Emperor, my August Master, have been won over to this view. In the conviction that this lofty aim is in conformity with the most essential interests and the legitimate views of all Powers, the Imperial Government thinks that the present moment would be a very favorable one for seeking, by means of international discussion, the most effectual means of insuring to all peoples the benefits of a real and durable peace, and, above all, of putting an end to the progressive development of the present armaments.

In the course of the last twenty years, the longings for a general appeasement have become especially pronounced in the consciences of civilized nations. The preservation of peace has been put forward as the object of international policy; in its name great States have concluded between [*sic*] themselves powerful alliances; it is the better to guarantee peace that they have developed, in proportions hitherto unprecedented, their military forces, and still continue to increase them without shrinking from any sacrifice.

All these efforts nevertheless have not yet been able to bring about the beneficent results of the desired pacification. The financial charges following an upward mark strike at the public prosperity at its very source.

The intellectual and physical strength of the nations, labor and capital, are for the major part diverted from their natural application and unproductively consumed. Hundreds of millions are devoted to acquiring terrible engines of destruction, which, though to-day regarded as the last word of science, are destined to-morrow to lose all value in consequence of some fresh discovery in the same field.

National culture, economic progress, and the production of wealth are either

221

paralyzed or checked in their development. Moreover, in proportion as the armaments of each Power increase so do they less and less fulfill the object which the Governments have set before themselves.

The economic crises, due in great part to the system of armaments *à l'outrance*, and the continual danger which lies in this massing of war material, are transforming the armed peace of our days into a crushing burden, which the peoples have more and more difficulty in bearing. It appears evident, then, that if this state of things were prolonged, it would inevitably lead to the very cataclysm which it is desired to avert, and the horrors of which make every thinking man shudder in advance.

To put an end to these incessant armaments and to seek the means of warding off the calamities which are threatening the whole world,—such is the supreme duty which is to-day imposed on all States. Filled with this idea, His Majesty has been pleased to order me to propose to all the Governments whose representatives are accredited to the Imperial Court, the meeting of a conference which would have to occupy itself with this grave problem.

This conference should be, by the help of God, a happy presage for the century which is about to open. It would converge in one powerful focus the efforts of all States which are sincerely seeking to make the great idea of universal peace triumph over the elements of trouble and discord.

It would, at the same time, confirm their agreement by the solemn establishment of the principles of justice and right, upon which repose the security of States and the welfare of Peoples. (signed) Count [Mikhail N.] Mouravieff

Notes

Abbreviations

AN	Archives nationales (Paris)
AN(EUR)	Archivio Nazionale-EUR (Rome)
BDIC	Bibliothèque du documentation internationale et contemporaine (Nanterre)
BHVP	Bibliothèque de l'histoire de la ville de Paris
BIP	Bureau internationale de la paix (Geneva)
BNC (F)	Biblioteca nazionale centrale (Florence)
BNC (R)	Biblioteca nazionale centrale (Rome)
BUP	Bibliothèque universitaire et publique (Geneva)
GLW/P	Garland Library of War/Peace
ICW	International Council of Women
IPU	Interparliamentary Union (Union interparlementaire)
ISRI	Istituto per la storia del Risorgimento italiano (Rome)
LDH	Ligue des droits de l'homme (Paris)
LPP	Library of the Peace Palace (The Hague)
NCW	National Council of Women (New York)
NLW	Archives of the National Library of Wales
PPP	Archives of the Préfecture de police, Seine
UPC	Universal Peace Congress (Congrès universel de la paix)
WILPF	Women's International League of Peace and Freedom

Introduction

1. Hans-Jörg Rudloff, chairman, Crédit Suisse-First Boston (London), quoted in Steven Greenhouse, "German Union Instills Vision of a Great Continent Reborn," *New York Times,* 3 April 1990, A1.

2. Houzeau de Lehaie to Christian Lange, 2 August 1914, IPU (Geneva), Letters of Lord Weardale, box 238.

3. See a general survey of peace plans in Sylvester John Hembleben, *Plans for World*

Peace Through Six Centuries (Chicago, 1943); repr. with new intro. by Walter F. Bense, GLW/P (New York, 1972).

4. Mercier's pacific prescriptions were offered in chap. 18, "The Ministers of Peace." American ed. trans. from French by W. Hooper (Philadelphia, 1795). Orig. title read 2440, not 2500.

5. Peter Brock, *Pacifism in Europe to 1914* (Princeton, NJ, 1972) is the standard study of the subject of Christian pacifism and antimilitarism; also *Freedom from War: Nonsectarian Pacifism 1814–1914* (Toronto, 1991).

6. Brock, *Pacifism in Europe,* 3.

7. Cloots wrote *La République universelle ou adresse aux tyrannicides* (1972); repr. with new intro. by James A. Thomas, Jr., GLW/P (New York, 1973). Kant's famous essay was originally *Zum ewigen Frieden: Ein philosophischer Entwurf* (Königsburg, 1795); it was altered in 1796 to include a supplement, "Secret Article for Perpetual Peace"; the first English trans. was made in that year. See Charles Chatfield, "Introduction" to *Perpetual Peace* by Immanuel Kant, GLW/P (New York, 1972), 5–6.

8. Moneta's speech to the VI Congresso nazionale della pace, Como, 18 September 1910, *La Vita internazionale,* 12, no. 18 (20 September 1910), 422.

9. André Perriollat to Henri La Fontaine, 12 December 1916, the Mundanum (Brussels), Henri La Fontaine Papers, box 2.

10. "Les Amis de la paix: Procès verbal de la réunion du 17 janvier," *Le Petit Clermontois,* 27 January 1892, 2. The meeting was in Puy-de-Dôme.

11. Adjutant V. Monefeldt to Henri La Fontaine, 26 December 1915, Henri La Fontaine Papers, box 2.

12. See, for instance, Jean de Bloch, *The Peace Societies: How to Widen Their Programme* (Glasgow, 1902); Jacques Novicow, "Orientation à donner au mouvement pacifique pour accroître son efficacité, mémoire," in *Peace and Civilization: Selections from the Writings of Jacques Novicow,* ed. S. E. Cooper, GLW/P (New York, 1972), 315–24; A. Fried, *Les Bases du pacifisme. Le Pacifisme réformiste et le pacifisme révolutionnaire* (Paris, 1909); repr. GLW/P (New York, 1972).

13. *"Carthago Delenda Est," Westminster Gazette* (1899); repr. in *Tolstoy on Civil Disobedience and Non-Violence* (New York, 1967), 98.

14. In 1975, an aging Signor Vezzoli, who worked in the tiny office of the Milanese Peace Society, told the author that he had persuaded a gang of Fascists to let him ransom the library of the Unione Lombarda per la pace (founded in 1887), Italy's main prewar peace society. The papers from the original office were burned, but many books and brochures were saved. Similarly, Jules Moch, the French socialist politician and son of Gaston Moch, a leading peace activist, reported that many family papers were deliberately destroyed in 1940 with the German occupation of France. He believed that his father's records (from 1889) were among those burned. The papers of E. T. Moneta were in the hands of a relative in the 1970s who insisted that there was nothing about the peace movement in them.

The rich treasure trove of the Brussels Mundanum, including a half-century of Henri La Fontaine's correspondence and the papers of Paul Otlet may not survive the conditions of storage that currently do not include any care. They are owned by a cultural organization and stored in a damp basement.

Chapter 1 The Debut of European Peace Movements, 1815–1850

1. Friedrich von Gentz, "Considerations on the Political System Now Existing in Europe, 1818," in *Five Views of European Peace,* ed. S. E. Cooper, GLW/P (New York,

1972), 71–72. A more recent version of the significance of Vienna as a model is Adda Bozeman, *Politics and Culture in International History* (Princeton, NJ, 1960).

2. The standard histories of the congress include Harold G. Nicolson, *The Congress of Vienna: A Study in Allied Unity, 1812–1822* (New York 1946); Hans G. Schenk, *The Aftermath of the Napoleonic Wars: The Concert of Europe, an Experiment* (London, 1947); Harold W. V. Temperly, *The Foreign Policy of Canning, 1822–1827* (London, 1925); and Ernest L. Woodward, *War and Peace in Europe, 1815–1870* (London, 1931). A copy of the Protocol of Troppau is reproduced in *The Concert of Europe,* ed. René Albrecht-Carrié (New York, 1968), 48, 52–55. See also Henry Kissinger, *A World Restored, Europe After Napoleon: The Politics of Conservatism in a Revolutionary Age* (New York, 1957, 1964).

3. See Edmund Silberner, *The Problem of War in Nineteenth-Century Economic Thought,* trans. from French by A. H. Krappe (Princeton, NJ, 1946); repr. with new intro. by Dennis Sherman, GLW/P (New York, 1972); also Helen Bosanquet, *Free Trade and Peace in the Nineteenth Century* (New York, 1924). Say's *Traité d'economie politique* appeared in 1803; his *Cours complet d'économie politique* was issued in 1828–1829.

4. Charles Fourier, *Triumvirat continental et paix perpétuelle sous trente ans* (Paris, 1803); published in *Oeuvres complétes,* vol. 1 (Paris, 1841–1845, 6 vols.). Comte Henri de Saint-Simon and Augustin Thierry, "De La Réorganisation de la société européenne, 1814," repr. in English in Cooper, *Five Views,* 26–28.

5. Hembleben, *Plans for World Peace.*

6. J. E. Cookson, *The Friends of Peace: Anti-War Liberalism in England, 1792–1815* (New York and London, 1982); W. H. van der Linden, *The International Peace Movement, 1815–1874* (Amsterdam, 1987), chaps. 1, 2, passim.

7. Cookson, *Friends of Peace,* chap. 1.

8. The creation of the early peace societies is described in Christina Phelps, *The Anglo-American Peace Movement in the Mid-Nineteenth Century* (New York, 1930); Merle Curti, *The American Peace Crusade, 1815–1860* (Chapel Hill, NC, 1929); A.C.F. Beales, *The History of Peace* (London, 1931), repr. with new intro. by Charles Chatfield, GLW/P (New York, 1971); Brock, *Pacifism in Europe;* see also van der Linden, *International Peace Movement,* chap. 1.

9. The founding of the American peace societies is discussed in Phelps, *Anglo-American Peace Movement;* Curti, *American Peace Crusade.*

10. A brief biography of Jean-Jacques, comte de Sellon, by S. E. Cooper is in *Biographical Dictionary of Modern Peace Leaders,* ed. Harold Josephson et al. (Westport, CT, 1985), 868–70.

11. Jean-Jacques Sellon, "Préface," *Reglement de la Société de la paix de Génève* (Geneva, 1831), 12 pp.

12. *Herald of Peace,* February 1819, 30.

13. "Proceedings of the First General Meeting of the Society of Christian Morals," in London Peace Society, *Annual Report,* 1822, no. 6, 17–18.

14. *Herald of Peace,* February 1819, 34.

15. Ibid.

16. Ibid., 36.

17. A. J. Whyte, *The Early Life and Letters of Cavour, 1810–1848* (Oxford, 1925); Ettore Passerin d'Entrèves, "Jean-Jacques de Sellon (1782–1839) e i fratelli Gustavo e Camillo di Cavour di fronte alla crisi politica europea del 1830," in *Ginevra e l'Italia,* ed. D. Cantimori et al. (Florence, 1959), 674–99.

18. P. E. Schazmann, "Napoléon III: Précurseur de la Société des nations: Lettre inédite de Louis Napoléon Bonaparte à Jean-Jacques Sellon," *Revue historique,* 179 (1937), 368–71.

19. J.-J. Sellon to the Marquis de Cordove, 27 August 1831, Biblioteca del Risorgimento, Milan, no. 36870.

20. *Archives de la paix,* no. 1 (1831), 18.

21. Ibid., no. 2 (1832), 101–3.

22. Jean-Jacques Sellon, *Réflexions sur les suites probables de l'arbitrage européen* (Geneva, 1829), 10.

23. Jean-Jacques Sellon, "Supplément," *Vœux adressés au futur congrès, 1 Novembre 1830* (Geneva, 1830), 15.

24. Jean-Jacques Sellon, *Les Institutions propres à remplacer le peine de mort et à éviter la guerre* (Geneva, 1836), 13; *Archives de le paix,* no. 4 (1837), 15–16.

25. Sellon, *Les Institutions,* 44.

26. J.-J. Sellon was not entirely supportive of the use of war by the Greeks for independence; his views troubled his nephew, Camillo di Cavour. D'Entrèves, "Jean-Jacques de Sellon," 682. See also Sellon, *Réflexions,* 15–16.

27. *Archives de la paix,* no. 2 (1832), 120, quotes Boucher de Perthes, "Opinion de M. Christophe (sur la guerre)."

28. *Archives de la paix,* no. 4 (1837), 73 ff.

29. Sellon, *Vœux adressé,* 12.

30. Ibid., 8–9.

31. M. Ramu to John Jefferson, 10 May 1843, *The Proceedings of the First General Peace Convention: Held in London, June 22, 1843, and the Two Following Days* (London, 1843), 90.

32. *Discours prononcé par la comtesse Valentine de Sellon, Congrès international de la paix, 4 octobre, 1878* (Paris, n.d.), 8 pp. Also Valentine de Sellon, *Comptes rendus de la presse sur les écrits de Valentine de Sellon: Lettres tirées de sa correspondance,* 3rd ed. (Paris, 1882).

33. Matthieu G. T. Villeneuve, *Le Duc de la Rochefoucauld-Liancourt* (Paris, 1827), 137–38; Frédéric Gaëtan, marquis de la Rochefoucauld-Liancourt, *Vie de la duc de La Rochefoucauld-Liancourt* (Paris, 1831), repr. in *Oeuvres* (Andelys, 1814–1845), vol. 2, 65 ff.; Ferdinand Dreyfus, *Un Philanthrope d'autrefois: La Rochefoucauld-Liancourt, 1747–1827* (Paris, 1903), 492–503.

34. "Torture en Algerie," in *Oeuvres,* vol. 2, 24 pp.

35. Phelps, *Anglo-American Peace Movement,* 47; Curti, *American Peace Crusade,* 132–33; *Herald of Peace,* April 1841, 284–85.

36. Matthieu G. T. de Villeneuve, *Société de la morale chrétienne: Rapport sur le concours, 18 avril, 1842* (Paris, 1842).

37. Ferdinand Durand, *Des Tendances pacifiques de la Société européenne et du rôle des armées dans l'avenir* (Paris, 1841; 2nd ed., 1845); repr. with intro. by Dennis Sherman, GLW/P (New York, 1971). Contantin Pecqueur's essays were published as *De La Paix, de son principe et de sa réalisation* (Paris, 1841); Constantin Pecqueur, *Des Armées dans leurs rapports avec l'industrie, la morale et la liberté* (Paris, 1842).

38. However, Pecqueur supported the aims of the 1843 general peace convention in London and urged future meetings be held each year. C. Pecqueur to S. Rigaud, 31 May 1843, in *Proceedings of the First General Peace Convention,* 91–92.

39. Frédéric Bastiat popularized Richard Cobden's writings in *Cobden et la ligue* (Paris, 1845). See also his *Sophismes économiques* (Paris, 1845–1848); *Le Libre-échange* (Paris 1846–1848); and *Paix et liberté ou le budget républicain* (Paris, 1849). Michel Chevalier's main work, *Cours d'économie politique* (Paris, 1844), included ideas developed earlier in "La Paix est aujourd'hui la condition de l'émancipation des peuples," *Le Globe* (January

1832), cited in Silberner, *Problem of War,* 100–103. Joseph Garnier wrote *Eléments de l'économie politique* (Paris, 1846). Gustave de Molinari belongs to the next generation. His main work, *Grandeur et décadence de la guerre* appeared in 1898; for years he served as editor of the *Journal des Économistes.*

40. Gustave d'Eichthal, *De L'Unité européenne* (Paris, 1840), 17.

41. A brief biography of Eugénie Niboyet by Laura S. Strumingher is in Josephson et al., *Biographical Dictionary,* 689–90.

42. Claire Goldberg Moses, *French Feminism in the 19th Century* (Albany, N.Y, 1984), 52, 56. Edith Thomas, *Les Femmes de 1848* (Paris, 1948), 11–12.

43. *La Paix des deux mondes,* 1, no. 1 (15 February 1844), 1.

44. Eugénie Niboyet, "De la politique pacifique du gouvernement de juillet," *La Paix des deux mondes,* 1, no. 12 (2 May 1844), 1–2.

45. "De la paix comme l'entendant certains chrétiens," *L'Avenir,* no. 42 (28 November 1844), 1.

46. "Adresse des ouvriers de l'Angleterre aux ouvriers de la France," in Rouchefou-cauld-Liancourt, *Oeuvres,* vol. 5, 6. Brock, *Pacifism in Europe,* 396–98.

47. A brief biography of Richard Cobden by William J. Baker is in Josephson et al., *Biographical Dictionary,* 171–74. Also J. A. Hobson, *Richard Cobden: The International Man* (New York and London, 1919); Nicholas C. Edsall, *Richard Cobden: Independent Radical* (Boston, 1986).

48. A brief biography of Frédéric Passy by S. E. Cooper is in Josephson et al. *Biographical Dictionary,* 730–32.

49. Nadine Lubelski-Bernard, "Les Mouvements et les idéologies pacifistes en Belgique, 1830–1914" (Ph.D. diss., Univ. libre de Bruxelles, 1977), vol. 1, 38.

50. *Proceedings of the First General Peace Convention,* 6.

51. Ibid., 12.

52. Ibid., 52.

53. William Ladd's essay was published in 1840.

54. A brief biography of Auguste Visschers by Nadine Lubelski-Bernard is in Josephson et al., *Biographical Dictionary,* 995–96.

55. *Peace Congress at Brussels on the 20, 21 and 22 September, 1848* (London, 1848), 13–14. A brief biography of Henry Richard by John V. Crangle is in Josephson et al., *Biographical Dictionary,* 803–5.

56. Two dozen entries competed for the prize of two thousand francs. Louis Bara's winning submission was *La Science de la paix,* repr. 1872 with an intro. by Charles Potvin; repr. with new intro. by S. E. Cooper, GLW/P (New York, 1972).

57. *Report of the Proceedings of the Second General Peace Congress Held in Paris on the 22, 23, 24 of August, 1849* (London, 1849), 14. Also Henry Richard, journal, "1849, France," entries 22–23 April 1849, NLW, no. 10200A.

58. *Journal des économistes,* 24 (August–November, 1849), 153n.

59. Conversation with Henry Richard, entry in Richard's journal, "1849, France," 64–66.

60. *Proceedings . . . Paris* (1849), 11.

61. Ibid., 13.

62. Ibid., 66–67.

63. Ibid., 39.

64. Ibid., 79.

65. Gustave d'Eichthal's speech, reported in *Journal des économistes,* 24 (1849), 169.

66. A brief biography of Joseph Sturge by William J. Baker is in Josephson et al., *Biographical Dictionary,* 916–18.

67. *Proceedings . . . Paris* (1849), 43–47; reported in *Journal des économistes,* 24 (1849), 160–64.

68. Bastiat's presentation was in *Proceedings . . . Paris* (1849), 49–52. Passy published his first economic essays in the late 1850s.

69. Ibid., 78.

70. Ibid., 88.

71. "Trois meetings des amis de la paix," *Journal des économistes,* 24 (1849), 427–28.

72. *Report of the Proceedings of the Third General Peace Congress Held in Frankfurt, 22, 23, and 24 August, 1850* (London, 1851), 43–44.

73. Ibid. ix.

74. Ibid., 14, 19.

75. Ibid., 51.

76. *Proceedings . . . Frankfurt (1850),* 44–51.

77. Théodore Karcher, "Paix et guerre," *La Voix du proscrit,* 27 October 1850, 216–217. *La Voix du proscrit* is preserved in LPP.

78. E. Antoine, "Chronique de l'étranger," *La Voix du Proscrit,* 221.

79. *La pace di Mauro Macchi* (Genoa, 1856), v–vi.

80. Aborigines Protection Society, *Proceedings at a Public Meeting, 11 November, 1851, on the Kaffir War* (London, 1851); repr. in *Internationalism in Nineteenth-Century Europe: The Crisis of Ideas and Purpose,* ed. S. E. Cooper, GLW/P (New York, 1976), 65–86.

81. Giuseppe Mazzini, *Lettere al congresso per la pace in Ginevra, 1867;* repr. Rome, 1891, 15 pp.

82. Victor Considérant, *La Dernière Guerre et la paix définitif en Europe* (Paris, 1850), in Cooper, *Five Views.*

83. For example, a German peace society, the Königsberger Friedensverein, functioned in the city associated with Immanuel Kant from September 1850 to May 1851. See van der Linden, *International Peace Movement,* 345–48.

84. Bara, *La Science de la paix,* was published in 1849 and repr. in 1872 by the Belgian freemason, Charles Potvin.

85. Alexander Tyrell, "Making the Millenium: The Mid-Nineteeth Century Peace Movement," *Historical Journal* 20, no. 1 (1978), 87; *Proceedings . . . Paris,* (1849), 79.

Chapter 2 Peace Movements and the Challenge of Nationalism, 1850–1889

1. Edmond Potonié-Pierre, *Histoire du mouvement pacifique,* intro. by E. Ducommun (Berne, 1899), 12–15. Potonié added Pierre to his name after 1880 when he and feminist Eugénie Pierre set up a home together, refusing to marry but sharing each other's names. Brief biographies of both by S. E. Cooper are in Josephson et al. *Biographical Dictionary,* 763–66.

2. *Correspondance cosmopolite* (1865?), no. 1, 6.

3. A brief biography of Rudolf Virchow by Brigette Goldstein is in Jacobson et al., *Biographical Dictionary,* 994–95.

4. The headquarters of Potonié's *ligue* was in Antwerp, where educated working-class participants, notably Jules Vincard, the editor of *La Mutualité,* supported it. Potonié's arguments later appeared in *Le Mirabeau* as well, an organ of the Association des francs-ouvriers (Verviers, 1867), which attained a maximum printing of four thousand copies in the following year. See Oscar Tessut, *Le Livre bleu de l'internationale* (Paris, 1871), 81.

5. *La Feuille d'Olivier,* June 1877, 27.

6. Potonié, *Histoire du mouvement pacifique,* 82.

7. Jacques Freymond et al., eds., *La Première internationale* (Geneva, 1962), vol. 1, 78–79. Tsarist Russia had destroyed Kossuth's republic in 1849, declared war in the Crimea, and in 1863–1864 quelled the Polish uprising. Socialists feared that a "disarmed" continent would be overrun by the Autocrat of the Russias. They preferred peoples' armies—armed militias to protect national independence during the long years of struggle that would take place before the transition from capitalism to socialism was complete. Potonié took no position on this argument; he focused on the threat that weapons presented to economic prosperity and social peace.

8. *Le Progrès,* 13 September 1870, in dossier Edmond Potonié, Paris, Préfecture de police, B A/1.22h, no. 28276.

9. A brief biography of J.-B. Coomans by Nadine Lubelski-Bernard is in Josephson et al., *Biographical Dictionary,* 176–77. Passy originally backed Potonié's efforts in 1865–1866 but in 1867 joined with a number of wealthy Parisians to organize a different kind of peace society.

10. *Correspondance cosmopolite* (1865?), 219–20.

11. Frédéric Passy, *Guerres et congrès ou le socialisme international: Extrait de l'Économiste belge, 19 novembre, 1859;* repr. Paris, 1899, 8 pp.

12. Ibid., 5–6.

13. Pierre-Joseph Proudhon, *War and Peace* (Brussels, 1861), repr. with intro. by Mark Weitz, GLW/P (New York, 1972), 2 vols.

14. Michel Chevalier, "La Guerre et la crise européenne," *Revue des deux mondes,* 2nd per., 63 (1866), 758–85, called for the creation of a federation like the United States. Without such, he predicted a future of endless war.

15. Henry Richard, journal, "1848, France" entry reports a conversation with George Sumner, 27.

16. Edouard Dolléans, *Histoire du mouvement ouvrier,* 6th ed. (Paris, 1957), vol. 1, *1830–1871,* 291–92.

17. Potonié, *Histoire du mouvement pacifique,* 114; Irwin Abrams, "A History of European Peace Societies, 1867–1899" (Ph.D. diss., Harvard Univ., 1938), 13.

18. A brief biography of Charles Potvin by Nadine Lubelski-Bernard is in Josephson et al., *Biographical Dictionary,* 766–67. See study of the Masonic ties to peace activism in Nadine Lubelski-Bernard, "Freemasonry and Peace in Europe, 1867–1914," in *Peace Movements and Political Cultures,* ed. Charles Chatfield and Peter van den Dungen (Knoxville, TN, 1988), 81–94.

19. For an account, see Abrams, "History of European Peace Societies," 18–19; Frédéric Passy, *Pour la paix: Notes et documents* (Paris, 1909); repr. with new intro. by Adolf Wild, GLW/P New York, 1972), 11–15.

20. Henry Richard, journal of a visit to Paris, entry for 8 February 1867, NLW, no. 10201A.

21. Potonié, *Histoire du mouvement pacifique,* 90.

22. Paul Passy, *Un Apôtre de la paix: La Vie de Frédéric Passy* (Paris, 1927).

23. In 1869, Henry Richard toured Europe—visiting Belgium, Prussia, and Paris particularly—to encourage the sponsorship of arms reduction proposals in European parliaments. See journal, 1869, pp. 233 ff., NLW, no. 10205B. His belief in the role of elected officials and established authorities to transform European relations was unshakeable.

24. Ligue internationale et permanente de la paix, *Première Assemblée générale, juin, 1868* (Paris, 1868), 77–87; see also *Le Comité de la Ligue internationale de la paix à ses adhérents, octobre, 1868* (Paris, 1868), 4 pp.

25. *L'Univers,* esp. 13 June 1868; Passy, *Pour la paix,* 32, 183–90. Henry Richard, journal, 1869, p 243.

26. Georges Seigneur, *La Ligue de la paix: Appel aux catholiques* (Paris, 1868), 71 pp.

27. Ligue international et permanente de la paix, *Première Assemblée générale,* 10–12. On paper the organization invited members from all religious backgrounds and both sexes, but the only recorded participation by a woman was the substantial donation given by Mme. Virginie Griess-Traut, a loyal supporter of progressive, republican, feminist, and peace causes during her long life. A brief biography of her by Patrick Kay Bidelman is in Josephson et al., *Biographical Dictionary,* 369–70.

28. Ligue international et permanente de la paix, *Première Assemblée générale,* 60.

29. The most important work in this series was Paul Leroy-Beaulieu's essay, "Les Guerres contemporaines." A close examination of the real human and material costs of warfare in the nineteenth century, it was translated into several languages and became a minor classic of its type. The English version, "Contemporary Wars (1853–1866)," is available in Cooper, *Internationalism in Nineteenth-Century Europe,* 387–435.

30. Beales, *History of Peace,* 100–101. The passage of this protocol was the result of discussions with the English delegate, George Villiers, Lord Clarendon. European governments viewed it as a vague and noncommittal promise, but it provided peace activists with an "antecedent" for the future.

31. Frédéric Passy to Jules Simon, 13 March 1870, Jules Simon Papers, AN 87 AP/6.

32. A brief biography of Henri Dunant by S. E. Cooper is in Josephson et al., *Biographical Dictionary,* 233–34; See also Daisy C. Mercanton, *Henri Dunant: Essai bio-bibliographique* (Geneva, 1971).

33. Passy, *Pour la paix,* 197.

34. For a discussion of this initiative, see Irwin Abrams, "Disarmament in 1870," *Die Friedens-Warte,* 54, 1 (Basel, 1957), 57–67.

35. Miklos Molnar, "La Ligue de la paix et de la liberté: Ses Origines et ses premières orientations," in *Mouvements et initiatives de paix dans la politique internationale, 1867–1928,* ed. Jacques Bariéty and Antoine Fleury (Berne, 1987), 18.

36. Barni persuaded the Section des sciences morales et politique of the Genevan National Institute to host the meeting, to follow the Lausanne conference of the First International in early September 1867. Jules Barni, "Preface," *Annales du Congrès de Génève, 9–12 septembre, 1867* (Geneva, 1868). Léon de Montluc, "La Vie de Charles Lemmonier," *Les États-Unis d'Europe* (1924), supplement to no. 8, 5.

37. Karl Marx and Friedrich Engels, *Collected Works, 1867–1870* (New York, 1985), vol. 20, 204.

38. Ibid., 426–27.

39. A complete bibliography of Garibaldi's involvement is in Anthony Perkins Campanella, *Bibliografia Garibaldiense* (1971), 62; see "Garibaldi, presidente del primo congresso internazionale della pace e della libertà a Ginevra nel 1867," 727–37, includes 112 published items.

40. Resolution on Permanent Armies of the First International Congress, Geneva, 1866 in *La Première Internationale,* ed. Jacques Freymond et al. (Geneva, 1962), vol. 1, 36.

41. Ibid., 122–23; Franca Pieroni Bortolotti, *La Donna, la pace, l'Europa: L'Associazione internazionale delle donne dalle origini alla prima guerra mondiale* (Milan, 1985), 31–34.

42. Freymond et al., *La Première internationale,* 124–25, 235.

43. J. Barni, ed., *Annales du Congrès de Génève,* 124–25.

44. Letter of Pius X, 2 October 1867, in *Annales du Congrès de Génève*, 378–79.

45. *Annales du Congrès de Génève*, 157–59.

46. Ibid., 284–94 and passim. César de Paepe also considered the nationalities issue as inconsequential, a distraction that would disappear in a federated Europe in the future.

47. Ibid., 172–74. Amand Goegg's view was argued by others.

48. A.P.J. Pictet-de-Sergy, *Les Ligues de la paix en face de la guerre: Lettre adressé à M. le professeur Jules Barni* (Geneva, 1870), 9.

49. A brief survey of the history of *Les États-Unis d'Europe* is in Molnar, "La Ligue de la paix et de la liberté," 18–20.

50. Bortolotti, *La Donna*, 43–45. The schools, inspired by the 1848–1849 upheavals, were denounced by the French bishop, Félix Dupanloup, because they left out religious education.

51. A biography of Amand Goegg by Alwin Hanschmidt and of Marie Goegg by S. E. Cooper is in Josephson et al., *Biographical Dictionary*, 336–39. For a discussion of the creation of the women's auxiliary of the peace society in Switzerland, see S. E. Cooper, "Women's Participation in European Peace Movements: The Struggle to Prevent World War I," in *Women and Peace: Theoretical, Historical and Practical Perspectives*, ed. Ruth Roach Pierson (London, 1987), 54–55; Bortolotti, *La Donna*, passim.

52. A brief biography of Clémence Royer by Linda L. Clark is in Josephson et al., *Biographical Dictionary*, 823–25.

53. Circular, 13 December 1867, Reform League, in files of *Les États-Unis d'Europe*, BUP.

54. Carte di Timoteo Riboli, Lega della pace e della libertà, ISRI, folders 495, 102 (11) and (12).

55. *Les États-Unis d'Europe, numéro-specimen* (December 1867), 37. Potonié delivered his records to Émile Accollas and Alfred Naquet in Paris. The imperial police decided to search the houses of the latter two and seize their papers. The records of Edmond Potonié's Ligue du bien public disappeared. See Potonié, *Histoire du mouvement pacifique*, 88.

56. Charles Lemonnier, *Les États-Unis d'Europe* (Paris, 1872), 108–9.

57. *Les États-Unis d'Europe* 1, 7 (February 1868), 18.

58. Ibid., no. 40 (4 October 1868), 157–58.

59. "The Herald of Peace" in *Les États-Unis d'Europe*, 1, no. 46 (15 November 1868), 182.

60. Barni and the founders of the *ligue* were conscious Kantians as well as forty-eighters. See Montluc, "Charles Lemonnier."

61. Freymond, *La Prèmiere internationale*, vol. 1, 388–89.

62. Ibid., 262.

63. *Deuxième Congrès de la paix et de la liberté convoqué pour le 22 septembre, 1868 à Berne*, attributed to Bakunin (n.p., n.d.), 4 pp., Columbia Univ., Seligman Archives. See also E. D. [Elie Ducommun], "Le Congrès de Berne," *Les États-Unis d'Europe*, 1, no. 35 (30 August 1868), 139; Marx Vuilleumier, "Bakunin, L'Alliance internationale de la démocratie socialiste et la Première internationale à Génève," *Cahiers Vilfredo Pareto* 1 (1964), 51–94.

64. *Les États-Unis d'Europe* 1, no. 45 (8 November 1868), 177.

65. *La Question sociale: Rapport présenté au Congrès de Lausanne, 27 janvier 1871* (Paris, 1871), 35 pp.

66. *Le Mirabeau (Verviers)* had a circulation of about four thousand. Tessut, *Le Livre bleu*, 81.

67. Marie Goeggs, "Proposition de créer une association internationale des femmes en

connexion avec la Ligue de la paix et de la liberté," *Les États-Unis d'Europe* 1, no. 10 (8 March 1868), 38. The attack appeared in August prior to the meeting, which accepted her proposal.

68. Marie Goegg, *Deux discours* (Geneva, 1878; repr. of 1868 speeches), 4–5.

69. Bortolotti, *La Donna*, 50–103, passim.

70. *Les États-Unis d'Europe* 1, no. 48 (29 November 1868), 189.

71. A brief biography of Ferdinand Buisson by Albert S. Hill is in Josephson et al., *Biographical Dictionary*, 123–24. See also Sandi E. Cooper, "Ferdinand Buisson—die Abrüstung des Hasses," in *Die Friedens-Nobelpreis von 1926 bis 1932,* ed. Michael Neumann, intro. by Harry Pross (Munich, 1990), 132–141.

72. Ferdinand Buisson, "L'Abolition de la guerre par l'instruction," *Les États-Unis d'Europe* 1, no. 17 (26 April 1868), 66.

73. Buisson helped design the Ferry laws that created the French public school system; he served as an undersecretary of education charged with curriculum and taught educational philosphy at the Sorbonne. Following the Dreyfus affair, he helped to write the laws separating church and state and also helped found and preside over the LDH. Buisson's distinguished career in the service of education and peace continued into the 1920s. He remained active in peace societies no matter what official post he held.

74. Opening speech by Victor Hugo, 14 September 1869; in *Actes et Paroles,* vol. 2, *Pendant l'exil, 1852–1870,* 407.

75. Pierre Angrand, *Victor Hugo, raconté par les papiers d'état* (Paris, 1961), 277. Initially, a confused Hugo thought the invitation was from the socialist International, ibid., 273–74.

76. Closing speech by Victor Hugo, 17 September 1869, in *Actes et paroles,* vol. 2, 469–70.

77. Ibid., 471.

78. *Les États-Unis d'Europe* 3, 7 (July 1870), 56.

79. Ibid., 65–66, 69.

80. "A Nos frères d'Allemagne" (circulated from July 1870); printed in *Les États-Unis d'Europe* 3, no. 8 (August 1870), 71. See also Edmond Potonié *Histoire du mouvement pacifique,* 91–92.

81. Potonié, *Histoire du mouvement pacifique,* 92–93.

82. Passy, *Pour la paix,* 49–50.

83. Passy, *Les États-Unis d'Europe* 3, no. 8 (1870), 71.

84. Letter of Marie Goegg in *Les États-Unis d'Europe* 3, no. 9 (October 1870), 82. (Special supplement.)

85. Amand Goegg et al., *Rapport au nom du comité central* (Lausanne, 1871), 5–7.

86. *Résolutions votées par les dix premiers congrès* (Geneva, 1877), 43; "Congrès de 1871," *Les États-Unis d'Europe* 4, no. 1 (11 April 1872), 3.

87. C. Lemonnier, *La Question sociale: Rapport présenté au Congrès de Lausanne, septembre, 1871* (Paris, 1871), 35 pp.

88. "Aux membres du Congrès de la paix à Lugano," in *Actes et paroles,* vol. 3, 283–84.

89. Lemonnier, *Les États-Unis d'Europe.*

90. *Les États-Unis d'Europe* 4, no. 2 (April 1872), 2.

91. Ibid., 115–18, 128–80, passim.

92. *Lettre à Messieurs les presidents et membres de la Conférence internationale de Bruxelles* (Geneva, 1875), 4–5.

93. Members appointed were the Italian jurist Frederic Sclopis; the Swiss Jacques

Staempfli; the Brazilian, Vicomte d'Itajuba; the American, Charles Francis Adams; and Alexander Cockburn, the British lord chancellor.

94. Adrian Cook, *The Alabama Claims: American Politics and Anglo-American Relations, 1865–1872* (Ithaca, NY, 1975), is a recent study. The work by Thomas W. Balch, *The Alabama Arbitration* (Philadelphia, 1900; repr. Freeport, NY, 1969), typified the use of the case by peace activists. The eminent international law scholar, J. C. Bluntschli wrote a major analysis of the subject in 1870; a study of Bluntschli's influence is found in Felix Lehner, *J. C. Bluntschlis Beitrag zur Lösung der Alabamafrage: Eine Episode im Werden der transatlantische Solidarität* (Zurich, 1957).

95. A brief biography of Samuel Baart de la Faille by J. H. Rombach is in Josephson et al., *Biographical Dictionary*, 47.

96. Charles Potvin et al., "Rapport sur la question de la paix, 10 mai, 1872," *La Chaîne d'Union de Paris, Journal de la maçonnerie universelle,* 9 (August 1872), 463–67; Potvin also published *Du Gouvernement de soi-même*, vol. 6, *Les Nations, droit international, la paix et la guerre* (Verviers, 1877), 92 pp.

97. Charles Potvin "Introduction" to Louis Bara, *La Science de la paix* (Brussels, 1872). Available with new intro. by S. E. Cooper GLW/P (New York, 1972). The work has been subject to periodic rediscoveries. See, for instance, G. B. Devos, *La Science supranationale de Louis Bara* (Paris, 1952), 32 pp.

98. F. Passy, *Revanche et relèvement* (Paris, 1872), 1.

99. Ibid., 12, 14, 20.

100. Frédéric Passy to François Mignet, secretary of the Academy of Moral Sciences, 20 February 1875, Deville Papers, AN 51 AP/2. The pretense that Passy's publication record was insufficient and nondistinguished continued to exclude him from recognition for some years. No matter how moderate and modest were his proposals for a new international vision, Passy was excluded from established circles. He was eventually admitted to the academy and to the Institut de France in the 1880s when he was a member of the Chambre des députés. This did not eliminate police surveillance.

101. A brief biography of Émile de Laveleye by Nadine Lubelski-Bernard is in Josephson et al., *Biographical Dictionary*, 198–200.

102. Speeckaert, *Coopération internationale;* Institut de droit international, *Livre du centenaire, 1873–1973: Évolution et perspective du droit international* (Basel, 1973), preface; Albéric Rolin, *Les Origines de l'Institut de droit international, 1873–1923* (Brussels, 1924). See also Abrams, "History of European Peace Societies," 93 ff.; and Passy, *Pour la paix,* 70.

103. James Lorimer, *The Application of the Principle of Relative or Proportional Equality to International Organization* (Edinburgh and London, 1867).

104. J. C. Bluntschli, "Die Organization das Europäischen Staatsvereins," in *Gegenwart* (1878). For a solid discussion of the main ideas, see F. H. Hinsley, *Power and the Pursuit of Peace: Theory and Practice in the History of Relations Between States* (Cambridge, 1963, 1967), 133–39.

105. Charles Lemonnier to Auguste Nefftzer, editor of *Le Temps,* 27 July 1876, AN, 113 AP/3.

106. Institut de droit international, *Livre du centenaire,* 7–9.

107. Speeckaert, *Coopération international,* 27–29.

108. Richard raised the subject of arbitration at Cologne (1881), Milan (1883), and London (1887). See "Further Progress of International Arbitration," in Association for the Reform and Codification of the Law of Nations, *Report of the Thirteenth Conference* (London, 25–28 July 1887), 91–101.

234   **Notes**

109. The radical Mme. André Leo (pseud. Léonie Béra, married to Grégoire Champ-seix) used the names of her sons for her public nom de plume. She was a well-known writer and champion of the Commune. I am grateful to Karen Offen for bringing Thérèse Moreau's paper, "Un Divorce: André Leo et la révolution bourgeoise" (delivered at Tou-louse, April 1989) to my attention.

110. *First Report and Balance Sheet of the Council of the Workman's Peace Associa-tion,* 10 July 1871, 1. W. R. Cremer became disenchanted with the First International, par-ticularly as Marx's influence had grown. In 1868, he supported the Ligue internationale de la paix et de la liberté when it was attacked in the First International Congress and he joined forces in 1870 with Edmond Beales and the Reform League in a campaign to keep Great Britain out of the Franco-Prussian War.

111. Howard Evans, *Sir Randal Cremer: His Life and Work* (London, 1909); repr. with new intro. by Naomi C. Miller, GLW/P (New York, 1973), 82–86.

112. W. R. Cremer to "friends of peace in France," 24 August 1872, IPU (Geneva), "Documents pour écrire une histoire," box 533.

113. Evans, *Sir Randal Cremer,* 88–90; Abrams, "History of European Peace Soci-eties," 145–47.

114. Beales, *History of Peace,* 144; Abrams, "History of European Peace Societies," 114–118.

115. A brief biography of Auguste Couvreur by Nadine Lubelski-Bernard is in Joseph-son et al., *Biographical Dictionary,* 178–79.

116. A brief biography of Chales Sumner by James B. Stewart is in Josephson et al., *Biographical Dictionary,* 919–21.

117. Beales, *History of Peace,* 147–49.

118. The English version of Adolf Fischhof's essays, "On the Reduction of Continental Armies," is in *Arms Limitation: Plans for Europe Before 1914,* ed. S. E. Cooper, GLW/P (New York, 1972), 7. The essays appeared originally in the *Neue Freie Presse,* 27, 28 September 1875. An excellent discussion of the political climate is in Richard R. Laurence, "The Problem of Peace and Austrian Society, 1889–1914: A Study in the Cul-tural Origins of the First World War" (Ph.D. diss., Stanford Univ., 1968), 138ff. See also Merze Tate, *The Disarmament Illusion* (New York, 1942), 39–42. A brief biography of Adolf Fischhof by Richard R. Laurence is in Josephson et al., *Biographical Dictionary,* 282–83.

119. Fischhof to Garibaldi, 9 December 1875, in ISRI Garibaldi Papers, folder 45 (27) 45. Garibaldi, tired and removed from the peace cause, politely sent approval, noting that "Our grandchildren will reap the reward someday." The words came too late to be included in the preface of the pamphlet reprinting Fischhof's essays. See also Richard Charmatz, *Adolf Fischhof* (Stuttgart and Berlin, 1910), 412.

120. Eduard Löwenthal, *Geschicte der Friedensbewegung: Mit Berücksichtigung der zweiten Haager Friedenskonferenz* (Berlin, 1907). See also Roger Chickering, *Imperial Ger-many and a World Without War: The Peace Movement and German Society, 1892–1914* (Princeton, NJ, 1975), 40–41.

121. Louis Maçon, *L'Origine de l'Union interparlementaire: Documents* (Lugano and Paris, 1909).

122. F. Le Doyen, *Extinction de la guerre au nom de la raison, de l'humanité et de la civilisation* (Paris, 1876), 11 pp.

123. Arturo de Marcoartu, *Internationalism* (London, 1876). A brief biography of Arturo de Marcoartu by Nancy A. Rosenblatt is in *Biographical Dictionary of Internation-alists,* ed. Warren Kuehl (Westport, CT, 1983), 472–74.

124. Sandi E. Cooper, "Patriotic Pacifism: The Political Vision of Italian Peace Move-

ments," in *Studies in Modern Italian History: From the Risorgimento to the Republic,* ed. Frank J. Coppa (New York, 1986), 204.

125. Congrès international des sociétés des amis de la paix, *Compte rendu sténographique, Paris, 26–30 septembre, 1 octobre, 1878* (Paris, 1880), 14–15.

126. Ibid., 16–17.

127. Lemonnier omitted mention of Edmond Potonié's Ligue du bien public, which elicited an intervention from Potonié himself.

128. *Compte rendu sténographique,* 29–30.

129. Ibid., 46–47.

130. Ibid., 47.

131. Ibid., 66–71.

132. Resolutions of the meeting are published in *Internationalism in Nineteenth Century Europe,* ed. S. E. Cooper, 225–31.

133. *Compte rendu sténographique,* 143.

134. Ibid., 129–30. A very uncomfortable Romanian delegate rose to plead for patience and understanding of his new country, where many backward and superstitious people lived who feared and hated Jews.

135. Ibid., 96.

136. Ibid., 89, 142.

137. Ibid., 59.

138. Sellon, *Discours prononcé par la comtesse Valentine de Sellon,* 7–8.

139. John V. Crangle, "The British Peace Movement and the Anglo-Egyptian War of 1882," *Quarterly Review of Historical Studies (India)* 15, no. 3 (1975–1976), 139–50; Crangle, "The British Peace Movement and the Intervention in the Sudan, 1884–1885," *Indiana Social Studies Quarterly* 30, no. 2 (1977), 22–37.

140. Charles Richet, "Edmond Thiaudière," *La Paix nar le droit,* 40 (1930), 479.

141. Reports of 20 February and 6 March 1874, PPP, B a/1214 no. 42494.

142. Printed in *Journal officiel,* 23 December 1885, and in Paul Passy, *Un Apôtre de la paix,* 43–46.

143. PPP, 13 December 1885, B a/1214 no. 42494.

144. Cremer's peace society lost membership when it attacked the government for the bombardment of Alexandria (1882). Evans, *Sir Randal Cremer,* 107–8.

145. A brief biography of Hodgson Pratt by John V. Crangle is in Josephson et al., *Biographical Dictionary,* 767–69.

146. A brief biography of Ernesto Teodoro Moneta by Richard Drake is in Josephson et al., *Biographical Dictionary,* 651–52. See also S. E. Cooper, "Patriotic Pacifism," 199–201.

147. Brief biographies of G. H. Perris by S. E. Cooper and Felix Moscheles by J. O. Baylen are in Josephson et at., *Biographical Dictionary,* 744–46 and 669–71, respectively. For Moscheles, see also Alfred H. Fried, *Handbuch der Friedensbewegung,* 2nd ed. (Berlin, 1913), vol. 2, 381–82; and *Who Was Who, 1916–1918* (London, 1929).

148. A brief biography of Fredrik Bajer by Peter van den Dungen is in Josephson et al., *Biographical Dictionary,* 49–50.

149. International Association for Arbitration and Peace, *Procès verbal de la conférence internationale tenue à Bruxelles, le 17, 18, 19 et 20 octobre, 1881* (London, 1883), 14.

150. Ibid., 136–37.

151. A brief biography of Jean-Baptiste-André Godin by Patrick Kay Bidelman is in Josephson et al., *Biographical Dictionary,* 334–36.

152. International Association for Arbitration and Peace, *Procès-verbal,* 48–49, 70–90, 96–97.

153. Ibid., 94. A minority argued Passy's position that the creation of an organized European peace was not "political" work.

154. Godin, speech to the Société de la paix, Familistère de Guise, *Le Devoir*, 10, no. 405 (13 June 1886), 225–26.

155. *Le Devoir*, 10, no. 396 (11 April 1886), 225–26.

156. Émile Beaussire, *Bulletin de la Société française des amis de la paix* (July 1885), 202–3, 205–6.

157. Frédéric Passy to Jules Simon, n.d. (probably January 1887), Jules Simon Papers, AN 87 AP/6.

158. Greeks have responsibilities as well as rights, Lemonnier noted dryly. See *Les États-Unis d'Europe*, 18, no. 45 (1 May 1886), 3.

159. Ibid., 1.

160. To Lemonnier arbitration treaties were acceptable as long as the signatories were republican states. He wanted a Swiss–U.S. agreement. Lemonnier had devised a model treaty in 1874, and he hoped to see it implemented. See Montluc, "Charles Lemonnier," 22–23.

161. Evans, *Sir Randal Cremer*, 126–27.

162. Abrams, "History of European Peace Societies," 230.

163. The French foreign minister made the silly remark, "It is not up to us, a defeated power, to make overtures," as if the United States had ever defeated France. Passy, *Pour la paix*, 89.

164. See, for instance, Passy to Simon, 18 September 1888, Delville Papers, AN 51 AP/2.

165. Unione lombarda per la pace e l'arbitrato internazionale, *La Festa della Società operaia e dei contadini in Vimercate, 15 maggio, 1887* (Milan, 1887), 39 pp. Also *L'Unione lombarda per la pace et l'arbitrato internazionale* (Milan, 1887), 4–5.

166. *Atti del congresso di Roma per la pace e per l'arbitrato internazionale, 12–16 maggio, 1889* (Citta di Castello, 1889).

167. The Swedish movement has entered the second century of its continued existence.

168. Ernesto Teodoro Moneta to Angelo de Gubernatis, 13 March 1889, BNC (F), A. De Gubernatis Papers, box 88, no. 43; see also Moneta to de Gubernatis, 10 September 1889. A brief biography of de Gubernatis by Sandi E. Cooper is in Josephson et al., *Biographical Dictionary*, 197–98.

169. Moneta was furious at the "new course" the government of Francesco Crispi had adopted—hostility to France, overseas expansion, and uncontrolled military expenditure. Crispi seemed to be willing to tie Italy so closely to the Triple Alliance that the country would lose its freedom of action, Moneta feared.

170. A brief biography of Klas Arnoldson by Peter van den Dungen is in Josephson et al., *Biographical Dictionary*, 39–41.

171. A brief biography of Priscilla Hannah Peckover by Thomas C. Kennedy is in Josephson et al, *Biographical Dictionary*, 736–38.

172. A brief biography of Charles Gide is in Josephson et al., *Biographical Dictionary*, 321–22.

173. Jacques Dumas, "Les Origines de la paix par le droit," *Paix par le droit*, 38, no. 3 (March 1928), 105–12; Henri Babut, "Les Origines de la paix par le droit," *Paix par le droit*, nos. 4/5 (April–May 1928), 169–75; Jules L. Puech, "La Paix par le droit (1887–1947)," *Paix par le droit* 51 (November–December 1947), 33–41.

174. Association de la paix par le droit, *Appel-programme-statuts* (Paris, 1912), 13 (esp. Art. 3).

175. See Godin in Josephson et al., *Biographical Dictionary*, 334–35.

176. Reports of January 1892 in *Le Petit Clermontois,* in the Mundanum (Brussels), Henri La Fontaine Papers, box 27 (clipping files).

177. *Le Petit Clermontois,* 5, no. 1 (1892), 1.

178. See police reports, PPP, no. 28276; *Le Travailleur,* 16 November 187ζ, 1–2, BIP, file 3, Q2; Congrès de la paix, Historique de M. Potonié; Potonié to Jules Simon, 24 June 1875, Letters of Jules Simon, AN.

179. A brief biography of Emile Arnaud by S. E. Cooper is in Josephson et al., *Biographical Dictionary,* 36–38.

180. At Simon's death, his widow asked Passy to write the biography, but Passy, citing age, had to decline. He wrote a brief biography for a pacifist journal, *La Paix par le droit.* Passy to Mme. Jules Simon, 17 December 1896, Letters of Jules Simon, AN 87 AP/16 IV.

181. Ruggiero Bonghi, "La Situazione europea e la pace," *Nuova antologia* 25, ser. 3 (17 September 1891), 20–21. A brief biography of Ruggiero Bonghi by S. E. Cooper is in Josephson et al., *Biographical Dictionary,* 92–93.

182. A brief biography of Edoardo Giretti by S. E. Cooper is in Josephson et al., *Biographical Dictionary,* 327–29.

183. A brief biography of May E. Wright Sewall by Michael Lutzker is in Josephson et al., *Biographical Dictionary,* 875–76.

184. The IPU has its headquarters in Geneva. The central office of the private peace organizations, the BIP, is in Geneva, though it is a different organization today than its ancestor of the same name.

Chapter 3   Pacifism and Internationalism: The Creation of a Transnational Lobby, 1889–1914

1. The word *pacifism* was first used in *L'Indépendance belge* (August 1901), quoted in Léon de Montluc, "Emile Arnaud," in *Les États-Unis d'Europe,* October 1922. (Special supplement)

2. See app. A for a list of peace societies.

3. For a recent discussion on the definition of *pacifism,* see Warren F. Kuehl, "Concepts of Internationalism in History," and Charles Chatfield, "Concepts of Peace in History," in *Peace and Change,* 11 (1986), 1–23. Complicating the definition of *pacifism* is the fact that its meaning has changed significantly since 1900, and its meaning is different from one country and culture to another. Moreover, dictionary editors have often inclined to adopt hostile definitions, such as the illustration offered in a French dictionary that quotes Proust: "Usually pacifism multiplies (the chances for) war and the indulgence of crime." A. Rey-Debove and J. Rey-Debove, *Le Petit Robert: Dictionnaire alphabétique et analogique de la langue française* (Paris, 1984). The *Oxford English Dictionary (OED)* prefers *pacificism* and illustrates *pacificist* with: the possibility that Germany might go "to war in order 'to demonstrate the futility of the dreams of the Pacificists.'" See *OED, Supplement,* vol. 3, O–Scz. The term *international law* often fares little better—an 1872 definition as "the limit of conscience of the strongest" appeared in the *OED,* vol. 5, as late as 1961. More neutral definitions, such as "love of peace," also occur. A balanced, recent discussion is Martin Ceadel, *Thinking About Peace and War* (Oxford, 1989), esp. chaps. 6 and 7.

4. For a brief description of leading pacifist personalities, see Verdiana Grossi, "Société européenne et pacifisme: Considérations sur une élite intellectuelle, 1867–1914," in Bariéty and Fleury, *Mouvements et initiatives de paix,* 59–79.

5. See, for instance, the ruling of the chair in 1890 at the London meeting when the motion to open with prayer was sent to a committee for consideration. UPC, *Proceedings*

... *London*, .. *1890* (London, 1890), 5–6. In 1891, the congress in Rome also refused to include religious services as part of the program and the English and American delegates were tempted to stalk out. "The Peace Congress at Rome: A Roman Journal on the Late Congress" by Dr. E. Darby and W. R. Cremer, privately printed, the Mundanum (Brussels), H. La Fontaine Papers, box 26.

6. Leo Tostoy to Bertha von Suttner, 28 August 1901, *Memoirs of Bertha von Suttner: The Record of an Eventful Life*, vol. 1, 372–73.

7. R. V. Sampson, *The Discovery of Peace* (New York, 1973), chap. 6.

8. A brief biography of Élie Ducommun by S. E. Cooper is in Josephson et al., *Biographical Dictionary*, 228–29. See also Ruedi Brassel-Moser, "Élie Ducommun—der unentbehrliche Vermittler," in *Der Friedens-Nobelpreis von 1901 bis heute*, ed. Michael Neumann (Munich, 1988), vol. 1, 136–47.

9. A brief biography of Albert Gobat by Sabine Jessner is in Josephson et al., *Biographical Dictionary*, 331–32. Also Hermann Böschenstein, "Albert Gobat—der unfriedliche Friedensförderer," in Neumann, *Der Friedens-Nobelpreis von 1901 bis heute*, 148–57.

10. *Die Waffen nieder* was originally published in 1889 by Pierson in Dresden. Over two hundred thousand German copies and over a million in other languages circulated by 1914. In English, *Lay Down Your Arms* was known as the *Uncle Tom's Cabin* of the peace movement. Irwin Abrams, "Introduction," to *Lay Down Your Arms* by Bertha von Suttner, GLW/P (New York, 1972), 8.

11. UPC, *Proceedings ... London 1890*, 19.

12. Richard R. Laurence, "The Peace Movement in Austria, 1867–1914, in *Doves and Diplomats*, ed. Solomon Wank (Westport, CT, 1978), 21–23.

13. See Bonghi in Josephson et al., *Biographical Dictionary*, 92–93.

14. Von Suttner, *Memoirs*, vol. 1, 359–60.

15. See Ducommun's *Report on the Work of the International Peace Bureau From Its Inauguration on December the 1st 1891 Until August the 31st 1893*, BIP Archives, IF folder, IPU/UPC Relations, I, no. 37.

16. See, for instance, Ducommun to von Suttner, 9 April 1895, BIP Archives, IF, Correspondance.

17. In the years when the UPC and the Interparliamentary Conference did not hold full congresses, delegate assemblies met. See app. B for a list of both groups' meetings.

18. By 1910, the membership of the Berne office actually included twenty-seven separate states from Europe, North and South America, North Africa, and Japan. Except for the groups from the United States and a small Australian organization, the majority of the non-European societies did not participate actively. The European states included Austria, Belgium, Denmark, France, Germany, Great Britain, and Ireland, Hungary, Italy, The Netherlands, Norway, Poland (actually at that time part of the Russian Empire), Portugal, Russia, Spain, Sweden, and Switzerland. The Algerian and Egyptian groups were headed by Europeans. There was also a Japanese society. In South America, committees existed in Argentina, Bolivia, Brazil, Chile, and Uruguay, and in North America, societies were in the United States and Canada. See BIP, *Annuaire du mouvement pacifiste pour l'année 1910* (Berne and Bienne, 1910).

19. Jeanne Mélin began her career in Flammarion's women's society in 1904–1905. See unpublished correspondance, Fonds Bouglé, Fonds Jeanne Mélin, BHVP, box 39, 4 June 1905; 8 October 1911.

20. A review of women's groups is in Cooper, "Women's Participation in European Peace Movements," in Pierson, *Women and Peace*, 51–75.

21. "Universal Peace from a Woman's Standpoint," *North American Review* 169

(1899), 50. For a recent essay that reads Bertha von Suttner's life from a more feminist-centered perspective, see Anne O. Dzamba, "Bertha von Suttner, Gender, and the Representation of War," in *Essays in European History: Selected from the Annual Meetings of the Southern Historical Association, 1986–1987*, ed. June K. Burton (New York and London, 1989), 61–72.

22. BIP, "Appel aux associations des dames," 12 May 1892, BIP Archives, V.A. 4.

23. Speech delivered in 1892 (n.d.), mss. in La Fontaine Papers, box 27.

24. A brief biography of Belva Lockwood by David Patterson is in Josephson et al., *Biographical Dictionary*, 570–71.

25. A brief biography of Jacques Novicow by S. E. Cooper is in Josephson et al., *Biographical Dictionary*, 705–7.

26. A brief biography of Alfred Fried by Roger Chickering is in Josephson et al., *Biographical Dictionary*, 303–5; also A. Gasser, "Alfred Hermann Fried," in *Die Friedensbewegung*, ed. H. Donat and K. Holl (Düsseldorf, 1983), 135–37.

27. A brief biography of Jean de Bloch [Ivan Bliokh] by Michael Bloch is in Josephson et al., *Biographical Dictionary*, 84–85.

28. Initially published in Russian and Polish in 1896, Bloch's *The Future of War in Its Technical, Economic and Political Relations* was soon translated into German and French.

29. Dario Biocca, "Il Pacifismo e la *grande illusione* di Norman Angell," *Studi storici* 21 (1980), 595–607.

30. Thomas Hayes Connor, "Parliament and the Making of Foreign Policy: France Under the Third Republic" (Ph.D. diss., Univ. of North Carolina, 1983) describes the tentative attempts to establish a role for elected representatives.

31. Congrès international de la paix, "Introduction" to *Troisième Congrès international de la paix* (Rome, 1892).

32. Fredrik Bajer, "Kopi Bog," Section "France" (1897), LPP (Unpublished diary.)

33. E. Langlade's speech to the National Peace Congress, Toulouse, 1902.

34. Henri Sée, *Histoire de la Ligue des droits de l'homme, 1898–1928* (Paris, 1929), 31ff. At its height in 1904, the *ligue* claimed to have 492 sections all over the country—groups interested in human and civil rights.

35. For example, eighteen individual sections in and around Paris passed arbitration resolutions in 1903. See LDH, *Bulletin*, 3 (Paris, 1903), index.

36. Ibid., 8 (1908), 1361–67.

37. Mathias Morhardt, *L'Oeuvre de la Ligue des droits de l'homme* (Paris, 1911), 18–19.

38. De Pressensé, who delivered a powerful criticism of the government's plans to trivialize The Hague Conference in 1907, first published his intent to interpellate the minister in the *ligue's Bulletin.* Other prominent founders were active in peace organizations or were authors of works supporting peace agendas—Yves Guyot, Charles Richet, Charles Seignebos, and Paul Passy (Frédéric's son and a leading Christian Socialist). The active support of Lucien Le Foyer, a prominent Mason and Radical politician, brought the peace message to Masonic circles and to the peace community a talented tongue.
A brief biography of Lucien Le Foyer by A. Hill is in Josephson et al., *Biographical Dictionary*, 551–54.

39. Short-lived groups included local organizations in Abbeville and Ponthieu established by Jules Tripier (1892) and small societies in Aubusson and Saint Colombe in 1893–1894; the Union de la paix founded by Auguste Desmoulins in 1891 lasted about a decade. A working-class membership group initiated by Antoine Pardoux in Puy-de-Dôme func-

tioned briefly in the 1890s as well. See "Liste et histoire des sociétés de la paix—table synoptique de E.D." in BIP Archives, 8, A. Also BIP, *Liste des organes du mouvement pacifiste* (Berne, 1895–1913), an annual publication.

40. A brief biography of Théodore Ruyssen by S. E. Cooper and B. C. Weber is in Kuehl, *Internationalists*, 647–48. Ruyssen, a professor of philosophy with a speciality in Kant, had chanced on a pacifist lecture in Munich given by Ludwig Quidde, himself a new recruit to the German movement.

41. *Sixième Congrès national des sociétés françaises de la paix, Reims, 30 mai—2 juin, 1909: Compte-rendu des séances* (Reims, 1909), 8.

42. VIIe Congrès national des sociétés françaises de la paix, Clermont-Ferrand, 4, 5, 6 et 7 juin, 1911, "Comité de patronage," Bibliothèque Marguerite Durand, Dos 72.

43. The Ligue internationale de la paix et de la liberté was represented in each Parisian arrondissement besides its thirty-eight branches around the country. The Association de la paix par le droit had eighteen branches; it merged with Passy's group, the Société française pour l'arbitrage entre nations in 1910.

44. BIP, *Annuaire du mouvement pacifiste pour l'année 1910* (Bienne, 1910), 43–60, and passim.

45. A brief biography of Baron d'Estournelles de Constant by Roger Chickering is in Josephson et al., *Biographical Dictionary*, 265–66. Also Adolf Wild, *Baron d'Estournelles de Constant (1852–1924): Das Wirken eines Friedensnobelpreisträgers für die deutsch-französische Verständigung und die europäische Einigung* (Hamburg, 1973).

46. Speakers ranged from Émile Durkheim to A. Merrheim, the union leader. See "École de la paix," BDIC, Fonds Gabrielle Duchêne, F ^Rés 222/2.

47. Jules Prudhommeaux to Jeanne Mélin, 8 December 1911, BHVP, Fonds Marie-Louise Bouglé, Fonds Jeanne Mélin, Correspondance, box 39.

48. The attacks by Ferdinand Brunetière, editor of *Revue des deux mondes;* the sarcasm of Émile Faguet in his book *Le Pacifisme;* and the denunciations by Paul Deschanel, president of the Chambre des députés typified center-right denunciations from intellectual and political sources. In 1913, the Action française opened a crusade against Théodore Ruyssen in Bordeaux that used more violent methods. See chap. 7.

49. Émile Faguet's book, *Le Pacifisme* (1908) popularized the word *pacifisme* among intellectuals and characterized its ideas as simplistic, utopian, childlike, and dangerous. Deschanel deliberately misrepresented pacifist debates that occurred at schoolteachers' congresses and meetings of French national peace congresses as treasonous.

50. Anatole Leroy-Beaulieu, *Les États-Unis d'Europe, Congrès des sciences politiques: rapport général* (Paris, 1904), 70 pp.

51. *Sur L'Internationalisme, libre entretiens, 2e série, 1905–1906* (Paris, 1906); repr. with intro. by S. E. Cooper, GLW/P (New York, 1971).

52. Chickering, *Imperial Germany*, 345, based on a calculation made by Alfred Fried.

53. The remaining fifty-five participants were lawyers, engineers, doctors, professors, journalists, landowners, industrialists, and bankers—an assemblage of politically conscious, educated middle- and upper-middle-class citizens.

54. *Atti del congresso di Roma per la pace e per l'arbitrato internazionale, 12–16 maggio, 1889* (Rome, 1889) 186 pp.

55. The society was forcibly closed by Fascist police in 1937, and most of its papers were burned. One devoted member, Signor Vezzoli, managed to save some of its library.

56. All copies of their publication, *La Pace internazionale,* have disppeared from libraries in Palermo.

57. BIP, *Annuaire* (1910), 74–76.

58. *Atti del congresso nazionale delle Società per la pace in Torino, 29, 30, 31 maggio e 2 guigno, 1904* (Turin, 1905) 8–18.

59. Bortolotti, *La Donna,* 183–93, and passim.

60. *La Vita internazionale* 10, no. 19 (5 October 1907), 433.

61. Ibid., 12, no. 21 (November 1909), 518–19.

62. V. Prestini and A. de Gubernatis to Albert Gobat, 16 June 1908, BIP Archives, VB, 4, "Unione internazionale per la pace." Also Angelo de Gubernatis Papers, BNC, box 155, "Pace" no. 2, *La Tribuna,* 4 December 1909.

63. A brief biography of alma dolens by S. E. Cooper is in Josephson et al., *Biographical Dictionary,* 220–21.

64. A brief biography of Rosalia Gwis-Adami by S. E. Cooper is in Josephson et al., *Biographical Dictionary,* 372–74.

65. *La Vita internazionale* 13, no. 12 (15 June 1910), 262.

66. Bortolotti, *La Donna,* 250.

67. See chap. 7 herein, for a discussion of the arguments for the Italian invasion.

68. alma dolens to A. Gobat, BIP Archives, Correspondence, 1912.

69. S. E. Cooper, "The Impact of Nationalism on European Peace Movements and Liberal Internationalists, 1848–1914," *Peace and Change* 6 (1980), 23–36.

70. Edoardo Giretti and Arcangelo Ghisleri (both 11 May 1913) to Henri La Fontaine, the Mundanum, La Fontaine Papers, box 26.

71. A discussion of this breakdown in the IPU is in chap. 7.

72. Von Suttner, *Memoirs,* vol. 1, 335. Laurence, "Problem of Peace and Austrian Society," 166–67.

73. The birth of the German movement is discussed in Chickering, *Imperial Germany.* See also Dieter Riesenberger, *Geschichte der Friedensbewegung in Deutschland, von den Anfängen bis 1933* (Göttingen, 1985), esp. 37–98.

74. Chickering, *Imperial Germany,* 44–52. Biographies of Adolf Richter, Franz Wirth, and Otto Umfrid by Roger Chickering and of Richard Feldhaus by Karl Holl are in Josephson et al., *Biographical Dictionary,* 809—10, 1019–20, 974–76, and 276–77, respectively; biographies of Richard Feldhaus, Adolf Richter, Otto Umfrid, and Franz Wirth by Karl Holl are in Donat and Holl, *Die Friedensbewegung,* 111–12, 327, 392–94, and 420, respectively. See also Karl Holl, *Pazifismus in Deutschland: Neue Historiche Bibliothek* (Frankfurt a.M. 1988), 41–54.

75. Chickering, *Imperial Germany,* 44–46; Holl, *Pazifismus in Deutschland,* 41–44.

76. See Richter in Josephson et al., *Biographical Dictionary,* 809–810.

77. See Wirth in Josephson et al., *Biographical Dictionary,* 1019–20.

78. Roger Chickering, "War, Peace and Social Mobilization in Imperial Germany," in Chatfield and van den Dungen, *Peace Movements,* 10–13.

79. Chickering, *Imperial Germany,* 59–61. See map (p. 60) for membership distribution. Also Friedrich-Karl Scheer, *Die Deutsche Friedensgesellschaft (1892–1933): Organisation, Ideologie, politische Ziele* (Frankfurt a.M., 1982), 58–62.

80. Chickering, *Imperial Germany,* 66–67.

81. Congresses were held in Jena (1908), Stuttgart (1909), Wiesbaden (1910), Frankfurt a.M. (1911), and Kaiserslautern (1914). See Fried, *Handbuch der Friedensbewegung,* vol. 2, 187.

82. "L'Allemagne et la paix," in *La Paix par le droit,* 17, 1 (January 1907), 11.

83. Théodore Ruyssen, "Ce Qu'on Pense de l'Allemagne," *Courrier Européen* 2, no. 56 (1 December 1905), 886.

84. M. L. Selenka, *Die internationale Kundgebung der Frauen zur Friedenskonferenz* (Munich, 1900).

85. *VII Deutsche Friedenskongress in Kaiserslautern* (Esslingen, 1914), 11–12.

86. A brief biography of Helen Stöcker by Amy Hackett is in Josephson et al., *Biographical Dictionary*, 904–6.

87. *Die Deutsche Friedenskongress in Wiesbaden 1910* (n.p., n.d.), copy in Hoover Institute, 11–12.

88. Scheer, *Die Deutsche Friedensgesellschaft*, 38–49, 230–35. Karl Holl, "Die Deutsche Friedensbewegung im Wilhelmischen Reich: Wirkung und Wirkinglosigkeit," in *Kirche zwischen Krieg and Frieden*, ed. Wolfgang Huber and Johannes Schwerdt Feger (Stuttgart, 1976) 321–72, esp. 328 ff.

89. Hans Wehberg, "Les Vingt premières années du mouvement pacifiste en Allemagne," *La Paix par le droit*, 23, no. 8 (25 April, 1913), 239–40.

90. Gobat, "Scattered Forces," in *The Peace Movement*, vol. 2, *1913*, 439.

91. Letter to Henri La Fontaine, 6 November 1913, the Mundanum, box 26.

92. See Walter Struve, *Elites Against Democracy: Leadership Ideals in Bourgeois Political Thought in Germany, 1890–1933* (Princeton, NJ, 1973), esp. chap. 1.

93. An excellent summary of the problem is Solomon Wank's "The Austrian Peace Movement and the Habsburg Ruling Elite," in Chatfield and van den Dungen, *Peace Movements*, 40–42.

94. Richard S. Laurence, "The Problem of Peace and Austrian Society, 1889–1914," 166–67.

95. Solomon Wank, "Diplomacy Against the Peace Movement: The Austro-Hungarian Foreign Office and the Second Hague Peace Conference of 1907," in Wank, *Doves and Diplomats;* also Laurence, "The Peace Movement in Austria 1867–1914," in Wank, *Doves and Diplomats*, 31–32.

96. Solomon Wank, "Introduction" to Hans Wehberg, *Die internationale Beschrankung der Rüstungen*, GLW/P (New York, 1972), 10–13; Laurence, "Peace Movement in Austria," in Wank, *Doves and Diplomats*, 26–27; "Viennese Literary Intellectuals and the Problem of War and Peace, 1889–1914," in *Focus on Vienna 1900: Change and Continuity in Literature, Music, Art and Intellectual History*, ed. Erika Nielsen (Munich, 1982), 12–22. Also Wank, "Diplomacy Against the Peace Movement," in Wank, *Doves and Diplomats*, 55–84.

97. A brief biography of Count Albert Apponyi by Gabor Vermes is in Josephson et al., *Biographical Dictionary*, 33–34.

98. Brief biographies of Anna Zipernowsky and Sándor Giesswein by Gabor Vermes are in Josephson et al., *Biographical Dictionary*, 322–23 and 1051–52, respectively.

99. A brief biography of Rosika Schwimmer by Edith Wynner is in Josephson et al., *Biographical Dictionary*, 862–64.

100. A brief, but succinct, discussion of British Quaker antiwar testimony at the opening of the twentieth century is Thomas Kennedy, "Why Did Friends Resist? The War, the Peace Testimony and the All-Friends Conference of 1920," *Peace and Change*, 14, no. 4 (October 1989), 356–58.

101. One affiliate, for instance, the National Pleasant Sunday Afternoon Society, had over a half-million members. BIP, *Annuaire*, (1910), 72–73.

102. Ibid., 69–72.

103. A. J. Anthony Morris, *Radicalism Against War, 1906–1914: The Advocacy of Peace and Retrenchment* (Totowa, NJ, 1972), esp. chap. 3.

104. Douglas J. Newton, *British Labour, European Socialism and the Struggle for Peace, 1889–1914* (Oxford, 1985), esp. 64–66.

105. A brief biography of Henri La Fontaine by Nadine Lubelski-Bernard is in Josephson et al., *Biographical Dictionary*, 538–39; see also "1913: Henri La Fontaine (1854–

1943)," in Irwin Abrams, *The Nobel Peace Prize and the Laureates: An Illustrated Biographical History, 1901–1987* (Boston, 1988), 76–78.

106. Circular, February 1890, quoted in Lubelski-Bernard, "Les Mouvements," 374. The society included Marie Popelin (the first woman doctor of laws in Belgium), who was refused permission to practice.

107. A brief biography of Paul Otlet by Nadine Lubelski-Bernard is in Josephson et al., *Biographical Dictionary,* 715–17. See also Jean Baugniet, "Deux Pionniers de la Coopération internationale et de la paix universelle: Henri La Fontaine et Paul Otlet," *Synthèses,* 25, no. 288 (1970), 44–48.

108. A brief biography of Edouard Descamps by Nadine Lubelski-Bernard is in Josephson et al., *Biographical Dictionary,* 209–10.

109. A brief biography of Auguste Beernaert by Nadine Lubelski-Bernard is in Josephson et al., *Biographical Dictionary,* 68–69.

110. The Belgian campaign to spread pacifism included an array of activities—formation of new societies, lecture tours, establishment of student organizations in universities, creation of materials for primary- and secondary-classroom use. See the Mundanum, La Fontaine Papers, esp. box 18.

111. *Compte rendu officiel du premier congrès national belge de la paix, Bruxelles, 8–9 juin, 1913* (Brussels, 1913), 30–32. The most thorough study of peace activism in Belgium is Lubelski-Bernard, "Les Mouvements."

112. A major figure in the feminist movement, Louis Frank also proposed a number of social projects, including the idea of transforming Brussels into the world's federal district. For a brief biography, see Nadine Lubelski-Bernard in Josephson et al., *Biographical Dictionary,* 300. See also his manuscript project for a global constitution and a federal authority, including architectural drawings for centers to be built in Brussels. See Bibliothèque Royale, Brussels, Frank Papers, II, 6053.

113. Louis Frank, "Plan des emplacements des Bureaux internationaux," Bibliothèque royale, Brussels, Louis Frank Papers, II, 6054. The drawings include structures to house international geographic and meteorologic institutes, statistical gathering organizations, as well as legislative centers.

114. G. P. Speeckaert, "Regards sur soixante années d'activité de l'Union des associations internationales," *Synthèses* 25, no. 288 (1970), 20–43.

115. H. Monnier, "Le Mouvement pacifique dans la Suisse Romande," in *Almanch de la paix pour l'année 1908* (Paris, 1909), 54.

116. BIP, *Annuaire . . . pour 1910,* 83–84.

117. H. Monnier, "Le Mouvement pacifique dans la Suisse française," in *Almanach de la paix pour l'année 1909* (Paris, 1910), 65.

118. "Liste des membres de la Société vaudoise de la paix," *La Paix* (March 1905), 6–8.

119. "Croyance en le pacifisme," *La Paix,* 1 (January 1908), 1.

120. Jonkheer B. de Jong van Beek en Donk, *History of the Peace Movement in The Netherlands* (The Hague, 1915); repr. with an intro. by S. E. Cooper, GLW/P (New York, 1972), 11, 21ff.

121. Brief biographies of Johanna Waszklewicz-van Schilgaarde and Cornelius van Vollenhoven by J. H. Rombach are in Josephson et al., *Biographical Dictionary,* 996–98, 1006–7, respectively.

122. Waszklewicz-van Schilgaarde to Henri La Fontaine, 20 May 1900, in the Mundanum, box 26.

123. When World War I broke out, the Dutch movement became the nucleus of the Center for a Durable Peace.

124. P. J. Eijkman to Louis Frank, 26 August 1907 in Bibliothèque royale, Brussels, Louis Frank Papers, II, 6057.

125. Cornelius van Vollenhoven, *De eendracht van het land* (1913).

126. A brief biography of Jacobus C. C. den Beer Poortugael by Peter van den Dungen is in Josephson et al., *Biographical Dictionary*, 206–7.

127. BIP, *Liste des organes*, 28–29.

128. Jasper Simonsen, "Bajer," in *The Interparliamentary Union from 1889–1939*, 223.

129. A brief biography of Klas P. Arnoldson by Peter van den Dungen is in Josephson et al., *Biographical Dictionary*, 39–41.

130. A brief biography of Björnstjerne Bjornson by William Shank is in Josephson et al., *Biographical Dictionary*, 80–82.

131. Oscar J. Falnes, *Norway and the Nobel Peace Prize* (New York, 1938; repr. New York, 1967), 16–19.

132. BIP, *Liste . . . pour 1907*, 50.

133. Nils Ivar Agoy, "Regulating Conscientious Objection in Norway from the 1890s to 1922," *Peace and Change*, 15, no. 1 (January 1990), 8–10.

134. Ibid., 21.

135. Wavrinsky to Ducommun, 4 July 1905, in BIP Archives, VA 1.2.

136. BIP, *Liste . . . pour 1907*, 48.

137. Sterzel, *Interparliamentary Union*, introduction.

138. *Almanach de la paix*, (Paris, 1893), 49.

139. Yves Guyot to E. Ducommun, 7 January 1894, BIP Archives, VA 5, "Propagande par des Sociétés ouvrières," no. 188.

140. *Bulletin officiel*, Antwerp, 1894, 77–79.

141. Ibid.

142. Jacques Novicow to A. H. Fried, Odessa, 30 August 1895, BIP Archives, Fried Correspondence, no. 87. The Erfurt program, adopted by the German Social Democratic party at its 1891 congress, affirmed pure Marxist principles. Among its proposed goals were direct suffrage, a militia to replace the standing army, equality of the sexes, compulsory secular education, free health care, the eight-hour day, prohibition of child labor, and social insurance under workers' control.

143. Sigma, "Le Parti pacifique et le peuple," *La Paix par le droit* 10, no. 1 (January 1900), 15. (Sigma was probably Jules Prudhommeaux).

144. "La Necessité de la coopération des classes ouvrières au mouvement pacifique" (1895), BIP Archives, VA 5.

145. *Bulletin officiel*, Budapest, 1896, 96. One vote per one hundred members was allowed with a maximum of ten per society. Émile de Vandevelde, a Belgian socialist present at the meeting, observed dryly that the peace community had little to fear because traveling expenses would prevent most socialists from attending meetings and overwhelming pacifist delegations. In a hostile description of the congress, a Hungarian writer called the peace activists "starry-eyed idealists" and evidently ignored the entire attempt to broaden the program. See Endre Ustor, "A Budapest Peace Congress in 1896," *New Hungarian Quarterly*, 22 (1981) 154–59.

146. Working-class involvement in the peace movement was debated from 1901 to 1910 at nearly every congress, as well as at Italian and French national meetings.

147. "Le Congrés de la paix en 1896," *Revue socialiste*, 24 (1896), 714–23.

148. *Bulletin officiel*, Berne, 1892, 106.

149. Originally in *Critica sociale*, 1892, 306; quoted in Antonio Valeri, "L'Idea federalista e l'internazionale nella 'Critica turatiana,'" *Critica sociale*, anno 64, 1 (1972), 12–14.

150. Valeri, "L'Idea federalista," 12. See also Franca P. Bortolotti, "Claudio Treves" in Josephson et al., *Biographical Dictionary,* 958–59.

151. French working-class leaders were not enthusiastic about The Hague conference, however. See letters to *La Paix par le Droit* 10, no. 3, (February 1900), 91. See also 119 ff.

152. "The Working Class and the Peace Movement," *Concord* (1900), BIP Archives, VA 5. (Clipping file.)

153. In 1902, the meeting was backed by the Independent Labour party, the General Federation of Trades Unions, the London Trades Council, the Metropolitan Radical Federation in Great Britain; from Belgium, the general council of the Belgian labor movement sent generic support and a national organization of Belgian youth assured him that they were radically antimilitarist. E. C. Wade, M. Maes, A. Daudé-Bancel, Henry Wolff to Ducommun, 1902–1903, BIP Archives, VA 5, no. 185.

154. "Le Congrès de Nîmes," in *La Paix par le droit* 14, no. 4 (1904), 135–37, 169. E. Giretti, "Per un accordo della società per la pace colle organizzazioni operaie," *Atti* (Turin, 1904), 69; repr. in *Giornali degli economisti,* 28 (1904), 543–54.

155. *Les Rapports du pacifisme et du mouvement ouvrier: Appel aux militants du prolétariat international et questionnaire* (Berne, March 1906), 2–3.

156. Report of Jules Prudhommeaux presented to UPC, *Bulletin officiel,* Milan, 1906, 209–12. Working-class leaders persisted in denouncing the movement as timorous and a disguise for preserving capitalist privilege, Prudhommeaux wearily reported.

157. See, for instance, Alfred Fried, "Der Amsterdamer Kongress und die Friedensbewegung," *Die Friedens-Warte,* September 1904, 165.

158. *Official Report,* London, 1908, 101–4, passim.

159. A brief biography of Hjalmar Branting is in Kuehl, *Internationalists,* 106–8.

160. *Bulletin officiel,* Stockholm, 1910, 270–71, 274.

161. Quoted in James Joll, *The Second International, 1889–1914* (New York, 1966), 196–98.

162. Céléstin Bouglé, "De La Haye à Stuttgart, la saison internationale," *La Grande Revue* 35 (1907), 62–72.

163. For a list of major pacifist periodicals, see app. B.

164. Perris to Ducommun, n.d., BIP Archives, VA 2h.

165. Chickering, *Imperial Germany,* 184–90.

166. Typical was the Union international de la presse pour la paix (founded in Brussels in October 1909), which was largely supported by journalists and intellectuals already committed to the movement—Fried, Perris, Paul Otlet, Horace Thivet, E. Séménoff (Moscow), La Fontaine.

167. E. Malcolm Carroll, *French Public Opinion and Foreign Affairs, 1870–1914* (orig. Chapel Hill, NC, 1931; repr. Hamden, CT, 1964), 272ff.

168. "Adresse à la presse en général," 1894, BIP Archives, VA 2, no. 131, 2; E. N. Rahusen and A. Gobat, "Adresse à la presse," The Hague, the Interparliamentary Council, 1894, 4 pp. (Typescript); L. Le Foyer, "Rapport," *Bulletin officiel,* 1913, The Hague. A survey of the Austrian press is found in Richard R. Laurence, "The Viennese Press and the Peace Movement, 1899–1914," *Michigan Academician* 13 (1980), 155–63.

169. Bertha von Suttner pointed out these two descriptions in the *Berlin Tageblatt* and *Neue Freie Presse* of 24 and 25 August 1892, respectively. Evidently, neither paper had a reporter present.

170. "Zukunstkrieg and Zukunstfriede," *Preussische Jahrbücher,* 96 (Berlin, April–June 1899) repr. in *Arbitration or War? Contemporary Reactions to the Hague Peace Conference of 1899,* ed. S. E. Cooper, GLW/P, (New York, 1972).

171. Quoted in Chickering, *Imperial Germany,* 135.

172. Quoted in Richard Drake, "The Theory and Practice of Italian Nationalism, 1900–1906, *Journal of Modern History* 53 (1981), 218. Interestingly, the conservative editor of *Revue des deux mondes,* Ferdinand Brunetière, attacked Immanuel Kant along with his admirers among peace activists and philosophers for threatening to turn France into "a China with Mandarins wearing crystal buttons." Letter in *Le Temps,* 3 April 1899.

173. Description in *Concord* (October 1899), 165–67. See chap. 4 herein.

174. Lord Weardale to Christian Lange, 21 May 1913, in IPU, Geneva, Archives, 1913, Weardale Letters.

175. *Bulletin officiel,* The Hague, 1913, 203.

176. See Charles Paix-Séailles, "La Conférence de Berne: Une journée historique, un grand acte révolutionnaire," *Le Courrier européen,* 10, no. 10 (16 March 1913), 147. See chap. 7 herein for a discussion of the Basel meeting.

177. *Bulletin officiel,* The Hague, 1913, 212–13.

178. Fonds M-L Bouglé, Fonds Jeanne Mélin, Correspondance 1913, SA 1918, box 39, Mélin to members of the International Peace Bureau.

179. BIP Archives, Crise de 1914, Conseil, Procès-verbal de sèance du 7 janvier 1915, 30. (Unpublished minutes.)

180. von Suttner, *Lay Down Your Arms,* 47–48.

181. Ducommun recommended a series of guidelines for writing comparative history, reducing chauvinism, and emphasizing the common experience of humankind. See *Bulletin officiel,* Antwerp, 86; Budapest, 7–8, 59.

182. *Bulletin officiel,* Antwerp, 1894, 86.

183. "Summary of the work of the NCW and the ICW on behalf of Peace and Arbitration," prepared by Mrs. May Sewell, in Archives, NCW, 5 pp. (Typescript.)

184. ICW, Committee on Peace and Arbitration, *Report, 1913,* 410.

185. Lady Aberdeen, *Report, 1899;* repr. in *Review of Reviews* (London 1900), 44.

186. *Paix par le droit,* 3, no. 1 (January 1893), 8–9.

187. "Le Congrès des instituteurs," *Le Matin,* 30 August 1905, Archives Nationales, F7 12524, police report of 31 August 1905. (Clipping file.)

188. Besides Passy, Arnaud, d'Estournelles de Constant, and Richet, lecturers included Émile Durkheim, Jean Longuet, Francis Delaisi, Paul Mantoux, Alphonse Merrheim, and several diplomats. The series ran from 1906 to 1914. Lists of lecturers preserved in BDIC, Fonds Gabrielle Duchêne, F^Rs 222/2.

189. A. Sève, *Cours d'enseignement pacifiste* (Paris, 1909).

190. *Official report,* Glasgow, 1901, 110.

191. *Atti* (Turin, 1904), 52. Another Italian, a woman, urged that the movement sponsor a society of educated women to serve as overseers of the historical education of the next generation. Proposal of Aurelia de San . . . (anon.), "Pace e donna," *Vita internazionale,* 11, no. 8 (20 April 1908), 174.

192. *Vita internazionale* 10, no. 5 (5 March 1907), 111.

193. *Bulletin officiel,* Milan, 1906, 57–63.

194. *Bulletin officiel,* Budapest, 1896, 23.

195. Ducommun to Ruyssen, 18 November 1893, Archives, "Propagande en France," VB 2.

196. Werner Simon, "The International Peace Bureau, 1892–1917: Clerk, Mediator, or Guide?" in Chatfield and van den Dungen, *Peace Movements,* 68–70.

197. "Programme pour la souscription en faveur du Bureau international de la paix," December 1891, BIP Archives, II, A. *La Correspondance autographiée,* no. 7 (15 April 1893), 2.

198. *La Correspondance autographiée*, followed by *La Correspondance bi-mensuelle*, is on microfiche, published by Clearwater.

199. The petition obtained 54,000 signatures, mainly in the Swiss Romande. "Une bonne nouvelle," *La Correspondance autographiée* (19 November 1893); the first payment came in January 1894.

200. Prudens (pseud.). "L'Avenir du bureau de Berne," *Paix par le droit* 16, no. 7 (July 1907), 257–62.

201. Comptes de l'exercise du ler juillet 1908 au 30 juin 1909, BIP Archives, I, 39.

202. *La Correspondance autographiée* 59 (10 October 1895), 1.

203. August Schou, "Introduction" to *Nobel: The Man and His Prizes* (Norman, OK, 1951), 477.

204. See Irwin Abrams, *The Nobel Peace Prize and the Laureates: An Illustrated Biographical History, 1901–1987* (Boston, 1988), xi–xii, 19–20, 22–30, passim, and app. A.

205. Neumann, *Der Friedens-Nobelpreis von 1901 bis heute*, describes Dunant, Passy, Ducommun, and Gobat in brief biographies; Abrams, *Nobel Peace Prize*, 37–50, 205. See also Bertha von Suttner to E. Ducommun, 23 January 1897, in The Hague, Archives, MS 451. Von Suttner wanted the prize winners to give their money to the central office.

206. Passy to Ducommun, 14 May 1899, BIP Archives, II A 3, Nobel file.

207. Abrams, *Nobel Peace Prize*, 47.

208. Ibid., 60–61, 79–80.

209. A. Gobat to Louis Frank, 26 September 1909, Louis Frank Papers, II, 6062. In 1904, Gobat headed a delegation of parliamentarians to President Theodore Roosevelt after the St. Louis meeting of the IPU where the group pleaded with the American president to initiate diplomatic moves for a second Hague Peace Conference. Roosevelt did, several months later. The "Englishman" in Gobat's letter is Philip Stanhope, Lord Weardale, who was influential in forcing the move and who followed Beernaert as chair of the group.

210. For a discussion of the differences between Ducommun and Gobat, see Werner Simon, "International Peace Bureau," in Chatfield and van den Dungen, *Peace Movements*, 67–72.

211. Statutes, International Institute of Peace, Art. I, *Comptes rendus de l'Institut international de la paix* (Monaco, 1903), nos. 1, 2.

212. Peter van den Dungen, *The Making of Peace: Jean de Bloch and the First Hague Peace Conference*, Center for the Study of Armament and Disarmanent. Occasional Papers, no. 12, ed. Udo Heyn (Los Angeles, 1983).

213. Originally in Russian, 6 vols. (St. Petersburg, 1898); trans. by R. C. Long (Boston, 1903); repr. with new intro. by S. E. Cooper, GLW/P (New York, 1973). An abridged English edition appeared in Boston, 1903; repr. GLW/P (New York, 1972).

214. Peter van den Dungen, "The International Museum of War and Peace at Lucerne," *Schweizerische Zeitschrift für Geschichte* 31 (1981), 185–202.

215. Report on the 1905 budget—the fourth year of its existence—in the Mundanum, La Fontaine Papers, box 3.

216. A brief biography of Andrew Carnegie by Joseph Frazier Wall is in Josephson et al., *Biographical Dictionary*, 143–45. See also Michael A. Lutzker, "The 'Practical' Peace Advocates: An Interpretation of the American Peace Movement, 1898–1917" (Ph.D. diss. Rutgers Univ., 1969), 217ff.

217. A brief biography Nicholas Murray Butler by David Patterson is in Kuehl, *Internationalists*, 130–33.

218. Butler to La Fontaine, 11 August 1911, the Mundanum, La Fontaine Papers, box 26.

219. Gobat to Butler, 28 September 1911, the Mundanum, La Fontaine Papers, box 26.

220. An American lawyer with occasional involvement in the New York Peace Society wrote to La Fontaine demanding a place on the *bureau's* executive committee now that American money was to be forthcoming! See Victor Hugo Duras, 20 October 1911, the Mundanum, La Fontaine Papers, box 26.

221. In English, it was called *The Peace Movement.*

222. Letters of Jacques Dumas, Passy, Gaston Moch, and Jules Prudhommeaux to La Fontaine, 6–15 November 1911, the Mundanum, La Fontaine Papers, box 26.

223. Jules Prudhommeaux to La Fontaine, 15 November 1911, the Mundanum, La Fontaine Papers, box 26.

224. Jules Prudhommeaux to J. Mélin, Fonds Mélin, 8 September 1911, Correspondence 1911, box 39.

225. "Rapport de gestion du Bureau international de la paix," 12 August 1912, BIP Archives, I, 39 "Organisation du bureau," esp. 6–7.

226. Letter from Gaston Moch to La Fontaine, 7 April 1912, indicates how "impossible" it had become to work with Prudhommeaux, Dumas, and the heads of the Dotation Carnegie, who want to control the entire national council and redirect it toward Carnegie objectives. The Mundanum, La Fontaine Papers, box 26.

227. Mlle. F. Montaudon to Henri La Fontaine, 30 November 1910. "I fear," she wrote, "that . . . those interested in the Bureau [will complain] that this manner of acting is entirely against the traditions of the Bureau since M. Ducommun always informed *all* the members of the Commission about what was happening. He never was influenced only by his sympathies and antipathies."

228. See letters of Victor Prestini to La Fontaine, esp. 15 February 1912, the Mundanum, La Fontaine Papers, box 26.

229. Gobat published *In Rei Memoriam* (1911), denouncing the Unione lombarda; the Dutch criticism came from De Pinto, "Confidential" of *Vrede door Recht,* Comité Central, 15 December 1912, 16 pp., to A. Gobat in Columbia University Library, Pamphlets, 1952, 212. (Printed pamphlet.)

230. La Fontaine to Elihu Root, 23 March 1914, the Mundanum, Henri La Fontaine Papers, box 26.

231. La Fontaine to the Commission, Berne Bureau, 14 May 1914, in the Mundanum, La Fontaine Papers, box 26.

232. Abrams, *Nobel Peace Prize,* 70–71.

233. A brief biography of Angelo Mazzoleni by S. E. Cooper is in Josephson et al., *Biographical Dictionary,* 617–18.

234. Angelo Mazzoleni letter in *La Paix par le droit* 4, no. 3 (February 1894), 55.

235. Angelo Mazzoleni, "Secrétariat international de la paix: Projet d'organisation, constitution et attributions du secrétariat," 3 pp., IPU, Archives, file "Rome, 1891."

236. Richard Reuter, "What Was the Best Way to Create an International Opinion Capable of Reacting Against Militarism," in Gustave Bjorklund, *Paix et désarmement* (1895), 80–81.

237. The UPC did authorize Ducommun to act in its name between meetings. See *Bulletin officiel,* Budapest, 1896, 43–47. The Interparliamentary Conference technically voted a similar resolution. Ludwig Quidde, "The Origins of the Interparliamentary Union," in *The Interparliamentary Union from 1889–1939,* 27–29; IPU, Session de 1897, *Compte rendu,* 64–67.

238. Statement of W. R. Cremer, 1891, the Mundanum, Henri La Fontaine Papers, box 26.

239. Élie Ducommun, "Programme pour l'organisation de la 4e Conférence interparlementaire et du 4e congrès universel de la paix à Berne en août, 1892," BIP Archives, IV, Conférence interparlementaire.

240. J. Binder to A. Gobat, 27 June 1892, IPU, Archives, file "Berne, 1892."

241. H. Pratt, "Creation of the Bureau international de la paix," *Concord* (16 March 1892), 47–48.

242. According to Pratt, Cremer saw this as "class pride"—people refusing to deal with him because of his working-class origins. Cremer to Passy, 17 April 1903, The Hague, mss. 45–1.

At one point, misunderstanding the proceedings during the Budapest peace congress in 1896, Cremer went as far as to attack his old friend, Passy, for claiming sole parentage of the peace movement. Passy, among the most modest of the pacifists, had done no such thing. Passy, "Explications amicales et pacifiques," BIP Archives, "Propagande en France," VB 1, 1897. (Confidential memorandum.) "Le Mauvais oeil," The Hague, mss. 49. (Typescript.)

243. *Concord* (16 March 1892), 47.

244. From 1891–1892, the Italian senator Beniamino Pandolfi had supported the office with his own money and the labor of his own family. After a year, Pandolfi wrote, "I have spent 5000 francs and for six months, I have worked like a dog and I have had the help of my two daughters and my son who know German and English perfectly. If I had had to pay for these secretaries, the cost would have been far greater." Pandolfi to Gobat, June 1892, IPU, Archives, file "Berne, 1892."

He had worked assiduously to increase the membership, circularizing countries where legislatures had not sent delegates. Von Suttner, *Memoirs,* vol. 1, 332–33. Also Pandolfi to "right Honorable President," U.S. Congress [*sic*], 1 February 1891, IPU (Geneva), Archives, file "Rome, 1891."

245. Moscheles to Gobat, June 1892, IPU, file "Berne, 1892."

246. Bajer, *Les Origines du Bureau international de la paix,* 16.

247. "Coordination des réunions organisées pacifiques," 6 March 1899, BIP Archives, IV, 6 Conférence interparlementaire, 1892–1899.

248. Cremer seemed to believe that Gobat, as secretary of the IPU, was plotting to merge the meetings of the union and the peace congress in Christiana (now Oslo) in 1899. BIP Archives, "Procès-verbal de séance de la commission du 5–6 mai, 1899," BIP Archives, "Berne, 1899," 5.

249. Activists in the union claimed some responsibility for influencing Tsar Nicholas II of Russia to issue the initial Rescript in 1898 that led to the meeting at The Hague. This claim arose from the request made by the parliamentary group at its Budapest meeting of 1896 to the tsar's government asking that some form of Russian representation be made at future meetings. The Russian consul-general in Budapest, Alexander Basily, provided his foreign office with a report on the organization, including a history and a description of its work. Members of the Interparliamentary Conference believed that this report was used by government ministers to persuade Tsar Nicholas to issue his Rescript as a way to answer a new increase in Austrian armaments without—in fact—increasing Russian weapons. See Hans Wehberg, "The Union and International Organization," in *The Interparliamentary Union from 1889 to 1939,* 41–42.

250. *La Conférence interparlementaire* 2, 18 (February 1895), 279.

251. Ibid., 4, 46 (1 December 1897), 653.

252. Sir Henry Campbell-Bannerman, aware that the tsar had dissolved the new Russian legislature, nonetheless cried, "The Duma is dead, long live the Duma." The publicity from this improper criticism of the internal affairs of another nation echoed across Europe.

253. Sterzel, IPU, 20ff.

254. Christian Lange, *Union interparlementaire: Rapport du sécretaire-général au conseil interparlementaire pour 1910* (Brussels, 1911), 20–21.

255. The death of Arturo de Marcoartu in 1904 ended the participation of any Spaniard in the peace movement.

256. Lange, *Union interparlementaire: Rapport.*

257. A brief biography of Philip Stanhope, Lord Weardale, by Gail L. Savage is in Josephson et al., *Biographical Dictionary,* 898–99.

258. Passy, *Pour la paix,* 140.

259. *Official Report,* London, 1908, 88.

260. "Preface," *Almanach de la paix* (Paris, 1901), 5.

261. Sir Thomas Barclay, "Peace," in *Encyclopaedia Britannica,* 11th ed., vol. 21, 4–17. The article on "International Arbitration" by Montague Hughes Crackenthorpe (ibid., vol. 22, 327–31) treated the subject with respect and seriousness.

262. Association de la paix par le droit, *Appel-programme-status* (Paris, 1914), 5.

263. Speech by Henri La Fontaine to the Belgian Senate, 25 March 1914, quoted in N. Lubelski-Bernard, *Les Mouvements,* 531—from *Annales parlementaires, sénat, 25 mars 1914,* 149–156.

264. Bertha von Suttner, "The Evolution of the Peace Movement," 18 April 1906; repr. in Frederick W. Haberman, *Nobel Lectures: Peace 1901–1925,* vol. 1 (Amsterdam, 1972), 88.

Chapter 4 Arbitration: The Search for Persuasive Propaganda

1. *Bulletin du premier congrès universel de la paix* (Paris, 1889), 10–13.

2. Gaston Moch, "L'Arbitrage universelle," in *Morale générale,* vol. 2 (Paris, 1903), 370–71n.

3. The English author M. H. Crackanthorpe catalogued over 170 cases in the nineteenth century in "International Arbitration," *Encyclopaedia Britannica,* 11th ed., vol. 2, 330.

4. Passy to Jules Simon, 18 September 1888, AN, Delville Papers, 51 AP/2, and 2 November 1888, 87 AP/6 reflect Passy's anxiety. All he would say to one journalist was that the meetings would cover the historical development of ideas of justice and arbitration.

5. *Procès-Verbaux, 1889,* 12–13, in Lange, *L'Union interparlementaire: Résolutions,* 33–34. The minutes of the organization from 1889 to 1897 are not available; Lange's summary remains the official record from that period as well as the journal, *La Conférence interparlementaire,* ed. Albert Gobat, published in Berne from 1893 to 1897.

6. Passy's enormous corpus of writings on political economy that developed this position included *Mélanges économiques* (Paris, 1857); *Leçons d'économie politique* (Paris, 1861); *La Question de la paix* (Paris, 1891); *La Paix internationale et la paix sociale* (Paris, 1892); and *L'Education pacifique* (Paris, 1902). In the 1860s, his support for Jean Macé's Ligue de l'enseignement was Passy's first public endorsement of public education.

7. The scholarly project of Leone Levi, for instance, that urged governments be pressured to select a standing panel of potential arbitrators, was presented to the Paris meeting in 1889 but not discussed. *Bulletin du premier congrès . . . 1889,* app.

8. *Proceedings of the Universal Peace Congrèss . . . ,* London, 1890, 8ff.

9. *Bulletin officiel,* Berne, 1892, 64–65.

10. Ibid., 71.

11. Ibid., 66.

12. Scholars, such as Michel Revon, whose prize-winning book urged a very cautious approach to arbitration aroused Pratt's rancor. See Revon's *L'Arbitrage international, son passé, son present, son avenir* (Paris, 1892). Revon's book won first prize from the Institut de France and helped get the young scholar a post as the first professor of international law at the University of Tokyo.

13. *Official Report,* Chicago, 1893, 176.

14. "Il Principio dell'arbitrato internazionale nelle varie sue forme e nei suoi modi d'applicazione," in *Atti* (Rome, 1889), 97–148; app., 148–81.

15. In particular, Émile de Laveleye, *Des Causes actuelles de guerre en Europe et de l'arbitrage* (Brussels, 1873); Eugène Goblet d'Alviella, *Désarmer ou déchoir: Essai sur les relations internationales* (Brussels, 1872); Revon's *L'Arbitrage international* as well as the international law tradition.

16. *Bulletin officiel,* Antwerp, 1894, 56ff. and app. I for the text.

17. *Bulletin officiel,* Hamburg, 1897, 36–40.

18. *Procès verbal,* Turin, 1898, 22.

19. *Bulletin officiel,* Hamburg, 1897, 44.

20. *La Paix par le droit* 8 (1898), 5–7. Evidently they were unaware that Hodgson Pratt had endorsed a similar tactic in 1898 at the Turin meeting of delegates from peace movements. Then, German delegates absolutely opposed any action by peace societies that appeared to intrude on government authority.

21. A brief biography of Edouard Descamps by Nadine Lubelski-Bernard is in Josephson et al., *Biographical Dictionary,* 209–10.

22. The members of the committee were Baron de Pirquet (Austria); Houzeau de Lehaie (Belgium); Bajer (Denmark); E. Labiche (France); Dr. Max Hirsch (Germany); Philip Stanhope, Lord Weardale; Cremer (Great Britain); Albert Apponyi (Hungary); Pandolfi (Italy); John Lund and Borg (Norway); E. H. Rahusen (the Netherlands); Urechia and Parumbaru (Romania); Edouard Wavrinsky (Sweden); and Gobat (Switzerland).

23. Edouard Descamps, *Essai sur l'organisation de l'arbitrage internationale: Mémoire aux puissances* (Brussels, 1896), 64 pp.

24. Ibid., 4.

25. Ibid., 33.

26. *La Conférence interparlementaire,* 2, 24 (1 September 1895), 348; *Compte rendu, Brussels, 1895* (Brussels, 1896), 35.

27. *La Conférence interparlementaire,* 2, 24 (1 September 1895), 348; *Conférence interparlementaire, Compte rendu, Brussels, 1896,* 35–36. Stanhope was particularly disappointed at the failure of the Anglo-American treaty.

28. *La Conférence interparlementaire,* 3, 31 (1 July 1896), 447–48.

29. Ibid., 41 (1 May 1897), 589.

30. "England and France: An Examination and an Appeal," *Contemporary Review,* 75 (1899) 153–60; quote is on p. 157.

31. "Settlement of the International Question," *International Journal of Ethics* 7, no. 1 (1896), 30–31.

32. "L'Arbitrage international et la codification des droit des gens," *Revue politique et parlementaire* 17 (1898), 465–515.

33. E. Rouard de Card, *Les Destinées de l'arbitrage international depuis la sentence rendue par le tribunal de Gènéve* (Paris, 1892), 214.

34. Quoted in *Européen* (November–December, 1902); repr. in *La Paix par le droit* 13 (1903), 5.

35. D. G. Ritchie, *Darwinism and Politics* (London, 1890), 36.

36. See app. C herein for the text.

37. Von Suttner, *Memoirs,* vol. 2, 188–89.

38. Ibid., 196.

39. See, for instance, "Adresse à S. M. l'Empereur de Russie," *Paix par le droit* 9 (1899), 227–29.

40. *Review of Reviews* (London), (1899), 131, 445.

41. *Paix par le droit* 9 (1899), 258; Selenka, *Die internationale Kundgebung,* ii–iii.

42. A brief biography of Waszklewicz-van Schilfgaarde by J. H. Rombach is in Josephson et al., *Biographical Dictionary,* 1006–7.

43. Selenka, *Die internationale Kundgebung,* x.

44. *La Paix par le droit* 9 (1899), 345–46.

45. Ibid., 433.

46. L'Alliance des savants et des philanthropes, "Suggestions sur les meilleurs moyens d'assurer la paix générale: Mémoire adressé au ministre des affairs etrangères par des nombreuses notabilités," *L'Humanité nouvelle* 4 (1899), 18 pp. (Special supplement); repr. in Cooper, *Arbitration or War?* GLW/P (New York, 1972).

47. "Le Projet du tsar et le parti de la paix," *La Paix par le droit* 9 (1899), 228.

48. *Review of Reviews* 8 (1898), 325; *Paix par le droit* 9 (1899), 16. See Joseph Baylen and P. G. Hogan, Jr., "Shaw, W. T. Stead and the International Peace Crusade, 1898–1899," *Shaw Review,* 6 (1963), 60–61.

49. Hodgson Pratt to Henri La Fontaine, 11 March 1899, the Mundanum, La Fontaine Papers, box 27.

50. W. T. Stead, *Chronique de la Conférence de La Haye, 1899: Accompagné du texte des conventions* (La Haye, 1900).

51. A substantial list of what was sent appeared in *Paix par le droit* 9 (1899), 20–22, 257–59.

52. "L'Initiative du tsar," *La Revue blanche* 17 (1898), 161–75.

53. "Die Philosophie des Friedens: Ein Wort an die Friedensconferenz im Haag," *Deutsche Rundschau,* (1899), 93.

54. "The Tsar's Eirenicon," *Contemporary Review* 74 (1898), 611–42; repr. Cooper, *Arbitration or War?*

55. M. Delbrück, "Zukunstkrieg and Zukunstfriede" *Preussische Jahrbücher* 96 (1899), 203–29; repr. Cooper, *Arbitration or War?*

56. Ibid., 219. British troops advancing up the Nile under Sir Herbert Kitchener, encountered at Fashoda on the Nile in July 1898 a French force under Jean-Baptiste Marchand that was moving east from the Congo. The incident nearly led to war until the French government, harassed by the Dreyfus affair, ordered Marchand's evacuation in November 1898. A diplomatic settlement was reached and lands were exchanged.

57. See, for instance, memo of the French ambassador in Berlin to the French foreign minister, Théophile Delcassé, in *Documents diplomatiques françaises,* vol. 15, 489 (no. 312); also memo of Paul Cambon (Constantinople) to Delcassé, ibid., 493–95 (no. 314); Bernhard von Bülow (Berlin) to Hatzfeld (London) in *Der Grosse Politik der Europäischen Kabinette,* vol. 15, 146 (no. 4217); Kaiser Wilhelm's note no. 4 on von Bülow to Wilhelm, 28 August 1898, ibid., 149–50; *Documenti diplomatici italiani,* 3rd ser., vol. 3 (1898–1900), 34.

58. Lord Salisbury to Scott, *British Documents on the Origins of the War, 1898–1914,* vol. 1, *The End of British Isolation,* ed. G. P. Gooch and Harold W. V. Temperly (London, 1932), 215.

59. Jost Düffler, *Regeln gegen den Krieg? Die Haager Friedens-Konferenzen 1899 und 1907 in der internationalen Politik* (Berlin, 1981), 36–69, and passim; Calvin D. Davis, *The United States and the Hague Peace Conference* (Ithaca, NY, 1961), 36–54, and passim;

William I. Hull, *The Two Hague Conferences and Their Contribution to International Law* (Boston, 1908); L. Telesheva, "Towards the History of the First Hague Conference," [trans. of Russian title], *Krasnyi Archiv* 50–51 (Moscow, 1932), 64–96; "New Material About The Hague Peace Conference of 1899," 54–55, *Krasnyi Archiv,* 49–79; T. K. Ford, "The Genesis of the First Hague Peace Conference," *Political Science Quarterly* 51 (1936), 354–82; S. E. Cooper, "Peace and Internationalism: European Ideological Movements Behind the Two Hague Conferences (1889 to 1907)" (Ph.D. diss., New York Univ., 1967), 289–300, and passim; David James Bettez, "France, Germany and The Hague Peace Conference of 1899 and 1907" (Ph.D diss. Univ. of Kentucky, 1982).

60. Rescript repr. in F. W. Holls, *The Peace Conference at The Hague and Its Bearings on International Law and Policy* (New York, 1900), 27.

61. Chickering, *Imperial Germany,* 220-21.

62. Norman Rich and M. H. Fischer, eds., *The Holstein Papers* (Cambridge, 1955–1963), vol. 4, 124–25, 135; Münster, 21 April 1899, in *Der Grosse Politik,* 186–87.

63. Note no. 2 by Kaiser Wilhelm on a communique in *Der Grosse Politik,* vol. 15, 145, (no. 4216).

64. Van den Dungen, *The Making of Peace,* 16–17.

65. *Der Gross Politik,* vol. 15, 235, 242–44.

66. Gooch and Temperly, *British Documents,* vol. 1, 228–29, Communiqué, 13 June 1899, Vienna to London. The work of Heinrich Lammasch was significant in convincing the Hapsburg government to support the limited arbitration arrangement under discussion.

67. *Documenti diplomatici italiani,* 3rd ser., vol. 3 (1898–1900), no. 278.

68. *Der Grosse Politik,* vol. 15, 354–55, 17 July 1899.

69. Bernhard von Bülow, *Memoirs,* 4 vols. (Boston, 1931–1932), vol. 1, 404; vol. 2, 230.

70. James Brown Scott, *The Hague Peace Conferences of 1899 and 1907,* vol. 2, *Documents* (Baltimore, 1909); repr. with an intro. by Warren Kuehl, GLW/P (New York, 1972), 89–110, for the text of the convention on the arbitration tribunal.

71. James Brown Scott, ed., *The Hague Conventions and Declarations of 1899 and 1907* (New York, 1918), 62.

72. William L. Langer, *The Diplomacy of Imperialism* (New York, 1935), vol. 2, 591.

73. Gooch and Temperley, *British Documents,* vol. 8, vii, forword.

74. Interview with E. T. Moneta, "Un Colloquio con l'ambasciatore Nigra," *La Vita internazionale* 2, no. 16 (20 August 1899), 99.

75. G. H. Perris et al., *A History of the Peace Congress at The Hague* (London, 1899) 11, repr. in Cooper, *Arbitration or War?*

76. Von Suttner, *Memoirs,* vol. 2, 239.

77. Resolution repr. in *La Paix par le droit* 9 (1899), 447.

78. A summary of the reports in the *Times* (London), *Spectator, Standard, Morning Post,* and *Pall Mall Gazette* is in *Concord* 14 (1899), 157.

79. *Pour la paix,* 165–66.

80. Union interparlementaire, *Compte rendu* (Paris, 1900), 9.

81. *La Paix par le droit,* 77 (1901), 24–29.

82. See, for instance, Edmund Monson (Paris) to Salisbury, in Gooch and Temperly, *British Documents,* vol. 1, no. 232, 24 October 1899, no. 284.

83. Council, International Arbitration League, Manifesto of September 1899, in IPU files, 1899–1900.

84. G. B. Clark to von Suttner, von Suttner, *Memoirs,* vol. 2, 356.

85. "The Transvaal Question: Manifesto for Members of the British Parliament," 4 October 1899, in IPU files, 1899–1900. Great Britain and the United States entered an

arbitration proceeding in 1895–1896 over the Venezuelan border. British willingness to use arbitration in what had become a nasty public confrontation avoided hostilities.

86. Reports in *Concord,* October 1899, 165–67; November 1899, 180–81; December 1901, 177–79.

87. Max Nordau, "Philosophy and Morals of War," *North American Review* 169 (1899), 788–89.

88. Letters, 28 May to 1 June, 1900 to La Fontaine, The Mundanum, Henri La Fontaine Papers, box 26.

89. *Proceedings,* Glasgow, 1901, 78–79.

90. Ibid., quoted 130–34; Wild, *D'Estournelles de Constant,* 93–98.

91. Interpellation, 29 January 1903, repr. in *La Paix par le droit* 13 (1903), 66–68.

92. A list of arbitration agreements between 1899 and 1908 is found in Scott, *The Hague Peace Conferences,* vol. 1, 813–15.

93. The parliamentarians exchanged visits in the summer of 1903.

94. IPU, *Compte rendu* (Vienna, 1903), 2.

95. "Preface," *Le Mouvement pacifique et le rapprochement Franco-Anglais: Les visites parlementaires de Londres et Paris, 22 juillet–26 novembre, 1903* (La Flèche, 1903), x.

96. Following a successful meeting of the IPU in St. Louis in 1904, a delegation visited the White House. The enthusiastic support of U.S. senator Richard Bartholdt was crucial in persuading President Roosevelt to take up the cause; however, this did not produce success for another three years. See Calvin Davis, *The United States and the Second Hague Peace Conference* (Chapel Hill, NC, 1975), 106–10.

97. Groupe parlementaire français de l'arbitrage international, *Le Bilan du groupe* (Paris, 1906–1910), app. 1. Over seventy bilateral treaties of arbitration signed between 1890 and 1906 essentially covered the areas proposed by the IPU.

98. *Official Report of the Fourteenth Interparliamentary Conference* (London, 1906), 117–18, 120–21.

99. Ibid., 107.

100. Quoted in Solomon Wank, "Diplomacy Against the Peace Movement: The Austro-Hungarian Foreign Office and the Second Hague Peace Conference of 1907," in Wank, *Doves and Diplomats,* 60.

101. *Bulletin officiel,* Milan, 1906, 76.

102. Ibid., 83.

103. J. Dumas, *Les Sanctions de l'arbitrage international* (Paris, 1906); and E. Duplessix, *Code de droit international public* (Paris, 1906), winner of the Thibault prize of L'Association la paix par le droit were the most influential. De Montluc disagreed with Duplessix in "La Loi des nations," in *Paix par le droit* 17 (1907), 17–23.

104. *Bulletin officiel,* Milan, 1906, 84.

105. Chickering, *Imperial Germany,* 229–30.

106. Biographies of T.M.C. Asser by Willen G. Zeylstra; of Heinrich Lammasch by Solomon Wank; of Frederic de Martens by J.W.H. Thijssen; and of James Brown Scott by Ralph D. Nurnberger are in Kuehl, *Internationalists,* 31–32, 413–15, 476–77, 660–62, respectively.

107. "A La Haye," *Paix par le droit* 17 (1907), 310.

108. Gooch and Temperly, *British Documents,* vol. 8, 267–68.

109. See Sir Edward Fry to Earl Grey, ibid., 215, 17 July 1907; Davis, *The United States and the Second Hague Conference,* 284.

110. *Bulletin officiel,* Munich, 1907, 37.

111. The American proposal included a complex system of rotation to select the judges; this failed to satisfy the smaller nations who feared being omitted. Beernaert also opposed

it on grounds that the task of sitting at The Hague waiting for cases would be so unappealing that only the most mediocre jurists would consider the appointment.

112. *Bulletin officiel,* Munch, 1907, 28–32, 35–6.

113. *La Vita internazionale* 11, no. 2 (20 January 1908), 53. See also 10, no. 15 (5 August 1907), 343–44.

114. *Bericht* (Munich, 1908), 122–23, 129, 132.

115. See, especially, Heinrich Lammasch, "L'Arbitrage obligatoire et les deux conférences de la Paix," *Revue générale de droit international public* 16 (1909), 689–98.

116. *Bericht,* 153–54.

117. "Les Résultats de la IIe Conférence de La Haye," *Paix par le droit* 18 (1908), 6.

118. Léon Bourgeois, *Pour La Société des nations* (Paris, 1910), 285–86.

119. See chap. 3, 85–86, herein.

120. Lammasch, "L'Arbitrage obligatoire," 689–98; L. Le Fur, "La Paix perpétuelle et l'arbitrage international," *Revue générale de droit international public* 16 (1909), 437–63.

121. Théodore Ruyssen, "A Propos d'un libre jaune: La Seconde Conférence de La Haye," *Paix par le droit* 19 (1909), 9–12.

122. Alfred Fried, "Les Voies nouvelles ouvertes au pacifisme," *Paix par le droit* 18 (1908), 155.

123. See esp. Jacques Novicow, *La Fédération de l'Europe* (Paris, 1901), repr. GLW/P (New York, 1973). Also "L'Avenir de la propagande pacifique," *La Revue (ancienne Revue des revues)* 38 (1901), 1–14.

124. Frédéric Passy, "Le Role de l'arbitrage," *La Revue (ancienne Revue des revues)* 18 (1908), 207–8.

125. *Bulletin officiel,* Stockholm, 1910, 47.

126. Ibid., complete code is in the app., 285–312.

127. Nicol, general secretary of the Comité d'action républicaine aux colonies françaises, began reporting to French national congresses in 1908. His essay, *Pacifisme et colonisation* (1911), summarized the miasma of French Colonial administration and predicted the coming native risings.

128. Ibid., 305.

129. In 1905 at Lucerne, the congress specifically criticized the Russo-Japanese peace treaty for ignoring the wishes of Korean and Manchurian peoples. In 1908 at London, the movement was asked to include policy statements protesting exploited peoples and the rights of national minorities beyond the European borders. See speech of Mrs. Drysdale, *Official Report,* 249–50. The most trenchant criticism of the movement for ignoring human rights had been written by Edoardo Cimbali, *Il Nuovo diritto internazionale e gli odierni congressi, conferenze, società e leghe per la pace, l'arbitrato e il disarmo* (Rome, 1910), esp. 7–8.

130. *Bulletin officiel,* Stockholm, 1910, 312.

131. The proposal for general strikes was developed by Charles Couet, "La Grève générale considerée comme sanction morale de l'arbitrage," *Paix par le droit* 17 (1907), 23–27.

132. A brief biography of Cornelius van Vollenhoven by J. H. Rombach is in Josephson et al., *Biographical Dictionary,* 996–98. Van Vollenhoven's work, "De Roeping van Holland," appeared originally in *De Gids* (1910).

133. See also Jong van Beek en Donk, *History of the Peace Movement in the Netherlands,* 21–24; repr. with an intro. by S. E. Cooper, ed., in *Peace Activities in Belgium and the Netherlands,* GLW/P (New York, 1972).

134. *Bulletin officiel,* Geneva, 1912, 103–4.

135. *Compte rendu officiel du premier congrès national belge de la paix (Brussels, 8–9 juin 1913)* (Brussels, 1913), 53.

136. A. Gobat, "The Need for Organising the Defence of Humanity" in *Peace Movement*, vol. 1, (1912), 135.

137. "Peace," in *Encyclopaedia Britannica*, 11th ed., vol. 21, 4.

138. See, for instance, A. G. de Lapradelle, "Compte rendu des travaux et appréciation critique: La Conférence de la paix," *Revue générale de droit international public* 6 (1899), 651–846; also, with N. Politis, "La Conférence de la paix: Origine, Convocation, Organisation," *Revue générale de droit international public* 16 (1909) 384–437.

Chapter 5   Arms Control: The Dilemna of Patriotic Pacifism

1. For the text of the Rescript, see app. C.

2. See p. 247, n. 213

3. van den Dungen, *The Making of Peace*, 12, and passim. See also chap. 3 herein.

4. Interestingly, the peace movement was criticized for its reticence by an anonymous author, "The Peace Movement," *Westminster Review* 151 (1899), 124–30.

5. Klas P. Arnoldson, *Pax Mundi: A Concise History of the Progress of the Movement for Peace by Means of Arbitration, Neutralization, International Law and Disarmament,* trans. by "A Lady" (London, 1892), 7–8.

6. *Die Waffen nieder,* 1897, no. 20, quoted in Wehburg, "The Union and International Organization," 15.

7. Max Nordau, "Philosophy and Morals of War," *North American Review* (1899), 787–97.

8. Solomon Wank, "The Austrian Peace Movement and the Habsburg Ruling Elite, 1906–1914," in Chatfield and van den Dungen, *Peace Movements,* 42–43.

9. Passy to Jules Simon, 21 December 1893, Jules Simon Papers, AN 87 AP/6.

10. *Union Interparlementaire: Résolutions des conférences et décisions principales du conseil,* 20.

11. A brief biography of Princess Gabrielle Wiesniewska by S. E. Cooper is in Josephson et al., *Biographical Dictionary,* 1021–23. See also Cooper, "Women's Participation in European Peace Movements," in Pierson, *Women and Peace,* 57.

12. Princess Wiesniewska to Austrian women, "Bibliothèque Marguerite Durand Archive, "Paix," n.d.

13. A brief biography of Sylvie Flammarion by S. E. Cooper is in Josephson et al., *Biographical Dictionary,* 283–84.

14. Caïel, *La Femme et la paix,* 53.

15. Reprinted in ibid., 49.

16. See, for instance, Lewis Appleton, *The Military and Financial Condition of Europe* (orig. London, 1882). (Distributed at the 1890 London congress.)

17. *Bulletin officiel,* 99.

18. Proposal in *Compte Rendu,* Brussels, 1897, 70–78; Lange, *Resolutions,* 19; *Compte rendu,* Paris, 1900, 5, 153–54.

19. Bajer carried the proposal to the UPC in 1902, see *Résolutions textuelles,* 15–18; to the French national peace congress in Toulouse, 1902, *Compte rendu,* 95–98; and again to the IPU, *Compte rendu,* Vienna, 1903, 32–33, 82.

20. *Compte rendu,* The Hague, 1913, 193–230.

21. F. Passy to Ducommun, 28 February, 1898, BIP, VB 1, "Propagande en France."

22. Auguste Hamon, *Psycologie du militaire professionel* (Paris, 1898), Italian trans., Milan, 1901. See also "À propos du désarmement" *L'Humanité nouvelle* 3 (1898), 427–45.

23. In the fall of 1898, Urbain Gohier was tried for *L'Armée contre la nation,* available with an intro. by Helena Lewis, GLW/P (New York 1972).

24. Passy to Ducommun, 28 February 1898, BIP, VB 1, "Propagande en France."

25. Chambre des députés, *Annales, Séance du 24 janvier, 1899,* 157.

26. Ibid., 134.

27. *Der Grosse Politik,* 15, no. 4222 (29 August 1898).

28. Gaston Moch, "Les Principles d'organisation militaire démocratique," *La Revue blanche* 17 (1898), 499–504.

29. Gaston Moch, "La Reduction du service militaire," *La Revue blanche* 12 (1898), 598–602.

30. Gaston Moch to "Madame et chère confrère," 8 August 1899, Jules Salvandi Papers, AN 152 AP/17

31. *L'Armée d'une démocratie,* 2nd ed. (Paris, 1900), 4–5, 81.

32. August Bebel, *Nicht stehendes Heer, sondern Volkswehr* (Stuttgart, 1898); repr. with new intro. by Claudia Koonz, GLW/P (New York, 1972), 88 pp.

33. Gaston Moch, *L'Alsace-Lorraine devant l'Europe,* 457.

34. See, for instance, Leonard Courtney, "The Approaching Conference," *Contemporary Review* 75 (May, 1899), 609–19; Arthur Desjardins, "Le Désarmement, étude de droit international," *Revue des deux mondes* 14 (1898), 668–79.

35. Gaston Moch, "La Philosophie de la Paix: l'Arbitrage universelle," in *Morale générale,* vol. 2 (Paris, 1903), 365.

36. Ibid., 370.

37. *Bulletin officiel,* Monaco, 1902, 10.

38. *Bulletin officiel,* Rouen and Le Havre, 1903, 143.

39. *Désarmons les Alpes! Vers la fédération d'occident.* (Paris, 1905).

40. Stefan Türr to Giuseppe Garibaldi, 20 January 1867, ISRI, Garibaldi Papers B52, no. 2(59).

41. *Atti . . . Roma,* 1889, 67.

42. Resolution repr. in *Atti . . . Roma,* 1889, 80–81.

43. "III Congresso nazionale della pace, Perugia, 20–22 settembre, 1907," *La Vita internazionale* 10, no. 19 (5 October 1907), 436.

44. "Il Convegno di Vienna dei pacifisti dei paesi della triplice," *La Vita internazionale* 10, no. 10 (20 May 1907), 217.

45. Paul Cambon to Henri Cambon, 8 August 1898, in *Paul Cambon, Correspondance, 1870–1914,* 3 vols., ed. Henri Cambon (Paris, 1940–1946), vol. 1, 438.

46. See, for instance, E. J. Dillon, "The Tsar's Eirenicon," *Contemporary Review* 74 (1898), 609–42; esp. 610; "A Soldier," "The Tsar's Appeal for Peace," 73 *Contemporary Review* (1898), 498–504; "The Looker-on," *Blackwood's Magazine* 164 (1899), 427–47. German diplomatic reaction is scattered in *Der Grosse Politik* 15 (1898), esp. no. 4219, (28 August 1898), Count von Bülow to the Kaiser, 149–50.

47. "Chronique des Faits Internationaux," *Revue générale de droit international public* 6 (1899), 78–79.

48. *Der Grosse Politik,* vol. 5, no. 4216 (26 August, 1898), 145.

49. Ibid., no. 4222 (29 August 1898), 151–52.

50. *Documenti diplomatici italiani,* 3rd ser., vol. 3, 179 (24 June 1899), 282.

51. Paul Cambon to Delcassé, *Documents diplomatiques françaises,* vol. 14, 495–96.

52. Van den Dungen, *The Making of Peace,* 12–17.

53. A brief biography of Frédéric [Fedor Fedorovich], de Martens by J.W.H. Thijssen is in Kuehl, *Internationalists,* 476–77.

54. *Der Grosse Politik,* vol. 15, no. 4216 (26 August 1898), 182.

55. Von Suttner, *Memoirs,* vol. 2, 228–29.

56. Gooch and Temperly, *British Documents,* vol. 1, no. 274, "Letter from the Admiralty to the Foreign Office," copy to Sir Julian Pauncefote, 224.

57. Ibid., 229–31, see advice of Lieutenant Colonel Charles Court, who also warned against naval cuts because the United States was soon to be a major Pacific rival of Great Britain.

58. The general hypocrisy of European nations in regard to the conference is a theme in Düffler, *Regeln gegen den Krieg?;* see also William F. Vollbrecht, "The Hypocrisy of the Powers on Disarmament in Connection with the First Hague Peace Conference, 1899," (Ph.D. diss., Univ. of Pennsylvania, 1935).

59. See, for instance, John W. Coogan, *The United States, Britain and Maritime Rights, 1899–1915* (Ithaca, NY, 1981), chap. 1.

60. Paul Cambon to Delcassé, *Documents diplomatiques françaises,* vol. 15, 495.

61. Quoted in Hull, *The Two Hague Conferences,* 58.

62. Paul M. Kennedy, *The Rise of the Anglo-German Antagonism, 1860–1914* (London, 1980, 1982), chaps. 12–15, and passim.

63. Thomas Hayes Conner, "Parliament and the Making of Foreign Policy: France Under the Third Republic, 1875–1914" (Ph.D. diss., Univ. of North Carolina, 1983).

64. See, for instance, Chambre des députés, *Annales, 19 janvier 1903,* 97–100. For the campaign launched by d'Estournelles de Constant, see Adolf Wild, "Introduction," *Arms Limitation: Plans for Europe Before 1914,* GLP/W (New York, 1972), 13–14. Also Tate, *The Disarmament Illusion* (New York, 1942), 306–7.

65. Chambre des députés *Annales, 19 janvier, 1903,* 617–18.

66. D'Estournelles de Constant, speech in the Chambre des députés, *Annales, 20 novembre, 1903,* 613.

67. Séverine, "Sylvie Flammarion," in *Le Congrès spiritualiste* 1, no. 7 (July 1908) (clipping in Bibliothèque Marquerite Durand, "Paix").

68. Brief biographies of Sylvie Flammarion by S. E. Cooper and of Séverine by A. Hill are in Josephson et al., *Biographical Dictionary,* 283–84 and 873–75, respectively.

69. Flammarion, speech of 20 April 1905; repr. in *La Paix par les femmes* (Paris, May 1905), BHVP, Fonds Marie-Louise Bouglé, Fonds Buisson.

70. Words by Edward Spalikowski, in *La Paix par les femmes* (Paris, May 1905), 20–21. The original French read:

Femmes, si vous aviez dire par fois aux hommes

Que c'est lâche et honteux de jeter vos enfants

Comme offrande à Moloch.

71. "Militarism in Politics and Lord Roberts' Army Reorganization," *Contemporary Review* 90 (1901), 761.

72. *Proceedings of the Universal Peace Congress,* Glasgow, 1901, 111–12. See also Perris's speech, *Bulletin officiel,* Monaco, 1902, 50.

73. Paul Allégret, "Refus de porter des armes," II Congrès national des sociétés françaises de la paix, Nîmes (7–10 April 1904), *Compte rendu,* 40–51.

74. See, for instance, the publication of Ferdinand Brunetière, "Le Mensonge du Pacifisme," *Revue des deux mondes,* 5 pér, 28 (1905); repr. in S. E. Cooper, ed., *Voices of French Pacifism.* See also Henri Tridon, *L'Antimilitarisme* (Tunis, 1906); Louis Petit, *Un Scandale à l'Hotel de Ville de Rouen à propos d'une conférence pacifiste de M. Charles Richet* (Paris, 1905), 12 pp. The scandal was that the City Hall was used for a peace activist's speech.

75. A brief biography of Gustave Hervé by James Friguglietti is in Josephson et al.,

Biographical Dictionary, 404–5. Hervé, a teacher and journalist, had been denouncing the French army in widely publicized articles since 1900. He urged youth to refuse to serve in the army, which only served the interests of the capitalist bourgeoisie and a state that exploited its poor and working class. An articulate spokesperson for the idea of permanent class warfare, Hervé stood outside the parliamentary socialist consensus and was attacked by Jaurès for his antipatriotism. *Hervéisme* became equivalent to antimilitarism, easily confused with the pacifist refusal to serve.

76. Passy to Ducommun, 21 October 1902, BIP, VB 1, Propagande en France.

77. *Atti* (Turin, 1905), 67.

78. Giovanni Artieri, *Cronaca del regno d'italia: Da porta pia all'intervento* (Rome, 1977), 886–87.

79. Pietro Mazzini, "La Paix armée en italie et l'extrême gauche," *Le Courrier européen* 2, no. 33 (23 June 1905), 521.

80. Ibid.

81. E. Giretti, "L'Enquête sur la marine en italie," *Le Courrier européen* 3, no. 8 (11 May 1906), 279. The Terni Corporation was a large steel producer.

82. The London meeting was widely publicized because delegates from the newly formed Russian Duma, a product of the Revolution of 1905, were present. During the meeting, news came that the tsar had dissolved the Duma, an act immediately recognized as counterrevolutionary. See p. 249, n. 252.

83. Report on the Limitation of Arms, IPU, *Official Report,* London, 1906, 142ff.

84. Ibid., 142.

85. Ibid.

86. Ibid. 144, 152.

87. A brief biography of Goblet d'Alviella by Nadine Lubelski-Bernard is in Josephson et al., *Biographical Dictionary,* 333–34.

88. Sénat de France, Session, 9 April 1906; repr. in *Revue de la paix* 11 (1906), 147.

89. "La Limitation des armaments," *Revue de la paix* 11 (1906), 171–72.

90. Brock, *Pacifism in Europe,* remains the most authoritative discussion of the absolute pacifist tradition. For an example of anarchist appropriation of peace society arguments, see Errico Malatesta, *Il nostro programma* (1905), and a brief biography of Malatesta by S. E. Cooper in Josephson et al., *Biographical Dictionary,* 598–99. Conscientious objection in Norway at the turn of the century is discussed in Agoy, "Regulating Conscientious Objection," 3–25.

91. *Annales* (7 June 1907), 401–2.

92. Ibid., 410.

93. See, for instance, Session, 15 January 1907, *Annales du Sénat,* 81, 96.

94. Wild, *D'Estournelles de Constant,* 288–89.

95. Stéphen Pichon, speech in Chambre des députés, quoted in Gooch and Temperly, *British Documents,* vol. 7, 241.

96. Sir F. Lascelles, dispatch, 16 August 1906, in Gooch and Temperly, *British Documents,* vol. 7, 192–93.

97. Paul Cambon to Pichon, 19 January 1907, *Documents diplomatiques françaises,* 2nd ser., vol. 10, 624–25.

98. Gooch and Temperly, *British Documents,* vol. 7, 191–92, 198.

99. *Der Grosse Politik,* vol. 23, I, 80–81.

100. Gooch and Temperly, *British Documents,* vol. 7, 192–93 (memo of 16 August 1906).

101. A. J. Anthony Morris, *Radicalism Against War, 1906–1914: The Advocacy of Peace and Retrenchment* (Totowa, NJ, 1972), remains a useful study.

102. Chickering, *Imperial Germany*, 223.

103. Von Bülow, conversation with Jules Cambon, 17 April 1907, quoted in *Documents diplomatiques françaises*, vol. 10, 748–50.

104. Richard Laurence, "Peace Movement in Austria," in Wank, *Doves and Diplomats*, 29.

105. Gooch and Temperly, *British Documents*, vol. 7, 209–210, 218–19; *Documents diplomatiques françaises*, vol. 10, 675.

106. Quoted in Solomon Wank, "Introduction" to Hans Wehburg, *Die internationale Beschränkung der Rüstungen*, GLW/P (New York, 1973), 13.

107. Laurence,"Peace Movement in Austria," 30.

108. Jusserand (Washington, DC) to Pichon, in *Documents diplomatiques françaises*, 2nd ser., vol. 10, no. 750–55.

109. Ibid., 197–98.

110. Bourgeois, *Pour la Société des nations*, 16, 287.

111. Charles Richet, "Le Service militaire et les amis de la Paix," *Revue de la paix*, (1907), 332; "Pace, Esercito e Patria," *La Vita internazionale* 10, no. 3 (5 February 1907), 49–53.

112. *Bericht*, Munich, 1907, 77.

113. Ibid., 70.

114. *La Paix par le droit* 17 (1907), 350–54.

115. *Proceedings*, London, 1908, 115–19.

116. Ibid., 116.

117. Ibid.

118. D'Estournelles de Constant to M. Picquart, 20 August 1908; repr. in *La Paix par le droit* 19 (1909), 50.

119. *Almanach de la Paix*, 1909, 59–64.

120. Charles Gide, "Les Aéroplanes," in *La Paix par le droit* 19 (1909) 55–58; Théodore Ruyssen, "Aéronefs, aéroplanes et pacifisme," in *La Paix par le droit* 18 (1908), 458.

121. Richet, in *La Paix par la droit* 19 (1909), 100–101.

122. VIe Congrès national des Sociétés françaises de la paix, Reims, 1909, 17.

123. Ibid., 48.

124. *Bulletin officiel*, Geneva, 1912, 142–43.

125. Ibid., 147.

126. *Compte rendu*, Geneva, 1912, 262.

127. Ferdinand Dreyfus, speech, *Compte-rendu*, 269–70.

128. A brief biography of Benjamin Trueblood by Calvin D. Davis is in Josephson et al., *Biographical Dictionary*, 961–62.

129. *Bulletin officiel*, Geneva, 1912, 96–97.

130. Ibid., 53.

131. *Bulletin officiel*, The Hague, 1913, 51.

132. Ibid., 180.

133. Ibid., 181

134. *La Paix par le droit* 23 (1913), 269–283; 12 (1913), 369–82.

135. Ibid., 374.

136. Ibid., 381

137. The text of the "Model Project" is available in IPU, *Compte rendu*, The Hague, 1913, 335–44.

138. The question of colonialism and of the problem of "backward" races was only an occasional issue at peace congresses. Quidde's attitude was not much different, for instance, than that of Ellen Key, a well-known Swedish feminist and pacifist. See *War, Peace and the Future: A Consideration of Nationalism and Internationalism, and of the Relationship of*

Women to War, trans. by Hildegard Norberg, (orig. 1916), Intro. by Berenice Carroll, GLW/P (New York, 1972), 52.

139. Brigette M. Goldstein, "Ludwig Quidde and the Struggle for Democratic Pacifism in Germany, 1914–1930" (Ph.D. diss., New York Univ., 1984), 42.

140. Ibid., 43, n.51.

141. "Les Dépenses de Guerre," in *Almanach de la Paix pour 1913* (Paris, 1914), 38.

142. *Bulletin officiel,* Geneva, 1912, 10–11.

143. A. T. Mahan, *Armaments and Arbitration, or the Place of Force in International Relations of States* (New York, 1912).

Chapter 6 War: The Anatomy of an Anachronism

1. A. H. Fried, *The Restoration of Europe,* trans. by L. S. Gannet (New York, 1916), 10, 16–17.

2. For a description of the breakdown of the peace movement, see chap. 8 herein.

3. Whether or not British Quakers of the pre-1914 generation were as sensitive to antiwar and antimilitarist attitudes as earlier generations had been is discussed in Kennedy, "Why Did Friends Resist? . . ." *Peace and Change* 14, no. 4 (October, 1989), 356–57.

4. Angelo Crespi, "Gli uomini e l'umanità," in *La Vita internazionale* 21, no. 5 (5 March 1918), 95–96.

5. Jacques Novicow, *La Politique internationale* (Paris, 1886).

6. Jacques Novicow, *Les Luttres entre sociétés et leures phases successives,* 2 vols. (Paris, 1893); repr. with a new intro. by S. E. Cooper GLW/P (New York, 1971).

7. Charles Richet, "Preface" to *L'Alsace-Lorraine: Obstacle à l'expansion allemande* by Novicow (Paris, 1913).

8. "Introduction" by Eugène Véron to *La Politique internationale,* 12.

9. *Théorie organique des sociétés: Défense de la organicisme* (Paris, 1899), 64; Novicow, *Conscience et volonté sociales* (Paris, 1897), 9.

10. *La Critique du Darwinisme sociale* (Paris, 1910), 3, 30–31, 41–42, 210–25; *Téorie organique,* 167–69.

11. Pyotr Kropotkin's *Mutual Aid* was originally published as articles in the *Nineteenth Century* during the 1890s and in book form in London, 1902.

12. Novicow, *Les Luttes,* 59.

13. Ibid. 647, n.1.

14. This point of view underlay all Novicow's work but was most specifically expressed in *Mécanisme et limites de l'association humaine* (Paris, 1912).

15. Novicow, *Les Luttes,* 445–47.

16. "L'Insignificance de la force brutale," *Revue internationale de sociologie* 1 (1893), 505–6.

17. Jacques Novicow, *War and Its Alleged Benefits,* with intro. by Norman Angell (London, 1912); repr. with intro. by S. E. Cooper, GLW/P (New York, 1971), 16–18. This work was a translation of *Les Guerres et ses bienfaits prétendus* (Paris, 1894).

18. Novicow, *Conscience et volonté sociales,* 230–35, 275–83; *La Possibilité du bonheur* (Paris, 1904), 22–23.

19. Novicow, *Conscience et volonté sociales,* 284–85.

20. Jacques Novicow, "Quelques paradoxes des amoreux de la guerre," *La Revue (ancienne Revue des revues)* 55 (1905), 457–68.

21. Jacques Novicow, *L'Affranchissement de la femme* (Paris, 1903); excerpted in Cooper, *Peace and Civilization,* 334–36, 362.

22. Novicow, *La Critique du Darwinisme sociale,* 3.

23. Novicow, *War and Its Alleged Benefits*, 115.

24. Novicow, *L'Affranchissement de la femme*, 339.

25. Report of Commission A, *Bulletin officiel*, Glasgow, 1901, 16–17.

26. Novicow, *La Fédération de l'Europe*, 667.

27. Ibid., 663–66. Also Novicow, *La Missione dell'Italia* (Milan, 1903).

28. "Organicism Applied," from Novicow, *Conscience et volonté sociales*, in Cooper, *Peace and Civilization*, 59.

29. Novicow, *La Possibilité du Bonheur*, 157–59, in Cooper, *Peace and Civilization*, 77.

30. Report of Commission A, *Bulletin officiel*, Glasgow, 1901, 16–17; report in *Bulletin officiel*, Monaco, 1902, 165–74.

31. Novicow, "Orientation à donner au mouvement pacifique pour accroître son efficacité," in Cooper, *Peace and Civilization*, 323.

32. Théodore Ruyssen, "De la methode dans la philosophie de la paix," in *Morale générale*, vol. 2, *Bibliothèque du congrès international de philosophie* (Paris, 1903), 342.

33. For a summary of Bloch's arguments, see S. E. Cooper, "Introduction," to *La Guerre* by J. de Bloch GLW/P (New York, 1973); also van den Dungen, *The Making of Peace*.

34. Bloch, *La Guerre*, vol. 1, 276.

35. Bloch, *The Future of War*, xvii.

36. Bloch, *La Guerre*, vol. 1, 277–80.

37. Bloch, *The Future of War*, 30.

38. Ibid. 142–43.

39. Interview in preface to the English one-volume edition of Bloch's *The Future of War*.

40. Bloch, *La Guerre*, vol. 2, 161; vol. 4, 326. (Here Bloch argued that Asians would also become heirs to Europe's world role.)

41. Conférence de Jean de Bloch, "Les Problèmes de la guerre et la politique d'expansion coloniale," BIP Archives, Misc. n.d. (probably 1900–1901), 1. (Typescript.)

42. Bloch, *La Guerre*, vol. 2, 163–64; vol. 4, 261–62; vol. 5, 136–37.

43. Ibid., vol. 5, 261–89, 645.

44. Ibid., vol. 4, 135.

45. This abridged edition of Bloch's *Future of War* contained an interview with W. T. Stead, the English journalist.

46. "The Tsar received de Bloch on several occasions to hear him expound his theories, which demonstrates that the Tsar not only knew the work but showed great interest in it," Van den Dungen, *The Making of Peace*, 6.

47. *The Work of the Peace Societies: How to Widen Their Programme* (Glasgow, 1901), 9–10.

48. Peter van den Dungen, "The International Museum of War and Peace at Lucerne," *Revue Suisse d'histoire* 31 (1981), 185–206; also "Peace Museums" in Linus Pauling et al., eds., *World Encyclopedia of Peace* (London, 1986), vol. 2, 234–43.

49. See, for instance, L. Cazé, "Les Armées du monde et le désarmement général," *Revue des revues (Paris)* 26 (1898), 623–31; René Lavalée, "Ce Que Coûte la paix armée," *L'Europe nouvelle* (May 1899), 1–28; "Looker-on," *Blackwood's Magazine* (April 1899), 762–68; Paul Louis, "Armements," *La Revue blanche (Paris)* 21 (1900), 386–88; E. Tallichet, "Le Désarmement et la Paix," *Bibliothèque universelle et revue suisse* 13 (1899), 149–65, 341–73. The moderate socialist editor Auguste Hamon published a special supplement, "À-Propos du désarmement," *L'Humanité nouvelle* 3 (1898), 427–65.

50. For instance, see *La Paix et l'enseignement pacifiste: Lecons professées à l'école des hautes études sociales* (Paris, 1906), 10–12.

51. A brief biography of Lucien Le Foyer by Albert Hill is in Josephson et al., *Biographical Dictionary,* 551–54.

52. Lucien Le Foyer et al., *Lettre à messieurs les membres de la Conférence de la paix de La Haye* (Paris, 1899), 16 pp.

53. Lucien Le Foyer, *La Guerre par les chiffres* (Paris, 1901), 10.

54. Ibid., 15.

55. Élie Ducommun, *Les Conséquences qu'aurait une guerre europíene* (Berne, 1906).

56. Ibid., 5–6.

57. Ibid., 11.

58. The argument was laid forth first in *La Passé de la guerre et l'avenir de la paix* (Paris, 1907), 66–67, 69. Also "Les Dépenses de la guerre," 38–39.

59. Richet, *Le Passé,* 79–81.

60. Ibid., 91.

61. Gustave de Molinari, *Grandeur et décadence de la guerre* (Paris, 1898), 58–63.

62. Ibid., 65. See also *The Society of Tomorrow: A Forecast of Its Political and Economic Organization* (London and New York, 1904), trans. by P. H. Lee Warner, intro. by Hodgson Pratt; repr. GLP/W (New York, 1971), 13–14.

63. Molinari, *Society of Tomorrow,* 16.

64. Molinari, *Grandeur,* 126.

65. A brief biography of Edoardo Giretti by S. E. Cooper is in Josephson et al., *Biographical Dictionary,* 327–29.

66. Giretti, speech, *Atti* (Turin, 1905), 67.

67. Gugliemo Ferrero, *Militarism* (London, 1902), repr. with an intro. by S. E. Cooper, GPW/P (New York, 1972), 87–88. The English edition was expanded to include chapters on the Spanish-American War and reflections on the implications of the Fashoda crisis.

68. Ibid., 96.

69. Ibid., 296.

70. Ibid., 166.

71. Fererro's response to Hamon, "Une Enquête sur la guerre et le militarisme," *L'Humanité nouvelle,* 166. (Special supplement.)

72. Police file in AN (EUR), Ministero dell'interno, direzione generale della pubblica sicurezza, divisione affari generali e riservato, Casellario politico centrale, no. 2033, "Ferrero."

73. John M. Robertson, "War at the Century's End," *Humane Review* (1901), 3–8.

74. Richet, *Le Passé,* 79–81.

75. Alfred Fouillée, "La Psychologie des peuples et l'anthropologie," *Revue des deux mondes* 127 (1895), 367.

76. A brief biography of Norman Angell by Louis Bisceglia is in Josephson et al., *Biographical Dictionary,* 27–31.

77. *The Great Illusion: A Study of the Relations of Military Power in Nations to Their Economic and Social Advantage* (London, 1910); repr. with new intro. by S. J. Stearns, GLW/P (New York, 1972).

78. Ibid., 3rd ed., 29–33, and passim.

79. Ibid., 4th ed. (1913), 12.

80. Philip D. Supina, "The Norman Angell Peace Compaign in Germany," *Journal of Peace Research* 9 (1972), 161–64.

81. Bisceglia, *Norman Angell,* 28. Also Biocca, "Il Pacifismo," 595.

82. G. Seregni, *Per la giustizia e la pace* (Milan, 1897), 5–6.

83. E. T. Moneta, "Ad un cattedratico della guerra," *La Vita internazionale* 2 (5 February, 1900), 57.

84. E. T. Moneta, "Cinquant'anni dopo, 1848–1898," *La Vita internazionale,* 1 (5

January, 1898) 1–5. See also Angelo Crespi, "Gli uomini e l'umanità," *La Vita internazionale* 20 (5 March 1898), 95–96.

85. Moneta, Speech, *Bulletin officiel,* Rouen and Le Havre, 1903, 144.

86. *Bulletin officiel,* Rouen, 1903, 139.

87. *Bulletin officiel,* Stockholm, 1910, 218–20.

88. Concomitant with their positions on the legitimate usages of war, Moneta and Gaston Moch led the "left wing" of the peace movement in favor of transformations of the military into militia. See Chapter 5 herein, 120–24.

89. *Official Report,* London, 1908, 167–71.

90. Ibid. 171.

91. *Bulletin officiel,* Stockholm, 1910, 61–71.

92. Carnegie Endowment for International Peace, *Yearbook for 1912* (Washington, DC, 1913), 85–95.

93. James C. Hunt, "Die deutschen Liberalen und ihre Versuche zur französische-deutschen Verständigung 1913–1914," in *Aspekte deutscher Aussenpolitik im 20. Jahrhundert: Aufsätze Hans Rothfels zum Gedächtnis,* ed. W. Benz and H. Graml (Stuttgart, 1977), 28–40.

94. *Mit der Kamera in der Schlachtfront! With the Greeks in the Firing Line! Avec la camera sous la mitraille!* Produced by Express-Film, GmBH, Freiburg iB.

95. Robert Schwobthaler to Henry La Fontaine, 22 December 1913, the Mundanum, Henry La Fontaine Papers, box. 26.

96. W.G.F. in the *Evening News* (London), 16 October 1913.

97. Comité du bureau international de la paix, Séance du 6 janvier 1915, BIP Archives, esp. 5–10. (Stenographic typescript.) Debate on the utility of a resolution condemning the Triple Alliance. See chap. 8 herein.

Chapter 7 Pacifism and Contemporary Crises

1. Alfred Fried, *The German Emperor and the Peace of the World* (New York and London, 1912), 40–41.

2. See, for instance, the speech of Professor J. de Louter welcoming delegates to the Universal Peace Congress, The Hague, 1913, in *Bulletin officiel,* The Hague, 1913, 3–4.

3. Charles Richet, *Le Passé de la guerre et l'avenir de la paix* (Paris, 1907), 126.

4. Paul Hyacinthe Loyson, "La Guerre latente," *Le Courrier européen* 10, no. 23 (12 September 1913), 361.

5. Rudolf Broda, *Le Rôle de la violence dans les conflits de la vie moderne, une enquête* (Paris, 1913), 91 pp.

6. Jacques Dumas, "Devenir un parti," *La Paix par de droit* 4 (1894), 1–4.

7. Ibid., 161–65.

8. Ruggiero Bonghi, *La Situazione europea e la pace* (Rome, 1891).

9. See Jules Simon, "International Peace Bureau," in Chatfield and van den Dungen, *Peace Movements,* 68–69.

10. Gaston Moch, "Memoire," 5 pp. BIP Archives, IF, Séance de la Commission du samedi 7 mai 1898: Ordre de jour. (Typescript.)

11. *Bulletin officiel,* Berne, 1892, 127.

12. Ibid. Passy insisted on this approach in private as well. See his letter to Jules Simon 21 December 1892, AN, Fonds Jules Simon, 87 AP 6.

13. *Bulletin officiel,* Paris, 1900, 99.

14. Moneta to the Central Committee, Berne, 1892, BIP, 14 June 1892, Archives, VI, A.1.a., "Nationalités."

15. European precedents encapsulated in the Treaty of Berlin (1884) were commonly invoked by pacifists. These agreements justified intervention to preserve civilized norms.

16. *Bulletin officiel,* Antwerp, 1894, 63.

17. Ibid., 157.

18. Letter (printed but circulated privately), "À Messieurs les membres des groupes parlementaires constitués de France et d'Italie, 13 octobre, 1893," signed by E. N. Rahusen, L. Trarieux, B. Pandolfi, and A. Gobat in AN, Fonds Jules Simon, 87 AP 6.

19. Christian Lange, *Resolutions,* 23. The most dramatic came later in 1911 during the Libyan War.

20. For a general discussion, see S. E. Cooper, "The Impact of Nationalism on European Peace Movements and Liberal Internationalism, 1848-1915," *Peace and Change* 6 (1980).

21. Robert Paine, UPC, *Proceedings,* Chicago, 1893, 299–300.

22. Jacques Novicow. "La Question d'Alsace-Lorraine ne sera jamais résolue par la guerre," *La Paix par le droit* 4 (1894), 106–9.

23. E. T. Moneta, *Dalla vera pace, la vera gloria* (orig. Milan: *Il Secolo,* 24, 8457, 20–21 October, 1889; repr. Milan, 1910), 15 pp.

24. Jean Heimweh, *Pensons-y et parlons-en* (Paris 1891), 4.

25. "La proposition de Gaston Moch," *La Paix par le droit* 4 (1894), 161–65. See also Unione lombarda, "Resolution," *La Paix par le droit* 5 (1895), 142–46.

26. Heimweh, *Pensons-y et parlons-en,* 18–28; Moch, *L'Alsace-Lorraine devant l'Europe,* 469.

27. A brief biography of Franz Wirth by Roger Chickering is in Josephson et al., *Biographical Dictionary,* 1019–20; see also Donat and Holl, *Die Friedensbewegung,* 420.

28. *La Paix par le droit* 6 (1896), 152–53.

29. Ibid., 207–13; *L'Alsace-Lorraine: Réponse à un pamphlet allemand* (Paris, 1895), repr. with intro. by S. E. Cooper, GLP/W (New York, 1972), 2–3. Also *La Paix par le droit* 6 (1896), 177–81.

30. Moch, *L'Alsace-Lorraine devant l'Europe,* 433–35.

31. *Bulletin officiel,* Budapest, 1896, 48.

32. Jacques Novicow to A. H. Fried, 30 August 1895, BIP Archives, Fried Correspondence, letter no. 87.

33. Gaston Moch to Ducommun, 15 April 1895, BIP Archives, VI A.1.a. "Nationalités."

34. Clothilde Dissart, *Réflexions en faveur du désarmement: La Question d'Alsace-Lorraine* (Paris, 1899) 11 pp.; August Lalance, "La Nouvelle triplice," *La Grande Revue,* 2 (1898), 253–70; Paul Fauchille, "L'Europe nouvelle," *Revue générale de droit international public* 6 (1899), 5–8.

35. *La Fédération de l'Europe* (Paris, 1901); repr. with intro. by S. E. Cooper, GLW/P (New York, 1972), 667; *Bulletin Officiel,* Monaco, 1902, 165–74; "Orientation à donner au mouvement pacifique," in Cooper, *Peace and Civilization,* 323.

36. Paul and Victor Marguerite urged French opinion to accept the vote of the Alsatian Landauschuss in 1904. See *La Paix par le droit* 15 (1905), 30–33, quoting *La Dépêche de Toulouse,* December 1904.

37. "Movimento pacifico internazionale, lettera dalla Francia," *La Vita internazionale* 5, no 7 (20 July 1902), 438.

38. It did not work. The normally radical French delegate Séverine (Carolyn Rémy)

bitterly attacked Novicow for his "intrigue" that would expose French pacifists to the predictable attacks in the nationalist press.

39. *Bulletin officiel,* Rouen, 1903, 119–20, 123.

40. These included Allégret, Arnaud, Beauquier, Le Foyer, Mérignhac, G. Moch, Richet, Passy, Weiss, and Spalikowski.

41. "La Question d'Alsace-Lorraine," app., Minutes of the Second National Congress of French peace societies at Nîmes; repr. in *La Paix par le droit* 14 (1904), 181–88.

42. "Pourquoi et comment la France devrait renoncer à l'Alsace-Lorraine," *La Paix par le droit* 15 (1905), 4–11.

43. "Le Rapprochement franco-allemand: Lettre ouverte à M. Alphonse Jouet," *La Paix par le droit* 14 (1904), 52.

44. Chickering, *Imperial Germany,* 193–97, 298.

45. "L'Allemagne et la France," *Internationalis Concordia* 10 (1904), 249–51, 251–54.

46. Alfred H. Fried, "Les Pacifistes allemands et la question d'Alsace-Lorraine," *La Paix par le droit* 14 (1904), 287–89.

47. *La Paix par le droit* 15 (1905), 451–54.

48. Ferdinand Bruntière, "Le Mensonge du pacifisme," *Revue des deux mondes,* 28 (1905), 278–95.

49. 3 December 1905.

50. Chambre des députés, *Annales,* 19 January 1906, reported in *La Paix par le droit,* 16 (1906), 12–24.

51. No matter what evidence to the contrary presented to Deschanel, he persisted in denouncing the movement as unpatriotic. Rightist journalists and politicans were aroused when they realized that pacifist ideas were making headway, especially among networks of French schoolteachers who had adopted positions resembling those of Moch and Heimweh—not the extremist antipatriotism of Gustave Hervé. In the widely publicized teachers' congress of 1905 at Lille, the question of what kind of history to teach exploded in a political confrontation between left and right. The police report on the Congress of Lille of 31 August 1905 is in AN F7 12524.

52. *La Paix par le droit* 15 (1905), 412.

53. *Bulletin officiel,* Lucerne, 1905, 38–39. See also Alphonse Jouet, "La Question d'Alsace-Lorraine au XIIIᵉ Congrès de la paix," *Internationalis Concordia* 11 (1904), 3–6.

54. From a mangled report in the *Neue Zürcher Zeitung,* reporters for the *Hamburgischer Korrespondant* (9 October 1905) transformed Quidde into a traitor. He was unable to answer any of the distortions in the German press and only *La Paix par le droit* (15 [1905]) provided him with a vehicle.

55. La Fontaine in *La Paix et l'enseignement pacifiste;* repr. in *Voices of French Pacifism,* ed. S. E. Cooper, 42–43.

56. Interview with "Quercus" in *Journal de Paris,* 16 August 1905, no. 4706 (Louis Frank Papers, clipping file, II, 6055).

57. Cooper, *Peace and Civilization,* 254–55, 262.

58. "La Nécessité d'un rapprochement franco-allemand," *Le Courrier européen* 2, no. 21 (31 March 1905), 325.

59. Théodore Ruyssen conducted a survey of German peace activists and intellectuals presumably close to the movement. Of hundreds of inquiries that he mailed, he received about thirty responses. See *La Paix par le droit* 16 (1907), 209–20.

60. E. T. Moneta to H. La Fontaine, 8 May 1913, the Mundanum, La Fontaine Papers, box 26.

61. Ignazio Scarabelli, *Cause di guerra in europa e rimedi* (Ferrara, 1890), 256–71, and passim.

62. Ibid., 262.

63. The original questionnaire appeared in *La Vita internazionale* 4, no. 12 (20 June 1901).

64. *La Vita internazionale* 4, no. 14 (20 July 1901), 437.

65. Ibid., 468–69, 499–500, 535.

66. *La Vita internazionale*, no. 19 (5 October 1901), 595–96. A brief biography by Edoardo Cimbali by Richard Drake is in Josephson et al., *Biographical Dictionary,* 167–68.

67. Edoardo Cimbali, *Rinnovamento della triplice* (Rome, 1902), 21.

68. Edoardo Cimbali, *Lo Stato secondo il diritto internazionale universale* (Rome, 1891), repr. as app. to *Rinnovamento,* 48.

69. Jacques Novicow, *La Missione dell'Italia* (Milan, 1901).

70. Four centuries earlier, the Italian peninsula was composed of a group of independent city-states whose leaders created an "international" arrangement at Lodi (1454) that was designed to reduce the endless warfare threatening Italian civilization. Although it lasted only a half-century, the Peace of Lodi, nevertheless, demonstrated that heads of state could be properly motivated to behave rationally. Italians in the nineteenth century again offered another model to Europe—establishing a unitary nation-state after centuries of control and dependency. (Novicow omitted the fact that the creation of Italy required several wars.)

See "L'Unità italiana: Modello della federazione Europea," orig., in *La Vita internazionale,* 5 (23 March and 5 April 1902), repr. in Cooper, *Peace and Civilization,* 286–311.

71. Among Italians who discussed his proposals most seriously, the most significant disagreement arose over his view of Russia. See E. Catellani, "Il Pericolo Russo," *La Vita internazionale* 4, no. 10 (20 March 1901), 305–8; also Alfredo Venturi, "Ideale e Realtà," *La Vita internazionale* 4, no. 7 (5 April 1901), 227–30; G. Prato, "Giacomo Novicow e l'avvenire d'Italia," *La Vita internazionale* 5, no. 7 (5 January 1902), 9–10.

72. The most immediate reflection of Novicow's prompting was the reinvigoration of the Franco-Italian League, which segments of both peace movements supported. At one of its gala banquets in Paris, the organization attracted support from a number of Italian politicians and feminists.

73. A. W. Salomone, *Italy in the Giolittian Era* (Philadelphia, 1945, 1960), esp. chap. 8, 86–94, and passim.

74. Giorgio Candeloro, *Storia dell'Italia moderna,* vol. 7, *1896–1914: La Crisi di fine secolo e l'età giolittiana* (Milan, 1974), 283.

75. Mario Pacor, *Italia e Balcani, dal Risorgimento alla resistenza* (Milan 1968), 26; Richard Webster, *Industrial Imperialism in Italy, 1908–1915* (Berkeley, 1975), 335.

76. Speech in *Atti* (Turin, 1905), 39–40.

77. Ibid., 36.

78. Ibid., 36–37.

79. Candeloro, *Storia dell'Italia moderna,* 288.

80. Giuseppe Tomé, "Che cosa resta da fare alla nazione italiana dopo l'annessione dell'Austria della Bosnia-Herzogivina," *La Vita internazionale* 11, no. 22 (20 November 1908), 507–9.

81. Alfred Fried, letter, October 1908 in *La Vita internazionale* 11, no. 20 (20 October 1908), 465–66.

82. *La Vita internazionale* 11, no. 21 (5 November 1908), 485–87.

83. *La Vita internazionale* 12, no. 4 (20 February 1909), 78–79.

84. E. T. Moneta, "La Pace assicurata," *La Vita internazionale* 12, no. 7 (5 April 1909), 146–49.

85. G. Salvemini, "La Politica estera dell'Italia e il pacifismo, replica a E. T. Moneta," in G. Salvemini, *Come siamo andati in Libia e altri scritti dal 1900 al 1915,* ed. by Augusto Torre (Milan, 1963, orig. 1914), 61.

86. Ercole Vidari, *La Vita internazionale* 12, no. 19 (5 October 1909), 436–38.

87. Arcangelo Ghisleri, speech at the Como congress, reported in *La Vita internazionale* 12, no. 20 (20 October 1910), 471–74.

88. L. Birondi, "Pacifismo e irredentismo," *Giovine Europa* 2, no. 2 (9 February 1914), 30–31.

89. E. Cimbali, *Il Nuovo Diritto internazionale e gli odierni congressi, conferenze, società e leghe per la pace, l'arbitrato e il disarmo* (Rome, 1910), 9–10, 15–16. Cimbali ignored the impressive growth of the new right, which established a party in Florence in 1910 announcing that "power, energy, authority, war [were] goals in themselves" and demanded a variety of "actions" to establish respect for Italy among the big powers. See Salomone, *Italy in the Giolittian Era,* 91.

90. E. T. Moneta, *Dal presente all'avvenire* (Milan, 1913), 6, 10.

91. In September 1911, both the UPC and the IPU had planned to hold their meetings in Rome to honor the fiftieth anniversary of Italian unification. Both meetings were summarily canceled. Angelo de Gubernatis, who had labored to make the occasions memorable, was enraged; pacifists who had begun to travel to Italy lost their money. It was a total fiasco.

92. S. E. Cooper, "The Impact of Nationalism," *Peace and Change* 6 (1980), 30. *La Vita internazionale* 14, no. 19 (5 October 1911), 491–92.

93. "L'Italia, Tripoli e la pace," *La Vita internazionale* 14, no. 19 (5 October 1911), 500–502.

94. *La Vita internazionale* 6, no. 11 (5 June 1911), 276–77. The argument against depopulation and favoring closer emigration was made even before the war broke out in pacifist circles.

95. Letters in *La Luce del pensiero* 5, nos. 1–2 (20 January 1912), 8; 5, no. 3 (10 February 1912), 14–15.

96. dolens to Gobat, BIP Archives, Correspondence, 1912; Maggiore to Gobat, 23 January, 23 February, 14 March 1912.

97. Prestini to Henri La Fontaine, 5 February 1912, lists "true" pacifists as E. Cimbali, Professor Ricciotti (editor of *Rivista del Lavoro*), Paolo Bacca *(Il Popolo pacifista),* and Domenico Maggiore *(La Luce del pensiero).* In the Mundanum, La Fontaine Correspondance, box 26.

98. *Bulletin officiel,* Geneva, 1912, 62–66, 147–50.

99. Rosalia Gwis-Adami to Angelo de Gubernatis, 11 September 1912, BNC(F), Angelo de Gubernatis Papers, box 67, no. 106.

100. Rosalia Gwis-Adami to Angelo de Gubernatis, 28 May 1912, BNC(F), box 67, no. 106.

101. Pasquale Ricciotti to Henri La Fontaine, 4 April 1912, in the Mundanum, La Fontaine papers, box 26.

102. *La Vita internazionale* 15, no. 8 (20 September 1912), 198.

103. Edoardo Giretti to Luigi Einaudi, 30 September 1912, Fondazione Luigi Einaudi (Turin), Archivio, busta 1, Carteggio Giretti.

104. Correspondence of Lord Weardale, letters to Christian Lange, IPU Archives, scattered, 1911–1912.

105. "The Need for Organizing the Defence of Humanity," *The Peace Movement* 1 (1912), 135.

106. Pietro Nenni, *Vent'anni di fascismo,* a cura di Gioette Dallò (Milan, 1964), 19–21.

107. Dutch objections to Gobat's activism were communicated in Ligue Générale Neerlandaise, Vrede door Recht, Comité Central, *Les Congrès internationaux de la paix à Génève et les réformes à apporter dans l'organisation de congrès suivants* (The Hague, 15 December 1912), 4–7, printed but not published.

108. *Bulletin officiel,* Budapest, 1896, 37.

109. *Bulletin officiel,* Hamburg, 1897, 27; *Procès-Verbal,* 1898, 4–5. Greek-supported insurrections against Turkish control of Crete in February 1896 and February 1897 eventually led to a war between Greece and Turkey, which was settled by Great Power intervention. The Greek army suffered heavy defeats and a widely publicized massacre of civilians occurred. A Greek governor eventually was named to head an autonomous Crete (May 1897).

110. *Bulletin officiel,* Paris, 1900, 35.

111. E. T. Moneta "Orrori dell'invasione delle truppe alleate in Cina," *La Vita internazionale* 3, no. 22 (20 November 1900), 675–80.

112. "Ausonius" (pseud. of Angelo Crespi), "Note Politico-Sociale," *La Vita internazionale* 3, no. 3 (5 July 1900), 411–12.

113. *La Paix par le droit* 10 (1900), 221–24.

114. *Bulletin officiel,* Paris, 1900, 69–76.

115. Rarely was an entire day given over to discussion of a contemporary issue. *Bulletin officiel,* Paris, 1900, 79–82.

116. *L'Eclair,* 4 June 1900.

117. "Le Problème international du XX siècle," *Le Courrier européen* 2 (1905), 882–83.

118. G. Sergi, "Les Droits de la race jaune," *Le Courrier européen* 2 (16 June 1905), 7.

119. *Bulletin officiel,* Paris, 1900, 95–99; *Proceedings,* Glasgow, 1901, 42, 45–47.

120. *Proceedings,* Glasgow, 1901, 82–83.

121. Stead was one of the most consistent anti-Boer War voices. The range of protest is excerpted in Stephen Koss, *The Pro-Boers* (Chicago, 1973).

122. See her appeals to H. La Fontaine, letter of 28 May 1900, the Mundanum, box 26.

123. Accounts in *Concord,* October 1899, 165–67; November, 1899, 180–81.

124. IPU, *Compte rendu,* (Paris, 1900), 92–93.

125. The Transvaal Question: Manifesto from the members of the British Parliament, IPU Archives, 2 pp. (Typescript.)

126. Examples of materials include International Arbitration League, Manifesto by Thomas Burt, W. R. Cremer et al., in IPU Archives, 1900.

127. *Some Lessons of the Transvaal War* (New York, n.d., 28 pp.); orig. *Contemporary Review* 79 (1900), 26–27.

128. *L'Eclair,* 4 August 1900.

129. *The War in South Africa: Its Causes and Effects* (London, 1900), 240, 310–16.

130. Gooch's critique is in *The War and Its Causes* ed. Cynthia Behrman, GLW/P (New York, 1972), 11–18.

131. Arthur Desjardins, "La Guerre Hispano-Américaine et le droit des gens," *Revue des deux mondes* 147 (1898), 518–49; "La Guerre de l'Afrique Australe et le droit des gens," *Revue des deux mondes,* 157 (1900), 38–78; "La Chine et le droit des gens" *Revue des deux mondes* 162 (1900), 522–49.

132. Paul Fauchille, "L'Europe Nouvelle," in *Revue générale de droit international public* 6 (Paris, 1899), 5–6.

133. Mario Borsa, "Il momento militarista inglese," *La Vita internazionale* 2, no. 22 (20 November 1899), 289.

134. "Ciò che insegna la guerra Anglo-Boero," *La Vita internazionale* 3, no. 6 (20 March 1900), 163.

135. "Ausonius," Note Politico-Sociale, *La Vita internazionale* 3, no. 6 (20 March 1900), 186.

136. Guglielmo Ferrero, "In che cosa l'Italia e la Francia sono superiori all'Inghilterra," *La Vita internazionale* 3, no. 11 (5 June 1900), 325–27.

137. The complexity of this issue is discussed by Claire Hirschfeld in "Blacks, Boers and Britons: The Anti-War Movement in England and the 'Native Issue,' 1899–1902," *Peace and Change* (1982), 21–34.

138. Hodgson Pratt, "The War and the Working Classes," *Concord,* December 1901, 177–79.

139. An anonymous union member reacted with the remark that the count possessed "the singular talent of creating . . . international complications" when none existed. Clipping from *Le Peuple,* 4 October 1903, preserved in IPU Archives (a translation from a piece in *Die Wage* (n.d.).

140. Novicow's attack on the bellicose behavior of the U.S. government during the Spanish-American War was based on the novel criticism that over three billion francs had been spent "to change the political and economic system of 631,000 men, of whom 528,000 were Negroes!" *La Fédération de l'Europe,* 41.

141. M. Rebérioux and G. Haupt, "L'Attitude de l'internationale," in "Le Socialisme et la question coloniale avant 1914," *Le Mouvement social* 45 (1963), 7–37. (Special number.)

142. *Bulletin officiel,* Antwerp, 1894, 65.

143. *Bulletin official,* Paris, 1900, 57–68.

144. Ibid., 102–19.

145. A series in *La Paix par le droit,* December 1905 through July 1907, was the best of its type. See esp. "La Colonisation rouge" 16 (1906), 69–76, including the Morel report and the photographs.

146. *Bulletin officiel,* Milan 1906, 87–88.

147. *La Paix par le droit* 17 (1908), 259–60. Also Pierre Clerget, "Colonisation et Civilisation," *La Paix par le droit* 16 (1906), 58–69.

148. Quoting the Duke of Mecklenberg, head of the German colonial society, in *Pacifisme et colonisation,* 28.

149. *VII Congrès national des sociétés françaises de la paix, Clermont-Ferrand, 4, 5, 6 et 7 juin 1911* (Clermont–Ferrand, 1911), 15–16, 76.

150. Code de la paix, in *Bulletin officiel,* Stockholm, 1910, 294–95.

151. *Proceedings* (London, 1908), 249.

152. *Bulletin officiel,* Geneva, 1912, 85.

153. Arcangelo Ghisleri, *La Guerra e il diritto delle genti* (Rome, 1913), 54. A brief summary of pacifist approaches to colonialism is found in Pierre Guillen, "Les Internationales et les crises coloniales avant 1914," in Pierre Milza, "Introduction," to *Les Internationales et le problème de la guerre au XXᵉ siècle* (Rome, 1987), 167–93.

154. Police dossier on the comité, AN F7 13331; also AN F7 12525 for the radical youth groups.

155. Conciliation internationale, *L'Assemblée générale du 30 mars 1912* (Paris, 1912), 24.

156. Wild, *D'Estournelles de Constant,* 377–78.

157. Haupt, *Socialism and the Great War,* 118–19.

158. Charles Sancerme, *Vers L'Entente* (Paris, 1913).

159. Ferdinand Buisson, speech in Paris, May 1913, to national conference of French pacifists, *La Paix par le droit* 22 (1913), 360.

160. M. L. Puech, "Vers l'Entente franco-allemande," *Almanach de la paix pour 1914* (Paris, 1914), 53.

161. Hunt, "Die deutschen Liberalen," 28–40.

162. D'Estournelles de Constant and Conrad Haussman, "Vers La Nouvelle 'Entente Cordiale' après Berne," *Le Courrier européen* 10 (1913), 148–49.

163. Ch. Paix-Séailles, "La Conférence de Berne: Une Journée historique; un grand acte révolutionnaire," *Le Courrier européen,* 10 (1913), 147.

164. Pour Mieux se connaître, *Appel,* Paris, 1912, 4 pp. In 1913, an appeal launched by the Ligue franco-allemand, Section française, made substantially the same points but seemed to have no follow-through.

165. L'Institut franco-allemand de la réconciliation, *Programme* (Paris, n.d.), 8 pp. Appeal, unpublished letter in BIP Archives, n.d.

166. A particularly urgent appeal came from Nathan-Larrier at the VIII Congrès national des sociétés françaises de la paix, May 1913.

167. G. Boll, editor of *Journal d'allemagne,* to H. La Fontaine, 29 March 1913, the Mundanum, La Fontaine Papers, box 26.

168. Lord Weardale to Christian Lange, 5 June 1913, Letters of Lord Weardale, IPU, Archives, box 28.

169. *Peace Theories and the Balkan War* (London, 1914), esp. 20 ff.

170. Winston Churchill speech delivered at Sheffield, quoted in Norman Angell, *Peace Theories and the Balkan Wars* (London, 1914), frontispiece.

171. *Bulletin officiel,* The Hague, 1913, 6–7.

172. Weardale to Lange, 10 March and 25 April, 1913.

173. For a discussion of parliamentary involvement in foreign policy, see Thomas Hayes Connor, "Parliament and the Making of Foreign Policy: France Under the Third Republic" (Ph.D. diss., Univ. of North Carolina, 1983).

174. "Le VIIIᵉ Congrès français de la paix," BIP Archives, VB 1, p 7; noted in *The Peace Movement* 2 (1913), 309.

175. "Les Traités secrets: Nécessité du contrôle du parlement et de l'opinion," VIII Congrès national de la paix, Paris, 1913, 1.

176. "Les Facteurs spirituels du rapprochement international: Extraits et resumé de la conférence faite à Strasbourg" (1913), The Hague Peace Library (pamphlet).

177. Quoted in Léon Boll, 46.

178. *L'Alsace-Lorraine et la paix* (Nîmes, 1913), 23.

179. Ligue des droits de l'homme, *Bulletin* 13, no. 6 (13 March 1913), 327–56.

180. *Les Rapports franco-allemands: Extrait de la Revue du mois* (May 1913), 7.

181. Tour of E. Riquiez, February and March 1913, *La Paix par le droit* 20 (1913), 347.

182. A reluctant German pacifist proposed that in return for autonomy, the French government sign the Treaty of Frankfurt again. *The Peace Movement* 2 (1913), 505.

183. "Lettre à un pacifiste allemagne," *La Paix par le droit* 24 (1914), 445–51.

184. Théodore Ruyssen, *La Philosophie de la paix,* 355.

185. "Why We Are Not Discouraged," *The Peace Movement* 1 (1912), 24.

186. Joseph Schumpeter, "The Sociology of Imperialism" (orig. 1919) in *Imperialism and Social Classes,* intro. by Bert Hoselitz, trans. by Heinz Norden (New York, 1958), 22, 92. The work of Arno Mayer, esp. *The Persistence of the Old Regime: Europe to the Great War* (New York, 1981) also reflects this tradition.

Chapter 8 The Collapse

1. Angell, *Peace Theories and the Balkan Wars,* 83.
2. Pacifists were amazed to learn that the German chancellor, Bernhard von Bülow opened a session of the Reichstag by insisting that love of peace did not imply an absence of patriotism. "There is a difference between peace at any price and peace founded on law and justice." Quoted by Hélène Stein, "La XV Conférence de l'Union interparlementaire à Berlin, 17–21 septembre, 1908," *Almanach de la Paix* (Paris, 1909), 57.
3. Henri La Fontaine, "What Pacifists Ought to Say" (Berne, November 1914), 4 pp. in the Mundanum, La Fontaine Papers, box 30.
4. Andrew Kelly, "Film as Antiwar Propaganda: *Lay Down Your Arms* (1914)," *Peace and Change* 16 (1991), 97–112. The film was shown in the United States in 1915.
5. Letter to Christian Lange, 31 August 1914, IPU, Lord Weardale Letters, "Crise européenne de 1914," box 238.
6. Laurence, "Viennese Press," 162–63.
7. The literature on the last days of peace is immense. See, for instance, Luigi Albertini, *The Origins of the War of 1914* (London and New York, 1952–1957, 1966); a brief treatment is Immanuel Geiss, ed., *July, 1914: The Outbreak of the First World War: Selected Documents* (New York, 1967).
8. *La Paix par le droit* 24 (1914), 401–4.
9. Délégation permanente des Sociétés belges de la paix, Statement of 29 July 1914, the Mundanum, La Fontaine Papers, box 18.
10. Reported in *La Vita internazionale* 17, no. 17 (5 August 1914), 412.
11. Telegrams of Lange to seventeen groups, 1 August 1914, urging that they convene and demand that their governments abide by The Hague Conventions. Nippold from Germany urged that six small neutral states led by the Dutch and Scandinavians lead a démarche to the Kaiser. In IPU, Lord Weardale Letters, "Crise européenne de 1914," box 238.
12. "Suprème effort," *La Paix par le droit* 24 (1914), 465.
13. See A. de Morsier, *La Paix par le droit et la guerre* (Geneva, 1915).
14. Ruyssen, "Suprème effort," *La Paix par le droit* 24 (1914), 467–68.
15. Houzeau de Lehaie to Lange, received 2 August 1914, IPU, Lord Weardale Letters, "Crise européenne de 1914," box 238.
16. Weardale to Lange, 4 August 1914, IPU, Lord Weardale Letters, "Crise européenne de 1914," box 238.
17. National Peace Council, Minute Book, "Minutes of the Special Meeting of the Council, Tuesday, August 4th, 1914 at 4 PM," pp. 295–96. (Unpublished.)
18. Weardale to Lange, 7 August 1914 in IPU, Weardale Papers, box 238.
19. Original unsigned letter in German to Golay, 8 August 1914, the Mundanum, Henri La Fontaine Papers, box 40; Golay's letter of 11 August 1914, the Mundanum, La Fontaine Papers, box 40.
20. La Fontaine to Golay, London, 14 October 1914, box 25.
21. Correspondance, 22 August 1914, BIP Archives, no. 7281.
22. G. Moch to Quidde via the Berne office, 20–24 August 1914, BIP Archives, "Crise de 1914."
23. *La Vita internazionale,* 17, no. 19 (5 October 1914), 518–21.
24. "Per la nostra neutralità," *Giovine Europa* 2 (1914), 138; *La Vita internazionale* 17, no. 15 (5 August 1914), 412.
25. "La Guerra europea," *La Vita internazionale* 17, no. 15 (5 August 1914), 401.
26. G. Sergi, *La Vita internazionale* 17, no. 16 (20 August 1914), 425.

27. Giretti to Luigi Einaudi, 24 September 1914, Einaudi Papers, Turin.

28. For a full discussion, see S. E. Cooper, "The Guns of August and the Doves of Italy," *Peace and Change* 7 (1981), 29–43.

29. "Zweites Kriegsflugblatt der Deutschen Friedensgesellschaft" (15 August 1914), repr. in Quidde, *Pazifismus im Weltkrieg,* quoted in Brigette Goldstein, "Ludwig Quidde and the Struggle for Democratic Pacifism in Germany, 1914–1930," 56–57.

30. Friedrich-Karl Sheer, *Die Deutsche Friedensgesellschaft (1892–1933),* 255ff.; James Shand, "Doves Among the Eagles: German Pacifists and Their Government During World War I," *Journal of Contemporary History* 10 (1975), 95–108.

31. G. Moch to Mlle. Montaudon or Mlle. Gobat, 23 August 1914, intended for L. Quidde, regarding a German child stranded in France. BIP Archives, no. 7287.

32. Letter to G. Moch, 3 September 1914, BIP Archives, Correspondance, no. 7289.

33. Charles Richet, "Les Représailles," *La Paix par le droit* 14 (1914), 443–44.

34. Théodore Ruyssen, "Lettre à un pacifiste d'Allemagne," *La Paix par le droit* 14 (1914), 450–51.

35. "What Pacifists Ought to Say," November 1914, 4 pp. The six significant points for a peace congress that La Fontaine urged were a world charter, the codification of international law, the creation of a unified money and measurement system, the creation of an international bank, "collective management of the globe," and international organization of study and research.

36. See entry 2 September 1914, Minute Book, p. 299.

37. Entry of 7 October 1914, Minute Book, p. 304.

38. National Peace Council, "To the Friends of International Peace" (Westminster, 4 November 1914), 2 pp.

39. D'Estournelles de Constant to Lange, 9 August 1914, arrived October 1914, IPU, Weardale Papers.

40. D'Estournelles de Constant to Lange, 10 August 1914, received 19 October 1914, IPU, Weardale Papers.

41. Text of Butler's speech, trans. into French, app. to letter to Lange, IPU, Weardale Papers.

42. "La France et la guerre," *La Paix par le droit* 10 (1914), 511.

43. With her sixty-nine-year-old parents, Jeanne Mélin was relocated several times; in July 1915, she petitioned the prefect in Cher for permission to move to Eure-et-Loir after several other moves. Letter, July 1915, in Fonds Marie-Louise Bouglé, Fonds Mélin, box 39, 1915.

44. Jeanne Mélin to R. Godefroy, Rouen, 21 August 1914, Correspondance, 1914, box 39.

45. G. Fiano, in *La Vita internazionale* 17, no. 17 (5 September 1914), 472–73.

46. Francesco de Luca, *La Vita internazionale* 17, no. 19 (5 October 1914), 509–13.

47. "Terminando l'anno," *La Vita internazionale* 17, no. 24 (20 December 1914), 645–46.

48. Henri Golay to Jeanne Mélin, 30 December 1914, Correspondance 1914, box 39.

49. "Lettre à un pacifiste d'Allemagne," *La Paix par le droit,* 24 (1914), 445–51.

50. 35,000 francs were to go to Alfred Fried and 12,500 to Ruyseen. See BIP, "Procès-verbal des séances du conseil tenues les 6 et 7 janvier 1915 au Bureau international de la paix à Berne," 6 January 1915, 65 pp. (Typescript.) Text varies from French to German.

51. There was some confusion during the meeting about whether or not it was actually petitioned for by eight or by nine members. 6 January 1915, afternoon session, pp. 1–2. (Typescript.)

52. Gaston Moch to Henri La Fontaine, 1 January 1915, 10 typed pages in BIP, "Crise de pacifisme."

53. Discussion, 6 January, pp. 2–4.

54. Ibid., 8 (of German text).

55. Ibid., 10.

56. Ibid., 11, 14.

57. Ibid., 13–14.

58. Ibid., 6.

59. Ibid., 31.

60. Ibid., 44–48.

61. Ibid., 49.

62. Ibid., 55.

63. Ibid., 62–63.

64. The minutes of 15 January, afternoon session, were handwritten, 32 pp.

65. Ibid., 32.

66. BIP, *Appel aux intellectuals du monde, 6–7 janvier, 1915* (Berne, 1915), 2 pp. preserved in BDIC, Fonds Passy.

67. In a long letter on 2 June 1916, the Swiss peace activist Bovet reported that Quidde was closely watched and would be arrested if he attempted any pacifist action.

68. "La Grande ora dell'Italia," *La Vita internazionale* 18, no. 10 (20 May 1915), 264. Also *Perchè sono per la guerra* (Rome, 1915).

69. Ruyssen to La Fontaine, 25 March 1915, La Fontaine Papers, box II.

70. Richet to Mélin, April 1915, in Fonds Marie-Louise Bouglé, Fonds J. Mélin, Correspondance, 1915, box 39.

71. Ruyssen to Mélin, 3 October 1916, in Correspondance, 1916.

72. *Bulletin,* 1 January–1 April 1915, 12.

73. Victor Basch, *Bulletin* 15 (1915), 162–75.

74. *Bulletin* 14 (1915), 200.

75. G. Moch to La Fontaine, 1 January 1915, BIP Archives, Commission de 1915.

76. L. Birondi, "Pacifismo e irredentismo," *Giovine Europa* 2, no. 2 (Milan, 9 February 1914), 30–31.

77. *La Vita internazionale* 17, no. 24 (20 December 1914), 646.

78. "Che faremo in caso di guerra?" *Giovine Europa* 3, no. 1 (1915), 8.

79. "La Grande Ora dell'Italia," *La Vita internazionale* (20 May 1915), 264, orig. in *Le Petit Journal* (Paris, 10 May 1915). See also *Perchè sono per la guerra.*

80. *La Vita internazionale* 18, no. 12 (20 June 1915), 305ff.

81. National Peace Council, Minute Book, 3 February 1915, 317.

82. Heath to La Fontaine 20 November 1915, the Mundanum, La Fontaine Papers, box II.

83. La Fontaine to Ruyssen, 6 September 1916, the Mundanum, La Fontaine Papers, box II. Ruyssen had pleaded for some help for his journal and had urged La Fontaine to convince the Americans that the kind of war under way in Europe would soon engulf them if it were not stopped in a fair manner.

84. La Fontaine to J. G. Phelps Stoke, 24 May 1917, the Mundanum, La Fontaine Papers, box II.

85. La Fontaine to Comrade John Spargo, 30 May 1917, the Mundanum, La Fontaine Papers, box II.

86. For a succinct summation of the split in the peace office during the war, see Werner Simon, "The International Peace Bureau," in *Peace Movements,* ed. Chatfield and van den Dungen, 75–78.

87. Editorial, "Les Pacifistes et la guerre," *La Voix de l'humanité*, no. 100 (Lausanne, 4–22 April 1917), 1–2.

88. G. Moch to La Fontaine, 1 January 1915, BIP Archives, "Crise," pp. 6, 8.

89. Gertrude Bussey and Margaret Tims, *Women's International League for Peace and Freedom* (London, 1965); Catherine Foster, *Women for All Seasons: The Story of the Women's International League for Peace and Freedom* (Athens, GA, 1989).

90. S. E. Cooper, "Women's Participation in European Peace Movements: The Struggle to Prevent World War I," in Pierson, *Women and Peace*, 51–52, 67–68.

91. Emmeline Pethick-Lawrence, quoted in Blanche W. Cook, "Introduction" to Marie Louise Degen, *The History of the Women's Peace Party*, GLW/P (New York, 1972), 7.

92. Aletta Jacobs, Chrystal Macmillan, telegram to Jeanne Mélin, March and April 1915, in Fonds Marie-Louise Bouglé, Fonds Jeanne Mélin, "Correspondance 1915."

93. Congrès International des femmes, 28 April–1 May 1915, The Hague, *Report-Rapport-Bericht* (Amsterdam, probably 1915), 106–11, 310–13. See also Marijik Mossink, "Womanly Pacifism, a Parable" (Univ. of Nijmegan, unpublished research paper, 1982), 3–5.

94. Ellen Key, *War, Peace and the Future: A Consideration of Nationalism and Internationalism, and of the Relation of Women to War*, 9–10.

95. Formation described by Mary Longman in "How German Women Met English Women," *Weekly Dispatch* (April 1915), clipping file, the Mundanum, La Fontaine Papers, box 16, "Les Femmes et la paix."

96. The group expected to be supported by Ellen Key and it emphasized the feminine aspects of pacific women. Brochure in the Mundanum, La Fontaine Papers, box 16.

97. Peter van den Dungen, "Introduction" to 1989 edition, Bart de Ligt, *The Conquest of Violence* (orig. 1937; London, 1989), xii.

98. Rosalia Gwis-Adami, *Nella mischia: Riposta di una donna a Romain Rolland* (Rome, 1918).

99. A brief biography of Jules Humbert-Droz by John M. Cammett is in Josephson et al., *Biographical Dictionary*, 437–39.

100. An example of Catholic action was the White Cross founded by Dr. M. J. Metzger in Augsburg in 1917. The standard study of religious pacifism, *Weltkirche und Weltfrieden* (1924) eventually landed its author, Franciscus Stratmann, in a Nazi prison.

101. A report on these new groups is in *La Paix par le droit*, February 1919.

102. Carl Heath, "Memorandum Regarding the Reorganizing of the Bureau International de la Paix," (31 March 1919), privately printed and circulated, Fonds Marie-Louise Bouglé, Fonds J. Mélin, "Articles (Thèmes) Paix." The new groups included the Center for a Durable Peace (the Netherlands), Union of Democratic Control, International Council of Women for a Durable Peace, the League for a New Nation (Germany), and WILPF.

103. Nearly all the meetings were organized by Henri Golay, who kept their minutes and published *Mouvement Pacifiste* for the twenty years that ended in 1939.

104. M. Gobat to La Fontaine 8 August 1920, the Mundanum, La Fontaine Papers, box 34.

105. La Fontaine to Marguerite Gobat, 12 June 1924, the Mundanum, La Fontaine Papers, box 34.

106. "L'Idée de la paix parmi les peuples: Un Resumé," unpublished ms., circulated privately by Clara Ragaz, February 1938, after Gobat's death. A surviving copy is in the Mundanum, La Fontaine Papers, box 20.

107. Irwin Abrams, "Permanent International Peace Bureau," *The Nobel Peace Prize and the Laureates*, 68.

108. The papers arrived in Geneva in 1920 from Berne. Letter of 12 July 1941, the Mundanum, La Fontaine Papers, box 28.

109. Golay to La Fontaine, 11 October 1942, the Mundanum, La Fontaine Papers, box 28.

Chapter 9 Conclusion

1. Revolutionary decree of 15 December 1792. See Georges Lefebvre, *The French Revolution: From Its Origins to 1793,* trans. by Elizabeth Moss Evanson (London and New York, 1962), 277.

2. Minutes of the meeting of 28 March 1913 of the Société de la paix, St. Petersburg, the Mundanum, La Fontaine papers, box 26.

3. E. T. Moneta, speech to the Sixth National Peace Congress, Como, September 1910, quoted in *La Vita internazionale* 13, no. 18 (20 September 1910), 411.

4. Alfred Fried, *The Restoration of Europe,* 11–12.

5. Gaston Moch to Ludwiq Quidde, 2 June 1912, BIP VB1, Propagande En France.

6. Biocca, "Il Pacifismo et la *Grande Illusione* di Norman Angell," 595.

7. Laurence LaFore, *The Long Fuse: An Interpretation of the Origins of World War I* (New York and Philadelphia, 1965), chap. 1, and passim; Jong van Beek en Donk, *History of the Peace Movement in The Netherlands,* 5.

8. Jacques Novicow, "Les Conquêtes successives de la femme." in Cooper, *Peace and Civilization,* 339.

9. Ruyssen to La Fontaine, 31 October 1912, the Mundanum, La Fontaine Papers, box 10.

10. "Per il diritto e la civiltà," *La Luce del pensiero* (Naples, 1912), extract in clipping file, the Mundanum, box 20.

11. Quoted in *Le National bruxellois, 2 juin, 1914,* the Mundanum, box 20, clipping file. alma dolen's tour covered Brussels, Ghent, Liège, and Arlon.

12. Cited in Morsier, *La Paix par le droit et la guerre,* 5–6.

Bibliography

Archives

Aberystwyth (Wales)
National Archives of Wales: Papers of Henry Richard

Brussels
Bibliothèque royale: Papers of Louis Frank
Mundanum: Papers of Henri La Fontaine

Florence
Biblioteca Nazionale Centrale: Papers of Angelo de Gubernatis

Geneva
Archives d'état
Bibliothèque des Nations Unies, Archives: Bureau international de la paix
Bibliothèque universitaire et public
Union interparlementaire, Archives

The Hague
Library of the Peace Palace

London
London School of Economics, Archives: Minute Book of National Peace Council

Milan
Biblioteca del Risorgimento

Paris
Archives nationales: Fonds Deville family, Fonds Étienne Lamy, Papers of Jules Salvandi, Fonds* Jules Simon
Bibliothèque de l'histoire de la ville de Paris Fonds Marie-Louise Bouglé (includes Fonds Ferdinand Buisson, Fonds Jeanne Mélin)
Bibliothèque de documentation internationale et contemporaine, Nanterre: Fonds Gabrielle Duchêne, Fonds Frédéric Passy, Fonds Jules Prudhommeaux
Bibliothèque Marguerite Durand
Bibliothèque nationale

*Collection.

Ligue des droits de l'homme
Préfecture de police (Seine)
Société de l'histoire du protestantisme français

Rome

Archivio Nazionale, EUR, Ministero dell'Interno, Direzione generale della pubblica
    sicurezza
Biblioteca Nazionale Centrale
Biblioteca di storia moderna e contemporanea
Istituto per la storia del Risorgimento italiano (Rome)

Turin

Fondazione Luigi Einaudi

United States

Columbia University, International Law, Nicholas Murray Butler Collection and Rare
    Book Room
New York Public Library
Stanford University, Library of the Hoover Institution
Swarthmore College, Peace Collection

Journals and Publications of Peace Societies

Danish

Fredsbladet, Dansk Fredsforening (Association pour la neutralisation du Danemark),
    founded 1892; edited by Fredrik Bajer.

Dutch

Review of Internationalism, The Hague (in four languages), founded 1907.
Vrede door Recht, Algemeene Nederlandsche Bond: Vrede door Recht, founded 1899;
    edited by Johanna Waszklewicz-van Schilfgaarde.

English

Herald of Peace, British Peace Society, founded 1816, usually monthly.
Concord, International Arbitration and Peace Association, 1886–1914, monthly; edited by
    Hodgson Pratt, George H. Perris.
Peace and Goodwill, Wisbech Peace Society, founded 1891; edited by Priscilla H. Peckover.

French

Bulletin de la Société des amis de la paix, organ of the Ligue internationale et permanente
    de la paix; founded 1867, Frédéric Passy, president; after 1878, changed to *Bulletin
    de la Société française des amis de la paix,* irregular
Correspondance cosmopolite, 1865–1867
Paix des deux mondes/L'Avenir, 1944.
Petits Plaidoyers contre la guerre, Ligue du bien public, founded 1859; irregular numbers;
    edited by Edmond and Eugénie Potonié-Pierre.
Les États-Unis d'Europe, Ligue de la paix et de la liberté, founded 1868 (until 1871 pub-
    lished in German also, usually monthly; editors, Charles Lemonnier, Émile Arnaud.
Almanach de la paix, Paris, Société des amis de la paix, 1872–1889, irregular. Became

Almanach illustrée de la paix, 1889; changed to *Almanach de la paix,* 1890–1908; and to *Almanach de la paix par le droit,* 1909–1917.

Le Devoir: Revue des questions sociales, Familistère de Guise, founded 1878, monthly; edited by Jean-Baptiste-André Godin.

La Paix par le droit, Association de la paix par le droit, founded 1887, monthly; edited by Charles Brunet, Jacques Dumas, Théodore Ruyssen, Lucien Le Foyer, Jules Prudhommeaux. Merged with *Revue de la paix* in 1910, (last issue, 1948). [Available on microfilm, Clearwater Publishing Co., New York]

Corréspondance autographée, Corréspondence bi-mensuelle, *Le Mouvement pacifiste* (also published as *The Peace Movement; Der Friedensbewegung*), Organ of the Bureau international de la paix, founded 1891; edited by Élie Ducommun, Albert Gobat. [available on microfilm, Clearwater Publishing Co., New York]

La Conférence interparlementaire, Interparliamentary Conference, founded 1893 (lasted to 1897); edited by Albert Gobat.

L'Arbitrage entre nations, Société française pour l'arbitrage entre nations, founded 1894, monthly; edited by Frédéric Passy, Charles Richet. Became *La Revue de la paix* in 1902 and merged with *La Paix par le droit* in 1909.

Concordia, Société d'études et de correspondance internationale, founded 1894, usually monthly; edited by Émile Lombard.

L'Universel, organ of Mouvement chrétien de la paix, founded by Henri Huchet, 1898. Irregular publication.

Le Courrier européen, Paris, 1904, usually semimonthly; an international board of editors established this journal after leaving *L'Européen: Courrier international hebdomadaire,* edited by Charles Seignebos, 1904.

Bulletin de la Société Gratry, Ligue catholique de la paix, 1907–1910.

La Correspondance de la paix, organ of the Délégation permanente des sociétés françaises de la paix, Paris, 1908–1914, monthly news bulletin.

La Réconciliation: Die Versöhnung. Revue franco-allemande. Paris and Berlin, Henriette Meyer, 1913–1914.

German

Die Waffen nieder, Oesterreiche Friedensgesellschaft, founded 1892, monthly; edited by Bertha von Suttner, Alfred H. Fried.

Der Friede, Schweizerischen Friedensverein, Berne, founded 1893.

Die Friedens-Warte, Berlin, founded 1899, weekly; edited by Alfred H. Fried.

Friedensblätter, Deutsche Friedensgessellschaft, Esslingen, founded 1900.

Italian

La Libertà e la pace, Società per la pace e l'arbitrato internazionale, Palermo, founded in 1890, irregular; edited by Elvira Cimino.

La Vita internazionale, Unione lombarda per la pace, Milan, founded 1897, semi-monthly; edited by E. T. Moneta.

Swedish

Fredsfanan, Svenska freds och skilgedoms-föreningen (Swedish Society for Peace and arbitration) monthly; edited by Edward Wavrinsky and others.

Bibliographical and Archival

Abrams, Irwin. "Bertha Von Suttner (1843–1914): Bibliographical Notes." *Peace and Change* 16 (1991), 64–73.

Albistur, Maité. *Catalogue des archives Marie-Louise Bouglé.* Paris: Bibliothèque de l'histoire de la ville de Paris, 1982.

Almond, N., and H. H. Fisher, comp. *Special Collections in the Hoover Library.* Stanford, CA, 1940.

Bibliothèque du Palais de la paix, *Index alphabetique du catalogue (1916) et du supplément (1922).* Leyden, 1920.

Brinton, Ellen Starr, et al., comps. *Guide to the Swarthmore College Peace Collection: A Memorial to Jane Addams.* Swarthmore, PA, 1947.

Bureau international permanent de la paix, *Catalogue d'ouvrages sur la paix et la guerre.* Berne, 1900, 19 pp.

Carroll, Berenice A., Clinton F. Fink, and Jane E. Mohraz. *Peace and War: A Guide to Bibliographies.* Urbana-Champaign, 1980.

Chmielewski, Wendy E., ed. *Guide to Sources on Women in the Swarthmore College Peace Collection.* Swarthmore, PA, 1988.

Cook, Blanche W. *Bibliography on Peace Research in History.* Preface by Charles Barker. Santa Barbara, CA, 1969.

Donat, H., and K. Holl, eds. *Die Friedensbewegung: Organisierter Pazifismus in Deutschland, Oesterreich und in der Schweiz.* Stuttgart, 1983.

Dungen, Peter van den, ed. *From Erasmus to Tolstoy: The Peace Literature of Four Centuries; Jacob ter Meulen's Bibliographies of the Peace Movement Before 1899.* Westport, CT, 1990.

Fried, Alfred H., ed. *Annuaire du mouvement pacifiste.* Berne: Bureau international de la paix, 1910, 1913.

Josephson, Harold, ed.-in-chief; Sandi E. Cooper, Solomon Wank, and Larry Wittner, assoc. eds. *Biographical Dictionary of Modern Peace Leaders.* Westport, CT, 1985.

Kuehl, Warren, ed. *Biographical Dictionary of Internationalists.* Westport, CT, 1983.

La Fontaine, Henri. *Bibliographie de la paix et de l'arbitrage internationale.* Monaco, 1904.

Pauling, Linus, Ervin Laszlo and Jong Youl Yoo, eds. *World Encyclopedia of Peace,* 4 vols. London, 1986.

Ter Meulen, Jacob and Arnoldus Lysen, eds. *Deuxième supplément (1929) au catalogue (1916) [de la] Bibliothèque du Palais de la paix.* Leyden, 1930.

Minutes of Congresses

General International Congresses

Peace Society (London). *The Proceedings of the First General Peace Convention: Held in London, June 22, 1843, and the Two Following Days.* London, 1843.

Peace Congress at Brussels on the 20, 21 and 22 September, 1848. London, 1848.

Report of the Proceedings of the Second General Peace Congress Held in Paris on the 22, 23, 24 of August, 1849. London, 1849.

Report of the Proceedings of the Third General Peace Congress Held in Frankfurt, 22, 23 and 24 August, 1850. London, 1851.

Annales du Congrès de Génève, 9–12 septembre, 1867. Intro. by Jules Barni. Geneva, 1868.

Ligue internationale de la paix et de la liberté. *Deuxième Congrès de la paix et de la liberté convoqué pour le 22 septembre, 1868 à Berne.* Geneva, n.d.

Ligue de la paix et de la liberté, Comité central. *Manifesto au peuple français et au peuple allemand.* Geneva, 1870, 1 p.

Geogg, Amand. *Rapport au nom du Comité central, Ligue de la paix et de la liberté.* Lausanne, 25 September 1871.

Congrès international des sociétés des amis de la paix. *Compte rendu sténographique, Paris, 26–30 septembre, 1 octobre, 1878.* Paris, 1880.

International Association for Arbitration and Peace. *Procès verbal de la conférence internationale tenue à Bruxelles, le 17, 18, 19 et 20 octobre, 1881.* London, 1883.

Association for the Reform and Codification of the Laws of Nations, *Report of the Thirteenth Conference.* London, 1887.

Richard, Henry. "Further Progress of International Arbitration." *Report of the Thirteenth Conference, London, Association for the Reform and Codification of the Law of Nations (25–28 July 1887).* London, 1887.

Institut international de la paix. *Comptes rendus de l'Institut international de la paix.* Monaco, 1903.

Internationaler Antimilitaristische Kongress. *Offizielles Protokoll des Internationalen Antimilitaristischen Kongresses.* Vienna, 1908.

Association médicale international contre la guerre. *Actes et manifestations diverses (1905–1910).* Paris, 1910.

First Universal Races Congress. *Papers on Inter-Racial Problems: First Universal Races Congress, London, 26–29 July, 1911.* London, 1911.

Bureau international de la paix. *Resolutions textuelles des Congrès universels de la paix tenus de 1843 à 1910 et les quatre Assemblées générales de 1898, 1899, 1909 et 1911.* Albert Gobat, ed. Berne, 1912.

Conciliation internationale: La Conciliation allemande (Verband für internationale Verstandigung). *Congrès de Heidelberg, 5–7 octobre, 1912.* Paris, 1913.

Conciliation internationale. *La Conférence franco-allemande de Berne–Mai, 1913.* Paris, 1913.

Conciliation internationale. *Le Palais de la Paix; Le Congrès de Nuremberg.* Paris, 1913.

International Council of Women, Committee on Peace and Arbitration. *Report, 1913.* London, 1914.

Congrès international des femmes, The Hague, 28 April–1 May 1915. *Report-Rapport-Bericht.* Amsterdam, 1915 [?].

Congrès Universels de la Paix

Congrès universel de la paix. *Bulletin du premier Congrès universel de la paix tenu à Paris, 1889.* Paris, 1900.

Congrès universel de la paix (Universal Peace Congress). *Proceedings of the Universal Peace Congress Held at Westminster Town Hall, London, 14–19 July, 1890.* London, 1890.

Congrès universel de la paix. *Troisième Congrès international de la paix, Rome, novembre, 1891.* Rome, 1892.

Congrès universel de la paix. *Bulletin officiel du IVᵉ Congrès universel de la paix tenu à Berne, 22–27 août, 1892.* Berne, 1892.

Congrès universel de la paix (Universal Peace Congress). *Official Report of the Fifth Universal Peace Congress, Chicago, August 14–20, 1893.* Chicago, 1893.

Congrès universel de la paix. *Bulletin officiel du VIᵉ Congrès international de la paix tenu à Anvers 29 août au 1 septembre 1894.* Antwerp, 1895.

Congrès universel de la paix. *Bulletin officiel du VIIᵉ Congrès universel de la paix tenu à Budapest 17–22 septembre 1896.* Berne, 1896.

Congrès universel de la paix. *Bulletin officiel du VIIIᵉ Congrès universel de la paix tenu à Hambourg du 12 au 16 août 1897.* Berne, 1897.

Congrès universel de la paix. Bureau international de la paix, *Procès verbal de l'Assemblée générale des délégués des sociétés de la paix tenue à Turin, 26–28 septembre, 1898.* Berne, 1898.

Congrès universel de la paix. *Bulletin Officiel du IXe Congrès universel de la paix tenu à Paris du 30 septembre au 5 octobre 1900.* Berne, 1901.

Universal Peace Congress. *Proceedings of the Tenth Universal Peace Congress held at St. Andrew's Hall, Glasgow, 10–13 September, 1901.* London and Berne, 1901.

Congrès universel de la paix. *Bulletin officiel du XIe Congrès universel de la paix tenu à Monaco du 2 au 5 avril 1902.* Berne and Monaco, 1902.

Congrès universel de la paix. *Bulletin officiel du XIIe Congrès universel de la paix tenu à Rouen et au Havre du 22 au 27 septembre 1903.* Berne, 1903.

Universal Peace Congress. *Official Report of the Thirteenth Universal Peace Congress Held at Boston, Massachusetts, October 3–8, 1904.* Boston, 1904.

Congrès universel de la paix. *Bulletin officiel du XIVe Congrès universel de la paix tenu à Lucerne, du 19 au 23 septembre 1905.* Berne, 1905.

Congrès universel de la paix. *Bulletin officiel du XVe Congrès universel de la paix tenu à Milan du 15 au 22 septembre 1906.* Berne, 1906.

Congrès universel de la paix. *Bulletin officiel du XVIe Congrès universel de la paix tenu à Munich du 9 au 14 septembre 1907.* Berne, 1908.

Universal Peace Congress. *Official Report of the Seventeenth Universal Peace Congress, Westminster, 27 July–1 August, 1908.* London, 1909.

Congrès universel de la paix, Bureau international permanent de la paix. *Procès-verbal de l'Assemblée générale des délégues des sociétés de la paix, Bruxelles, 1909.* Brussels, 1910.

Congrés universel de la paix. *Bulletin officiel du XVIIIe Congrès universel de la paix à Stockholm du 1 au 5 août 1910.* Stockholm, 1911.

Congrès universel de la paix. *Bulletin officiel du XIXe Congrès universel de la paix tenu à Genève du 22 au 28 septembre 1912.* Berne, 1912.

Congrés universel de la paix. *Bulletin officiel du XXe Congrès universel de la paix tenu à La Haye du 18 au 23 août 1913.* Berne, 1913.

Union Interparlementaire

Union interparlementaire [pour l'arbitrage]. *Séances de 29–30 juin, 1889.* Paris, 1889, 17 pp.

Union interparlementaire. *Resumé de l'histoire du mouvement interparlementaire pour l'arbitrage et pour la paix. Extraits des rapports officiels des Comités d'organisation de Paris et de Londrès.* Beniamino Pandolfi, ed. Padua, 1891. 20 pp.

Union interparlementaire pour l'arbitrage. *Compte rendu de la VIIIe conférence tenue à Bruxelles août 1897.* Braine-le-Comte, 1898.

Union interparlementaire. *Resolutions Voted by the First Eight Conferences and Supplements.* Berne, 1899.

Union interparlementaire. *Compte rendu de la Xe conférence tenue à Paris, Palais du sénat, 31 juillet–3 août, 1900.* Paris, 1901.

Union interparlementaire. *Compte rendu de la XIe conférence tenue à Vienne, Palais du Reichsrat du 7 au 9 septembre 1903.* Vienna, 1903.

Union interparlementaire. *Compte rendu de la XIIe conférence tenue à St. Louis, Missouri du 12 au 14 septembre 1904.* Washington, DC, 1905.

Union interparlementaire. *Compte rendu de la XIIIe conférence tenue à Bruxelles, 28–31 août 1905.* Brussels, 1905.

Union interparlementaire (Interparliamentary Union). *Official Report of the Fourteenth Conference held in the Royal Gallery of the House of Lords, London, 23–25 July, 1906.* London, 1906.

Union interparlementaire. *Bericht über die XV Conferenz in Berlin, 17–19 Sept. 1908.* Berlin and Leipzig, 1908.

Union interparlementaire. *Compte rendu de la XVIᵉ conférence tenue à Bruxelles du 30 août au 1 septembre 1910*. Brussels, 1910.

Union interparlementaire. *L'Union interparlementaire: Résolutions des conférences et décisions principales du conseil*. Christian Lange, ed., Brussels, 1911.

Union interparlementaire. *Compte rendu de la XVIIᵉ conférence tenue à Genève du 18 au 20 septembre 1912*. Brussels, 1913.

Union interparlementaire. *Compte rendu de la XVIIIᵉ conférence tenue à La Haye du 3 au 5 septembre 1913*. Brussels, 1914.

English Peace Congresses

London (later British) Peace Society. *Annual Report*. London, 1820–1822.

Aborigines Protection Society. *Proceedings at a Public Meeting, 11 November, 1851 on the Kaffir War*. London, 1851.

Liverpool and Birkenhead Women's Peace and Arbitration Society, *Annual Report*. Liverpool, 1895.

Great Britain. National Peace Council, "Minute Book (August 1908–February 1916)." Archives, Library of the London School of Economics.

French Peace Congresses

Société de la morale chrétienne (Paris). *Assemblée générale annuelle, 10 mai, 1824*. Paris, n.d.

Ligue internationale et permanente de la paix. *Première Assemblée générale, juin 1868*. Paris, 1868.

Délégation nationale des sociétés françaises de la paix. *Premier Congrès national des sociétés françaises de la paix, Toulouse, octobre 1902*. Toulouse, 1903.

Délégation nationale des sociétés françaises de la paix. *Deuxième Congrès national des sociétés françaises de la paix, Nîmes,, 7, 8, 9 et 10 avril 1904: Compte rendu des séances*. Nîmes, 1904.

"Congrès international de la libre pensée, la libre pensée et le pacifisme: Contre la guerre par le désarmement et l'arbitrage." *Action* (8 September 1905), 1–3.

"Le Vᵉ Congrès national de la paix, La Rochelle, 7, 8 et 9 juin 1908." *La Paix par le droit* 18 (June 1908), 247–68, 297–315.

Sixième Congrès national des sociétés françaises de la paix, Reims, 30 mai–2 juin, 1909; Compte-rendu des séances. Reims, 1909.

Délégation nationale des sociétés françaises de la paix. *VIIᵉ Congrès national des sociétés françaises de la paix, Clermont-Ferrand, 4, 5, 6 et 7 juin 1911: Compte Rendu du congrès par P. D.* Clermont-Ferrand, 1911.

Union interparlementaire. *Le Groupe français de l'arbitrage international et l'union interparlementaire*. Paris 1912.

Délégation nationale des sociétés françaises de la paix. *VIIIᵉ Congrès national de la paix, Paris, 11, 12, et 13 mai 1913*. Paris, 1913.

S.F.I.O. (Section française de l'Internationale ouvrière). *Manifeste du Congrès national, 25–29 décembre 1915*. Paris, 1916.

Italian Peace Congresses

Lega italiana. *Libertà, fratellanza e pace, atti della lega italiana. Il primo comizio della pace in Italia nel 1898: Il secondo comizio nel 1879. (Resconto stenografico)* Milan, 1880.

Unione lombarda per la pace. *La Festa della Società operaia e dei contadini in Vimercate, 15 maggio 1887*. Milan 1887. 39 pp.

Unione lombarda, *Per la pace e l'arbitrato: Relazione all'assemblea generale 9 dicembre 1888*. Milan, 1888. 47 pp.

Atti del Congresso di Roma per la pace e l'arbitrato internazionale, 12–16 maggio, 1889. Città di Castello, 1889.
Atti del Congresso nazionale delle Società per la pace in Torino, 29, 30, 31 maggio e 2 giugno 1904. Turin, 1905.

German Peace Congresses

Der Deutsche Friedenskongress, Jena, 1908. Bericht über den Kongress. Esslingen, 1908.
Der Deutsche Friedenskongress in Wiesbaden, 1910. n.p. 1910.
VII Deutsche Friedenskongress in Kaiserslautern 1913. Esslingen, 1914.

Miscellaneous

Archives de la paix. (1831–1837), Geneva.
Compte rendu officiel du premier Congrès national belge de la paix, Bruxelles, 8–9 juin, 1913. Brussels, 1913.

Anthologies and Documentary Collections

Cooper, Sandi E., ed. *Militarism, Politics and Working-Class Attitudes.* New York, 1971, GLW/P.
————, *Arms Limitation: Plans for Europe Before 1914.* New York, 1972, GLW/P.
————. *Five Views of European Peace.* New York, 1972, GLW/P.
————, *Peace Activities in Belgium and The Netherlands.* New York, 1972, GLW/P.
————. *Voices of French Pacifism.* New York, 1973, GLW/P.
————. *Internationalism in Nineteenth-Century Europe: The Crisis of Ideas and Purpose.* New York, 1976, GLW/P.
————. *Peace and Civilization: Selections from the Writings of Jacques Novicow.* New York, 1976, GLW/P.
Freymond, Jacques, et al., eds. *La Première internationale,* 2 vols. Geneva, 1962.
Haberman, Frederick W., ed. *Nobel Lectures: Peace 1901–1925,* vol. 1. Amsterdam, 1972.
Moorhus, Roger, ed. *European Socialism and the Problem of Internationalism Before World War I.* New York, 1972, GLW/P.
Weitz, Mark, ed. *European Socialism and the Problems of War and Militarism: A Sample of Opinions Before the First World War.* New York, 1972, GLW/P.
Wild, Adolf, ed. "Introduction." *Arms Limitation Plans for Europe Before 1914.* New York, 1972, GLW/P.

Pacifist and Anti-pacifist Literature

Abrami, Léon. "Le Traité d'arbitrage du 14 octobre 1903 et les relations anglo-françaises." *Revue politique et parlementaire,* 38 (1903), 535–55.
L'Alliance des savants et des philanthropes. "Suggestions sur les meilleurs moyens d'assurer la paix générale: Mémoire adressé au ministre des affaires etrangères par des nombreuses notabilités." *L'Humanité nouvelle 4* (1899). 18 pp. (Special supplement.)
American Peace Society. *The Teaching of History in the Public Schools with Reference to War and Peace: Report of a Committee.* Boston, 1906. 27 pp.
Amos, Sheldon. *Political and Legal Remedies for War.* London and New York, 1880.
Angell, Norman. *The Great Illusion: A Study of the Relations of Military Power in Nations to Their Economic and Social Advantage,* London, 1910; New York, 1972.
————. *Peace Theories and the Balkan Wars.* London, 1914.

Appleton, Lewis. *The Military and Financial Condition of Europe.* London, 1882.
———. *Fifty Years of Disarmament.* London, 1899.
Apponyi, Albert. "Unser Krieg vom Standpunkte der interparlamentarischen Union." *Nord und Sud* 151 (1914), 151–55.
Arnaud, Émile. *L'Organisation de la paix.* Berne, 1899.
———. "Le Mouvement pacifiste." *La Grande Revue,* 8th year, 31 (1904), 416–21.
———. "Le Pacifisme et ses détracteurs." *La Grande Revue,* n.s., 37, (1906), 160–88.
———. "La Deuxième Conferénce de La Haye." *La Grande Revue,* n.s., 40, (1906), 41–50.
———. "La Deuxième Conférence de La Haye." *La Grande Revue,* n.s., 42 (1907), 156–65.
Arnoldson, Klas P. *Pax Mundi: A Concise Account of the Progress of the Movement for Peace by Means of Arbitration, Neutralization, International Law and Disarmament.* Trans. by "A Lady." London, 1892.
Association de la paix par le droit. *Appel-programme-statuts.* Paris, 1914.
Bajer, Fredrik. "Kopi Bog" (1897). (unpublished diary.) Library of the Peace Palace, The Hague.
———. *Les Origines du Bureau international de la paix.* Berne, 1904.
Bakunin, Mikhail. *Deuxième Congrès de la paix et de la liberté convoqué pour le 22 septembre, 1868 à Berne.* N.p., n.d., (probably 1868). Seligman Archive, Columbia Univ.
Bara, Louis. *La Science de la paix.* Intro. by S. E. Cooper. New York, 1972, GLW/P. (Orig. Brussels, 1872.)
Barclay, T[homas]. "New Treaties of Arbitration and Diplomacy." *Fortnightly Review* 82 (1904), 602–7.
———. "The Second Hague Conference," *Fortnightly Review,* 87 (1907), 967–76; 88 (1907) 551–61.
———. "Peace." *Encyclopaedia Brittanica,* vol. 21, 4–17. New York, 1910.
Barraute de Plessis. *La Patrie blanche.* Paris. 1909. 12 pp.
Bastiat, Frédéric. *Cobden et la ligue.* Paris, 1845.
———. *Sophismes économiques.* Paris, 1845–1848.
———. *Le Libre-échange.* Paris, 1846–1848.
———. *Paix et liberté ou le budget republicain.* Intro. by Dennis Sherman. New York, 1974, GLW/P. (Orig. Paris, 1849.)
Bebel, August. *Nicht Stehendes Heer Sondern Volkswehr!* Intro. by Claudia Koonz. New York, 1972, GLW/P (orig. Stuttgart, 1898).
Beer Portugael, J.C.C. den. *Le Droit des gens en marche vers la paix et la guerre de Tripoli.* The Hague, 1912.
Bellot, Hugh H. L. "The Hague Conference," *Westminster Review* 168 (1907), 187–92.
Bernard, Charles. "Considérations sur le désarmement." *Revue de Belgique,* ser. 2, 26 (1899), 5–19.
Bernhardi, General Friedrich von. *On War of Today.* Trans. from German by Karl von Donat; new intro. by Trumbull Higgins. New York, 1972, GLP/W.
Besson, Emmanuel. "L'Arbitrage international et la codification des droit des gens." *Revue politique et parlementaire* 17 (1898), 465–515.
Bienstock, W. "Le Mouvement anti-militariste." *La Revue blanche (Paris)* 21 (1900), 429–434.
Bjorklund, Gustave. *Paix et désarmement.* Stockholm, 1895.
Blanqui, Adolphe. *Précis élémentaire de l'économie politique.* Paris, 1846.
Bloch, Jean de. "Les Problèmes de la guerre et la politique d'expansion coloniale—Conférence." Typescript. Archives, Bureau international de la paix, misc. n.d.

——. *La Guerre,* 6 vols. Paris, 1898; intro. by S. E. Cooper. New York, 1973. GLW/P.

——. "L'Armée franco-russe et la guerre du Transvaal." *La Revue (ancienne Revue des revues),* 3rd ser. 36 (1901), 507–25.

——. "Militarism in Politics and Lord Roberts' Army Organization Scheme." *Contemporary Review* 80 (1901), 761–93.

——. *The Work of the Peace Societies: How to Widen Their Programme.* Glasgow, 1901. 35 pp.

——. *The Future of War in Its Technical, Economic and Political Relations.* Trans. from French by R. C. Long (Orig. Boston, 1902.), intro. by S. E. Cooper. New York, 1972, GLW/P.

Bluntschli, Johann Caspar. *Das moderne Kriegsrecht der civilisirten* [sic] *Staaten als Rechtsbuch.* Nördlingen, 1866.

——. "Opinion impartiale sur la question de l'Alabama et sur la manière de la résoudre." *Revue de droit international et de législation comparée.* vol. 2, (1870), 452–85.

——. *Das Beuterecht im Krieg und das Seebeuterecht inbesondere: Eine volkerrechtliche Untersuchung.* Nördlingen, 1878.

Bollack, Léon. "Faits et documents: Vers l'arbitrage international." *La Revue (ancienne Revue des revues),* 47 (1903), 524–25, 785–87.

——. "Faits et documents: Vers l'entente universelle," *La Revue (ancienne Revue des revues),* 49 (1904), 497–99.

——. "Faits et documents: Vers l'entente universelle." *La Revue (ancienne Revue des revues)* 54 (1905), 269–72.

Bonghi, Ruggiero. "La Situazione europea e la pace." *Nuova antologia* 35, ser. 3 (1891), 207–26.

Bouglé, Celestin. "De La Haye à Stuttgart: La Saison internationale." *La Grande Revue,* n.s., 45 (1907), 62–72.

Bourgeois, Léon. *Pour la Société des nations.* Paris, 1910.

Bresca, G. N. *La Unione interparlamentare per la pace: Considerazioni e proposte.* Potenza, 1898.

Broda, Rudolf. *Le Rôle de la violence dans les conflits de la vie moderne.* Paris, 1913.

Brunetière, Ferdinand. "Le Mensonge du pacifisme." In *Voices of French Pacifism.* Sandi E. Cooper, ed. New York, 1973, GLW/P.

Brusa, E. "La Question du désarmement et la note du Tsar Nicholas II." *Revue générale du droit international public* 5 (1898), 729–43.

Buisson, Ferdinand. "L'Abolition de la guerre par l'instruction"." *Les États-Unis d'Europe* 7, (1868), 66–68.

Bureau international de la paix. *Les Rapports du pacifisme et du mouvement ouvrier: Appel aux militants du prolétariat international et questionnaire.* Berne, 1906.

Caïel [sic]. *La Femme et la paix: Appel aux mères portugaises.* Lisbon, 1898. 55 pp.

Castelar, Emilio de. *La Cuestion social y la paz armada en Europa.* Madrid, 1890.

Catellani, Enrico. *Realtà ed utopie della pace.* Turin, 1899.

——. "I trattai d'arbitrato e la attuali garanzie della pace." *Revista istituto Veneto* 3, no. 2 (1904), 841–63.

Cazé, L. "Les Armées du monde et le désarmement général." *Revue de revues et Revue d'Europe et d'Amérique* 26 (1898), 623–31.

——. "L'Enfer de la guerre." *La Revue (ancienne Revue des revues),* 3rd ser. 74 (1908), 99–109.

Challaye, Félicien. *Les Rapports franco-allemands: Extrait de la Revue du mois.* Paris, 1913. 25 pp.

Charmatz, Richard. *Adolf Fischhof.* Stuttgart and Berlin, 1910.

Charriaut, Henri. "Le Mouvement pacifique." *Revue socialiste* 38 (1903), 370–77.

Chavet, Gabriél. *Justice sociale et justice internationale.* Paris, 1900. 40 pp.

Chevalier, Michel. "Organisation industrielle de l'armée; politique d'association; système de la Méditerranée." *Religion saint-simonienne: Politique industrielle et système de la Méditerranée.* Paris, 1832.

———. *Cours d'économie politique.* Paris, 1844.

———. "La Guerre et la crise européenne." *Revue des deux mondes,* 2nd per. 63 (1866), 758–85.

———. "Les États-Unis d'Europe et la paix." *Journal des économistes* 15 (1869), 76–91.

Cimbali, Edoardo. *Rinnovamento della triplice.* Rome, 1902. 67pp.

———. *Il Nuovo Diritto internazionale e gli odierni congressi, conferenze, società e leghe per la pace: L'Arbitrato e il disarmo.* Rome, 1910.

Clarke, G. S. "Reply to 'Should Europe Disarm?'" *Nineteenth Century* 44 (1898), 697–706.

Clerget, Pierre. *La Question sociale et la paix.* Chaux-de-Fonds, 1903. 38 pp.

Cloots, Anacharsis. *La République universelle ou adresse aux tyrannicides.* Intro. by James A. Thomas, Jr. New York, 1973, GLW/P. (Orig. Paris, 1793.)

Cobden, Richard. *The Political Writings of Richard Gobden.* 2 vols. Intro. by Naomi Churgin Miller. New York, 1973, GLW/P (orig. London, 1903).

Comte, Auguste. *Cours de philosophie positive, 1830–1842,* 6 vols. Paris, 1843.

"Conférences, correspondances, notes: Deuxième Conférence de la paix." *Archives diplomatiques,* 3rd ser., vol. 105 (1908), 21–230.

Conseil national des femmes françaises: Section de la paix. *Simples Réponses à de fréquentes objections du pacifisme.* Paris, 1913. 16 pp.

Considérant, Victor. *La Paix ou la guerre.* Paris, 1829.

———. *De la politique générale et du rôle de la France en Europe.* Paris, 1840.

———. "La Dernière Guerre et la paix définitif en Europe." In *Five Views of European Peace.* Sandi E. Cooper, ed. New York, 1972, GLW/P. (Orig. Paris, 1850.)

Corbet, W. J. "Can a War of Aggression Be Justified." *Westminster Review* 155 (1901), 274–84.

Courtney, Leonard. "The Approaching Conference." *Contemporary Review* 75 (May 1899), 609–19.

Courtney of Penwith. "Peace or War?" *Contemporary Review* 96 (1909), 385–400, 513–26.

Crispi, Francesco. "La Conferenza pel disarmo." *Nuova antologia* 81, ser. 4 (1899), 360–66.

Crucé, Eméric. *The New Cyneas of Emeric Crucé,* Trans. from French and ed. by Thomas W. Balch. Philadelphia, 1909. (Orig. Paris, 1623.); intro. by C. F. Farrell, Jr., and E. R. Farrell. New York, 1972, GLW/P.

d'Aguanno, Giuseppe "L'Ideale scientifico della pace internazionale." *Rivista di sociologia* 1 (1894), 241–58.

d'Eichthal, Eugène. "La Paix internationale." *Revue politique et parlementaire* 10 (1900), 27–41.

d'Eichthal, Gustave. *De l'unité européenne.* Paris, 1840.

Darby, W. E. *Historical Outline of the Modern Peace Movement.* London, 1890.

———. *Popular Responsibility in Declaring War.* London, 1892.

———. *Reactionary Ethics.* London, 1898.

———. *International Tribunals,* 4th ed. London, 1904.

———. *The Claim of "The New Pacifism."* London, 1913. 12 pp.

Davis, H., ed. *Among the World's Peacemakers.* New York, 1907.

De Jongh, Charles. *L'Allemagne et les conventions de la Haye: Pacifisme et démocratie.* Lausanne, 1915.

Delbrück, Hans. "Zukunftskrieg und Zukunftsfriede." *Preussische Jahrbücher* 6 (April–June 1899), 203–229.

Delhassé, Félix, and T. Théophile. *Contre la guerre! Études historiques sur la guerre dans l'antiquité et au Moyen Âge.* Brussels, 1855.

Descamps, Edouard, le Chevalier. *Essai sur l'organisation de l'arbitrage internationale: Mémoire aux puissances.* Brussels, 1896. 64 pp.

Desjardins, Arthur. "Le Désarmement, étude de droit international." *Revue des deux mondes,* 4 per., 149 (1898), 668–79.

———. "La Guerre hispano-américaine et le droit des gens." *Revue des deux mondes,* 4th per., 147 (1898), 518–49.

———. "La Chine et le droit des gens." *Revue des deux mondes,* 4th per., 162 (1900), 522–49.

———. "La Guerre de l'Afrique australe et le droit des gens." *Revue des deux mondes,* 4th per., 158 (1900), 38–78.

Despagnet, F. "La Question du désarmement et la note du Tsar Nicholas II." *Revue générale du droit international public* 5 (1898), 710–21.

Dillon, E. J. "The Tsar's Eirenicon." *Contemporary Review* 74 (1898), 609–42.

———. "International Parliament of Good Intentions." *Contemporary Review* 92 (1907), 269–74.

———. "True Story of the Genesis of the Hague Conference." *Contemporary Review* 91 (1907), 879–82.

Dissart, Clothilde. *Réflexions en faveur du désarmement: La Question d'Alsace-Lorraine.* Paris, 1899. 11 pp.

Dolens, Noël. "Le Problème de désarmement." *Revue socialiste* 23,24 (1907–1908), 52–67, 490–505.

Dreyfus, Ferdinand. "La Conférence interparlementaire de La Haye et le mouvement pacifique." *Revue politique et parlementaire* 2 (1894), 273–84.

Ducommun, Élie. "Memorandum for a History of the Inter-Parliamentary Union." Bureau international de la paix, Conférence interparlementaire. Archives, United Nations Library, Geneva.

———. "Le Congrès de la paix in 1896." *Revue socialiste,* 24, (1896), 714–23.

———. *Rôle de la guerre et de la paix dans les progrès de la civilisation.* Berne, 1899. 20 pp.

———. *The Probable Consequences of a European War.* London, 1906. 24 pp.

Dumas, Jacques. "De la responsibilité du pouvoir executif considerée comme l'une des sanctions de l'arbitrage international." *Revue politique et parlementaire* 29 (1901), 312–20.

———. *La Colonisation: Essai de doctrine pacifiste.* Paris, 1904.

———. "De la fédération considerée comme l'une des sanctions de l'arbitrage international." *Revue international de sociologie* 13 (1905), 289–98.

———. *Les Sanctions de l'arbitrage international.* Paris, 1906.

Dumesnil, Henri. *La Guerre: Etude philosophique.* Paris, 1872.

Dunant, Henri. *Memoir of Solferino.* Geneva, 1862.

Duplessix, E. *Code de droit international public.* Paris, 1906.

———. *La Loi de nations.* Paris, 1906.

Durand, Ferdinand. *Des Tendances pacifiques de la société européenne et du rôle des armées dans l'avenir.* Intro. by Dennis Sherman. New York, 1972, GLP/W (Orig. Paris, 1841; 2nd ed., 1845.)

Duras, Victor Hugo. *La Paix par l'organisation internationale.* Paris, 1910.

Durkheim, Émile. *Sur l'internationalisme.* Paris, 1906.

Egidy, Moritz von, and Gaston Moch. *L'Ere sans violence.* Paris, 1899.

Estournelles de Constant, Paul Henri, Baron d'. *La Conciliation internationale: Les Deux Politiques.* Paris, 1905.

———, ed. *Le Mouvement pacifique et le rapprochement franco-anglais: Les Visites parlementaires de Londres et Paris, 22 juillet–26 novembre, 1903.* La Flèche, 1903.

———. "Les Deux Politiques." *La Revue (ancienne Revue des revues)* 59 (1905), 501–5.

———. *Report on the Limitation of Armaments.* London, 1906.

Evans, Howard. *Sir Randal Cremer: His Life and Work.* London, 1909.

Faguet, Émile. *Le Pacifisme.* Paris, 1908.

Fauchille, P. "La Question du désarmement et la note du Tsar Nicholas II." *Revue générale du droit international public* 5 (1898), 687–94.

———. "L'Europe nouvelle." *Revue générale de droit international public* 6 (1899), 5–8.

Ferrari, Celso. *La Guerre, essai de pathologie sociale.* Paris, 1896.

———. *La Nazionalità e la vita sociale.* Palermo, 1896.

———. *Nazionalismo e internazionalismo.* Milan, 1906.

Ferrero, Guglielmo. *Militarism.* Trans. from Italian. Intro by S. E. Cooper. New York, 1972, GLW/P. (Orig. Milan, 1898; orig. Eng. ed., London, 1902.)

———. "L'Europe de demain." *Revue des revues et Revue d'Europe et d'Amérique* 28 (1899), 1–10.

———. "Le Patriotisme italien." *La Revue (ancienne Revue des revues),* 40 (1902), 265–72.

Fiore, Pasquale. *Un Appel à la presse et à la diplomatie, l'empereur d'Allemagne, la France, la question européenne: Une Solution.* Paris, 1890. 40 pp.

———. "Settlement of the International Question." *International Journal of Ethics* 7 (1896), 20–32.

———. "L'Imperatore di Russia e la conferenza." *Nuova antologia* 80, ser. 4 (1899), 167–81.

Fischhof, Adolf. *On the Reduction of Continental Armies.* London, 1875. 34 pp.

Follin, H. L. "Interpatriotisme." *La Grande Revue,* 7th year, 28, (1903), 398–405.

———. "La Crise de la civilisation politique." *La Grande Revue,* 8th year, 31 (1904), 324–63.

"Foreign Affairs: A Chronique." *Fortnightly Review* 87 (1907), 740–45.

Forest, Louis. "L'Antimilitarisme en Allemagne." *La Revue (ancienne Revue des revues)* 36 (1901), 125–45; 260–71.

Fouillée, Alfred. "La Psychologie des peuples et l'anthropologie." *Revue des deux mondes* 127 (1895), 365–96.

Fourier, Charles. *Triumvirat continental et paix perpétuelle sous trente ans.* Paris, 1803.

Fox-Bourne, H. R. *European Rivalries.* London, 1896.

Frank, Louis. *Les Belges et la paix.* Brussels, 1905.

———. *La Paix et le district fédéral du monde: L'Avenir de Belgique au point de vue internationale.* Intro. by Sandi E. Cooper. New York, 1972, GLW/P (Orig. Paris, 1910).

Fried, Alfred. *Die moderne Friedensbewegung.* Leipzig, 1907.

———. *Les Bases du pacifisme: Le Pacifisme réformiste et le pacifisme révolutionnaire,* Intro. by Sandi E. Cooper. New York, 1972, GLW/P (Orig. Paris, 1909.)

———. *The German Emperor and the Peace of the World.* New York and London, 1912.

———. *Handbuch der Friedensbewegung,* 2nd ed., 2 vols. Intro. by Daniel Gasman. New York, 1972, GLW/P (Orig. Berlin, 1913.)

———. *The Restoration of Europe.* Intro. by Sandi E. Cooper. New York, 1971, GLW/P (Orig. New York, 1916.)

———, ed. *Amerika gegen die Rüstungen.* Berlin, 1909.

Garnier, Joseph. *Eleménts de l'économie politique.* Paris, 1846.

Gavet, André. "L'Idée de patrie." *Revue politique et parlementaire* 45 (1905), 433–50.

Gentz, Friedrich von. "Considerations on the Political System Now Existing in Europe, 1818." In *Five Views of European Peace,* Sandi E. Cooper, ed. New York, 1972, GLW/P.

Ghisleri, Arcangelo. *La Guerra e il diritto delle genti.* Rome, 1913.

Giradin, Émile de. *Paix et liberté: Questions de l'année 1863.* Paris, 1864.

Giretti, Edoardo. *Sei anni di protezionismo in Italia.* Milan, 1893.

———. *Il Popolo e la lotta contra il militarismo.* Bologna, 1900.

———. "Per Un Accordo della società per la pace colle organizzazioni operaie." *Giornale degli economisti* 28 (1904), 543–54.

———. "Letters to Luigi Einaudi." Einaudi Archive, Turin. (Scattered, 1909–1913.)

———. *Perchè sono per la guerra.* Rome, 1915.

Goblet d'Alviella, Eugène. *Désarmer ou déchoir.* Brussels, 1872.

Goegg, Marie. "Proposition de créer une association internationale des femmes en connexion avec la Ligue de la paix et de la liberté." *Les États-Unis d'Europe* 1 (March 8, 1868), 2–3.

———. *Deux discours.* Geneva, 1878. (Repr. of 1868 speeches.)

Gohier, Urbain. *L'Armée contre la nation.* Paris, 1899.

———. "The Danger of Militarism." *Independent* 52 (1900), 233–56.

———. *L'Antimilitarisme et la paix.* Intro. by Helena Lewis. New York, 1972, GLW/P. (Orig. Paris, 1905.)

Gooch, G. P. *The War and Its Causes.* Intro. by Cynthia F. Behrman. New York, 1972, GLW/P. (Orig. Westminster, 1900).

Goyau, Georges. "La Conférence de La Haye et le Saint-Siège." *Revue des deux mondes* 154 (1899), 590–611.

———. *L'École et la patrie.* Paris, 1906.

Griess-Traut, Virginie. *Arguments en faveur de la transformation des armées guerrières-destructives en armées pacifiques-productives,* 2nd ed. N.p., 1893.

Groupe parlementaire français de l'arbitrage international. *Le Bilan du groupe.* Paris, 1906–1910.

Hamelle, Paul. "Guerre à la guerre." *La Revue blanche (Paris)* 19 (1899), 19–29.

Hamon, Auguste. "Á-propos du désarmement," *L'Humanité nouvelle,* 3 (1898), 427–45.

———, ed. "Enquête sur la guerre et le militarisme." *L'Humanité nouvelle* 4 (1899). (Special supplement.) Intro. by Sandi E. Cooper. New York, 1972, GLW/P (orig. 1899).

Hanotaux, Gabriel. "Une Préface—l'arbitrage international." *Questions diplomatiques et coloniales* 17 (1904), 341–46.

Heimweh, Jean. *Pensons-y et parlons-en.* Paris, 1891.

———. *Allemagne, France, Alsace-Lorraine.* Paris, 1899.

Higgins, Alexander P. *The Hague Conference and Other International Conferences Concerning the Laws and Usages of War.* London, 1904.

Hirst, F. W. *The Arbiter in Council.* London, 1906.

Hobson, John. *The War in South Africa: Its Causes and Effects.* Intro. by Cynthia F. Belman. New York, 1972, GLW/P (orig. London, 1900).

Hodgson, Harry. "Coming Hague Conference." *Westminster Review* 166 (1906), 135–43.

———. "Formation of an International Arbitration Court." *Westminster Review* 166 (1906), 368–74.

Holland, T. E. "Some Lessons of the Peace Conference." *Fortnightly Review* 72 (1899), 944–57.

Holls, Frederick W. *The Peace Conference at The Hague and Its Bearings on International Law and Policy.* New York, 1900.

Hron, K. *Abrüstung, Panslavismus und Deutschthum.* Vienna, 1898.

Hugo, Victor. *Actes et paroles,* 3 vols. Paris, 1881–1884.

L'Institut franco-allemand de la réconciliation. *Programme.* Paris, n.d. 6 pp.

Jacques, Léon. *De Quelques considérations sur la "res publica" européenne.* Paris, 1910.

Jaurès, Jean. *L'Armée nouvelle, l'Organisation socialiste de la France.* Paris, 1910.

J.B.W.C. "Substitutes for War." *Westminster Review* 146 (1896), 676–80.

Jevons, H. S. "Development of an International Parliament." *Contemporary Review* 92 (1907), 305–26.

Jouet, Alphonse. "Le Pacifisme et sa phase actuelle." *La Grande Revue* 7th year, 27 (1903), 141–54.

Karcher, Théodore. "Paix et guerre." *La Voix du proscrit,* 27 October 1850, 216–77.

Key, Ellen. *War, Peace and the Future: A Consideration of Nationalism and Internationalism, and of the Relation of Women to War.* Trans. by Hildegard Norberg; intro. by Berenice A. Carroll. New York, 1972, GLW/P (Orig. 1916).

Koht, Halvdan. *Histoire du mouvement de la paix en Norvège.* Christiana (now Oslo), 1900.

Lafargue, Paul. *Le Patriotisme de la bourgeoisie.* Paris, n.d. 16 pp.

Lagneau, G. *Conséquences démographiques pour la France des guerres.* Paris, 1892.

Lagorgette, Jean. *Le Rôle de la guerre.* Paris, 1906.

La Grasserie, Raoul de. *Des Moyens Pratiques pour parvenir à la suppression de la paix armée et de la guerre.* Paris, 1894. 100 pp.

Lalance, August. "La Nouvelle triplice." *La Grande Revue* 2 (1898), 253–70.

Lammasch, Heinrich. "L'Arbitrage obligatoire et les deux conférences de la paix." *Revue générale de droit international public* 16 (1909), 689–98.

Landry, A. "La Paix et l'enseignement pacifiste." *Revue d'économie politique* 19 (1905), 267–86.

Lavallée, René. "Ce Que Coûte la paix armée." *L'Europe nouvelle* (May 1899),762–68.

Laveleye, Émile de. *Des Causes actuelles de guerre en Europe et de l'arbitrage.* Brussels, 1873.

Lawrence, Thomas J. *International Problems and Hague Conferences.* London, 1908.

Le Doyen, F. *Extinction de la guerre au nom de la raison, de l'humanité et de la civilisation.* Paris, 1876.

Le Foyer, Lucien. "Le XI Congrès de la paix et la mouvement pacifique." *Revue politique et parlementaire* 33 (1902), 546–58.

Le Fur, L. "La Paix perpétuelle et l'arbitrage international." *Revue générale de droit international public* 16 (1909), 437–63.

Legrand, Louis. "L'Internationalisme et l'idée de patrie." *Revue politique et parlementaire* 7 (1897), 245–61.

Lemonnier, Charles. *La Question sociale: Rapport présenté au Congrès de Lausanne, septembre, 1871.* Paris, 1871, 35 pp.

———. *Les États-Unis d'Europe.* Paris, 1872.

———. *Lettre à messieurs les presidents et membres de la Conférence internationale de Bruxelles.* Geneva, 1875.

———. *The Problem of European Peace and Its Progressive Solution by Means of Tribunals of International Justice Based on Federations of European States.* London, 1887.

Lémonon, Ernest. "La Second Conférence de la paix." *Revue politique et parlementaire* 54 (1907), 304–19.

L'Ermite, Pierre. *La Paix armée.* Paris, 1906. 34 pp.

Leroy-Beaulieu, Anatole. "La Russie, la Finlande, et la Conférence de la Haye." *Revue des revues* et *Revue d'Europe et d Amérique* 29 (1899), 333–40.
––––––. *Les États-Unis d'Europe, Congrès des sciences politiques: Rapport général.* Paris, 1904.
––––––. "Pacifisme, christianisme et antimilitarisme." *La Revue (ancienne Revue des revues),* 3rd series, 61 (1906), 181–87.
Leroy-Beaulieu, Paul. "Contemporary Wars (1853–1866)." In *Internationalism in Nineteenth-Century Europe: The Crisis of Ideas and Purpose.* Ed. S. E. Cooper. New York, 1976, GLW/P. 387–435.
Libertas, Justitia, Pax. Milan, 1895.
Libres entretiens: Sur l'internationalisme, 1905–1906. Deuxième ser. Paris 1906.
Lockwood, Belva. *La Création d'un bureau international de la paix.* Berne, 1892.
Loewenthal, Eduard. *Geschichte der Friedensbewegung: Mit Berücksichtigung der zweiten Haager Friedenskonferenz.* Berlin, 1907.
Lorimer, James. *The Application of the Principle of Relative or Proportional Equality to International Organisation.* Edinburgh and London, 1867.
Louis, Paul. "Désarmement?" *Revue socialiste* 28 (1898), 251–62.
––––––. "La Conférence de la Haye," *Revue socialiste* 29 (1899), 658–63.
––––––. "L'Angleterre et l'Europe," *La Revue blanche (Paris)* 21 (1900), 615–17.
––––––. "Armements." *La Revue blanche (Paris)* 21 (1900), 386–88.
Low, S. "Should Europe Disarm?" *Nineteenth Century* 44 (1898), 521–30.
––––––. "Hypocrisies of the Peace Conference." *Nineteenth Century* 45 (1899), 689–98.
Loyson, Paul-Hyacinthe. "La Langue de la paix." *La Grande Revue,* n.s., 39 (1906), 663–64.
Macchi, Mauro. *La Pace di Mauro Macchi.* Genoa, 1856.
Macdonell, J. "Rules of Neutrality and the Future Hague Conference." *Contemporary Review* 88 (1905), 848–56.
Maciejewski, Casimir. *La Crise du pacifisme actuel.* Paris, 1913.
––––––. *Distinction des diverses catégories du pacifisme et son importance pratique.* Paris, 1913.
Maday, André de. *Sociologie de la paix.* Paris, 1913.
Mahan, [Admiral] Alfred Thayer. *Armaments and Arbitration, or the Place of Force in International Relations of States.* New York, 1912.
Mahy, F. de. "Le Désarmement." *Questions diplomatiques et coloniales* 5 (1898), 65–70.
Maineri, B. E. *Le Plébiscite international pour l'arbitrage et pour la paix.* Rome, 1892, 16 pp.
Manning, T. F. "Causes of Wars." *Westminster Review* 152 (1899), 597–607.
Martens, F. de. "La Question des armements dans la relation entre la Russie et l'Angleterre." *Revue de droit international et du législation comparée* 26 (1894), 573–85.
––––––. "International Arbitration and the Peace Conference at The Hague." *North American Review* 69 (1899), 604–24.
Martin, Archibald. *Why Nations Cannot Live at Peace: A Realistic View of the Peace Movement.* Aberdeen, 1910.
Marzorati, *Guerra e pauperismo.* Milan 1878.
Masini, Pier Carlo, ed. *La Scapigliatura democratica: Carteggi di Arcangelo Ghisleri, 1875–1890.* Milan, 1961.
Mazzini, Giuseppe. *Lettere al Congresso per la pace in Ginevra, 1867.* Rome, 1891, 15 pp.
––––––. "Europe: Its Condition and Prospects." In *Five Views of European Peace,* Sandi E. Cooper, ed. New York, 1972, GLW/P (Orig. London, 1852).

Mazzoleni, Angelo, *L'Italia nel movimento per la pace.* Milan, 1891, 73 pp.

Meale, Gaetano. See Umano.

Melville, R. D. "Prospects of International Arbitration." *Westminster Review* 147 (1897), 367–77.

Mérignhac, A. "La Conférence internationale de la paix (Conférence de La Haye) de 1899." *Revue politique et parlementaire* 24 (1900) 681–702.

———. "Les Traités d'arbitrage permanent au XX siècle: Accords franco-anglais et franco-italien des 14 octobre et 25 décembre 1903." *Revue politique et parlementaire* 29 (1904), 281–311.

Merttens, F. *Militarism and Wages.* War and Peace Pamphlet, no. 3, Garton Foundation. London, 1913. 16 pp.

Mezières, M. L. *De la polémomanie ou folie de la guerre dans l'Europe actuelle.* Paris, 1872.

Mielle, Paul. "Patriotisme et internationalisme." *Revue des revues* et *Revue d'Europe et d'Amèrique* 33 (1900), 557–68.

Millet, René. "La Paix à tout prix." *Revue politique et parlementaire* 39 (1904), 267–80.

M. L. "La Question du désarmement." *Revue scientifique* 2 (1894), 6–15, 48–52.

Moch, Gaston. *L'Alsace-Lorraine: Réponse à un pamphlet allemand.* Intro. by Sandi E. Cooper. New York, 1972. GLW/P (Orig. Paris, 1895).

———. *Autour de la Conférence interparlementaire.* Intro. by Sandi E. Cooper. New York, 1972, GLW/P (Orig. Paris, 1895).

———. "Les Principes d'organisation militaire démocratique." *La revue blanche* (Paris) 17 (1898), 499–504.

———. "La Réduction du service militaire." *La Revue blanche* (Paris) 17 (1898), 598–602.

———. *L'Armée d'une démocratie.* Intro. by Sandi E. Cooper. New York, 1972, GLW/P (Orig. Paris, 1900).

———. "La Philosophie de la paix: L'Arbitrage universel." In *Morale générale,* vol. 2. Paris, 1903, 362–76.

———. *Vers La Fédération d'occident: Désarmons les Alpes!* Paris, 1905.

Molinari, Gustave de. *Questions d'économie politique et de droit public,* 2 vols. Brussels, 1861.

———. *Grandeur et décadence de la guerre.* Paris and Brussels, 1898.

———. "Les Problems du XX siècle." *Revue d'économie politique* 1 (1902), 370–72.

———. *The Society of Tomorrow: A Forecast of Its Political and Economic Organisation.* Intro. by Sandi E. Cooper. New York, 1971, GLW/P (Orig. London and New York, 1904).

Moneta, E. T. *Garibaldi contro le guerre e per la federazione Europea.* Milan, 1911, (orig. 1860). 7 pp.

———. "Un Appel en faveur de la paix." *Revue socialiste* 7 (1888), 191–94.

———. *Dalla vera pace, la vera gloria.* Milan, 1910 (orig. 1889). 15 pp.

———. *Patria e umanità: Orrori dell'invasione delle truppe alleate in Cina.* Milan, 1900.

———. *Le Guerre, le insurrezioni e la pace nel secolo XIX,* 4 vols. Milan, 1903–1910.

———. *La Pace ed il diritto nella tradizione italiana.* Milan, 1909.

———. *L'Italia e la conferenza dell'Aja.* Milan, 1911.

Montluc, Léon de. "L'Arbitrage obligatoire dans les rapports internationales," *La Grande Revue,* 8th year, 30 (1904), 451–57.

———. "La Vie de Charles Lemonnier." *Les États-Unis d'Europe* (Paris, 1924–1925). Supplements.

Morhardt, Mathias, *L'Oeuvre de la Ligue des droits de l'homme. 1898-1908.* Paris, 1911.

Morley, J. "Arbitration With America." *Nineteenth Century* 40 (1896), 320–37.

Morsier, A. de. *La Paix par le droit et la guerre: Abrégé historique et documents.* Geneva, 1915.

Moynier, Gustave. *Les Bureaux internationaux des unions universelles.* Geneva, 1892.

Nattan-Larrier, Pierre. "Les Assurances sur la vie et le risque de guerre." *La Grande Revue,* 9th year 34 (1905), 540–61.

Nordau, Max. "Philosophy and Morals of War" *North American Review* 169 (1899), 787–97.

Notovitch, Nicholas. *La Pacification de l'Europe et Nicholas II.* Paris, 1899.

Novicow, Jacques. *La Politique internationale.* Paris, 1886.

———. *Les Luttes entre sociétés et leurs phases successives,* 2 vols. Intro. by Sandi E. Cooper. New York, 1971, GLW/P (Orig. Paris, 1893).

———. "L'Insignificance de la force brutale." *Revue internationale de sociologie* 7 (1893), 495–506.

———. *Les Gaspillages des sociétés modernes: Contribution à l'étude de la question sociale.* Paris, 1894.

———. *La Fédération de l'Europe.* Intro. by Sandi E. Cooper. New York, 1972, GLW/P (Orig. Paris, 1901).

———. *Conscience et volonté sociales.* Paris, 1897.

———. *Théorie organique des sociétés: Défense de la organicisme.* Paris, 1899.

———. "Comment se fera la fédération de l'Europe," *Revue internationale de sociologie* 8 (1900), 561–77.

———. *L'Affranchissement de la femme.* Paris, 1903.

———. *La Possibilité du bonheur.* Paris, 1904.

———. "Quelques Paradoxes des amoreux de la guerre." *La Revue (ancienne Revue des revues),* 3rd ser., 55 (1905), 457–68.

———. "Les Prétendus Difficultés du désarmement." *La Revue (ancienne Revue des revues),* 67 (1907), 449–59.

———. *La Critique du Darwinisme sociale.* Paris, 1910.

———. *War and Its Alleged Benefits.* Intro. by Sandi E. Cooper. New York, 1971, GLW/P (Orig. London, 1912).

———. *Mécanisme et limites de l'association humaine.* Paris, 1912.

———. *L'Alsace-Lorraine: Obstacle à l'expansion allemande.* Paris, 1913.

Office central des associations internationales. *L'Union des associations internationales.* Brussels, 1912.

Passy, Frédéric. Documents pour écrire une histoire, Union interparlementaire. Archives, Interparliamentary Union, Geneva.

———. "Le Mauvais Oeil." Archives, Library of the Peace Palace, The Hague, no. D699, Ms. 49.

———. *Mélanges économiques.* Paris, 1857.

———. *Guerres et congrès ou le socialisme international: Extrait de l'économiste belge, 19 novembre, 1859.* Paris, 1899 (orig. Paris, 1859).

———. *Leçons d'économie politique.* Paris, 1861.

———. *La Guerre et la paix.* Paris, 1867.

———. *Revanche et relèvement.* Paris, 1872.

———. "Le Congrès interparlementaire de la paix, 1889." *Journal des économistes* 4 (1889), 84–90.

———. *La Question de la paix.* Paris, 1891.

———. *La Paix internationale et la paix sociale.* Paris, 1892.

———. "Peace Movement in Europe." *American Journal of Sociology,* 2 (1896), 1–12.

————. "La Guerre impossible." *Journal des économistes* 14 (1899), 242–48.

————. "Quelques Souvenirs de ma propagande pacifique" *Revue des revues* et *Revue d'Europe et d'Amérique* 34 (1900), 357–68.

————. *Histoire du mouvement de la paix.* Paris, 1904. 64 pp.

————. "Les Causes économiques de la guerre." *La Grande Revue,* 9th year, 39 (1905), 437–42.

————. *La Paix et l'enseignement pacifiste: Leçons professées à l'école des hautes études sociales.* Paris, 1906.

————. "Le Triomphe de la paix." *La Revue (ancienne Revue des revues)* 71 (1907), 176–78.

————. *Pour la paix: Notes et documents.* Intro. by Adolf Wild. New York, 1972, GLW/P. (Orig. Paris, 1909).

Pecqueur, Constantin. *Economie sociale.* Paris, 1839.

————. *Des Armées dans leurs rapports avec l'industrie, la morale et la liberté.* Paris, 1842.

————. *De La Paix, de son principe et de sa réalisation.* Paris, 1842.

Perris, George H. *For an Arrest of Armaments: A Note for the Second Hague Conference.* London, 1906. 24 pp.

————. *Protectionist Peril.* London, 1910.

————et al. *A History of the Peace Congress at The Hague.* London, 1899.

Petit, Louis, *Un Scandale à l'Hotel de Ville de Rouen.* à propos d'une conférence pacifiste de M. Charles Ricket. Rouen, 1905. 13 pp.

Picard, René. "La Question de la limitation des armaments de nos jours." (M.A. thesis, Univ. of Paris, 1911).

Pictet-de-Sergy, A. P. J. *Les Ligues de la paix en face de la guerre: Lettre adressé à M. le professeur Jules Barni.* Geneva, 1870.

Pol, Stéfan. "Le Préjugé des races et le pacifisme." *La Grande Revue,* 9th year, 35 (1905), 213–19.

Pollack, Sir Frederick. "The Modern Law of Nations and the Prevention of War." *Cambridge Modern History, vol. 12, The Latest Age.* Cambridge, 1910, 703–29.

Potonié-Pierre, Edmond. *Un Peu Plus Tard.* Paris: 1893.

————. *Histoire du mouvement pacifique.* Intro. by E. Ducommun. Berne, 1899.

Potonié-Pierre, Eugénie, and Edmond Potonié-Pierre. *Petits Plaidoyers contre la guerre.* Paris, 1890–1898. (Issued irregularly.)

Potvin, Charles. "Rapport sur la question de la paix, 10 mai, 1872." *La Châine d'union de Paris, Journal de la maçonnerie universelle* 9 (1872), 463–67.

Pratt, Hodgson. *International Arbitration.* London, 1898. 13 pp.

————. *War and the Working Classes.* London, 1901.

Pressensé, Francis de. "England and France." *Contemporary Review* 75 (1899), 153–60.

Prudhomme, Sully. "Patrie et humanité." *La Revue (ancienne Revue des revues)* 48 (1904), 1–20.

Prudhommeaux, Jules. *Coopération et pacification.* Paris, 1904. 82 pp.

Reuter, Richard. "Der Friedensgedanke in Deutschland. Regierung und Reichstag." *Die Friedens-Warte* 5 (1904), 141–45.

Revon, Michel. *L'Arbitrage international, son passé, son présent, son avenir.* Paris, 1892.

————. "Le Problème de la guerre." *La Nouvelle revue,* 77 (1892), 5–26, 244–58.

Richard, Henry. *Memoirs of Joseph Sturge.* London, 1864.

Richet, Charles. "Chimère de la paix et chimère de la guerre." *Revue scientifique* 77 (1899), 773–77.

————. "Blancs Contre Jaunes (autour de la guerre Russo-Japonaise)." *La Revue (ancienne Revue des revue)* 49 (1904), 133–37.

————. "Philosophie de la paix et de la guerre." *Revue de la Paix* (1905), 84–88, 120–26.

————. *Le Passé de la guerre et l'avenir de la paix.* Paris, 1907.

Ritchie, D. G. *Darwinism in Politics,* 2nd ed. London, 1909.

Robertson, E. "Question of Disarmament." *Nineteenth Century* 57 (1905), 145–56.

Robertson, John M. "War at the Century's End." *Humane Review* (1901), 1–15.

Rochefoucauld-Liancourt, Frédéric Gaëtan, marquis de la. *Vie du duc de la Rochefoucauld-Liancourt. Oeuvres,* vol. 2 (orig. Paris, 1831; Andelys, 1814–1845).

Rouanet, Gustave. "Les Unions de la paix et le socialisme." *Revue Socialiste* 20 (1895), 708–14.

Rouard de Card, E. *Les Destinées de l'arbitrage international depuis la sentence rendue par le tribunal de Genève.* Paris, 1892.

Rouxel, F. "La Guerre au point de vue économique." *Journal des économistes* 15 (1900), 392–99.

Ruyssen, Théodore. "De La Methode dans la philosophie de la paix." In *Morale générale,* Bibliothèque du Congrès international de philosophie. Paris, 1903, vol. 2, 295–320.

————. *Rapport sur les congrès nationaux de la paix et leurs relations avec les Congrès internationaux de la paix.* Toulouse, 1903. 6 pp.

Saint Georges d'Armstrong, Thomas de. *Principles généraux du droit international public: De L'Utilité de l'arbitrage.* Paris, 1890.

Saint-Maurice, Comte de. "Notes sur la conférence de La Haye." *La Grande Revue,* n.s., 11th year, 45 (1907), 162–69.

Saint-Simon, Comte Henri de, and Augustin Thierry. "De La Réorganisation de la société européenne, 1814." In *Five Views of European Peace.* Sandi E. Cooper, ed. New York, 1972, GLW/P. 26–28.

Salvemini, Gaetano. *Come siamo andati in Libia e altri scritti dal 1900–1915.* Intro. by Augusto Torre. Milan, 1963 (Orig. Florence, 1914).

Sancerme, Charles. *Vers l'entente.* Paris, 1913.

Santallier, F. *L'Union de la paix entre tous les peuples civilisées: Proposition adressée au monde entier,* 3rd ed. 15 pp. Le Havre, 1867.

Sarolea, Charles. "A propos du message du czar en faveur du désarmement." *Revue de Belgique,* ser. 2, 24 (1898), 5–15.

Say, Jean-Baptiste. *Traité d'économie politique.* Paris: 1803.

Scarabelli, Ignazio. *Cause di guerra in Europa e rimedi.* Ferrera, 1890.

Schaeffle, Albert. "Die Friedenskonferenz im Haag: Beiträge zu einer sozialwissenschaftlichen Theorie des Krieges." *Zeitschrift für die gesamte Staatswissenschaft.* 55 (1899), 705–48.

Schlief, Eugen. *Zeitungskrieg und Volkerfrieden.* Munich, 1899.

Schücking, Walther. *Die Organisation der Welt.* Leipzig, 1909.

————. *The International Union of The Hague Conferences.* Oxford, 1918.

Scott, James Brown. *The Hague Peace Conferences of 1899 and 1907.* Intro. by Warren Kuehl. New York, 1972, GLP/W. (Orig. 1909).

Seigneur, Georges. *La Ligue de la paix: Appel aux catholiques.* Paris, 1868. 71 pp.

Seillière, E. *La Philosophie de l'impérialisme.* Paris, 1903–1908.

Selenka, Margarethe L. *Die internationale Kundgebung der Frauen zur Friedenskonferenz.* Munich, 1900.

Sellon, Jean-Jacques. *Réflexions sur les suites probables de l'arbitrage européen.* Geneva, 1829.

——. *Lettre sur la guerre*. Geneva, 1830.

——. *Vœux adressés au futur congrès, 1 novembre, 1830*. Geneva, 1830. 15 pp.

——. *Réglement de la Société de la paix de Genève*. Geneva, 1831. 12 pp.

——. Letter to the Marquis de Cordove, 27 August 1831. Biblioteca del Risorgimento, Milan, no. 36870.

——. *Adresse aux chrétiens*. Geneva, 1834.

——. *Les Institutions propres à remplacer le peine de mort et à éviter la guerre*. Geneva, 1836.

Sellon, Valentine de, Comtesse. *Discours prononcé par la Comtesse Valentine de Sellon, Congrès international de la paix, 4 octobre, 1878*. Paris, n.d. 8 pp.

——. *Comptes rendus de la presse sur les écrits de Valentine de Sellon: Lettres tirées de sa correspondance*, 3rd ed. Paris, 1882.

Sembat, Marcel. *Faites un Roi, sinon faites la paix*. Paris, 1913.

Seregni, G. *Per la giustizia e la pace*. Milan, 1897.

Serrigny, Bernard. *Les Conséquences économiques et sociale de la prochaine guerre*. Paris, 1909.

Sève, A. *Cours d'enseignement pacifique: Principes et applications du pacifisme*. Paris, 1910.

——. *Notions d'enseignement pacifiste (avant-propos par Ferninand Buisson)*. Paris, 1912.

Sewall, May. "Summary of the Work of the NCW and the ICW in behalf of Peace and Arbitration." Archives, National Council of Women. (Typescript.)

Simon, Jules. "Les Amis de la paix." *Le Matin* (November 3, 1888), 3–4.

Skarvan, Dr. "Le Refus du service militaire." *La Revue blanche, (Paris)* 18, (1899), 561–69.

Société d'économie politique. *Le Pacifisme devant la science économique*. Paris, 1906. 31 pp.

Stead, W. T. *The United States of Europe on the Eve of the Parliament of Peace*. Intro. by Sandi E. Cooper. New York, 1971, GLW/P. (Orig. 1899.)

——. *The Truth About the [South African] War*. London, 1900.

——. *La Chronique de la Conférence de La Haye, 1899*. The Hague, 1901.

——. *The Americanization of the World or the Trend of the Twentieth Century*. Intro. by Sandi E. Cooper. New York, 1972, GLW/P. (Orig. 1910.)

——. "Créons un budget de la paix." *La Revue, (ancienne Revue des revues)*, 3rd ser., 62 (1906), 29–44.

——. "Impressions from The Hague." *Contemporary Review* 92 (1907), 721–30.

——. *Le Parlement de l'humanité (la Conférence de la paix à La Haye) 1907*. Amsterdam, 1907.

——. "Le Pélerinage de la paix." *La Revue (ancienne Revue des revues)*, 67 (1907), 222–25.

——. ed. *Courrier de la Conférence de la paix*. (15 June–20 October 1907). The Hague, 1907.

Stengel, Karl von. *Weltstaat und Friedensproblem*. Berlin, 1909.

Stoika, N. M. *La Question de l'arbitrage obligatoire aux conférences de la paix*. Parix, 1909.

Sully, Maximilien de Béthune, Duc de. *Le Grand Dessein de Henri IV*, 2 vols. Paris, 1638, 1662.

Suttner, Bertha von. *Lay Down Your Arms*. Intro. by Irwin Abrams. New York, 1971, GLW/P (Orig. Dresden, 1889).

——. *Die Haager Friedensconferenz. Tagebuchblätter*. Dresden, 1901.

————. *Memoirs of Bertha von Suttner: The Record of an Eventful Life,* 2 vols. Intro. by Irwin Abrams. New York, 1972, GLW/P. (Orig. Boston, 1910.)

————. *Der Kampf um die Vermeidung des Weltkriegs: Randglossen aus zwei Jahrzehnten zu den Zeitereignissen vor der Katastrophe.* Alfred Fried, ed. Zurich, 1917.

Sydenham, G. S. C., and J. G. Rogers. "The Tsar's Proposed Conference and Our Foreign Affairs." *Nineteenth Century* 44 (1898), 697–717.

Tallichet, E. "Le Désarmement et la paix." *Bibliothèque universelle et revue suisse* 13 (1899), 149–65, 341–73.

————. *La Question de la paix et sa solution.* Paris, Lausanne, 1907.

Tarbel, Jean. "Pacifisme et antimilitarisme." *La Nouvelle Revue,* n.s., 26 (1906), 184–98, 378–92.

Tchéraz, Minas. "Les Martyrs arméniens devant la Conférence de La Haye." *Revue des revues et Revue d'Europa et d'Amérique* 29 (1899), 234–42.

Tessut, Oscar. *Le Livre bleu de l'internationale.* Paris, 1871.

Tolstoy, L. N. *La Guerre et le service obligatoire.* Brussels, 1896.

————. "Le Militarisme et la religion." *La Revue blanche* (Paris) 20 (1899), 379–83.

————. *The War Between Russia and Japan.* New York, n.d. (Orig. 1904.)

————. *War–Patriotism–Peace.* Intro. by Scott Nearing. New intro. by Ralph T. Terplin. New York, 1973, GLW/P (Orig. 1926).

Tridon, Henri. *L'Antimilitarisme.* Tunis, 1906.

Trueblood, Benjamin F. *The Federation of the World.* Boston, 1899.

————. *International Arbitration at the Opening of the Twentieth Century.* Boston, 1909. 23 pp.

Turiello, Pasquale. "La Conferenza dell'Aja." *Nuova antologia,* 82 ser. 4 (1899). 727–37.

Umano (pseud. Gaetano Meale). *La Fine delle guerre nella federazione dei popoli,* 3rd ed. Milan, 1896.

————. *Essai de constitution internationale: Solution positive et pratique du problème des armements et des guerres.* Paris, 1907.

Umiltà, Angelo. *L'Oeuvre de la Ligue internationale de la paix et de la liberté.* Neuchâtel, 1891, 29 pp.

Un Européen, *Les États-Unis d'Europe et la question d'Alsace-Lorraine.* Paris, 1902.

L'Union lombarde pour la paix. *Concours pour le prix de la paix: Rapport de la commission d'examen.* Modena, 1890. 18 pp.

Vecchio, Giorgio del. *Il Fenomeno della guerra e l'idea della pace,* 2nd ed. Turin, 1911.

Verband für internationale Verständigung, *Ziele und Aufgaben.* Berlin, 1913.

Verdier Winteler de Weindeck, H. *De la paix: Du Désarmement et de la solution du problème social.* Paris, 1903.

Vesnitch, M. R. "La Question du désarmement et la note du Tsar Nicholas II—la question d'Alsace-Lorraine: Est-elle insoluble?" *Revue générale du droit international public* 5 (1898), 744–49.

Villeneuve, Matthieu G. T. *Société de la morale chrétienne. Rapport sur le concours, 18 avril 1842.* Paris, 1842.

Vollenhoven, Cornelis van. *War Obviated by an International Police.* The Hague, 1915.

Vries, I. H. de. *Pour la paix: Une Presse mondiale.* Paris and Brussels, 1911.

Wallon, J. "Sciences: La science contre la guerre." *Revue des revues* 28 (1899), 440–45.

Waszklewicz-van Schilfgaarde, J. *Internationale Ontwapening: Ein vrouloenzaak en ein vrouloenbelan.* Amsterdam, 1899.

Wybrouboff, G. *Le Congrès de la paix (Ext. de la Philosophie Positive).* Versailles, 1867. 14 pp.

Secondary Sources

Abrams, Irwin. "A History of European Peace Societies, 1867–1899." Ph.D. diss., Harvard Univ., 1938.

———. "Disarmament in 1870." *Die Friedens-Warte* 54 (1957), 57–67.

———. "Bertha von Suttner and the Nobel Peace Prize." *Journal of Central European Affairs* 22 (1962), 286–307.

———. "The Transformation of the Nobel Peace Prize." *Peace and Change* 10 (1984), 1–25.

———. *The Nobel Peace Prize and the Laureates: An Illustrated Biographical History, 1901–1987.* Boston, 1988.

Albrecht-Carrié, René, ed. *The Concert of Europe.* New York, 1968.

Andrews, James R. "The Rationale of Nineteenth-Century Pacifism: Religious and Political Arguments in the Early British Peace Movement." *Quaker History* 57 (1968), 17–27.

Angrand, Pierre. *Victor Hugo raconté par les papiers d'état.* Paris, 1961.

Anitchkow, Mikhail. *War and Labour.* London, 1900.

Auspitz, Katherine. *The Radical Bourgeoisie: The Ligue de l'enseignement and the Origins of the Third Republic, 1866–1885.* Cambridge, 1982.

Baker, Robert P. "The Belgians and the European Peace Movement, 1889–1914." M.A. thesis, Stanford Univ., 1962.

Balch, Thomas W. *The Alabama Arbitration.* Freeport, NY, 1969. (Orig. Philadelphia, 1900.)

Barbier, J-B. *Le Pacifisme dans l'histoire de France (de l'an mille à nos jours).* Paris, 1966.

Barclay, Thomas. *New Methods of Adjusting International Disputes and the Future.* London, 1917.

Bariéty, Jacques, and Antoine Fleury, eds. *Mouvements et initiatives de paix dans la politique internationale, 1867–1928.* Berne, 1987.

Barkeley, Richard. *Die Deutsche Friedensbewegung, 1870–1933.* Hamburg, 1948.

Barnes, Harry Elmer. "A Sociological Criticism of War and Militarism: An Analysis of the Doctrines of Jacques Novicow." *Journal of International Relations* 12 (1921), 238–65.

Barraclough, Geoffrey. *European Unity in Thought and Action.* Oxford, 1963. 60 pp.

Baudin, Louis. *Frédéric Bastiat.* Paris, 1962.

Bauer, Riccardo. *Il Movimento pacifista e i lavoratori.* Milan, 1972.

Baugniet, Jean. "Deux Pionniers de la coopération internationale et de la paix universelle: Henri La Fontaine et Paul Otlet." *Synthèses* 25 (1970), 44–48.

Baylen, Joseph O. "W. T. Stead and the Boer War: The Irony of Idealism." *Canadian Historical Review* 40 (1959), 304–14.

———. *W. T. Stead: A Life.* London, 1982.

Baylen, Joseph, and P. G. Hogan, Jr. "Shaw, W. T. Stead and the International Peace Crusade, 1898–1899." *Shaw Review* 6 (1963), 60–61.

Beales, A. C. F. *The History of Peace.* Intro. by Charles Chatfield. New York, 1971, GLP/W. (Orig. London, 1931).

Becker, Jean-Jacques. *Comment les français sont entrés dans la guerre.* Paris, 1977.

———. *The Great War and the French People.* Trans. by Arnold Pomerans. Warwickshire, Eng., 1985.

Berghahn, V. R. *Militarism: The History of an International Debate, 1861–1979.* Cambridge, 1981.

Bernstein, Samuel. "Jean Jaurès and the Problem of War." *Science and Society* 4, (1940), 127–64.

Berthrong, Merrill Gray. "Disarmament in European Diplomacy, 1816–1870." Ph.D. diss., Univ. of Pennsylvania, 1961.

Best, Geoffrey. *Humanity in Warfare: The Modern History of the International Law of Armed Conflicts.* London, 1980.

Bettez, David James. "France, Germany and The Hague Peace Conferences of 1899 and 1907." Ph.D. diss., Univ. of Kentucky, 1982.

Biocca, Dario. "Il Pacifismo e la *Grande Illusione* di Norman Angell." *Studi storici* 21 (1980), 595–607.

Bisceglia, Louis. "Norman Angell and the 'Pacifist' Muddle." *Bulletin of the Institute of Historical Research* 45 (1972), 104–21.

Bock, Helmut. "Pazifistische und marxistche Fruhwarnungen vor dem ersten Weltkrieg." *Zeitschrift Geschichtswissenschaft* 37 (1989), 35–49.

Bolchini, Piero. "Milano: 1915, il socialismo e la guerra." *Movimento operaio e socialista* 16 (1970), 261–91.

Bonnard, L. C. *Essai sur la conception d'une Société des nations avant le XX siècle.* Paris, 1921.

Bortolotti, Franca Pieroni. *La Donna, la pace, l'Europa: L'Associazione internazionale delle donne dalle origini alla prima guerra mondiale.* Milan, 1985.

Bosanquet, Helen. *Free Trade and Peace in the Nineteenth Century.* New York, 1924.

Bouglé, Célestin. *Un Moraliste laïque: Ferdinand Buisson.* Paris, 1933.

Bozeman, Adda. *Politics and Culture in International History.* Princeton, NJ, 1960.

Braker, Regina. "Bertha Von Suttner as Author: The Harriet Beecher Stowe of the Peace Movement." *Peace and Change* 16 (1991), 74–96.

Brock, Peter. *Pacifism in the United States From the Colonial Era to the First World War.* Princeton, NJ, 1968.

———. *Pacifism in Europe to 1914.* Princeton, NJ, 1971.

———. *Freedom from War: Nonsectarian Pacifism, 1814–1914.* Toronto, 1991.

Bussey, Gertrude, and Margaret Tims. *Pioneers for Peace: Women's International League for Peace and Freedom 1915–1965.* London, 1965.

Carnegie Endowment for International Peace, *Institutes of International Affairs.* New York, 1953.

Carroll, E. Malcolm. *French Public Opinion and Foreign Affairs, 1870–1914.* Hamden, CT, 1964. (Orig. Chapel Hill, NC, 1931).

Carsten, F. L. *War Against War: British and German Radical Movements in the First World War.* Berkeley, CA, 1982.

Ceadel, Martin. *Pacifism in Britain 1914–1945: The Defining of a Faith.* Oxford, 1980.

———. *Thinking About Peace and War.* Oxford, 1989.

Chatfield, Charles, and Peter van den Dungen, eds. *Peace Movements and Political Cultures.* Knoxville, TN, 1988.

Chickering, Roger P. "Pacifism in Germany, 1900–1914: A Study of Nationalism and Wilhelmine Society." Ph.D. diss., Stanford Univ., 1968.

———. "A Voice of Moderation in Imperial Germany." *Journal of Contemporary History* 8 (1973), 147–64.

———. *Imperial Germany and a World Without War: The Peace Movement and German Society, 1892–1914.* Princeton, NJ, 1975.

Christ, Franz. *Gestalt und Geschichte des europäischen Friedensgedankens.* Ronco-Ascona, 1968.

Combi, Maria. *Ernesto Teodoro Moneta, premio Nobel per la pace.* Milan, 1968.

Conner, Thomas Hayes. "Parliament and the Making of Foreign Policy: France Under the Third Republic." Ph.D. diss., Univ. of North Carolina, 1983.

Coogan, John W. *The United States, Britain and Maritime Rights, 1899–1915.* Ithaca, NY, 1981.

Cook, Adrian. *The Alabama Claims: American Politics and Anglo-American Relations, 1865–1872.* Ithaca, NY, 1975.

Cookson, J. E. *The Friends of Peace: Anti-War Liberalism in England, 1792–1815.* New York and London, 1982.

Cooper, Sandi E. "The Impact of Nationalism on European Peace Movements and Liberal Internationalists, 1848–1914." *Peace and Change* 6, (1980), 23–36.

———. "The Guns of August and the Doves of Italy." *Peace and Change* 7, (1981), 29–43.

———. "Patriotic Pacifism. The Political Vision of Italian Peace Movements." In *Studies in Modern Italian History: From the Risorgimento to the Republic,* Frank J. Coppa, ed. New York, 1986, 197–230.

———. "The Work of Women in Nineteenth-Century Continental Peace Movements." *Peace and Change* 9 (1984), 11–28.

Crangle, John V. "The British Peace Movement and the Anglo-Egyptian War of 1882." *Quarterly Review of Historical Studies (India)* 15 (1975–1976), 139–50.

———. "The British Peace Movement and the Intervention in the Sudan 1884–1885." *Indiana Social Studies Quarterly* 30 (1977), 22–37.

Curcio, Carlo. *Europa: Storia di un'idea,* 2 vols. Florence, 1958.

Curti, Merle. *The American Peace Crusade, 1815–1860.* Durham, NC, 1929.

d'Allemagne, H. R. *Les Saint-simoniens, 1827–1837.* Paris, 1930.

Davis, Calvin D. *The United States and the First Hague Peace Conference.* Ithaca, NY, 1962.

———. *The United States and the Second Hague Peace Conference.* Chapel Hill, NC, 1975.

De Bueger-van Lierde, Françoise. "Louis Frank, pionnier du mouvement féministe belge." *Revue belge d'histoire contemporaine* 4 (1973), 377–92.

Defrasne, Jean. *Le Pacifisme.* Paris, 1983.

Degan, Marie Louise. *The History of the Women's Peace Party.* Intro. by B. W. Cook. New York, 1972, GLW/P. (Orig. Baltimore, MD, 1939).

Dehio, Ludwig. *Germany and World Politics in the Twentieth Century.* New York, 1959.

Delassus, A. *Précis d'enseignement pacifiste: Ouvrage présenté au concours ouvert par le Bureau international permanent de la paix.* Monaco, 1910.

Descamps, E. F. E. *The Origin of International Arbitration.* London, 1907.

Descamps, E. F. E., and Louis Renault, eds. *Recueil international des traités du XIX siècle.* Paris, 1901.

Desjardins, Paul, and H. F. Stewart. *French Patriotism in the Nineteenth Century.* Cambridge, 1923.

Devos, G. B. *La Science supranationale de Louis Bara.* Courtrai [Kortrijk] and Paris, 1952.

Dickinson, G. Lowes. *War: Its Nature, Causes and Cures.* London, 1923.

———. *The International Anarchy, 1904–1914.* London, 1926.

Dickmann, Fritz. *Friedensrecht und Friedenssicherung: Studien zur Friedensproblem in die Geschichte.* Göttingen, 1971.

Dolléans, Edouard. *Histoire du mouvement ouvrier, 1830–1871,* vol. 1, 6th ed. Paris, 1957.

Donat, H., and K. Holls, eds. *Die Friedensbewegung.* Düsseldorf, 1983.

Drachkovitch, Milorad M. *Les Socialisme française et allemand et le problème de la guerre, 1870–1914.* Geneva, 1953.

Drake, Richard. "The Theory and Practice of Italian Nationalism, 1900–1906." *Journal of Modern History* 53 (1981), 213–41.

Dreyfus, Ferdinand. *Un Philanthrope d'autrefois: La Rochefoucauld-Liancourt, 1747–1827.* Paris, 1903.

Düffler, Jost. *Regeln gegen den Krieg? Die Haager Friedens-Konferenzen 1899 und 1907 in der internationalen Politik.* Berlin, 1981.

Dungen, Peter van den. *The Hidden History of a Peace 'Classic': Eméric Crucé's "Le Nouveau Cynée."* London, 1980. 52 pp.

————. "The International Museum of War and Peace at Lucerne." *Revue suisse d'histoire* 31 (1981), 185–206.

————. *The Making of Peace: Jean de Bloch and the First Hague Peace Conference.* Occasional papers, 12. Udo Heyn. ed., Los Angeles, 1983. 57 pp.

————. "Peace Research and the Search for Peace." *International Journal on World Peace* 2 (1985), 35–52.

————. "Peace Museums." *World Encyclopedia of Peace,* vol. 2, 234–43. London, 1986.

Duroselle, Jean B. *L'Idée d'Europe dans l'histoire.* Paris, 1965.

Dzamba, Anne O. "Bertha von Suttner, Gender, and the Representation of War." In *Essays in European History: Selected from the Annual Meetings of the Southern Historical Association, 1986–1987.* June K. Burton, ed. New York and London, 1989. 61–72.

Eagleton, Clyde. *Analysis of the Problem of War.* New York, 1937.

Earle, Edward M., ed. *Makers of Modern Strategy: Military Thought from Machiavelli to Hitler.* Princeton, NJ, 1944.

Echard, William E. *Napoleon III and the Concert of Europe.* Baton Rouge, 1983.

Edsall, Nicholas C. *Richard Cobden: Independent Radical.* Boston, 1986.

Eickhoff, Richard. *Die Interparlamentarische Union, 1889–1914.* Geneva, 1921. 40 pp.

Eisenbeiss, Wilfried. *Die burgerliche Friedensbewegung in Deutschland wahrend des Ersten Weltkrieges. Organisation, Selbstverstaendnis und politische Praxis, 1913/14–1919.* Frankfurt, a.M., 1980.

Ellis, Jack. *The French Socialists and the Problem of Peace, 1904–1914.* Chicago, 1967.

Englund, Steven Louis. "The Origin of Oppositional Nationalism in France (1881–1889)." Ph.D. diss., Princeton Univ., 1981.

Evans, Richard. *The Feminists.* London, 1977.

————. *Comrades and Sisters: Feminism, Socialism and Pacifism in Europe, 1870–1945.* New York, 1987.

Fakkar, Rouchdi. *Sociologie, socialisme et internationalisme prémarxiste.* Neuchâtel, 1968.

Falnes, Oscar J. *Norway and the Nobel Peace Prize.* New York, 1938, 1967.

Faries, J. C. *Rise of Internationalism, 1829–1913.* New York, 1915.

Feis, Herbert. *Europe, the World's Banker 1870–1914.* London, 1930.

Ferrero, Guglielmo. *The Problems of Peace: Holy Alliance to League of Nations.* New York, 1919.

Fink, Clinton. "Peace Education and the Peace Movements Since 1815." *Peace and Change* 5 (1980), 66–73.

Fletcher, Roger. *Revisionism and Empire: Socialist Imperialism in Germany, 1897–1914.* London, 1987.

Flourney, F. R. "British Liberal Theories on International Relations." *Journal of the History of Ideas* 7 (1946), 195–217.

Ford, T. K. "The Genesis of the First Hague Peace Conference." *Political Science Quarterly* 51 (1936), 354–82.

Foster, Catherine. *Women for All Seasons: The Story of the Women's International League for Peace and Freedom.* Athens, GA, 1989.

Fraise, Geneviève. "Et Si Les Mères désertaient la guerre . . . Madeleine Vernet (1879–

1949): Pacifisme et féminisme." *Les Cahiers de GRIF: Violence* 14/15 (1976), 34–39.

Frick, Stephen. "Joseph Sturge and the Crimean War: Pt. II, The Founding of the Morning Star." *Journal of the Friends Historical Society (London)* 53 (1975), 335–58.

Fuchs, Gustav. *Der deutsche Pacifismus in Weltkrieg.* Stuttgart, 1928.

Fuller, J. F. C., Major-General. *War and Western Civilization 1832–1932: A Study of War as a Political Instrument and the Expression of Mass Democracy.* London, 1932.

Gallavresi, Giuseppe. "Le Centenaire d'un précurseur: Jean-Jacques de Sellon." *Revue internationale de la Croix-Rouge (Geneva)* (May 1931), 348–58.

Ganci, Salvatore Massimo. "L'Opposizione democratico-borghese, repubblicani e radicali," in *Storia della società italiana: La Crisi di fine secolo (1880–1900).* Giovanni Cherubini et al., eds. Milan, 1980, 213–34.

Garber, Elizabeth S. "L'Arbitrage international devant le mouvement socialiste français, 1890–1914." *Revue socialiste* 105 (1957), 293–313.

Goedeckemeyer, Albert. *Die Idee von ewigen Frieden.* Leipzig, 1920.

Goldstein, Brigette. "Ludwig Quidde and the Struggle for Democratic Pacifism in Germany, 1914–1930." Ph.D. diss., New York Univ., 1984.

Gollwitzer, Heinz. *Europe in the Age of Imperialism, 1880–1914.* New York, 1969.

Gooch, George P. *Recent Revelations of European Diplomacy.* London, 1928.

Gosselin, Anne. "Antimilitarisme et pacifisme des femmes en France, 1906–1920." Mémoire de maîtrise, Univ. de Paris, VII, 1980.

Gosses, Frans. *The Management of British Foreign Policy Before the First World War.* Leyden, 1948.

Gues, André. "Schema historique sur la non-violence." *Écrits de Paris,* 33 (1974), 63–75.

Guillen, P., ed. *La France et l'Italie pendant la première guerre mondiale.* Actes du colloque tenu a l'Université des sciences sociales de Grenoble, les 28, 29 et 30 septembre 1973. Grenoble, 1976.

Guillen, Pierre. "Les Internationales et les crises coloniales avant 1914." In *Les Internationales et le problème de la guerre au XX siècle.* Pierre Milza, ed. Rome, 1987.

Halasz, Nicholas. *Nobel: A Biography.* New York, 1959.

Hamann, Brigitte. *Bertha von Suttner: Ein Leben für den Frieden.* Munich, 1986.

Hamburger, Maurice. *Léon Bourgeois, 1851–1925.* Paris, 1932.

Hassner, Pierre. "Les Concepts de guerre et de paix." *Revue française des science politique* 2 (1961), 642–70.

Haupt, Georges. *Socialism and the Great War: The Collapse of the Second International.* Oxford, 1972.

Heiss, Gernot, and Heinrich Lutz, eds., *Friedensbewegungen: Bedingungen und Wirkungen.* Vienna, 1984.

Hembleben, Sylvester John. *Plans for World Peace Through Six Centuries,* Intro. by Walter F. Bense. New York, 1972, GLW/P. (Orig. Chicago, 1943.)

Henderson, Gavin B. "The Pacifists of the Fifties." *Journal of Modern History* 9 (1937), 314–41.

Hering, Sabine, and Cornelia Wenzel. *Frauen Riefen, aber Man Hörte sie Nicht: Die Rolle der Deutschen Frauen in der Internationalen Frauenfriedensbewegung zwischen 1892 und 1933,* 2 vols. Kassel, 1986.

Hinsley, F. H. *Power and the Pursuit of Peace: Theory and Practice in the History of Relations Between States.* Cambridge, 1963, 1967.

Hirschfeld, Claire. "Blacks, Boers and Britons: The Antiwar Movement in England and the 'Native Issue,' 1899–1902." *Peace and Change* 8 (1982), 21–34.

Hoblitzelle, Harrison. "War Against War in the Nineteenth Century: A Study of the Western Background of Ghandian Thought." Ph.D. diss., Columbia Univ., 1959.

Hobsbawm, Eric. *The Age of Empire, 1875–1914.* New York, 1987.

Hobson, J. A. *Richard Cobden: The International Man.* London, 1919 (New York, 1968.)

Hodé, Jacques. *L'Idée de Fédération internationale dans l'histoire.* Paris, 1921.

Holl, Karl. "Die Deutsche Friedensbewegung im Wilhelmischen Reich, Wirkung und Wirkunglosigkeit." In *Kirche zwischen Krieg und Frieden.* Wolfgang Huber and Johannes Schwerdt Feger, eds. Stuttgart, 1976. 321–72.

———. *Pazifismus in Deutschland: Neue Historische Bibliothek.* Frankfurt a.M., 1988.

Howard, Michael E. *War and the Liberal Conscience.* New Brunswick, NJ, 1978.

Hubert, M.-F. *L'Idée d'Europe dans la littérature française de 1830 à 1848.* Strasbourg, 1981.

Hull, William I. *The Two Hague Conferences and Their Contribution to International Law.* Intro. by Warren F. Kuehl. New York, 1972, GLW/P. (Orig. Boston, 1908.)

Hunt, James C. "Die deutschen Liberalen und ihre Versuche zur franzosische-deutschen Verständigung 1913–1914." In *Aspekte deutscher Aussenpolitik im 20. Jahrhundert: Aufsatze Hans Rothfels zum Gedachtnis.* W. Benz and H. Graml, eds. Stuttgart, 1977, 28–40.

Institut du droit international. *Livre du centenaire, 1883–1973. Evolution et perspective du droit international.* Basel, 1973.

Interparliamentary Union, Bureau, *The Inter Parliamentary Union: Its Work and Organization.* Geneva, 1921.

Jaray, G. L. *La Politique franco-anglaise et l'arbitrage internationale.* Paris, 1904.

Joll, James. *The Second International, 1889–1914.* New York, 1966.

Jones, Goronwy J. *Wales and the Quest for Peace.* Cardiff, 1969.

Kaldor, Mary, ed. "Women and Peace." *End: Journal of European Nuclear Disarmamaent* 14 (1985), 30.

Kaplan, Sheila. "Great Britain and The Hague Conference: An Episode in Internationalism." Ph.D. diss., City Univ. of New York, 1973.

Kelly, Andrew. "Film as Antiwar Propaganda: *Lay Down Your Arms* (1914)." *Peace and Change* 16 (1991), 97–112.

Kelsen, Hans. "Compulsory Adjudication of International Law." *American Journal of International Law* 37 (1943), 397–407.

———. *Peace Through Law.* Chapel Hill, NC, 1944.

Kempf, Beatrix. *Suffragette for Peace: The Life of Bertha von Suttner.* London, 1972.

Kennedy, Paul. *The Rise of the Anglo-German Antagonism 1860–1914.* London, 1980.

Kennedy, Thomas C. "The Quaker Renaissance and the Origins of the Modern British Peace Movement, 1895–1920." *Albion* 16 (1984), 243–72.

———. "Why Did Friends Resist? The War, the Peace Testimony and the All-Friends Conference of 1920." *Peace and Change* 14 (1989), 355–71.

Kissinger, Henry. *A World Restored, Europe After Napoleon: The Politics of Conservatism in a Revolutionary Age.* New York, 1957, 1964.

Klein, Fritz. "Sozialistische und Pazifistische Friedenskonzeptionen vor 1914." In *Politik und Gesellschaft im Alten und Neuen Österreich: Festschrift für Rudolf Neck zum 60. Geburtstag.* Isabella Ackerl et al., eds. Vienna, 1981, 324–37.

Koss, Stephen, ed. *The Pro-Boers: The Anatomy of an Anti-War Movement.* Chicago, 1973.

Krehbiel, Edward. *Nationalism, War and Society.* New York, 1916.

Kroll, Ulrich. *Die internationale Buren-Agitation, 1899–1902. Haltung der offentlichkeit und Agitation Zugunsten der Buren in Deutschland, Frankreich, und den Niederlanden wahrend des Burenkrieges.* Munich, 1973.

Kukiel, M. *Czartoryski and European Unity, 1770–1861.* Princeton, NJ, 1955.

Lagny, Jean. "Un Conseilleur général de Saint-Germain, premier prix Nobel de la paix, Frédéric Passy (1822–1912)." *Histoire et archéologie dans les Yvelines* 4 (1979), 21–30. (Supplement.)

Lange, Christian. *The Conditions of a Lasting Peace.* Cristiana [Oslo], 1917.

———. *Histoire de la doctrine pacifique.* Académie de droit international. *Recueil des cours.* 1927. 171–426.

Lange, Christian and August Schou. *Histoire de l'internationalisme,* 3 vols. Oslo, 1919, 1954, 1963.

Langer, William L. *The Diplomacy of Imperialism,* 2nd ed. New York, 1956.

Langhorne, Richard. *The Collapse of the Concert of Europe.* New York, 1981.

Lapradelle, Geouffre A. de. "Compte rendu des travaux et appréciation critique: La Conférence de la paix." *Revue générale de droit international public* 6 (1899), 651–846.

———. *La Paix moderne (1899–1945) de La Haye à San Francisco.* Paris, 1947.

Latané, John H., ed. *The Development of the League of Nations Idea: Documents and Correspondence of Theodore Marburg,* 2 vols. New York, 1932.

Laurence, Richard R. "The Problem of Peace and Austrian Society, 1889–1914: A Study in the Cultural Origins of the First World War." Ph.D. diss., Stanford Univ., 1968.

———. "The Peace Movement in Austria, 1867–1914" In *Doves and Diplomats.* Solomon Wank, ed. Westport, Ct., 1978.

———. "The Viennese Press and the Peace Movement, 1899–1914." *Michigan Academician* 13 (1980), 155–63.

———. "Viennese Literary Intellectuals and the Problem of War and Peace, 1889–1914." In *Focus on Vienna, 1900: Change and Continuity in Literature, Music, Art and Intellectual History.* Erika Nielsen, ed. Munich, 1982.

Le Pointe, Gabriel. "Le Mouvement vers la conciliation et l'arbitrage en droit international au début du XX diècle: L'Action de d'Estournelles de Constant." In *Recueils de la Société Jean Bodin pour l'histoire comparative des institutions,* vol. 15, *La Paix,* (1961), 557–80.

Ledermann, Laszlo. *Les Précurseurs de l'organisation internationale.* Neuchâtel, 1945.

Lehner, Felix. *J. C. Bluntschlis Beitrag zur Lösung der Alabamafrage: Eine Episode in Werden der transatlantische Solidarität.* Zurich, 1957.

Leuch-Reineck, Annie. *Le Féminisme en Suisse.* Lausanne, 1929.

Libby, Violet K. *Henry Dunant: Prophet of Peace.* New York, 1964.

Lovett, Clara. *The Democratic Movement in Italy, 1830–1876.* Boston, 1982.

Lovett, Perry Glenn. "Justifying War: The Just War Tradition Until 1919." Ph.D. diss., Univ. of Oklahoma, 1982.

Low, S. "Should Europe Disarm?" *Nineteenth Century* 44 (1898), 521–30.

Lubelski-Bernard, Nadine. "Les Débuts du pacifisme féminin." *Les Cahiers de GRIF: Violence* 14/15 (1976), 30–34.

———. "Les Mouvements et les ideologies pacifistes en Belgique, 1830–1914," 3 vols. Ph.D. diss., Univ. libre de Bruxelles, 1977.

———. "Freemasonry and Peace in Europe, 1867–1914." In *Peace Movements and Political Cultures.* Charles Chatfield and Peter van den Dungen, eds. Knoxville, TN, 1988, 81–94.

Lussu, Joyce, et al. *Donna, guerra e società.* Ancona, 1982.

Lutzker, Michael. "The 'Practical' Peace Advocates. An Interpretation of the American Peace Movement, 1898–1917." Ph.D. diss., Rutgers Univ., 1969.

———. "The Pacifist as Militarist: A Critique of the American Peace Movement, 1898–1914." *Societas* 5 (1975), 87–104.

Lyons, F. S. *Internationalism in Europe, 1815–1914.* Leyden, 1963.

Macon, Louis. *L'Origine de l'Union interparlementaire: Documents.* Lugano and Paris, 1909. 25 pp.

Madariaga, Salvador de. *Disarmament.* New York, 1929.

———. *Portrait of Europe.* London, 1967.

Manning, G. A. W., ed. *Peaceful Change: An International Problem.* London, 1937.

Marriot, Sir John A.R. *Commonwealth or Anarchy? A Survey of the Projects of Peace From the Sixteenth Century to the Twentieth Century.* London, 1937.

Martin, David A. *Pacifism: An Historical and Sociological Study.* New York, 1966.

Martin, William. *Disarmament and the Interparliamentary Union.* New York, 1931.

Maurois, André. *Victor Hugo.* London, 1956.

Mayer, Arno J. *The Persistence of the Old Regime: Europe to the Great War.* New York, 1981.

Maza, Herbert. *Neuf Meneurs internationaux de l'initiative individuelle dans l'institution des organisations internationales pendant le XIX et le XX siècles.* Paris, 1965.

Melamud, S. M. *Theorie, Ursprung und Geschichte der Friedensidee.* Stuttgart, 1909.

Mélandri, Pierre. "Pacifisme." *Universalie,* 95–103. Paris, 1983.

Mercanton, Daisy C. *Henri Dunant: Essai bio-biographique.* Geneva, 1971.

Merle, Marcel, ed. *Pacifisme et internationalisme.* Paris, 1966.

Meulen, Jacob ter. *Les Français à la recherche d'une Société des nations depuis le roi Henri IV jusqu'aux combattants de 1914.* Paris, 1920.

———. *Der Gedanke der Internationalen Organisation in seiner Entwicklung,* 3 vols. The Hague, 1917, 1919, 1940.

Michel, Andrée, ed. *La Militarisation et les violences à l'égard des femmes. Nouvelles questions féministes.* Paris, 1985.

Miller, Kenneth E. "John Stuart Mill's Theory of International Relations." *Journal of the History of Ideas* 22 (1961), 493–514.

Millis, Walter, and James Real. *The Abolition of War.* New York, 1963.

Moë, Ragnvild. *Le Prix Nobel de la paix et l'Institut Nobel norvégien,* 2 vols. Oslo, 1932.

Morandi, Carlo. "'L'Idea dell'unità d'Europa nel XIX e XX secolo." In *Questioni di storia contemporanea.* 2 vols. Ettore Rota, ed. Milan, 1952.

Morgan, Kenneth. "Peace Movements in Wales, 1899–1945." *Welsh Historical Review* (1981), 398–430.

Morris, A. J. Anthony. "The English Radicals' Campaign for Disarmament and The Hague Conference of 1907." *Journal of Modern History* 43 (1971), 368–93.

———. *Radicalism Against War, 1906–1914.* London, 1972.

Mowat, R. B. *The Life of Lord Pauncefote: First Ambassador to the United States.* London, 1929.

Musto, Ronald G. *The Catholic Peace Tradition.* Maryknoll, New York, 1986.

Nettleship, Martin, R. Dale Givens, and A. Nettleship, eds. *War, Its Causes and Correlates.* The Hague, 1975.

Neumann, Michael, ed. *Der Friedens-Nobelpreis von 1901 bis heute.* Munich, 1988.

Newton, Douglas J. *British Labour: European Socialism and the Struggle for Peace, 1889–1914.* Oxford, 1985.

Nicolson, Harold G. *The Congress of Vienna: A Study in Allied Unity, 1812–1822.* New York, 1946.

Nuttall, Geoffrey. *Christian Pacifism in History.* Berkeley, CA, 1971.

Otlet, Paul. *L'Organisation internationale et les associations internationales.* Brussels, 1910.

———. *Les Problèmes internationaux et la guerre.* Geneva and Paris, 1916.

Pacor, Mario. *Italia e balcani: Dal Risorgimento alla resistenza.* Milan, 1968.

Papa, Antonio. "Edoardo Giretti." *Belfagor* 25 (1969), 50–70.

Passerin d'Entrèves, Ettore. "Jean-Jacques de Sellon (1782–1839) e i fratelli Gustavo e Camillo di Cavour di fronte alla crisi politica europea del 1830." In *Ginevra e l'Italia,* D. Cantimori et al., eds. Florence, 1959, pp. 674–99.

Passy, Paul. *Un Apôtre de la paix: La Vie de Frédéric Passy.* Paris, 1927.

––––––. *Souvenirs d'un socialiste chrétien.* Issy-les-Moulineaux, 1930.

Payne, E. A. "Illusion and Failure? Efforts for Peace Before World War I." *Baptist Quarterly (Great Britain)* 28 (1980), 302–13.

Pegg, Carl H. *Evolution of the European Idea, 1914–1932.* Chapel Hill, NC, 1983.

Perris, H. S. *Pax Brittanica: A Study of British Pacification.* New York, 1913.

Phelps, Christina. *The Anglo-American Peace Movement in the Mid-Nineteenth Century.* New York, 1930.

Pierson, Ruth Roach, ed. *Women and Peace: Theoretical, Historical and Practical Perspectives.* London, 1987.

Pinkerton, Florence. "The Concept of National Character: Its Historical Development, Study and Its Relevance to International Relations." Ph.D. diss., New York Univ., 1960.

Pipkin, C. W. *Social Politics and Modern Democracy,* 2 vols. New York, 1931.

Playne, Caroline E. *Bertha von Suttner and the Struggle to Avert the World War.* London, 1936.

Posthumus van der Goot, W. H. "Les Efforts féminins pour l'organisation de la paix aux XIX et XX siécles." *Recueils de la Société Jean Bodin pour l'histoire comparative des institutions,* vol. 15. *La Paix.* Brussels, 1961, 581–610.

Puech, J. L. *Tradition socialiste en France et la Société des nations.* Paris, 1921.

––––––. "La Paix per le droit (1887–1947)." *La Paix par le droit* 51 (1947), 33–41.

Pye, E. M. *Peace Movement in France.* London, 1932.

Quidde, Ludwig, Christian Lange et al. *The Inter-Parliamentary Union from 1889–1939.* Geneva, 1939.

––––––. *Der Deutsche Pazifismus während des Weltkrieges, 1914–1918: Aus dem Nachlass Ludwig Quidde.* Karl Holl and H. Donat, eds. Boppard am Rhein, 1979.

Rabaut, Jean. *L'Anti-militarisme en France, 1810–1975: Faits et documents.* Paris, 1975.

Rahm, Berta. "Marie Goegg-Pouchoulin, 1824–1899." Radio script, 1 March 1968. Zurich, Radiosendung. Bibliothèque universitaire et public (Geneva).

Rajewsky, Christiane, and Dieter Riesenberger, eds. *Wider den Krieg: Grosse Pazifisten von Immanuel Kant bis Heinrich Boll.* Munich, 1987.

Raumer, Kurt von. *Ewige Friede: Friedensrufe und Friedenspläne seit der Renaissance.* Munich, 1953.

Rayward, Boyd. "The Evolution of an International Library and Bibliographic Community." *Journal of Library History* 16 (1981), 449–62.

Reardon, Betty. *Sexism and the War System.* New York, 1985.

Rebérioux, M., and G. Haupt, "L'Attitude de l'internationale: Le Socialisme et la question coloniale avant 1914." *Le Mouvement social* 45 (1963), 7–37. (Special number.)

Renouvin, Pierre. "L'Idée d'États-Unis d'Europe pendant la crise de 1848." In *Actes du Congrès historique du centenaire de la révolution de 1848.* Paris, 1948, 31–45.

––––––. *L'Idée de Fédération Européenne dans la pensée politique du XIX siècle.* Oxford, 1949.

Riesenberger, Dieter. "Die Behandlung der Historischen Friedensbewegung im Geschichtsunterricht." *Geschichtsdidaktic* 5 (1980), 55–66.

Riley, Patrick. "Kant as a Theorist of Peace Through International Federalism." *World Affairs* 136 (1973), 121–31.

Robbins, Keith. *The Abolition of War: The "Peace Movement" in Britain, 1914–1919.* London, 1976.

Robert, Daniel. "Les Protestants français et la guerre de 1914–1918." *Francia, Forschungen zur westeuropäischen Geschichte,* 2 (1974), 415–30.

Robinson, Margaret. *Arbitration and The Hague Peace Conferences of 1899 and 1907.* Philadelphia, 1936.

Rochefoucauld, Jean-Dominique de la, Claudine Wolikow, and Guy Ikni. *Le Duc de la Rochefoucauld-Liancourt, 1747–1827.* Paris, 1980.

Rolin, Albéric. *Les Origines de l'Institut de droit international, 1873–1923.* Brussels, 1924.

Romein, Jan. *The Watershed of Two Eras: Europe in 1900.* Middletown, CT, 1978.

Rota, Ettore. "I Movimenti pacifisti dell'800 e del'900 e le organizzazioni internazionali." In *Questioni di storia contemporanea.* Ettore Rota, ed. Milan, 1954, vol. 2, 1963–2018.

Rougement, Denis de. *Vingt-huit siècles d'Europe: La Conscience européenne à travers les textes d'Hesiode à nos jours.* Paris, 1961.

———. *The Idea of Europe.* New York, 1966.

Ruyssen, Théodore. *De la guerre au droit.* Paris, 1920.

———. *La Société internationale.* Paris, 1950.

———. *Les Sources doctrinales de l'internationalisme,* 3 vols. Paris, 1961.

———. *Itinéraire spirituel: Histoire d'une conscience.* Paris, 1966.

Sager, Eric W. "The Working-Class Peace Movement in Mid-Victorian England." *Histoire sociale/Social History* 12 (1979), 122–44.

———. "Social Origins of Victorian Pacifism." *Victorian Studies* 23 (1980), 211–36.

Saitta, Armando. *Dalla Respublica Christiana agli Stati Uniti di Europa: Sviluppo dell'idea pacifista in Francia nei secoli XVII–XIX.* Rome, 1948.

———, ed. "L'Idea di Europa dal 1815 al 1870." In *Aspetti e momenti della civiltà Europea.* Naples, 1971, 171–234.

Salomone, A. W. *Italy in the Giolittian Era.* Philadelphia, 1945; 2nd ed., 1960.

Salvemini, Gaetano. *Mazzini.* London, 1956.

Sampson, R. V. *The Discovery of Peace.* New York, 1973.

Schazmann, P. E. "Napoléon III: Précurseur de la Société des Nations: Lettre inédite de Louis Napoléon Bonaparte à Jean-Jacques de Sellon." *Revue historique* 179 (1937), 368–71.

Scheer, Friedrich-Karl. *Die Deutsche Friedensgesellschaft (1892–1933): Organisation, Ideologie, politische Ziele.* Frankfurt a.M., 1981.

Schenk, Hans G. *The Aftermath of the Napoleonic Wars: The Concert of Europe, an Experiment.* London, 1947.

Schou, August. *Nobel: the Man and His Prizes.* Norman, OK, 1951.

Schück, H., R. Sohlman et al. *Nobel: The Man and His Prizes.* Norman, OK, 1951.

Schücking, Walther M. A. *The International Union of The Hague Conferences.* Trans. by Charles G. Fenwick. Oxford, 1918.

Schumpeter, Joseph, *Imperialism and Social Classes.* Trans. by H. Norden. New York, 1958.

Scott, James B. "Public Opinion in Relation to War and Peace: The Word of Non-Official Organizations." In *The Problems of Peace.* Institute of International Relations. Geneva, 1926; London, 1927, 313–25.

Sée, Henri. *Histoire de la Ligue des droits de l'homme, 1898–1928.* Paris, 1929.

Semmel, Bernard. *Liberalism and Naval Strategy: Ideology, Interest and Sea Power During the Pax Brittanica.* London, 1987.

Shand, James. "Doves Among the Eagles: German Pacifists and Their Government During World War I." *Journal of Contemporary History* 10 (1975), 95–108.

Sheehan, James J. *German Liberalism in the Nineteenth Century.* Chicago, 1978.

Shotwell, James R. *Plans and Protocols to End War.* New York, 1925. 35 pp.

――――. *The Autobiography of James T. Shotwell.* Indianapolis, 1961.

Silberner, Edmund. *The Problem of War in Nineteenth-Century Economic Thought.* Trans. from French by A. H. Krappe. Intro. by Dennis Sherman. New York, 1972, GLW/P. (Orig. Princeton, NJ, 1946.)

Simon, Werner, "The International Peace Bureau, 1892–1917: Clerk, Mediator, or Guide?" In Charles Chatfield and Peter van den Dungen, eds.. *Peace Movements and Political Cultures.* Knoxville, TN, 1988, 67–80.

Singer, Barnett. "From Patriots to Pacifists: The French Primary School Teachers, 1880–1940." *Journal of Contemporary History* 12 (1977), 413–34.

Sinopoli, Nicola. *Una Donna per la pace: Bertha von Suttner accanto ad Alfred Nobel—cronache, scritti, idee.* Rome, 1986.

Société Jean Bodin pour l'histoire comparative des institutions. *Peace (La Paix)* vol. 2. Brussels, 1962.

Souleyman, Elizabeth V. *The Vision of World Peace in Seventeenth- and Eighteenth-Century France.* New York, 1941.

Spadolini, Giovanni. *I Radicali dell'ottocento (da Garibaldi à Cavallotti),* 3rd ed. Florence, 1972.

Speeckaert, G. P. "Regards sur soixante années d'activité de l'Union des associations internationales." *Synthèses* 25, 288, Brussels (January–June, 1970), 20–43.

――――. *Le Premier siècle de la coopération internationale, 1815–1914.* Brussels, 1980.

Sterzel, Fredrik. *The Interparliamentary Union.* Stockholm, 1968.

Stevenson, R. C. "Evolution of Pacifism." *International Journal of Ethics* 44 (1934), 437–51.

Stiewe, Dorothee. "Die bürgerliche deutsche Friedensbewegung als soziale Bewegung bis zum Ende des Ersten Weltkrieges." Ph.D. diss., Univ. of Freiburg, Switz., 1972.

Stone, Judith. *The Search for Social Peace: Reform Legislation in France, 1890–1914.* Albany, NY, 1983.

Stromberg, Roland N. "The Intellectuals and the Coming of War in 1914." *Journal of European Studies* 3 (1973), 109–22.

Struve, Walter. *Elites Against Democracy: Leadership Ideals in Bourgeois Political Thought in Germany 1890–1933.* Princeton, NJ, 1973.

Summerton, N. W. "Dissenting Attitudes to Foreign Relations, Peace and War, 1840–1890." *Journal of Ecclesiastical History,* 28 (1977), 151–78.

Supina, Philip D. "The Norman Angell Peace Campaign in Germany." *Journal of Peace Research* 9, (1972), 161–64.

Swerdlow, Amy. "Teaching About Peace, War and Women in the Military." *Women's Studies Quarterly* 9 (1984), 51.

Tamborra, Angelo. *Garibaldi e l'Europa: Impegno militare e prospettive politiche.* Rome, 1983.

Tate, Merze. *The Disarmament Illusion.* New York, 1942.

Thibaud, Paul. "Pacifism and Its Problems." *Telos* 59 (1984), 150–62.

Thomas, Edith, *Les Femmes de 1848.* Paris, 1948.

Tyrell, Alexander. "Making the Millennium: The Mid-Nineteenth Century Peace Movement." *Historical Journal* 20 (1978), 75–95.

Vaisse, Maurice. "Le Passé insupportable, les pacifismes 1984, 1938, 1914." *XXe Siècle* 3 (1984), 27–43.

Valeri, Antonio. "L'Idea federalista e l'internazionale nella 'Critica turatiana.'" *Critica Sociale* 64 (1972), 12–14.

van der Linden, W. H. *The International Peace Movement, 1815–1874.* Amsterdam, 1987.

Villeneuve, Matthieu G. T. *Le Duc de la Rochefoucauld-Liancourt.* Paris, 1827.

Vuilleumier, Marx. "Bakunin, L'Alliance internationale de la démocratie socialiste et la Première internationale à Genéve" *Cahiers Vilfredo Pareto* 4 (Paris, 1964), 51–94.

Waltz, Kenneth. *Man, the State and War: A Theoretical Analysis.* New York, 1959.

Wank, Solomon. "The Austrian Peace Movement and the Habsburg Ruling Elite, 1906–1914." In Charles Chatfield and Peter van den Dungen, eds. *Peace Movements and Political Cultures.* Knoxville, TN, 1988, 40–63.

―――. *Doves and Diplomats: Foreign Offices and Peace Movements in Europe and America in the Twentieth Century.* Westport, CT, 1978.

Wehberg, Hans. *Die Führer der deutschen Friedensbewegung, 1980 bis 1923.* Leipzig, 1923.

―――. "Graf Sellon, ein Vorkaempfer des Volkerbundes." *Friedens-Warte* 30 (1930), 354–56.

―――. "Die Genfer Friedensgesellschaft den Grafen Sellon." *Friedens-Warte* 31 (1931), 42–45.

―――. "La Contribution des conférences de la paix à La Haye au progrès du droit international." Academy of International Law, The Hague. *Recueil des cours,* no. 3 (1931), 527–669.

―――. *Die internationale Beschrankung der Rüstungen.* Intro. by Solomon Wank. New York, 1973, GLW/P (Orig. 1919).

Weill, Georges. *L'École saint-simonienne: Son histoire, son influence jusqu'à nos jours.* Paris, 1896.

Weisz, Leo. *Jean-Jacques de Sellon.* Zurich, 1929.

Weitzel, R. L. "Pacifists and Anti-Militarists in New Zealand 1909–1914." *New Zealand Journal of History* 7 (1973), 128–47.

Whyte, A. J. *The Early Life and Letters of Cavour, 1810–1848.* Oxford, 1925.

Whyte, F. *The Life of Stead.* London, 1925.

Wild, Adolf. *Baron d'Estournelles de Constant (1852–1924): Das Wirken eines Friedensnobelpreisträgers für die deutsch-französische Verständigung und die europäische Einigung.* Hamburg, 1973.

Winock, Michel. "Socialisme et patriotisme en France (1891–1894)." *Revue d'histoire moderne et contemporaine* 20 (1973), 376–423.

Woodward, Ernest L. *War and Peace in Europe, 1815–1870.* London, 1931.

Woolf, Leonard. *International Government.* London, 1916.

―――. *The Framework of a Lasting Peace.* London, 1917.

Young, Nigel. "Why Peace Movements Fail: An historical and social overview." *Social Alternatives* 4 (1984), 9–16.

―――. "The Peace Movement: A Comparative and Analytical Survey." *Alternatives* 10 (1986), 185–217.

Zampaglione, Gerardo. *The Idea of Peace in Antiquity.* Notre Dame, IN, 1973.

Zorn, Philip. "Deutschland und die beiden Haager Friedensconferenzen." *Deutsche Revue* 44 (1918), 25–34, 117–29, 222–40, 19–32, 127–37.

Zouaoui, Ahmed. *Constantin Pecqueur, aspects de sa doctrine socialiste: Contribution à l'internationalisme.* Geneva, 1964.

Index

Aborigines Protection Society, 70, 177, 179, 205

Action française, 65, 183, 210

Activists, peace, 9, 204. *See also* International peace movement; Peace movements
activities of, 60–61
confrontational tactics of, 210
diverse nationalities of, 62, 238n.18
as elites vs. broader groups, 14, 17, 29
in German-speaking countries, 62
growth in number of, 60, 62
media treatment of, 77–78
and Boer War protests, 104, 176
non-mainstream values of, 52
Passy on influence of, 51
proposals from, 206
women as, 8, 62–63, 211. *See also* Women

Addams, Jane, 82, 200

Aehrenthal, Alois Lexa von, 107, 132

Africa
Congo abuses, 76, 112, 178, 209
Sellon on penetration of, 18

Agnelli, 173

Air power, 134–35
prohibition of missiles from ballons, 126, 132–33, 159

Alabama arbitration, 45–46, 96–97, 104

Albert I (prince of Monaco), 82

Alcan, Félix, 141

Alexander, Joseph G., 187, 195, 198

Alexander I (tsar of Russia), 15

Alexander II (tsar of Russia), assassination of, 146

Algemeen Nederlandsche Vredebond (renamed Vrede door Recht), 216

Allard, Maurice, 127

Allégret, Paul, 65, 128

Allen, William, 15

Alliance des femmes pour la paix. *See* Alliance universelle des femmes pour la paix et pour le désarmement

Alliance des femmes pour la paix par l'education, 215

Alliance des savants et des philanthropes, 214

Alliance system, 150, 161–62, 170, 191

Alliance universelle des femmes, 72

Alliance universelle des femmes pour la paix, 71
section norvégienne, 217

Alliance universelle des femmes pour la paix et pour le désarmement (renamed Alliance universelle des femmes pour la paix par l'education), 98, 117–18, 214
Netherlands section of, 216

alma dolens (pseud. of Teresita Pasina dei Bonfatti), 63, 67, 173, 187, 207, 211, 216

Almanach de la paix, 64

Almanach des jeunes amis de la paix, 9

Alsace-Lorraine, 164–68, 183
Bonghi on, 62, 163
and Hague Conference, 98, 100
in Moch's analysis, 121
and Passy's viewpoint, 46, 209
Ruyssen lectures on, 182–83

Alveydra, Marquis Saint-Yves d', 54

Alviella, Goblet d', 130

Alziator, Adèle, 67, 80, 216

America. *See* United States

American Peace Society, 15

American Union Against Militarism, 201

Amis de la paix in Puy-de-Dôme, Les, 57

Anarchism. *See also* Socialism and socialists
appeals by, 133
arms race as supporting (Bloch), 148
and conscientious objection, 130
direct-action groups in Italian war against Turkey, 174
and Ligue international de la paix et de la liberté, 40
militarism justified by danger of, 124
pacifism charged with abetting (Deschanel), 167
war as supporting (Bloch), 147

Andler, Charles, 66

Angell, Norman, 4, 64, 156–57, 181, 185, 210

Anglo-American peace movement, 7, 15–16, 28
and defensive war, 158
and European movements, 29
and international court, 93
and justifiable-war debate, 10, 29, 158–59
and Moch on popular militias, 124

and national honor or vital interests, 94
and treaties, 94
and Code de la paix (1910), 111–12, 158, 179
at emergency World War I Bureau meeting, 187
and Hague Conference, 108, 109–10
and international court, 107
lecture of, 97
and Lemonnier on social-change issue, 207
and *ligue* move, 72
and militarism, 133, 207
in newspaper control group, 77
on "pacifism," 60
and Quidde on war measures, 188
and von Suttner on tsar's Rescript, 97
World War I service of, 189
Arnaud, Maxime (son), 189
Arnoldson, Klas B., 54, 56–57, 58, 73, 81, 117
Asia (Far East). *See also* China; Japan
arms race in, 129
European militarism of benefit to, 118, 209
Asser, Tobias M. C., 47, 81, 108
Association des femmes de Suède pour la paix, 217
Association internationale des amis de la paix (renamed Ligue internationale de la paix et de la liberté, Belgian section), 215
Association internationale des femmes (later Solidarité des femmes), 41, 51
Association des jeunes amis de la paix (renamed Association de la paix par le droit), 57, 214
Association des journalistes amis de la paix, 77, 214
Association marseillaise de la paix, 215
Association montalbanaise de la paix par le droit, 215
Association for the Neutralization of Denmark, 73, 217
Association 'la paix et le désarmement par les femmes,' L', 63, 118, 214
Association de la paix par le droit, L', 162, 186, 214
Association pour la réforme et le codification du droit des gens, 47
Association for the Reform and Codification of International Law, 91
Association toulousaine de la paix, 215
Associazione per l'arbitrato e per la pace internazionale, 216
Associazione nazionale pro arbitrato e disarmo, 67
Augusta Victoria (queen of Prussia), 35
Aulard, Alphonse, 202
Australia, activists in, 60
Austria
and arms control, 132
in Bloch's analysis of war, 148
Bosnia-Herzegovina annexed by, 171–72

peace societies in, 217–18. *See also specific organizations*
socialism in, 75
Austrian Peace Society (Oesterreicher Friedensgesellschaft), 67–68, 69–70, 217
Austro-Hungarian Empire
and alliance system, 161
and *Italia irredenta,* 169
peace movement in, 69–70

Babut, Henri, 74
Bachiene, Philip Johannes, 46
Bajer, Fredrik, 54, 56, 73
and Dansk Fredsforening, 217
and 1899 Congress meeting, 219
and Hague Conferences, 104, 109, 110
and neutrals, 74, 118–19
Nobel Peace Prize to, 54, 81
and Universal Peace Congress/ Interparliamentary Union, 85
Bakunin, Mikhail, 36, 40
Balance of power, 161, 188. *See also* Alliance system
Balkans, and peace societies, 6
Balkan Wars, 78, 115, 137, 159, 161, 181
moving pictures of, 159–60, 209
Banks, and war, 27, 136–37
Bara, Louis, 24, 29, 46
Barbosa, Ruy, 109
Barclay, Thomas, 106, 114
Baring, Evelyn (Lord Cromer), 180
Barni, Jules, 36, 40, 42, 214, 215
Barnier, Louis, 57
Barrès, Maurice, 162
Bartholdt, Richard, 110, 220
Barthou, Louis, 65
Basch, Victor, 64, 197
Basel
1913 French-German meeting at, 159, 180, 211
parliamentarians' conference in, 78
Bastiat, Frédéric, 7, 21, 22, 24, 26, 27, 34
Bauer, Claire, 62, 71, 80
Bebel, August, 41, 43, 44, 121
Beccaria, Cesare, 16
Beccaris, Bava, 154
Beek en Donk, Jong van, 187
Beernaert, Auguste, 71
and air power, 135
death of, 86, 183
and Hague Conferences, 101, 103–4, 109
as Interparliamentary Council president (1894), 85
as Interparliamentary Union presiding officer (1897, (1905, (1910), 220
as Nobel Peace Prize winner, 65, 81
Belgium
arbitration treaty for proposed, 71
arms spending in, 129
and Congo massacres, 76, 112, 178, 209
English peace activists in, 15–16